ZAGATSURVEY®

1998

NEW YORK CITY RESTAURANTS

Published and distributed by
ZAGAT SURVEY, LLC
4 Columbus Circle
New York, New York 10019
212 977 6000
E-mail: zagat@zagatsurvey.com

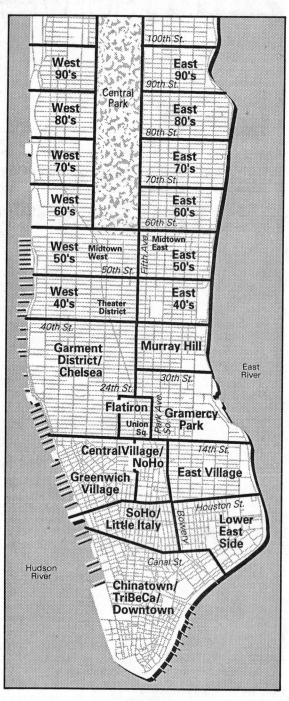

Third Printing
© 1997 Zagat Survey, LLC
ISBN 1-57006-105-X

Contents

Introduction

Here are the results of our *1998 New York City Restaurant Survey* covering 1,933 restaurants in what we believe is the best and most varied restaurant scene in the world, including London and Paris for which we now do *Surveys*.

By annually surveying large numbers of regular restaurant-goers, we think we have achieved a uniquely current and reliable guide. We hope you agree. This year, 17,182 people participated in this *Survey*, eating over 3 million restaurant meals, an average of well over 1,000 meals per restaurant surveyed. Since the participants dined out an average of 3.4 times per week, this *Survey* is based on over 8,300 meals per day.

Of the surveyors, the breakdown by age is 19% in their 20s, 27% in their 30s, 21% in their 40s, 20% in their 50s and 13% in their 60s or above; 55% are women, 45% are men. We want to thank each respondent. They are a most diverse group in every respect but one – they are food lovers all. This book is really "theirs."

To help guide our readers to NYC's best meals and best buys, we have prepared a number of lists. See, for example, New Yorkers' Favorites (page 9), Top Ratings (pages 11–17), Best Buys (pages 18–20) and Prix Fixe Menus (pages 21–22). We have also included a Traffic Report (page 10) listing the restaurants most frequently visited by our surveyors in the past year. On the assumption that most people want a "quick fix" on the places at which they are considering eating, we have tried to be concise and to provide handy indexes by cuisine type, neighborhoods and special features and appeals. For the first time this past year, we published a NYC dining map as a companion to this guide.

To be a reviewer in our 1999 *Survey*, simply send a stamped, self-addressed, business-size envelope to ZAGAT SURVEY, 4 Columbus Circle, New York, NY 10019, so we can contact you. Each participant will receive a free copy of our *1999 New York City Restaurant Survey* when published.

Your comments, suggestions and even criticisms of this *Survey* are also solicited. There is always room for improvement, but we depend on your help.

New York, New York   Nina and Tim Zagat
November 10, 1997

Foreword

In keeping with the city's strong economy, the New York restaurant industry has enjoyed a banner year:

1. Dining frequency increased from 3.2 to 3.4 times (i.e. 6.3%) per week and average spending per meal increased from $29.28 to $30.69 (i.e. 4.8%). At the 20 most expensive "fine dining restaurants", per meal spending rose from $65.08 to $69.33 (i.e. 6.5%).

2. At the top, Daniel jumped three places to win this year's No.1 Food Rating, while Lespinasse repeated its last year's performance as Highest Overall Rated (averaging food, decor and service), and Union Square Cafe retained its title as NYC's Most Popular restaurant.

3. This past year's openings outpaced closings 276 to 92, a marked improvement over last year's 265 to 129 record. The two most prominent debuts were clearly Jean Georges, rated No.5 for its Food, and Le Cirque 2000 (which dropped in its *Survey* standings from two years ago despite enormous press attention). Following the pattern of the past 10 years, most newcomers fall into the BATH (Better Alternative to Home) category featuring three characteristics: modest pricing, casual ambiance and homey, healthy cuisine.

4. Culinary diversity remains the city's greatest strength. Exemplifying this was the expansion of Austrian, Belgian, Greek, Soul Food and Vietnamese eateries.

5. Prix fixe menus are proliferating with over 500 places offering bargain menus year-round and even more in summer. See pp. 21-22 for lists of the best of these.

6. Service remains the main problem area for the local industry. The average service rating of all restaurants surveyed was only 16.8, whereas the average food rating was 18.6. When asked what irritated them most about dining in New York, 43% of surveyors stressed service. In contrast, concerns about noise and price, the second and third most serious irritants, were cited by only 17% of surveyors, and smoking issues were targeted by only 3% of surveyors.

7. Finally, surveyors indicated that fully 60% of all the meals they consumed were made outside the home either at restaurants or prepared food shops. This obviously is a good portent for the NYC restaurant industry's future.

New York, New York   Nina and Tim **Zagat**
November 10, 1997

Key to Ratings/Symbols

This sample entry identifies the various types of information contained in your Zagat Survey.

(1) Restaurant Name, Address & Phone Number

(2) Hours & Credit Cards

(3) ZAGAT Ratings

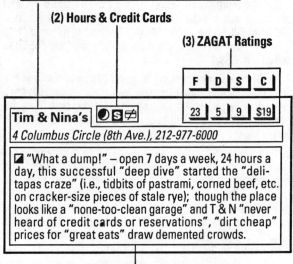

	F	D	S	C
Tim & Nina's ◐ Ⓢ ⊄	23	5	9	$19

4 Columbus Circle (8th Ave.), 212-977-6000

◪ "What a dump!" – open 7 days a week, 24 hours a day, this successful "deep dive" started the "deli-tapas craze" (i.e., tidbits of pastrami, corned beef, etc. on cracker-size pieces of stale rye); though the place looks like a "none-too-clean garage" and T & N "never heard of credit cards or reservations", "dirt cheap" prices for "great eats" draw demented crowds.

(4) Surveyors' Commentary

The names of restaurants with the highest overall ratings, greatest popularity and importance are printed in **CAPITAL LETTERS**. Address and phone numbers are printed in *italics*.

(2) Hours & Credit Cards

After each restaurant name you will find the following courtesy information:

◐ .... *serving after 11 PM*

Ⓢ .... *open on Sunday*

⊄ .... *no credit cards accepted*

(3) ZAGAT Ratings

Food, Decor and **Service** are each rated on a scale of **0** to **30**:

F	D	S	C

F .... *Food*
D .... *Decor*
S .... *Service*
C .... *Cost*

23	5	9	$19

0 - 9	....	*poor to fair*
10 - 15	....	*fair to good*
16 - 19	....	*good to very good*
20 - 25	....	*very good to excellent*
26 - 30	....	*extraordinary to perfection*

∇ 23	5	9	$19

∇ .... *Low number of votes/less reliable*

The **Cost (C)** column reflects the estimated price of a dinner with one drink and tip. Lunch usually costs 25% less.

A restaurant listed without ratings is either an important **newcomer** or a popular **write-in**. The estimated cost, with one drink and tip, is indicated by the following symbols.

–	–	–	VE

I .... *$15 and below*
M .... *$16 to $30*
E .... *$31 to $50*
VE .... *$51 or more*

(4) Surveyors' Commentary

Surveyors' comments are summarized, with literal comments shown in quotation marks. The following symbols indicate whether responses were mixed or uniform.

◨ .... *mixed*
◼ .... *uniform*

NYers' Favorite Restaurants

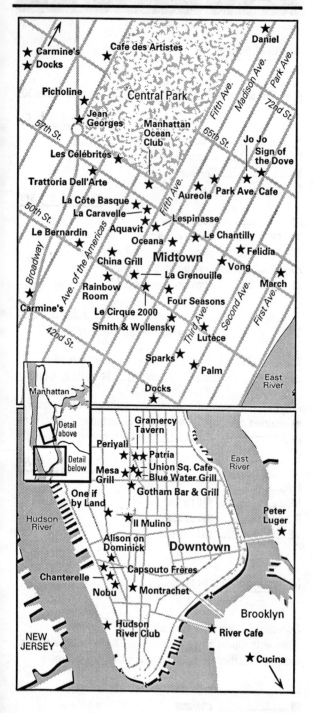

Carmine's
Docks
Cafe des Artistes
Daniel
Picholine
Central Park
Jean Georges
Manhattan Ocean Club
Fifth Ave.
Madison Ave.
Park Ave.
72nd St.
57th St.
65th St.
Jo Jo
Les Célébrités
Sign of the Dove
Trattoria Dell'Arte
Aureole
Park Ave. Cafe
La Côte Basque
La Caravelle
Fifth Ave.
Lespinasse
50th St.
Aquavit
Le Chantilly
Le Bernardin
Oceana
Felidia
Ave. of the Americas
China Grill
Midtown
Vong
Broadway
La Grenouille
March
Rainbow Room
Second Ave.
First Ave.
Carmine's
Le Cirque 2000
Four Seasons
42nd St.
Smith & Wollensky
Third Ave.
Lutèce
Sparks
Palm
East River
Docks

Manhattan
Detail above
Detail below

Gramercy Tavern
Periyali
Patria
East River
Mesa Grill
Union Sq. Cafe
Blue Water Grill
Gotham Bar & Grill
One if by Land
Hudson River
Il Mulino
Peter Luger
Alison on Dominick
Downtown
Capsouto Frères
Chanterelle
Nobu
Montrachet
Brooklyn
Hudson River Club
River Cafe
NEW JERSEY
Cucina

8

New Yorkers' Favorite Restaurants

Each of our reviewers has been asked to name his or her five overall favorite restaurants. The 50 spots most frequently named, in order of their popularity, are:

1. Union Square Cafe
2. Aureole
3. Gotham Bar/Grill
4. Gramercy Tavern
5. Café des Artistes
6. Le Bernardin
7. Lespinasse
8. Four Seasons
9. Peter Luger
10. Chanterelle
11. Daniel
12. Nobu
13. La Côte Basque
14. La Grenouille
15. One if by Land, TIBS
16. Aquavit
17. Il Mulino
18. Sign of the Dove
19. Park Avenue Cafe
20. Mesa Grill
21. Picholine
22. River Cafe
23. Vong
24. Lutèce
25. Carmine's
26. Patría
27. Rainbow Room
28. Montrachet
29. Jean Georges
30. Capsouto Frères
31. March
32. Les Célébrités
33. Jo Jo
34. Oceana
35. Felidia
36. Manhattan Ocean Club
37. La Caravelle
38. Hudson River Club
39. Palm
40. Sparks
41. China Grill
42. Trattoria Dell'Arte
43. Blue Water Grill
44. Le Cirque 2000
45. Alison on Dominick
46. Docks Oyster Bar
47. Periyali
48. Cucina
49. Le Chantilly
50. Smith & Wollensky

It's obvious that most of the above restaurants are expensive, but New Yorkers also love a bargain. Fortunately, our city has an abundance of wonderful ethnic restaurants and other inexpensive spots that fill the bill. Thus, we have listed over 100 "Best Buys" on pages 18–20 and both Prix Fixe and Pre-Theater Bargains on pages 21–22. In fact, despite New York's reputation as an expensive place to live, its vast size and less pricey outer boroughs offer far more affordable and diverse dining options than any other US city.

Traffic Report

This Traffic Report indicates the 50 spots most often visited by our surveyors, and the number of visits in the past year:

4,500	Café des Artistes	2,237	Le Bernardin
4,426	Union Square Cafe	2,222	America
4,051	Carmine's	2,164	Nobu
3,625	Gotham Bar/Grill	2,158	Park Avenue Cafe
3,380	Aureole	2,103	China Grill
3,314	Gramercy Tavern	2,092	Ollie's
3,295	EJ's Luncheonette	2,086	Rainbow Room
3,288	Carnegie Deli	2,030	Vong
3,169	Peter Luger	2,016	Zen Palate
3,086	Arizona 206 & Cafe	2,004	Daniel
3,007	Tavern on the Green	1,993	Ess-a-Bagel
2,984	Docks Oyster Bar	1,993	Tribeca Grill
2,791	John's Pizzeria	1,960	Dallas BBQ
2,751	Four Seasons	1,950	Becco
2,724	California Pizza Kitchen	1,950	Second Avenue Deli
2,636	Starbucks	1,930	Bryant Park Cafe
2,623	Sarabeth's	1,922	Oyster Bar
2,572	Aquavit	1,912	Palm
2,512	Jackson Hole	1,874	Lespinasse
2,489	Mesa Grill	1,863	Manhattan Ocean Club
2,428	Smith & Wollensky	1,850	Cité
2,386	Cafe Un Deux Trois	1,836	One if by Land, TIBS
2,321	Sign of the Dove	1,829	Chanterelle
2,290	La Côte Basque	1,802	Virgil's Real BBQ
2,288	Trattoria Dell'Arte	1,801	Blue Water Grill

The above numbers represent simple volume (or where people actually eat most), i.e. the number of our reviewers who have gone to these places. Since the typical surveyor visited each restaurant 7.1 times on average, the number of meals eaten in the above restaurants is enormous. For example, that would mean our surveyors dined at Café des Artistes nearly 32,000 times in the past year – that's over 85 people a day.

It's clear that these restaurants are not high traffic spots solely for their food; some of them have either been bashed by professional food critics or simply ignored; what this Traffic Report reflects is that other features besides food, such as ambiance, convenience and value, very often determine where people choose to eat. See the Teflons index for more such restaurants.

Top Ratings*

Top 50 Food Ranking

28 Daniel
Le Bernardin
Lespinasse
Aureole
Jean Georges
27 Chanterelle
Nobu
Peter Luger
La Grenouille
Les Célébrités
Union Square Cafe
Gotham Bar/Grill
Il Mulino
Soup Kitchen Intl.
Tomoe Sushi
La Côte Basque
26 March
Gramercy Tavern
La Caravelle
Yama
Four Seasons
Lutèce
Montrachet
Oceana
Sushisay

25 Totonno Pizzeria
Patsy Grimaldi's
Picholine
Felidia
Sparks
Piccola Venezia
Le Cirque 2000
Arcadia
Iso
Jo Jo
Hasaki
Honmura An
Tuscany Grill
Il Giglio
Manhattan Ocean Club
River Cafe
Le Régence
Aquavit
One if by Land, TIBS
Park Avenue Cafe
Blue Ribbon Sushi
Patría
Vong
Palm
Nick's Pizza

Top Spots by Cuisine

Top American
28 Aureole
27 Union Square Cafe
Gotham Bar/Grill
26 March
Gramercy Tavern
25 Arcadia

Top American Regional
24 Mesa Grill/SW
Hudson River Club/NY
23 Cooking With Jazz/Cajun
An American Place/NE
22 Tropica/FL
Michael's/CA

Top Breakfast
23 Carlyle
Café Pierre
20 Sarabeth's
Regency (540 Park)
19 Good Enough to Eat
17 Anglers & Writers

Top Brunch
25 River Cafe
Le Régence
Park Avenue Cafe
24 Mesa Grill
Petrossian
Café des Artistes

Top Business Lunch
28 Le Bernardin
Jean Georges
26 Four Seasons
Oceana
25 Sparks
Le Cirque 2000

Top Cafes
27 Union Square Cafe
Gotham Bar/Grill
25 River Cafe
Park Avenue Cafe
24 New City Cafe
Café des Artistes

---

* Excluding restaurants with low voting.

Top Caviar & Champagne
24 Petrossian
23 Caviarteria
21 Rainbow Room
20 FireBird
19 King Cole Bar
16 Pravda

Top Chinese
24 Shun Lee Palace
    Canton
23 Tse Yang
    Joe's Shanghai
    Chin Chin
    Szechuan Kitchen

Top Coffeehouses/Desserts
23 Veniero's
22 Emack & Bolio's
21 Cupcake Cafe
20 Palm Court
19 Sant Ambroeus
    Cafe Lalo

Top Continental
26 Four Seasons
25 One if by Land, TIBS
24 Two Two Two
    Petrossian
23 Sign of the Dove
    Carlyle

Top Delis
22 Barney Greengrass
21 Second Avenue Deli
20 Carnegie Deli
19 Stage Deli
18 Katz's Deli
    Pastrami King

Top French
28 Daniel
    Le Bernardin
    Lespinasse
    Jean Georges
27 Chanterelle
    La Grenouille

Top French Bistros
26 Montrachet
25 Jo Jo
24 Alison on Dominick
    Chez Michallet
23 La Bouillabaisse
    Raphaël

Top Greek/Mideast
24 Periyali
23 Elias Corner
    Telly's Taverna
22 Ithaka
    Deniz a la Turk
    Moustache

Top Hamburgers
21 Wollensky's Grill
    "21" Club
20 Corner Bistro
19 Island Burgers
18 Cal's
16 Joe Allen

Top Hotel Dining
28 Daniel/Surrey
    Lespinasse/St. Regis
    Jean Georges/Trump Intl.
27 Les Célébrités/Essex Hse.
26 La Caravelle/Shoreham
25 Le Régence/Plaza Athénée

Top Indian
24 Jackson Diner
22 Dawat
    Shaan
21 Salaam Bombay
    Mavalli Palace
    Diwan Grill

Top Italian
27 Il Mulino/Aquila
25 Felidia/Trieste
    Pic. Venezia/Venice
    Tuscany Grill/Florence
    Il Giglio/Rome
24 Pó/Pistoia
    Cucina/Florence
    Il Nido/Lucca
    Da Umberto/Florence
    Rao's/Naples
    Rosemarie's/multi
    Campagna/multi
22 Gennaro/Lipari

Top Japanese
27 Nobu
    Tomoe Sushi
26 Yama
    Sushisay
25 Iso
    Hasaki

Top Korean
24 Hangawi
23 Mirezi
22 Woo Chon
21 Won Jo
   Kang Suh
   Dok Suni

Top Kosher
21 Second Avenue Deli
   Tevere 84
   Levana
20 Va Bene
19 Le Marais
   Abigael's

Top Late Dining
24 Blue Ribbon
22 Raoul's
21 Wollensky's Grill
   NY Noodle Town
   Balthazar
20 Carnegie Deli

Top Mediterranean
25 Picholine
23 Savoy
   Verbena
21 Pitchoune
   Café Crocodile
   Matthew's

Top Mexican/Tex-Mex
23 Rosa Mexicano
22 Mi Cocina
21 Zarela
20 Zócalo
   Canyon Road
   Gabriela's

Top Newcomers/Rated
28 Jean Georges
25 Le Cirque 2000
24 Quilty's
23 Gennaro
   Ocean Grill
   Mirezi

Top Newcomers/Unrated
   Bouley Bakery
   Gertrude's
   Grill Room
   Milos
   Molyvos
   Union Pacific

Top Noodle Shops
25 Honmura An
21 NY Noodle Town
20 Big Wong
19 Sam's Noodle Shop
   Menchanko-tei
18 Bo-Ky

Top Old New York
27 Peter Luger/1887
25 Palm/1926
24 Rao's/1896
   Café des Artistes/1917
23 Café Pierre/1931
22 Oyster Bar/1913

Top People-Watching
27 La Grenouille
25 Le Cirque 2000
22 Fresco by Scotto
   Circo
   Blue Water Grill
21 Balthazar

Top Pizza
25 Totonno Pizzeria
   Patsy Grimaldi's
   Nick's Pizza
24 Lombardi's
23 Joe's Pizza
21 John's Pizzeria

Top Power Scenes
26 Four Seasons
25 Sparks
21 Gabriel's
   Patroon
   "21" Club
20 Regency (breakfast)

Top Private Rooms
28 Le Bernardin
27 La Grenouille
   Les Célébrités
   La Côte Basque
26 Gramercy Tavern
   Four Seasons

Top Pub Dining
21 Wollensky's Grill
20 Corner Bistro
   Cité Grill
16 Joe Allen
   J.G. Melon
15 Walker's

Top Quick Fixes
27 Soup Kitchen Intl.
22 Oyster Bar (counter)
21 Second Avenue Deli
20 Hale & Hearty Soups
Così Sandwich Bar
Carnegie Deli

Top Seafood
28 Le Bernardin
26 Oceana
25 Manhattan Ocean Club
24 Aquagrill
SeaGrill
23 Elias Corner

Top Sleepers
26 Carol's Cafe
24 Kum Gang San
Little Szechuan
Vittorio Cucina
Nadaman Hakubai
23 Ubol's Kitchen

Top Southern/Soul
20 Jezebel
Cafe Beulah
19 Shark Bar
18 B. Smith's
Sylvia's
Bubby's

Top Spanish
23 Bolo
22 El Cid
Marichu (Basque)
21 Solera
Francisco's C.V.
El Charro

Top Steakhouses
27 Peter Luger
25 Sparks
Palm
24 Post House
23 Morton's of Chicago
Mike & Tony's

Top Sunday Dinner
27 Union Square Cafe
Gotham Bar/Grill
La Côte Basque
26 March
Gramercy Tavern
Montrachet

Top Tasting Menus
28 Daniel ($69 & up)
Lespinasse ($130)
Aureole ($85)
Jean Georges ($95)
27 Chanterelle ($89)
Nobu ($60 & up)

Top Thai
25 Vong
24 Plan Eat Thailand
23 Thailand Rest.
22 Topaz Thai
21 Rain
Jai-Ya Thai

Top Trips to the Country*
28 Xaviar's, NY
Maxime's, NY
Saddle River Inn, NJ
Ryland Inn, NJ
27 Jean-Louis, CT
Mill River Inn, LI

Top 24-Hour
22 Woo Chon
21 Kang Suh
19 Uncle George's
17 Gray's Papaya
Kiev
16 L'Express

Top Vegetarian
24 Hangawi
21 Mavalli Palace
20 Vatan
19 Angelica Kitchen
Zenith
Zen Palate

Top Vietnamese
22 Viet-Nam
Le Colonial
21 Nha Trang
20 Indochine
Saigon Grill
MeKong

Top Wild Cards
25 Aquavit/Scandinavian
Patría/Nuevo Latino
24 Blue Ribbon/Eclectic
Sonia Rose/Eclectic
22 Chur. Plataforma/Brazilian
21 Turkish Kitchen/Turkish

---

* See *Zagat Long Island, New Jersey* and *Connecticut/Southern New York State Surveys.*

Tops by Neighborhood*

Chelsea/Garment Dist.
24 Luma
   Da Umberto
22 Le Madri
   Chelsea Bistro
   El Cid
   Woo Chon

Chinatown
24 Canton
23 Thailand Rest.
   Joe's Shanghai
22 Viet-Nam
   Wong Kee
21 NY Noodle Town

East Village
25 Iso
   Hasaki
23 Veniero's
   Il Bagatto
22 O.G.
   Bambou

Flatiron/Union Square
27 Union Square Cafe
26 Gramercy Tavern
25 Patría
24 Periyali
   Mesa Grill
   Campagna

Gramercy Park
26 Yama
24 Sonia Rose
23 Tatany
   Verbena
   I Trulli
22 Park Bistro

Greenwich Village
27 Gotham Bar/Grill
   Il Mulino
   Tomoe Sushi
25 One if by Land, TIBS
24 Pó
   Chez Michallet

Midtown - East 40s & 50s
28 Lespinasse
27 La Grenouille
26 March
   Four Seasons
   Lutèce
   Oceana

Midtown - West 40s & 50s
28 Le Bernardin
27 Les Célébrités
   La Côte Basque
26 La Caravelle
25 Manhattan Ocean Club
   Aquavit

Murray Hill
24 Hangawi
23 An American Place
22 Water Club
   Villa Berulia
21 Le Grenadin
   Wu Liang Ye

Outer Boroughs
27 Peter Luger/Bklyn
25 Piccola Venezia/Qns
   Tuscany Grill/Bklyn
   River Cafe/Bklyn
24 Cucina/Bklyn
   New City Cafe/Bklyn

SoHo/Little Italy
25 Honmura An
   Blue Ribbon Sushi
24 Alison on Dominick
   Aquagrill
   Lombardi's
   Blue Ribbon

TriBeCa/Downtown
27 Chanterelle
   Nobu
26 Montrachet
25 Il Giglio
24 Hudson River Club
   Rosemarie's

Upper East Side - 60s & Up
28 Daniel
   Aureole
25 Arcadia
   Jo Jo
   Le Régence
   Park Avenue Cafe

Upper West Side - 60s & Up
28 Jean Georges
25 Picholine
24 Two Two Two
   Terrace
   Café des Artistes
23 Gennaro

---

* Based on Food ratings.

Top 50 Decor Ranking

28 Lespinasse
   Rainbow Room
   Les Célébrités
   La Grenouille
   Le Régence
27 FireBird
   River Cafe
   Le Bernardin
   Four Seasons
   One if by Land, TIBS
   Café des Artistes
   Terrace
   Café Botanica
26 La Côte Basque
   King Cole Bar
   Hudson River Club
   Cellar in the Sky
   Water's Edge
   Sign of the Dove
   View
   Carlyle
   Aureole
   Chanterelle
   Kings' Carriage House
   Windows on the World

   Box Tree
   Top of the Tower
   Hangawi
   Gramercy Tavern
25 March
   La Caravelle
   Water Club
   Daniel
   57, 57
   Palio
   Jean Georges
   Aquavit
   Jezebel
   Tavern on the Green
   Balthazar
   Nirvana
   Vong
   Mark's
   Temple Bar
   Morgan Court Cafe
24 Lutèce
   Gotham Bar/Grill
   Bouterin
   Café Pierre
   Palm Court

Top Gardens

American Festival
Aureole
Barbetta
Barolo
Boathouse Cafe
Bryant Park Cafe/Grill
Cloister Cafe
Flowers
Gascogne
Grove
I Trulli
La Cigale
Lattanzi
Le Jardin Bistro

Le Petit Hulot
M & R Bar-Dining Rm.
March
Maria Elena
Marichu
Metropolitan Cafe
Miracle Grill
Provence
Rialto
SeaGrill
Tavern on the Green
Trattoria Venti Tre
Verbena
Vittorio Cucina

Top Romantic

Arcadia
Box Tree
Café des Artistes
Cafe Nicholson
Erminia
Jezebel
King Cole Bar
La Belle Epoque
La Colombe d'Or
La Grenouille

Le Refuge
Les Célébrités
Mark's
One if by Land, TIBS
Rainbow Room
River Cafe
Sign of the Dove
Temple Bar
Terrace
Water's Edge

Top Rooms

Aquavit
Aureole
Balthazar
Bouley Bakery
Bouterin
Café des Artistes
Carlyle
Chez Es Saada
Circo
FireBird
Four Seasons
Gage & Tollner
Gotham Bar/Grill
Gramercy Tavern
Hudson River Club
Jean Georges
La Côte Basque
La Grenouille
Le Bernardin
Le Cirque 2000
Les Célébrités
Lespinasse
Lutèce
March
Metronome
Milos
Palio
Rainbow Room
Redeye Grill
Torre di Pisa NY
Union Pacific
Zen Palate/Union Sq.

Top Views

Boathouse Cafe
Cellar in the Sky
Grill Room
Harbour Lights
Hudson River Club
Nirvana
Pier 25A
Rainbow Room
River Cafe
Spirit Cruises
Tavern on the Green
Terrace
Top of the Tower
View
Water Club
Water's Edge
Windows on the World
World Yacht

Top 50 Service Ranking

28 Lespinasse
27 Les Célébrités
   Le Bernardin
   Chanterelle
   La Grenouille
26 Jean Georges
   Aureole
   Four Seasons
   La Caravelle
   Union Square Cafe
   Le Régence
   La Côte Basque
   March
25 Lutèce
   Gramercy Tavern
   Daniel
   Gotham Bar/Grill
24 Le Perigord
   Carlyle
   Oceana
   One if by Land, TIBS
   Cellar in the Sky
   Hangawi
   Nobu
   Terrace

   Montrachet
   Café Pierre
   Box Tree
   La Reserve
   River Cafe
23 Leopard
   Aquavit
   Mark's
   Il Tinello
   Le Cirque 2000
   Il Mulino
   Arcadia
   Grifone
   Café des Artistes
   Hudson River Club
   57, 57
   Alison on Dominick
   Rainbow Room
   Erminia
   Café Botanica
   Villa Berulia
   Water's Edge
   Petrossian
   La Baraka
   Sign of the Dove

Best Buys

Top 100 Bangs For The Buck*

This list reflects the best dining values in our *Survey*. It is produced by dividing the cost of a meal into the combined ratings for food, decor and service.

1. Krispy Kreme	51. California Burrito
2. Emack & Bolio's	52. Excellent Dumpling Hse.
3. Daily Soup	53. Angelica Kitchen
4. Papaya King	54. El Pollo
5. Ess-a-Bagel	55. Comfort Diner
6. Gray's Papaya	56. John's Pizzeria
7. Emerald Planet	57. Wong Kee
8. Cosí Sandwich Bar	58. Le Pain Quotidien
9. Vinnie's Pizza	59. La Taza de Oro
10. Fresco Tortillas	60. Mee Noodle Shop
11. Veniero's	61. Tsampa
12. Hale & Hearty Soups	62. Vynl Diner
13. Pommes Frites	63. Yaffa Cafe
14. Eisenberg Sandwich	64. V&T Pizzeria
15. Freddie & Pepper's	65. Sam's Noodle Shop
16. Island Burgers	66. Taqueria de Mexico
17. Cafe Lalo	67. Kings Plaza Diner
18. Cupcake Cafe	68. Stingy Lulu's
19. Nick's Pizza	69. Goodfella's
20. It's a Wrap	70. New Pasteur
21. City Bakery	71. Bo-Ky
22. Soup Nutsy	72. Benny's Burritos
23. Thé Adoré	73. Noodles on 28
24. Joe Jr.'s	74. Dojo
25. Kitchenette	75. Van West
26. Cafe Mona Lisa	76. Old Devil Moon
27. Pintaile's Pizza	77. Picasso Cafe
28. Corner Bistro	78. Blockhead's
29. Columbus Bakery	79. Burger Heaven
30. Caffe Reggio	80. Viet-Nam
31. Patsy Grimaldi's	81. Caravan of Dreams
32. Big Wong	82. Silver Spurs
33. Edgar's Cafe	83. Cafe Gitane
34. Two Boots	84. Ben's Kosher Deli
35. Totonno Pizzeria	85. Tea & Sympathy
36. Jackson Diner	86. Lupe's East L.A. Kitchen
37. Soup Kitchen Intl.	87. Mangia
38. Rose of India	88. Brawta Caribbean Cafe
39. Burritoville	89. Pink Tea Cup
40. Moustache	90. Lamarca
41. Mama Buddha	91. Thai House Cafe
42. Veselka	92. Sammy's Noodle Shop
43. Plan Eat Thailand	93. Patsy's Pizza
44. Chez Brigitte	94. Morgan Court Cafe
45. Joe's Pizza	95. Tanti Baci Caffé
46. Flor de Mayo	96. Hallo Berlin
47. Quantum Leap	97. Teresa's
48. Lombardi's	98. Bodega
49. ABC Parlour Cafe	99. Arturo's Pizzeria
50. Manganaro's Hero-Boy	100. Tea Box

* We have excluded coffeehouses from the above list because coffee, not food, is their main attraction; however, we have listed Top Coffeehouses on the following page.

Bang For Buck – By Cuisine

American
Kitchenette
ABC Parlour Cafe
Stingy Lulu's
Silver Spurs

Bar-B-Q
Waterfront Ale House
Dallas BBQ
Brothers BBQ
Virgil's Real BBQ

Breakfast
Cupcake Cafe
City Bakery
Columbus Bakery
Le Figaro Cafe

Brunch
Yaffa Cafe
Aggie's
Good Enough to Eat
Popover Cafe

Burgers
Island Burgers
Corner Bistro
Burger Heaven
Silver Spurs

Burritos
Burritoville
California Burrito
Benny's Burritos
Blockhead's

Cafes
Veniero's
Cafe Lalo
Cafe Mona Lisa
Edgar's Cafe

Cajun/Creole
Two Boots
Great Jones Cafe
Baby Jake's
Acadia Parish

Caribbean/So. American
El Pollo
Brawta Caribbean Cafe
Rice 'n' Beans
Old San Juan

Central/Eastern Europe
Veselka
Hallo Berlin
Teresa's
Kiev

Chinese
Big Wong
Mama Buddha
Excellent Dumpling Hse.
Wong Kee

Coffeehouses
DT•UT
New World Coffee
Drip
Pasqua Coffee Bar

Delis
Ess-a-Bagel
Eisenberg Sandwich Shop
Ben's Kosher Deli
Katz's Deli

Diners/Coffee Shops
Joe Jr.'s
Comfort Diner
Vynl Diner
Kings Plaza Diner

Family Dining
Jackson Diner
Ollie's
Green Field
Main Street

French
Thé Adoré
Chez Brigitte
Le Gamin
Tartine

Greek
Kings Plaza Diner
Uncle George's
Uncle Nick's
Ithaka

Health Food
Quantum Leap
Angelica Kitchen
Yaffa Cafe
Caravan of Dreams

Hotels
Edison Cafe/Edison
C3/Washington Sq.
Sarabeth's/Wales
King Cole Bar/St. Regis

Indian
Jackson Diner
Rose of India
Haveli
Windows on India

Italian
Manganaro's Hero-Boy
Picasso Cafe
Mangia
Lamarca

Japanese
Dojo
Tea Box
Menchanko-tei
Souen

19

Malay/Indonesian
Franklin Station Cafe
Bali Nusa Indah
Penang
Malayboo

Mexican/Tex-Mex
Fresco Tortillas
Taqueria de Mexico
Lupe's East L.A. Kitchen
Bodega

Middle Eastern
Moustache
Khyber Pass
Magic Carpet
Afghan Kebab House

Newcomers
Emerald Planet
Pommes Frites
It's a Wrap
Ben's Kosher Deli

Noodle Shops
Mee Noodle Shop
Sam's Noodle Shop
Bo-Ky
Noodles on 28

Pastarias
Lamarca
Tanti Baci Caffé
Ecco-La
Bella Donna

Pizza
Vinnie's Pizza
Freddie & Pepper's
Nick's Pizza
Pintaile's Pizza

Pubs
Corner Bistro
Old Town Bar
McSorley's
Ear Inn

Sandwiches
Cosí Sandwich Bar
Eisenberg Sandwich Shop
Thé Adoré
Manganaro's Hero-Boy

Seafood
Ocean Palace
Frutti di Mare
Cucina di Pesce
Telly's Taverna

Soup
Daily Soup
Hale & Hearty Soups
Soup Nutsy
Soup Kitchen Intl.

Southern/Soul Food
Old Devil Moon
Pink Tea Cup
Bubby's
Acme Bar & Grill

Spanish/Cuban
Flor de Mayo
La Taza de Oro
La Caridad 78
Ñ 33 Crosby

Steakhouses
Embers
Moran's Chelsea
Knickerbocker
Gage & Tollner

Sushi
Haru
Hasaki
Jo-An Japanese
Sushi Hana

Teens
EJ's Luncheonette
Jekyll & Hyde
Official All Star Cafe
Hard Rock Cafe

Thai
Plan Eat Thailand
Vynl Diner
Thai House Cafe
Thailand Restaurant

Vietnamese
New Pasteur
Bo-Ky
Van West
Viet-Nam

Bargain Prix Fixe Menus*

• Lunch •

Adrienne	$34.00	La Reserve	$32.00
Akbar	14.95	Layla (Fri. only)	19.98
Anche Vivolo	13.95	Le Beaujolais	14.25
Aquagrill	14.50	Le Cirque 2000	35.00
Aquavit	29.00	L'Ecole	17.99
Arizona 206	19.98	Le Perigord	32.00
Arqua	19.98	Le Quercy	19.95
Artos	17.50	Le Régence	22.50
Aureole (after 2PM)	19.98	L'Ermitage	15.75
Becco	16.95	Les Pyrénées	19.00
Bombay Palace	12.95	Levana	19.98
Bouterin	18.97	Le Veau D'Or	19.95
Café Botanica	28.00	Lutèce	38.00
Café des Artistes	23.00	Manhattan Grille	17.95
Cafe Luxembourg	19.98	Mark's	19.98
Café Pierre	32.00	Nirvana	16.95
Capsouto Frères	19.95	Nobu	19.98
Carlyle	32.00	Novitá	19.98
Chanterelle	35.00	Oceana	38.00
Chin Chin	19.98	Odeon	23.00
Churrascaria Plataforma	25.00	Palio	29.00
Cinquanta	24.00	Palm	19.97
Circus	17.00	Park Bistro	23.00
Daniel	35.00	Pen & Pencil	22.95
Darbar	17.95	Petrossian	22.00
Dawat	13.95	Picholine	19.98
Destinée	28.00	Quatorze Bis	14.00
Duane Park Cafe	19.98	René Pujol	25.00
Fantino	24.95	San Domenico	19.98
Felidia	27.50	Sardi's	29.50
Ferrier	19.98	Shaan	15.95
Fifty-Seven Fifty-Seven	37.00	Sign of the Dove	19.98
Gotham Bar/Grill	19.98	Solera	32.00
Gramercy Tavern	33.00	Sonia Rose	23.00
Halcyon	19.98	Table d'Hôte	17.50
Harry Cipriani	26.00	Tapika	19.98
Honmura An	18.00	Tavern on the Green	19.98
Jean Lafitte	22.50	Terrace (Tues.-Fri.)	25.00
Jimmy Sung's	22.95	Toscana	22.00
Jo Jo	25.00	Tribeca Grill	19.98
Kings' Carriage Hse.	12.95	Trois Jean	19.98
La Caravelle	36.00	Tse Yang	25.75
La Côte Basque	33.00	Tuscan Square	22.50
La Mediterranée	24.00	"21" Club	25.00
La Petite Auberge	21.95	Vong	25.00

* This list shows the lowest prix fixe menus available; there may be higher-priced options. Since prix fixe prices may change or be canceled at any time, check on them when reserving. Nearly all Indians serve an AYCE (all-you-can-eat) buffet lunch for $15 or less.

• Dinner •

Adrienne*	$35.00	Le Colonial*	$32.00
Alison on Dominick*	19.98	Le Perigord*	38.00
American Festival	22.50	Le Quercy**	23/28
Anche Vivolo*	19.95	L'Ermitage*	19.75
Ansonia*	26.50	Les Pyrénées	27.00
Aquavit**	39.00	Levana	19.98
Arcadia*	30.00	Le Veau D'Or	19.95
Aria*	24.95	Manhattan Grille*	17.95
Arqua	35.00	Mark's*	29.00
Artos*	21.50	Michael's*	29.50
Barbetta*	41.00	Mi Cocina* (Mon.–Thurs.)	15.00
Bar Six*	16.50	Montebello*	26.75
Bay Leaf*	12.95	Montrachet	34.00
Becco	19.95	Nirvana	22.95
Bombay Palace*	19.95	Odeon	25.00
Café Botanica**	34/38	Palio*	49.00
Cafe Centro**	18/28	Park Bistro*	23.00
Café des Artistes	37.50	Pen & Pencil*	29.95
Cafe Luxembourg	29.50	Petrossian	35.00
Café Pierre*	34.00	Rainbow Room*	42.00
Charlotte*	32.50	Raphaël*	32.00
Chelsea Bistro*	35.00	Regency*	35.00
Chez Michallet*	19.95	René Pujol	36.00
Christer's*	27.00	Riodizio	24.95
Churrascaria Plataforma	27.00	San Domenico*	29.50
Cibo	24.95	Sardi's*	41.50
Cinquanta	24.00	SeaGrill	39.00
Cité*	39.50	Sette MoMA	22.50
Darbar*	22.95	Shaan*	21.95
Delia's	35.00	Sign of the Dove*	34.00
Fantino*	29.00	Sonia Rose	38.00
Ferrier*	19.98	Supper Club*	25.00
44*	39.95	Table d'Hôte*	19.95
Four Seasons*	43.50	Tapika*	26.00
Gascogne*	25.00	Tavern on the Green	23.50
Halcyon**	32/34	Terrace (Tues.–Thurs.)	42.00
Harry Cipriani	45.00	Thomas'*	14.95
Helena's*	19.99	Torre di Pisa*	26.95
Indochine*	25.00	Toscana*	22.00
Jean Lafitte	27.50	Trois Canards*	21.95
Kings' Carriage Hse.	34.00	Trois Jean	39.50
La Caravelle*	40.00	Tropica Bar	29.00
La Mediterranée**	24/28	Tuscan Square	38.50
La Petite Auberge	21.95	"21" Club*	29.00
La Reserve*	39.50	Two Two Two*	36.00
Layla	28.00	Vatan	19.95
Le Beaujolais	21.00	Vong*	35.00
L'Ecole	24.99	Willow*	19.98

* Pre-theater only.
**Prices divided by a slash are for pre-theater and normal hours.

Alphabetical
Directory of
Restaurants

Abbracciamento on the Pier (Brooklyn) S
15 | 18 | 17 | $33

2200 Rockaway Pkwy. (exit 13 off Belt Pkwy.), 718-251-5517

■ The "lovely seaside setting" and weekend music are the big draws at this midpriced Canarsie Pier Italian; detractors call it "overpriced" and lament "if only the food were half as good as the view."

ABC Parlour Cafe S
17 | 22 | 13 | $19

38 E. 19th St. (bet. B'way & Park Ave. S.), 212-677-2233

■ "Sink down into an overstuffed chair" in the wonderful "shabby chic" ambiance of this Flatiron furniture store's "sweet retreat"; it's best for an affordable "light" lunch or coffee and cake.

Abigael's S
19 | 17 | 18 | $37

9 E. 37th St. (bet. 5th & Madison Aves.), 212-725-0130

■ You can "say goodbye to chopped liver and gefilte fish" at this casual Murray Hill glatt kosher cafe where the "really good" American menu is "a pleasant surprise", but the tab is not so pleasant.

Acadia Parish (Brooklyn) S
19 | 11 | 16 | $22

148 Atlantic Ave. (bet. Clinton & Henry Sts.), 718-624-5154

■ Bringing "a bit of the Big Easy to Brooklyn", this "kick-ass" Cajun "home cooking" specialist offers a "very tasty" menu, e.g. alligator, jambalaya and "jumbo gumbo with no mumbo jumbo"; "BYO keeps costs down", but it's "very cramped" and far from pretty.

Acappella
23 | 21 | 22 | $48

1 Hudson St. (Chambers St.), 212-240-0163

■ The "prices are as high as the loft ceiling" but the menu is "superb" say reviewers of this TriBeCa Italian; the "witty" waiters "cannot be more attentive" – to the point of "joining in your conversation" – and diners warn it's often "too dark to see your food."

Acme Bar & Grill S
14 | 11 | 13 | $20

9 Great Jones St. (bet. B'way & Lafayette St.), 212-420-1934

■ "Classic rough around the edges" NoHo Cajun offering fried, blackened and barbecued Southern comfort food that's described as "the best heart attack on a plate"; toss down a couple of their margaritas and you won't notice the "funky" "gas station decor."

Across the Street S
22 | 15 | 20 | $43

444 E. 91st St. (bet. 1st & York Aves.), 212-722-4000

■ Eli Zabar's newcomer ("like a very classy girl in a plain dress") draws high praise for "delicious, fresh and innovative" American food, with a limited menu that changes daily; "you'd expect to find this kind of comfortable, amiable place in the Hamptons", which helps explain why "the elite meet to eat" here.

Adrienne S
22 | 24 | 23 | $51

Peninsula Hotel, 700 Fifth Ave. (55th St.), 212-903-3918

■ The "very good" French Classic food with an Asian influence at this "totally civilized" mezzanine plays second fiddle to the "dignified", "beautiful" setting; diners tout the prix fixe lunch and pre-theater specials, but say it can be disquietingly empty.

Aesop's Tables (Staten Island)
▽ 22 | 19 | 19 | $33

1233 Bay St. (Maryland Ave.), 718-720-2005

■ "Each dish is an artwork" at this "warm-feeling", midpriced French-Mediterranean bistro; besides winning kudos for its outdoor garden and "gracious, congenial service", diners report it's "worth staying on SI for – that's a switch!"

F	D	S	C

Afghan Kebab House — 17 | 9 | 14 | $17
1345 Second Ave. (bet. 70th & 71st Sts.), 212-517-2776 [S]
764 Ninth Ave. (bet. 51st & 52nd Sts.), 212-307-1612 ⊄
155 W. 46th St. (bet. 6th & 7th Aves.), 212-768-3875
◪ "Ignore the dreary, dark decor" at these "aromatic" BYO Middle Eastern standbys – the "addictive" food is "exotic, spicy and cheap" and the waiters will offer a "free history of Afghanistan"; in sum, this is "as authentic an Afghan as you can get without land mines."

Aggie's [S] ⊄ — 16 | 9 | 12 | $16
146 W. Houston St. (MacDougal St.), 212-673-8994
◪ "Survive the seating frenzy and service troubles and you're in for a good brunch" at this cheap West Village American; standouts include omelets and French toast, but "don't go if you're allergic to cats."

Agrotikon ◐ [S] — 21 | 14 | 16 | $28
322 E. 14th St. (bet. 1st & 2nd Aves.), 212-473-2602
■ "Forget Astoria", there's "finally a good Greek in Manhattan" rave acolytes of this reasonable East Village taverna; but reviewers say be prepared for "an Odyssey-long wait" for the "melt in your mouth fish."

Aja [S] — 21 | 21 | 17 | $44
937 Broadway (22nd St.), 212-473-8388
■ Architectural Amerasian fusion cuisine that's "as good as it is tall" and the sexy setting draw a "hip Flatiron crowd" to this comfortable spot; while possibly "too trendy for its own good" and too pricey, a martini at this "poseur bar" can't be beat.

AJ's Niota ◐ [S] — ▽ 20 | 19 | 18 | $28
337 W. Broadway (Grand St.), 212-431-6222
■ "Cool den decor", "good karma" and an owner whose "hair looks like Don King's" greet patrons of this midpriced SoHo Indian duplex yearling; most patrons praise "delicious and spicy fare" that's "full of surprises", but a disappointed few say it's "not there yet."

Akbar [S] — 19 | 19 | 19 | $32
475 Park Ave. (bet. 57th & 58th Sts.), 212-838-1717
■ A "dark, mysterious and luxurious" "place for plots and intrigues", this Midtown Indian serves food that can be "sublime" but disappoints those who say it has "seen better days" and has reached a state of "advanced entropy"; N.B. don't miss the bargain prix fixe lunch.

Akroyiali (Queens) ◐ [S] — ▽ 21 | 14 | 18 | $27
33-04 Broadway (33rd St.), 718-932-7772
■ "Manhattanites should head to Astoria" for the "simple, fresh, well-seasoned" food at this unpretentious, affordable Greek yearling; the staff "tries hard to please" and the fish is not to be missed.

Al Bacio [S] — - | - | - | M
1679 Third Ave. (94th St.), 212-828-0111
With a wide-ranging, moderately priced pasta and pizza menu, this Upper East Side Italian newcomer has a lot of something for everyone; the word is out – it's quickly becoming a local favorite.

Al Bustan [S] — 18 | 16 | 18 | $34
827 Third Ave. (bet. 50th & 51st Sts.), 212-759-8439
◪ Expect "great appetizers" and honeyed desserts at this Midtown East Middle Eastern popular with UN diplomats; though some say it could be "more exciting", it's interesting, especially "with a little Arabic."

Al Dente [S] — 17 | 11 | 15 | $25
417 Amsterdam Ave. (80th St.), 212-362-1180
◪ The food is easy to chew and "so is the bill" at this "cute" Italian "hole-in-the-wall" on the Upper West Side; locals tout its "flavorful budget pastas" but others call it only "average."

	F	D	S	C

Alexandre ◐
123 E. 54th St. (bet. Lexington & Park Aves.), 212-688-6888
"Great decor and sensational food" is the initial reaction to this
promising Midtown Mediterranean newcomer; the question is whether
NYers will be able to find its tucked-away, subterranean space.

▽	19	21	16	$40

Alexi on 56 🅂
25 W. 56th St. (bet. 5th & 6th Aves.), 212-767-1234
☑ Most surveyors praise the "expensive but delicious" glatt kosher
food at this Midtown Eclectic newcomer; however, skeptics only go
so far as to say there is potential "if they could get their act together."

15	19	17	$41

Algonquin Hotel, The 🅂
The Algonquin Hotel, 59 W. 44th St. (bet. 5th & 6th Aves.), 212-840-6800
■ "Impress intellectuals from out of town" over tea or drinks in the
"charming" wood-paneled lobby of this Midtown institution or check
out the cabaret in the Oak Room but skip the American food – it "would
have annoyed Dorothy Parker."

24	21	23	$52

ALISON ON DOMINICK STREET 🅂
38 Dominick St. (bet. Hudson & Varick Sts.), 212-727-1188
■ Taxis may get lost on the way to Alison Price's SoHo hideaway, but
it's well worth the trip and steep tab for "the understated setting and
[country French] gourmet meals" that are "pure romance."

15	15	15	$28

Allegria 🅂
66 W. 55th St. (bet. 5th & 6th Aves.), 212-956-7755
☑ Summer outside dining is the main draw at this modestly priced
Midtown Italian; though some surveyors like the "excellent pasta",
more say the food and service are "nothing special."

18	19	18	$30

Alley's End 🅂
311 W. 17th St. (bet. 8th & 9th Aves.), 212-627-8899
■ "An affordable oasis" say fans of this aptly named Chelsea New
American – the cozy atmosphere and "delightful hidden garden" feel
make it a "great date place" even if you're already married; regulars
rate it ideal "for no special occasion."

17	15	16	$29

Allora 🅂
1321 First Ave. (71st St.), 212-570-0384
■ Surveyors say it's a "notch above" other East Side Italians and
suggest sitting in the cozy interior or outdoors for meals of tasty fish
or pasta; it's modestly priced so families flock here.

14	12	14	$19

All State Cafe ◐🅂⌿
250 W. 72nd St. (bet. B'way & West End Ave.), 212-874-1883
■ "The perfect dive for a burger and a beer" à la *Cheers*, this West
Side pub is "as comfortable as an old shoe"; it can get "smoky" and
crowded but the fried chicken is "addictive" and the price is right.

			M

Alonzo's ◐
302 E. 45th St. (bet. 1st & 2nd Aves.), 212-808-9373
An old newcomer, this Italian classic-cum-bar scene, located for 18
years on West 44th Street, has moved to the UN area; it serves the
full range of Italian standards at very fair prices.

19	17	17	$37

Alva ◐🅂
36 E. 22nd St. (bet. B'way & Park Ave. S.), 212-228-4399
☑ The American bistro fare at this darkly attractive Flatiron spot is as
"innovative as its namesake", Thomas Alva Edison, but critics warn
"you can barely taste the food" for the cigar smoke.

Amarone ●◐S
— — — M

686 Ninth Ave. (bet. 47th & 48th Sts.), 212-245-6060
Fitting comfortably into the burgeoning Hell's Kitchen dining scene, this Italian newcomer has attractively upgraded an old storefront as a backdrop for its midpriced pastas, fish, game and namesake wines.

Ambassador Grill S
20 20 20 $42

Regal UN Plaza Hotel, 1 UN Plaza (bet. 1st & 2nd Aves.), 212-702-5014
■ "Watch the diplomats preen" at this mirrored American cafe opposite the UN; though not cheap, the food is "consistently good" and the Sunday brunch is an "endless orgy."

America ●◐S
13 15 13 $24

9 E. 18th St. (bet. B'way & 5th Ave.), 212-505-2110
◪ With a menu that goes "from steak to Fluffernutters", this loud, stadium-sized Flatiron standby with its huge, elevated, people-watcher's bar is ideal for starving singles, party-goers and families with kids, but the decibel level may "make your ears bleed"; detractors say it "does nothing especially well", but doesn't charge much either.

American Festival Cafe S
15 19 16 $35

Rockefeller Plaza, 20 W. 50th St. (Rock. Ctr. Skating Rink), 212-332-7620
◪ There's a "great view of Prometheus but the food is not of the gods" at this handsome Rockefeller Center "tourist trap"; in winter by the skating rink or in summer at an outdoor table, the vibe is "very NY" but the American "coffee shop" cuisine falls short of the location.

Amy's Bread ⊉
— — — I

672 Ninth Ave. (bet. 46th & 47th Sts.), 212-977-2670
Chelsea Market, 75 Ninth Ave. (bet. 15th & 16th Sts.), 212-462-4338 S
Best known for its myriad fine breads, this Ninth Avenue bakery has recently spun off to the Chelsea Market; with tasty, original sandwiches and breakfasts, they're drawing a full, if small, house.

An American Place
23 21 21 $46

2 Park Ave. (32nd St.), 212-684-2122
◪ "Always a treat" say the many fans of chef Larry Forgione; though "often overlooked", it's "a safe bet" for "amazing" Regional American fare in an "elegant, spacious room" with "attentive service"; critics find it too noisy (at lunch), too quiet (at dinner) and "overpriced."

Anche Vivolo ●
18 17 18 $33

222 E. 58th St. (bet. 2nd & 3rd Aves.), 212-308-0112
◪ "The price is right" at this "unreconstructed old-world Italian" that draws an older crowd; the East Side space, staffed by "efficient and helpful waiters", is "cozy" and the food is "very reliable."

Andrusha S
18 14 17 $31

1370 Lexington Ave. (bet. 90th & 91st Sts.), 212-369-9374
◪ "A welcome change from the pasta circuit" near the 92nd Street Y, this Russian cafe offers "heavy, comforting food – like a blanket", served by "charming" staffers who are "trying hard."

Angelica Kitchen S⊉
19 14 16 $18

300 E. 12th St. (bet. 1st & 2nd Aves.), 212-228-2909
■ Despite its "holier than thou vibe", this "crowded" East Villager could be "the best Vegetarian in town"; its "macrobiotic, granola-ladened" patrons say it "feels like a Grateful Dead concert", and even critics admit it's "better than a trip to the gym."

Angelina's (Staten Island) S
— — — E

26 Jefferson Blvd. (Drumgoole Rd.), 718-227-7100
Forget the strip mall SI location and you'll "believe you're in Manhattan" at this stylish, new, pricey but promising Italian; the middle-aged, gold-chain crowd and polite, tuxedoed waiters seem made for each other.

Angelo & Maxie's ●⊟ — 20 | 20 | 18 | $40
233 Park Ave. S. (19th St.), 212-220-9200
■ "If you love hunks of meat", this "trendy", "noisy", handsome high-ceilinged Flatiron steakhouse newcomer with "excellent" service is your spot, but the "real beef is at the bar", which is "filled with cigar-smoking yuppies" and B&Ters looking to hook up.

Angelo's of Mulberry Street ●⊟ — 20 | 13 | 17 | $33
146 Mulberry St. (bet. Grand & Hester Sts.), 212-966-1277
☑ "For that old-time Italian feeling" stop by this "touristy" midpriced Little Italy red sauce institution; though it has become "less enchanting" and more "plastic" over the years, "good" "classic" dishes served by "attentive" waiters keep customers coming back.

Angels ●⊟ — 17 | 12 | 15 | $21
1135 First Ave. (bet. 62nd & 63rd Sts.), 212-980-3131
☑ "Be prepared to be stuffed" at this popular East Side mainstay; an often long wait and some "angel overkill" in the decor don't stop fans, who say "St. Peter would be proud" of the pastas, sauces and prices; critics suspect "devils have arrived in the kitchen."

Anglers & Writers ●⊟⊅ — 17 | 20 | 17 | $23
420 Hudson St. (St. Luke's Pl.), 212-675-0810
☑ The "cozy", "homey" ambiance and "slow" service make this touch of "rustic" "Wisconsin on Hudson Street" perfect for "procrastinating while writing the great American novel"; reviews are mixed on the "hearty" American food, but brunch is benign.

Annam ⊟ — – | – | – | M
38 Carmine St. (bet. Bleecker & Bedford Sts.), 212-243-8428
Inviting, creative West Village French-Vietnamese newcomer; the back garden has a waterfall you won't want to miss.

Annie's ●⊟ — 16 | 15 | 15 | $25
1381 Third Ave. (bet. 78th & 79th Sts.), 212-327-4853
☑ Skeptics say this "casual", "affordable" East Side American is "not thrilling" and "only for the baby carriage trade", but most praise its "wonderful" breakfasts, brunch and salads.

Ansonia ●⊟ — 21 | 19 | 18 | $45
329 Columbus Ave. (bet. 75th & 76th Sts.), 212-579-0505
☑ "Some meals are lyrical" at this "stylish" New American yearling where "everything is lofty – the prices, the upstairs seating and the attitude"; true, it may seem to "belong in SoHo", but it's "a great addition to the Upper West Side" and the long bar is a scene.

Anton's ●⊟ — ▽ 20 | 16 | 19 | $30
259 W. Fourth St. (Perry St.), 212-675-5059
■ "One of the West Village's best-kept secrets", this "cozy" (aka "small") Eclectic with enjoyable outdoor seats serves "well-priced" "food that tastes homemade"; chef-owner "Anton is a sweetheart."

Aperitivo — 19 | 16 | 20 | $42
29 W. 56th St. (bet. 5th & 6th Aves.), 212-765-5155
■ The "best veal chop in town", "quiet" quarters and "friendly" waiters draw an "older crowd" to this midpriced Midtown "classic Italian"; "it fits" most customers "like an old shoe."

Aquagrill ⊟ — 24 | 18 | 20 | $40
210 Spring St. (6th Ave.), 212-274-0505
■ "A godsend in the age of hype", this well-priced SoHo "poor man's Le Bernardin" draws "aqualades" for its "fab raw bar", "oh so fresh" fish, "courteous" staff and outdoor terrace; P.S. it's been discovered.

AQUAVIT 🅂

25 | 25 | 23 | $52

13 W. 54th St. (bet. 5th & 6th Aves.), 212-307-7311

■ The striking indoor waterfall and "serene" "postmodern" decor are "as cool as chilled vodka and just as smooth" at this popular, highly rated Midtown Scandinavian; chef Marcus Samuelsson's "melt-in-your-mouth" salmon, "herring from heaven" and "hushed, attentive service" "could make Ingmar Bergman smile"; for a quicker, less expensive taste try the upstairs cafe.

ARCADIA

25 | 23 | 23 | $57

21 E. 62nd St. (bet. 5th & Madison Aves.), 212-223-2900

■ For "a charming reminder of what a fine civilized restaurant can be" try Anne Rosenzweig's "innovative" New American Eastsider; in the small but beautiful muraled dining room the tables are packed and it can be noisy, but most say this is "a class act all the way."

Areo (Brooklyn) ●🅂

22 | 17 | 17 | $36

8424 Third Ave. (85th St.), 718-238-0079

■ "Seems like Venice" say admirers of this Bay Ridge Italian with excellent food; however, it's getting too well known, bringing long waits and so much noise "you can't hear yourself chew."

Aria 🅂

20 | 17 | 20 | $39

253 E. 52nd St. (2nd Ave.), 212-888-1410

◪ "From the minute you enter, you feel comfortable" at this "never crowded" Midtown Italian sleeper, where "the food and service are always worth the price"; however, the fare might "seem better with improved ambiance" – as it is, many ask "where is everybody?"

Arioso 🅂

▽ 19 | 19 | 14 | $27

120 W. 23rd St. (bet. 7th & 8th Aves.), 212-807-6391

◪ This new, "undiscovered" Chelsea Mediterranean "oasis" hidden away behind the Milan cafe may be "a little disorganized", but voters still sanction it as "perfect for a power lunch" or quiet dinner.

ARIZONA 206 & CAFE 🅂

19 | 17 | 16 | $34

206 E. 60th St. (bet. 2nd & 3rd Aves.), 212-838-0440

◪ A cozy adobe ambiance, great margaritas and creative SW kitchen are still pulling people to this staple near Bloomingdale's; it may be "noisy", "cramped" and "slipping", but "imaginative food combos that sound strange but work" keep it ever-"trendy."

Arlecchino ●🅂

18 | 15 | 18 | $30

192 Bleecker St. (bet. MacDougal St. & 6th Ave.), 212-475-2355

◪ Surveyors tout this "tiny" West Village Italian "jewel box" for its "yummy food" at "gentle" prices; but service by "flirtatious" Italian waiters can be "slow" so don't go "if you're in a hurry."

Armani Cafe 🅂

15 | 15 | 15 | $26

601 Madison Ave. (bet. 57th & 58th Sts.), 212-715-0500

◪ The light food is "more affordable than the clothes" at this "sleek" Italian cafe in the basement of Emporio Armani; it's "great for lunch", but "glacial" service causes some to say "stick with suits, Giorgio."

Arqua 🅂

22 | 20 | 20 | $43

281 Church St. (White St.), 212-334-1888

■ "The simple decor belies the sophisticated food" at this pricey TriBeCa Italian whose ruddy walls and "golden" food remind one of dining in an Italian hill town.

Arté 🅂

18 | 19 | 19 | $35

21 E. Ninth St. (bet. 5th Ave. & University Pl.), 212-473-0077

■ "A real charmer" with "good, authentic Italian" fare, a "lovely garden" and "congenial" if somewhat older crowd is the word on this Central Villager; the "friendly staff" and cozy fireplace add appeal.

F | D | S | C

Artepasta ◐[S]⌿ — 15 | 14 | 14 | $21
106 W. 73rd St. (bet. Amsterdam & Columbus Aves.), 212-501-7014
81 Greenwich Ave. (Bank St.), 212-229-0234
◪ "There could be more art to the pasta" at this "cheap and steady" pair, but the "bargain Italian" cuisine and "upscale" decor keep the young and hungry coming back in spite of "uneven" service.

Artos [S] — 20 | 22 | 20 | $39
307 E. 53rd St. (bet. 1st & 2nd Aves.), 212-838-0007
■ This "sophisticated" East Side Greek with breads "to die for" and "great fresh fish" is "like a Mediterranean vacation"; with "warm, sunny" decor and "unpretentious" service it invites you to "stay and enjoy for hours", but leaves some asking "why isn't it busier?"

Arturo's Pizzeria ◐[S] — 18 | 10 | 13 | $17
106 W. Houston St. (Thompson St.), 212-677-3820
◪ Don't let the "garage sale decor" and "strange mix of people" scare you away from some of the "best coal-oven pizza in Manhattan"; still, it's like "eating in the rec room of a friend's house."

Artusi — 21 | 18 | 20 | $42
36 W. 52nd St. (bet. 5th & 6th Aves.), 212-582-6900
■ Surveyors enjoy the Italian food at this "undiscovered", "creative" Midtown yearling while lamenting the "boring" decor that "looks like a boardroom" – that and "fast service" could be the reason it's "excellent for a business lunch", but "too quiet on weekends."

Asia de Cuba ◐[S] — – | – | – | E
Morgans Hotel, 237 Madison Ave. (bet. 37th & 38th Sts.), 212-726-7755
Brand-new, superstylish, all-white, Philippe Starck–designed, multilevel Murray Hill Asian-Cuban; there's a 45-foot hologram of a waterfall, communal seating option, working fireplaces and an endless selection of rums; N.B. it's the sister restaurant to China Grill, but twice as hip.

Asiana [S] — ▽ 16 | 16 | 14 | $20
53 Ave. A (bet. 3rd & 4th Sts.), 212-674-3538
◪ "A bit like Disneyland" with tiki torches and faux bridges, this East Village Pan-Asian yearling draws mixed reviews: "excellent tastes" vs. "disappointingly bland"; service doesn't help, but low prices do.

Athens Cafe (Queens) ◐[S] — ▽ 18 | 16 | 17 | $20
32-07 30th Ave. (32nd St.), 718-626-2164
◪ Most people enjoy the "casual Mediterranean atmosphere" and "major people-watching" at this Astoria "Greek hangout"; but many prefer to "go in the summer when you can sit outside."

August Moon [S] — ▽ 21 | 19 | 19 | $31
145 W. 58th St. (bet. 6th & 7th Aves.), 212-581-2288
■ This "serene" Midtown Chinese yearling has "solicitous" service and "healthy" cuisine, even if "portions are small for the price."

Au Mandarin [S] — 19 | 15 | 17 | $28
World Financial Ctr., 200-250 Vesey St. (West St.), 212-385-0313
◪ Rather than eat in the "loud WFC setting", "investment bankers live by the takeout" from this "excellent" upscale Chinese; it's not bad for a "lunch meeting with your boss."

AUREOLE — 28 | 26 | 26 | $68
34 E. 61st St. (bet. Madison & Park Aves.), 212-319-1660
■ "Everything you've heard is true and more" at Charlie Palmer's "top-notch" East Side star; surveyors say the "sensational" New American cuisine and "architectural" desserts are "worth every truffled cent" and the service is "sublime"; the back garden and "beautiful" flowers make it "a place to propose"; P.S. the new post–2 PM $19.98 prix fixe menu has to be NYC's best fine dining buy.

Au Troquet 🔲
| 21 | 18 | 20 | $41 |

328 W. 12th St. (Greenwich St.), 212-924-3413

■ "Really French feeling without French snootiness", this standby in the West Village serves "truly delicious" bistro cuisine in a "romantic" setting; as good as it is, the kitchen is no trailblazer.

Avenue A ◑🔲
| 18 | 15 | 14 | $24 |

103 Ave. A (bet. 6th & 7th Sts.), 212-982-8109

◪ "Black walls, neon hair and good sushi" draw the "I'm too sexy for my sushi crowd" to this affordable East Village Japanese; the DJ spinning "loud" music and "service with an attitude" can "try the nerves", but the fish pieces are "bigger and fresher than elsewhere."

Azure 🔲
| – | – | – | E |

484 Amsterdam Ave. (bet. 83rd & 84th Sts.), 212-721-1000

Write-ins tout this relaxing, azure-colored Upper West Side "new twist on" Mediterranean; it's packed nightly with a smart after-work crowd enjoying a small but "top-quality" menu.

Azusa of Japan
| ▽ | 17 | 15 | 18 | $30 |

3 E. 44th St. (bet. 5th & Madison Aves.), 212-681-0001

◪ There's "no fuss, just fresh" sushi at this Midtown Japanese popular for its $9.75 lunch; still, foes would prefer more fish and improved decor.

Baby Jake's ◑🔲
| 16 | 11 | 13 | $19 |

14 First Ave. (bet. 1st & 2nd Sts.), 212-254-2229

■ A cheap East Village Cajun with a young crowd; there's not much decor but the "spicy", "hearty" fare causes gasps of "Holy Cholesterol!"

Baci 🔲
| 18 | 15 | 16 | $32 |

412 Amsterdam Ave. (bet. 79th & 80th Sts.), 212-496-1550

◪ Most surveyors feel you get your "money's worth" at this "crowded", "closet-size", "always delicious" West Side Sicilian pasta place with "flowers all over" and service by "Euro-slick Romeos."

Bali Nusa Indah 🔲
| 18 | 11 | 15 | $21 |

651 Ninth Ave. (bet. 45th & 46th Sts.), 212-265-2200

◪ There's "great satay and rijsttafel" and "hefty portions" at this Hell's Kitchen "bargain" Indonesian joint; it's a good "pre-theater alternative" despite service that's "slow of tongue, wit and foot."

Ballato's 🔲
| 17 | 12 | 17 | $29 |

55 E. Houston St. (bet. Mott & Mulberry Sts.), 212-274-8881

◪ This "homey" East Village storefront with a garden serves "cheap, decent pasta" and is "good from door to dessert"; but it's often "crowded" and old-timers say it's "not up to when John Ballato ran it."

BALTHAZAR ◑🔲
| 21 | 25 | 18 | $44 |

80 Spring St. (bet. Crosby St. & B'way), 212-965-1414

■ Surveyors rave over the "romantic, retro" bistro decor at Keith McNally's "bustling", "trendy with a capital T" new SoHo-based "Parisian-style brasserie"; they hail the "surprisingly good food" but dis the "attitude à la carte" service; as for the crowd, "Holy Models, Batman!" – "are we cool enough" to get in?

Baluchi's 🔲
| 21 | 17 | 17 | $25 |

1565 Second Ave. (bet. 81st & 82nd Sts.), 212-288-4810
283 Columbus Ave. (bet. 73rd & 74th Sts.), 212-579-3900
240 W. 56th St. (bet. B'way & 8th Ave.), 212-397-0707
361 Sixth Ave. (Washington Pl.), 212-929-2441
193 Spring St. (bet. Sullivan & Thompson Sts.), 212-226-2828

■ There are now five outlets of this "standout" Indian minichain with "fresh, cheap", "spicy" food that "answers your mantra" by being "good at all locations"; everyone loves the "amazing half-price lunch deal", but decor and service appear to be "uneven."

Bambou
22 24 19 $43

243 E. 14th St. (bet. 2nd & 3rd Aves.), 212-358-0012

■ This yearling East Village "black celeb hangout" with "beautiful", "relaxing tropical" decor has "the best Caribbean food in NYC"; despite a few grumbles about the "limited menu" and staff that still "needs training", it's like "a quick trip to the islands."

Bamcafe (Brooklyn) ⊅
– – – M

Brooklyn Academy of Music, 30 Lafayette Ave. (Ashland Pl.), 718-636-4100

With Michael Ayoub (of Cucina) behind it, this International newcomer (currently only open on performance days) has to be taken seriously.

Bamiyan S
▽ 18 14 16 $23

358 Third Ave. (26th St.), 212-481-3232

☑ "Dependable" East Side "Afghan bargain" with good food, "friendly staff" and a section with "floor-cushions" that impresses "out-of-towners."

Bangkok Cafe S
17 13 15 $22

27 E. 20th St. (bet. B'way & Park Ave. S.), 212-228-7681

☑ A "find in pricey Gramercy", especially for the affordable prix fixe, this "neighborhood Thai" has a "friendly staff", "good specials" and is "excellent for takeout"; a few call it simply "average."

Bangkok Cuisine ●S
18 13 15 $24

885 Eighth Ave. (bet. 52nd & 53rd Sts.), 212-581-6370

☑ A "reliable", "tangy" veteran Theater District Thai; surveyors savor the "slurpable soups", fish fresh from tanks and the thrice-weekly bargain lunch buffet, but not the "dreary", "dark" decor.

Bar and Books ●S
11 21 18 $27

1020 Lexington Ave. (73rd St.), 212-717-3902
889 First Ave. (50th St.), 212-980-9314
Cityspire Ctr., 156 W. 56th St. (bet. 6th & 7th Aves.), 212-957-9676
636 Hudson St. (bet. Horatio & Jane Sts.), 212-229-2642

☑ The place for a martini and a good cigar, this minichain of "Ralph Lauren–style library bars" offers "elegant" decor as a backdrop for the fashionable "LBD (little black dress)" crowd, but given the "nuked", "prefab" Eclectic food, you may want to eat elsewhere.

Baraonda ●S⊅
17 18 13 $35

1439 Second Ave. (75th St.), 212-288-8555

☑ At this art-filled, "always happening", "sleek pasta place" on the East Side, some say the "fun begins at midnight" when "people dance on tables"; "the [Italian] food is good", but "most go to see and be seen."

Barbetta ●
19 24 20 $48

321 W. 46th St. (bet. 8th & 9th Aves.), 212-246-9171

☑ "What a pleasant surprise"; this upmarket Restaurant Row classic Italian, entering its 10th decade, exudes "old-world charm" though "at 90, you'd be tired too"; eating in the garden is "heavenly" – even if some suspect they "pipe in recorded bird-chirping" – and the "pre-theater specials are a good value"; however, the "very good food" could be better for the price.

Barcelona S
16 15 18 $36

1291 Madison Ave. (bet. 91st & 92nd Sts.), 212-860-2300

☑ Respondents report that this pricey new Carnegie Hill tapas place is "still having beginner's problems" ("watery sangria", for example), but is "one to watch", especially for its "superb $12.95 lunch."

Bardolino S
– – – M

1496 Second Ave. (bet. 77th & 78th Sts.), 212-734-9050

With good Italian food at "prices you can afford every night", this cozy Eastsider is the quintessential cheap date spot: candlelight sets the mood, and servers don't rush or hover.

Bar 89 ◐[S] 14 | 23 | 14 | $24
89 Mercer St. (bet. Broome & Spring Sts.), 212-274-0989
◩ Critics snipe at the pub fare and service at this SoHo "models' hangout"; though "you can't say much for the food", everyone loves the "must-see" "techno" bathrooms and the drinks (have a cosmopolitan).

Barking Dog Luncheonette ◐[S]≠ 16 | 14 | 15 | $19
1678 Third Ave. (94th St.), 212-831-1800
■ "Casual", "almost too cute", "kid-friendly" East Side luncheonette serving sandwiches, burgers and "better meat loaf than Aunt Sadie's"; brunch attracts the "hangover crowd"; critics sniff "for the dogs."

Barney Greengrass [S]≠ 22 | 7 | 13 | $20
541 Amsterdam Ave. (bet. 86th & 87th Sts.), 212-724-4707
■ "He ain't the sturgeon king for nothing" say fans of this West Side Jewish deli classic that looks like "your grandparents' old kitchen"; it makes a "memorable breakfast" and is "great for brunch, but the [weekend] lines are crazy"; no dinner.

Bar Nine ◐[S] 17 | 19 | 16 | $26
807 Ninth Ave. (54th St.), 212-399-9336
◩ There's "funky", "Transylvanian" lounge decor and "passable" to "good" American food at this "inexpensive", "host-driven", "Hell's Kitchen godsend"; locals like the fact that "they don't rush you out."

Barocco ◐[S] 20 | 16 | 17 | $35
301 Church St. (Walker St.), 212-431-1445
■ "Predictably good even if black duds are mandatory" and decor is a bit "dilapidated", this "chic" TriBeCa trattoria is "a survivor" that remains "one of the art world's favorites" for fine fish and pasta.

Barolo ◐[S] 18 | 21 | 16 | $41
398 W. Broadway (bet. Broome & Spring Sts.), 212-226-1102
◩ Diners enthuse over the "beautiful, huge garden", "supermodels", "weekday lunches", "great risotto" and wine list at this "stylish" SoHo Italian but grumble about prices and "snooty", "slow" staff.

Bar Pitti ◐[S]≠ 20 | 15 | 16 | $27
268 Sixth Ave. (bet. Bleecker & Houston Sts.), 212-982-3300
■ For "great Village dining" at "unbeatable prices" try this Tuscan with sidewalk seats; there's "supertasty pasta" and "good people-watching."

Bar Six ◐[S] 15 | 16 | 13 | $27
502 Sixth Ave. (bet. 12th & 13th Sts.), 212-691-1363
◩ The style at this "crowded" French-Moroccan Village bistro/bar scene is "twentysomething/darkish/smoky/actor", but so loud it's touted as a date place only "if you don't want to talk"; "right this way, Mr. Pitt."

Basilica ◐[S] ▽ 18 | 15 | 16 | $29
676 Ninth Ave. (bet. 46th & 47th Sts.), 212-489-0051
◩ Surveyors agree that this new "unpretentious" Theater District Italian is a "friendly", "good value", but while some praise the "excellent fish", others find the grub only "adequate."

Basta Pasta [S] 17 | 15 | 17 | $29
37 W. 17th St. (bet. 5th & 6th Aves.), 212-366-0888
◩ "Udon meets semolina" at this "chic" modern Italian in the Flatiron District; fans find it "a kick" with "good value at lunch, not as good at dinner", but critics claim it's "weird" for "Japanese to make Italian."

Bayamo ◐[S] 13 | 15 | 13 | $23
704 Broadway (bet. 4th St. & Washington Pl.), 212-475-5151
◩ This "funky" "cheapo Chino-Latino" "barnlike" "dive" near NYU may be "fun if you're 21", but the older and hopefully wiser find it "noisy", "bland" and "overpriced" except for the $4.50 early-bird.

Bay Leaf ⬛
20 | 17 | 18 | $32
49 W. 56th St. (bet. 5th & 6th Aves.), 212-957-1818
◪ There's "different, delicious" Indian food at this Midtown venue, especially at the "great value" lunch buffet and pre-theater prix fixe; some find the interior "lovely", others "boring."

B Bar ◑⬛
13 | 16 | 10 | $32
(fka Bowery Bar)
40 E. Fourth St. (bet. Bowery & Lafayette St.), 212-475-2220
◪ "Good luck getting any service" at this "trendy" Downtown New American "over the top" meet market; if "great for fashion-watchers", it irks diners with its "bland and scant" food; P.S. for best results, "tell them you're from *People* magazine."

Beatrice Inn
16 | 14 | 18 | $29
285 W. 12th St. (bet. 8th Ave. & W. 4th St.), 212-929-6165
◪ Italian West Village standby that has a "homey" atmosphere and good solid food; the back room is good for private parties.

Becco ◑⬛
20 | 16 | 19 | $34
355 W. 46th St. (bet. 8th & 9th Aves.), 212-397-7597
■ "Best buy in the Theater District" – Joe Bastianich's Restaurant Row Italian offers an "excellent" $19.95 AYCE pasta dinner served by "nice people" in attractive townhouse digs; "reserve early" for pre-theater when it's busy, but check it out "after 8 PM" too.

Bel-Air ◑⬛≠
– | – | – | M
110 St. Marks Pl. (bet. 1st Ave. & Ave. A), 212-477-3311
Airy East Village French-American newcomer that has the potential to impress with its charming interior and basic, hearty, midpriced eats.

Bella Blu ◑⬛
18 | 18 | 15 | $36
967 Lexington Ave. (bet. 70th & 71st Sts.), 212-988-4624
◪ At this "noisy" East Side Italian "scene" cafe, the "young and would-be-young" crowd touts the "witty" multicolored decor and food; even the "spacey" waiters are said to be "improving."

Bella Donna
18 | 9 | 15 | $19
1663 First Ave. (bet. 86th & 87th Sts.), 212-534-3261 ⬛≠
307 E. 77th St. (bet. 1st & 2nd Aves.), 212-535-2866 ◑⬛≠
18 E. 23rd St. (Madison Ave.), 212-505-3678 ◑
◪ The prix fixe lunch and "cheap pasta" in the evening are the "way to go when your plastic is maxed out", which helps account for the "long lines" at these "cramped", "no atmosphere" East Side Italians.

Bella Luna ⬛
17 | 15 | 16 | $27
584 Columbus Ave. (bet. 88th & 89th Sts.), 212-877-2267
◪ Neighbors keep coming to this "consistent, inexpensive" Upper West Side Italian where "they take care of children too"; a minority finds the experience "boring – but good", i.e. "a fine *local* restaurant."

Bellissima ⬛
16 | 12 | 15 | $22
1409 Second Ave. (bet. 73rd & 74th Sts.), 212-535-3030
1179 Second Ave. (bet. 62nd & 63rd Sts.), 212-751-1536 ≠
◪ This pair of "best buy" "cozy" East Side Italian bistros have "solid" food and "friendly service", but the location near Bloomie's (which is BYO) has only 20 seats – "my closet is larger."

Bello
20 | 16 | 19 | $35
863 Ninth Ave. (56th St.), 212-246-6773
■ Strategically located between the Theater District and Lincoln Center, and providing free parking, this "always busy" "old-fashioned Italian" offers "solid food" and "attentive service" at fair prices.

Belluno
▽ 23 | 17 | 20 | $38

340 Lexington Ave. (bet. 39th & 40th Sts.), 212-953-3282

■ A "great new addition" to the Murray Hill scene, this reasonably priced Northern Italian has "pretty, airy decor" and a "staff that tries"; fans salute the salads, steaks and thin-crust pizzas.

Ben Benson's S
22 | 17 | 19 | $48

123 W. 52nd St. (bet. 6th & 7th Aves.), 212-581-8888

◢ It's "no Peter Luger" and "no bargain", but "Ben still makes great steaks" and "the stiffest drinks in the city" served with "big sides", including highly touted potatoes, at his Midtown "men's club"; expect "lots of noise and testosterone" along with plenty of good eats.

Benihana of Tokyo S
16 | 15 | 18 | $32

120 E. 56th St. (bet. Lexington & Park Aves.), 212-593-1627
47 W. 56th St. (bet. 5th & 6th Aves.), 212-581-0930

◢ "Avoid the flying shrimp tails" and enjoy the samurai chefs' "good floor show" at this pair of "slice and dice" Midtown teppanyaki houses; some say "keep it for kids' birthday parties" and for tourists.

Benito I S
18 | 12 | 16 | $27

174 Mulberry St. (Broome St.), 212-226-9171

◢ "A good choice for Little Italy", this "cramped" old bastion of "earthy Sicilian cooking" has "no finesse" but is a "good deal."

Benito II S⇄
18 | 11 | 16 | $29

163 Mulberry St. (bet. Broome & Grand Sts.), 212-226-9012

◢ There's "lotsa garlic" at this "dress-down", "fair-priced" Little Italy homestyle Southern Italian; it's "a treat if you don't have to wait."

Benny's Burritos ◐S⇄
17 | 9 | 12 | $15

113 Greenwich Ave. (Jane St.), 212-727-3560
93 Ave. A (6th St.), 212-254-2054

■ An upgrade in the "SW kitsch garage-sale decor" "would ruin the charm" of these popular, "cramped", "great value" Village Mexicans; "yummy" "monster burritos" draw a "hip", young, beer-drinking crowd.

Ben's Kosher Deli S
18 | 12 | 15 | $18

209 W. 38th St. (7th Ave.), 212-398-2367
Bay Terrace, 211-37 26th Ave., Queens, 718-229-2367

◢ The well-known "eat till you plotz" Long Island kosher deli chain has now leaped the East River and landed in the Garment District (convenient "before Garden events"); so "pass the mustard" and remember delis aren't supposed to be pretty, just "clean."

Between the Bread
16 | 10 | 12 | $18

141 E. 56th St. (bet. 3rd & Lexington Aves.), 212-888-0449

◢ This "soup and sandwich" lunch place with "tiny, crowded tables" splits surveyors; some call it "delicious, casual and quick"; others say it's "expensive and offensive", but admit "the muffins are good."

Bice ◐S
20 | 19 | 17 | $45

7 E. 54th St. (bet. 5th & Madison Aves.), 212-688-1999

◢ "There are better restaurants around", but Euros and other fans love this "fashionable", "show me the money" Midtown Milanese with the "best suntanned legs in town"; the food is "high level", ditto the prices and noise; but critics "don't know how all the egos fit."

Bienvenue
19 | 14 | 19 | $31

21 E. 36th St. (bet. 5th & Madison Aves.), 212-684-0215

■ This "charming" Murray Hill French bistro has "warm, friendly" service and a "new chef who's improved" the already good food; a recent remodeling may also help this "cramped" "old standby."

F	D	S	C

Big Wong [S]≠ 20 | 4 | 9 | $11
67 Mott St. (bet. Bayard & Canal Sts.), 212-964-0540
■ A "happy tummy comes cheap" at this Chinatown "cafeteria-like" "dump" with "lines for lunch"; ignore the "cheeky waiters" and enjoy "hearty" "BBQ and noodles that set the standard for authenticity."

Bill Hong's [S] 20 | 13 | 19 | $35
227 E. 56th St. (bet. 2nd & 3rd Aves.), 212-751-4048
◪ "If you can't get to Canton", try this Midtown Cantonese "grande dame"; while regulars lavish praise on the "fabulous lobster roll", some say the food is "humdrum" and the decor "needs a face-lift."

Billy's ◐[S] 16 | 13 | 17 | $35
948 First Ave. (bet. 52nd & 53rd Sts.), 212-753-1870
◪ There's "nothing nouvelle, only good" simple steak and fish at this "friendly" wood-paneled Sutton Place American saloon; though "loved by the older generation", younger diners say it's strictly "yesteryear."

Biricchino 20 | 12 | 18 | $30
260 W. 29th St. (8th Ave.), 212-695-6690
◪ The "best Italian near the Garden", this "great little NY secret" is best known for its "superb homemade sausage" but also wins kudos for antipasti, pastas and free chocolate truffles; hopefully, renovations will spruce up its "mundane" decor.

Bissaleh ◐[S] 17 | 13 | 14 | $20
1435 Second Ave. (bet. 74th & 75th Sts.), 212-717-2333
127 W. 72nd St. (bet. Columbus & Amsterdam Aves.), 212-724-0377
◪ "Welcome to Israel"; these "haimish", "noisy, crowded" kosher dairy joints serve "sharing-is-a-must" portions of good Middle Eastern food.

Bistro Carré [S] – | – | – | M
1590 First Ave. (bet. 82nd & 83rd Sts.), 212-717-7575
Cozy, new eight-table East Side French bistro offering an intimate setting and a something-for-everyone menu including such unique entrees as beet gnocchi with goat cheese sauce.

Bistro du Nord [S] 19 | 16 | 17 | $38
1312 Madison Ave. (bet. 92nd & 93rd Sts.), 212-289-0997
■ A lunch and pre-theater "standby" in Carnegie Hill, this "charming French sardine can" inhabits an "itsy-bitsy" jewel box; fortunately, the "pricey", "very French" food is "attractive and good."

Bistro Latino ◐[S] 19 | 16 | 18 | $37
1711 Broadway, 2nd fl. (54th St.), 212-956-1000
■ Like a "glamorous speakeasy", this second-floor "Latin Rainbow Room" is a rare Midtown place for "civilized" dining and dancing, offering "interesting food", including steaks and empanadas, and doing the tango and cha-cha-cha to a live band; it's "cheesy" but can be "fun."

Bistro Le Steak ◐[S] 18 | 14 | 16 | $33
1309 Third Ave. (75th St.), 212-517-3800
■ A "good value for basic steak frites", this "modest" but "delicious" East Side yearling is a "great addition to the neighborhood"; it can be "a little too crowded", but that's because it's "consistently good."

Bistro 39 [S] – | – | – | M
720 Second Ave. (39th St.), 212-696-1654
Dark, cozy, brick-walled Midtown French bistro presided over by chef James Rafferty (ex Bouley); plan on a relaxing meal at modest prices.

Bistrot Margot [S]≠ 19 | 16 | 17 | $26
26 Prince St. (bet. Elizabeth & Mott Sts.), 212-274-1027
■ "Like a small Paris bistro", this "snug", "noisy" but "relaxed" SoHo place has "amazingly authentic" food but only "adequate" service.

Blockhead's S
954 Second Ave. (bet. 50th & 51st Sts.), 212-750-2020
499 Third Ave. (bet. 33rd & 34th Sts.), 212-213-3332
322 W. 50th St. (bet. 8th & 9th Aves.), 212-307-7070

15 | 10 | 13 | $15

☑ "Burritos the size of burros" are the main draw at these "cheap", "generic" Cal-Mexicans; critics say "you have to be a blockhead" to eat the "landfill" they serve.

BLUE RIBBON ◑S
97 Sullivan St. (bet. Prince & Spring Sts.), 212-274-0404

24 | 17 | 19 | $39

■ "If you can get a table, which you can't, you'll love the food", especially the "excellent fresh seafood" at this "crowded, noisy", "trendy", "models galore" SoHo Eclectic; go before 6 or after 11 to avoid a "nasty wait."

BLUE RIBBON SUSHI ◑S
119 Sullivan St. (bet. Prince & Spring Sts.), 212-343-0404

25 | 19 | 19 | $40

■ "Best sushi in NY" and "great sake" rave numerous aficionados about this "sleek and cool" Blue Ribbon spin-off; but it takes no reservations, often resulting in "killer waits."

BLUE WATER GRILL ◑S
31 Union Sq. W. (16th St.), 212-675-9500

22 | 22 | 19 | $39

■ "A delight in every way" sums up this Union Square seafood cafe in a "classic old bank" with fish, pasta and a raw bar; for conversation and people-watching, stay upstairs, for music and a cool bar, go downstairs.

Boathouse Cafe, The S
Central Park Lake (East Park Dr. & 72nd St.), 212-517-2233

14 | 24 | 15 | $34

☑ It's a "lovely setting" overlooking Central Park Lake, so "who cares about" the American food?; most tout it "for a date or out-of-town friend", but wonder if the food was "caught in the lake."

Bobby Van's Steakhouse S
230 Park Ave. (46th St), 212-867-5490

20 | 18 | 19 | $48

☑ "Lots of suits, smoke and excellent steaks" is the general verdict on this Grand Central–area beef emporium; some surveyors say it's "strictly for the rich and to-be-seen crowd."

Boca Chica S
13 First Ave. (1st St.), 212-473-0108

18 | 13 | 14 | $22

☑ The food at this "funky", low-budget East Village "carnival" is Brazilian-Latin (including "the best rice and beans") and the decor is "eye-popping zebra"; but there are "long waits" on weekends when "ear-popping music" leads to "shoulder shaking" on the dance floor.

Bodega ◑S
136 W. Broadway (bet. Duane & Thomas Sts.), 212-285-1155

16 | 14 | 15 | $19

☑ Popular with both families and "arty types", this new "change of pace" TriBeCa Eclectic has "cheap, good", "diverse" food, including sandwiches, burritos, fried chicken and "delicious fruity sodas"; critics call it "hiply mediocre."

Bo-Ky S⌿
80 Bayard St. (bet. Mott & Mulberry Sts.), 212-406-2292

18 | 4 | 9 | $12

☑ Cheap Chinatown Vietnamese "jury duty payback" joint with great noodle dishes and roast duck for chicken feed.

BOLO S
23 E. 22nd St. (bet. B'way & Park Ave. S.), 212-228-2200

23 | 21 | 20 | $44

■ Serving Spanish food "as snappy as castanets", this "noisy, trendy", "upscale" Flatiron venue with "flamenco flair", "stylish decor" and "people-watching" is "hitting its stride" under the aegis of chef Bobby Flay; fans hail the lamb shank as "superb" and the paella as NY's "best."

Bombay Palace 🅂

F	D	S	C
18	18	18	$29

30 W. 52nd St. (bet. 5th & 6th Aves.), 212-541-7777

■ Reviewers praise the $11.95 lunchtime buffet "that's worth every penny" upstairs at this resurrrected Midtown Indian where even the à la carte price is right; despite the "lighter feel" of the new decor. some surveyors say it's a case of "sikh transit gloria."

Bona Fides 🅂

16 | 15 | 16 | $22

60 Second Ave. (bet. 3rd & 4th Sts.), 212-777-2840

☑ It's "nice and dark inside" and there's a "beautiful garden" at this "quiet", "off-the-beaten-track" East Village Italian "bargain hunter's dream"; skeptics say it proves "anyone can open a restaurant."

Bondini

20 | 21 | 20 | $38

62 W. Ninth St. (bet. 5th & 6th Aves.), 212-777-0670

■ Surveyors like "the gorgeous main room with high ceilings and flowers" at this Village Italian "treasure"; regulars say it's "tried and true" and "a perfect first-date place" though "a bit pricey."

Boom ◑🅂

15 | 16 | 13 | $34

152 Spring St. (bet. W. B'way & Wooster St.), 212-431-3663

☑ Booming when it first opened six years ago as a SoHo hot spot, this "modern ethnic" Eclectic has now become "a staple" local "haunt"; P.S. the "chic, sexy, twentysomething crowd" appears "after 10 PM."

Bora

▽ 21 | 13 | 20 | $36

179 Madison Ave. (bet. 33rd & 34th Sts.), 212-725-3282

■ There's "upscale food" at this "congenial", "respectfully formal" Murray Hill Northern Italian "sleeper"; local business people appreciate its "efficient" lunch.

Borgo Antico ◑🅂

20 | 19 | 21 | $35

22 E. 13th St. (bet. 5th Ave. & University Pl.), 212-807-1313

■ "Upscale" Village Northern Italian with a "charming room", "delicious pasta" and game specialties; still, "it's not a destination place – you just end up there."

Bosco 🅂

15 | 14 | 16 | $31

1049 Lexington Ave. (bet. 74th & 75th Sts.), 212-535-8400

■ Prix fixe menus ($10 for lunch, $14.95 at dinner and $19.98 for the nightly lobster special) are complemented by a rosy, candlelit setting that makes this Italian Eastsider an always "pleasant" venue.

Botany, The 🅂

▽ 22 | 18 | 20 | $34

55 Greenwich Ave. (bet. 6th & 7th Aves.), 212-243-5655

■ Surveyors tout the "gracious owner", "cozy ambiance", "freshest fish" and "decadent mashed potatoes" at this Village American newcomer; give it a try.

BOULEY BAKERY ◑🅂

– | – | – | E

120 W. Broadway (bet. Duane & Reade Sts.), 212-964-2525

Having opened too late to be in this year's voting and being too small to permit many reservations anyway, this semi-informal TriBeCa newcomer proves that the original Bouley was no fluke: look for wonderful baked-on-premises breads and the freshest organic ingredients exquisitely cooked and served in a lovely space; go!

BOUTERIN 🅂

22 | 24 | 21 | $52

420 E. 59th St. (bet. 1st Ave. & Sutton Pl.), 212-758-0323

☑ Chef Antoine Bouterin's Provençal restaurant near the Queensboro Bridge has "wonderful food", "excellent wine" and is "great for a special night out"; though "expensive", it's "getting better each time."

BOX TREE S 24 | 26 | 24 | $68
250 E. 49th St. (bet. 2nd & 3rd Aves.), 212-758-8320
☑ A "gorgeous", highly rated French in an art nouveau room "dripping with romantic energy"; if money is no object, it's a "perfect proposal place" with handy upstairs rooms if the answer is 'yes'; P.S. dissenters dis it as a "pretentious" "rip-off" at its prix fixe price of $86 for dinner.

Brasilia S 16 | 13 | 15 | $29
7 W. 45th St. (bet. 5th & 6th Aves.), 212-869-9200
☑ "A taste of samba in every mouthful" say enthusiasts about this Midtown down-home Brazilian serving "meat, meat and more meat" as well as seafood; others insist it "isn't very good."

Bravo Gianni ●S 21 | 17 | 20 | $50
230 E. 63rd St. (bet. 2nd & 3rd Aves.), 212-752-7272
☑ Regulars cite "welcoming owner", Gianni, at this "intimate, clubby", "lots of kisses" East Side "classic Italian"; the "careful cooking and attentive service justify high prices."

Brawta Caribbean Cafe (Brooklyn) S 19 | 12 | 14 | $18
347 Atlantic Ave. (Hoyt St.), 718-855-5515
☑ "One bite and you're in the islands" at this "quick, clean", "cheap" Downtown Brooklyn Caribbean; surveyors praise the "blazing jerk chicken" and roti, but as ratings show, not the decor or service.

Bricco Ristorante S 19 | 18 | 17 | $30
304 W. 56th St. (bet. 8th & 9th Aves.), 212-245-7160
■ This "cozy" Southern Italian trattoria between the Theater District and Lincoln Center has "good prices", a "gregarious host" and "great thin pizza and pasta"; it's also "good for business lunch."

Bridge Cafe ●S 21 | 17 | 19 | $34
279 Water St. (Dover St.), 212-227-3344
■ A "charming", "historic"-looking American bar/cafe near South Street Seaport with a "creative menu", "super brunch" and "pleasant staff"; fans say it has "just the right mix of casual atmosphere and really good food."

Bright Food Shop S⊅ 18 | 10 | 15 | $19
216 Eighth Ave. (bet. 21st & 22nd Sts.), 212-243-4433
■ With a "successful fusion" of Asian and SW grub (as in "Mexican moo shu"), this "hip", 45-seat, cash-only Chelsea venue is "totally devoid" of ambiance; brunch is best, but any meal can be counted on to be "spicy", "cheap and good."

Brio S 18 | 15 | 17 | $34
786 Lexington Ave. (bet. 61st & 62nd Sts.), 212-980-2300
☑ This small, "midpriced" East Side Italian is "a charming refuge for the Bloomie's crowd" offering "good and dependable" food. "casual" ambiance and "service with a smile"; Brio Forno, around the corner, has a wood-burning oven.

Brooklyn Diner USA ●S 14 | 15 | 14 | $24
212 W. 57th St. (bet. B'way & 7th Ave.), 212-581-8900
☑ "Goulash as good as mom made" and Texas-size hot dogs are among the wide-ranging choices at this "upscale", "'50s-style" Carnegie Hall–area diner; critics would send dem bums back to Brooklyn.

Broome Street Bar ●S 14 | 12 | 13 | $20
363 W. Broadway (Broome St.), 212-925-2086
■ This affordable "SoHo institution" serves "better burgers and sandwiches than you would expect at a bar" and "always has someone interesting to talk with"; look for local art types on weekdays and gallerygoers on weekends.

Brother Jimmy's BBQ ◑Ⓢ
15 10 13 $20
1644 Third Ave. (92nd St.), 212-426-2020
1461 First Ave. (76th St.), 212-288-0999
■ "Their dry-rubbed ribs are the reason cows were invented" say fans of these beer-swilling, low-budget East Side "frat parties"; they're among the best in their class, that is, if you don't mind dining with "a noisy twentysomething crowd" watching "ACC basketball."

Brothers BBQ Ⓢ
15 12 13 $20
225 Varick St. (Clarkson St.), 212-727-2775
■ "Put some South in your mouth", including "tangy" ribs, pulled pork and a "great catfish sandwich", at this "little bit of Memphis" in the Village; it draws a "postcollege crowd" drinking out of "fishbowls."

Bruce Ho's Four Seas ◑Ⓢ
19 16 20 $35
116 E. 57th St. (bet. Lexington & Park Aves.), 212-753-2610
☑ "Bruce is the nicest man" and his "classic '50s" Cantonese food is "served with TLC" at this East Side "haven"; modernists complain about "very plain food", but most surveyors say simply "delicious."

Bruno Ristorante ◑
21 18 20 $44
240 E. 58th St. (bet. 2nd & 3rd Aves.), 212-688-4190
■ This "old standby" Italian on the East Side has "slick decor", "professional service" and "solid" food; surveyors tout the lively "piano bar scene" in the evening, but point out that "there are better for less."

Bryant Park Grill Ⓢ
18 22 16 $35

Bryant Park Cafe ◑Ⓢ
16 21 15 $31
25 W. 40th St. (behind NY Public Library), 212-840-6500
☑ You "cannot beat the setting" at this Bryant Park New American pair; respondents rate the dining experience surprisingly good, but better and more expensive at the "appealing" Grill; outdoor seating becomes "wall-to-wall yuppies" after work and the best place to find "a Brooks Brothers man" in a "Midtown oasis" that "makes a sunny day sunnier."

B. Smith's Ⓢ
18 17 17 $36
771 Eighth Ave. (47th St.), 212-247-2222
■ Owner Barbara Smith is widely regarded as "the most charming lady in town", which helps make her "elegant" Soul Fooder-cum-bustling buppie bar ideal "for pre- or post-theater"; the aurally sensitive chide the "high noise level."

Bubble Lounge, The ◑
13 21 14 $31
228 W. Broadway (bet. Franklin & White Sts.), 212-431-3433
■ With a choice of 280 champagnes – 20 by the glass – this "dark, mysterious" TriBeCa lounge "with comfy couches" is a place where "anyone can look cool"; "who cares about the [American] food when the champagne is always cold" and the "singles shopping" so good; here, "B&T crowd" often means beautiful and tall.

Bubby's ◑Ⓢ
18 13 14 $20
120 Hudson St. (bet. Franklin & N. Moore Sts.), 212-219-0666
☑ Serving "homestyle" American "comfort food", this "very popular" TriBeCa "neighborhood place" (with outdoor seating) attracts the likes of JFK, Jr., De Niro and Keitel; go for one of the "best breakfasts in Manhattan" or weekend brunch.

Bull & Bear ◑Ⓢ
18 19 18 $42
Waldorf-Astoria, 570 Lexington Ave. (49th St.), 212-872-4900
☑ Evoking "a time when meat was king", this somewhat "stuffy", "men's club" steakhouse with "magnificent wood decor" in the Waldorf is "surprisingly good" if "you're on someone else's expense account"; a minority reports the "bull tastes more like bear" and "the bar is best."

Bull Run 🅂   ▽ 17 | 17 | 15 | $31
52 William St. (Pine St.), 212-859-2200
☑ Wall Streeters like this "sleek", "much-needed" Continental
newcomer because "it can do a sit-down lunch in 30 minutes" and
has a "lively, fun bar"; food quality is rated "ok."

Burger Heaven 🅂   14 | 8 | 12 | $13
9 E. 53rd St. (bet. 5th & Madison Aves.), 212-752-0340
20 E. 49th St. (bet. 5th & Madison Aves.), 212-755-2166
291 Madison Ave. (bet. 40th & 41st Sts.), 212-685-6250
536 Madison Ave. (bet. 54th & 55th Sts.), 212-753-4214
☑ Management has attempted to deal with decor problems with a spiff-
up at these "fast", "cheap" "pit stops" for burgers and sandwiches;
philosophers shrug "sometimes you gotta eat."

Burritoville 🅂   15 | 5 | 11 | $11
1606 Third Ave. (bet. 90th & 91st Sts.), 212-410-2255
1489 First Ave. (bet. 77th & 78th Sts.), 212-472-8800
166 W. 72nd St. (bet. Columbus & Amsterdam Aves.), 212-580-7700 ◗
264 W. 23rd St. (bet. 7th & 8th Aves.), 212-367-9844 ◗
141 Second Ave. (bet. 8th & 9th Sts.), 212-260-3300 ◗
36 Water St. (Broad St.), 212-747-1100
144 Chambers St. (bet. Greenwich Ave. & W. B'way), 212-571-1144
☑ "Blimp-sized burritos" are the staple at these popular "kick-ass"
Mexicans with "negative decor" where you listen to "loud music"
and "eat a ton for almost nothing"; critics call it "blandville."

Busby's 🅂   15 | 15 | 15 | $33
45 E. 92nd St. (Madison Ave.), 212-360-7373
☑ Most praise the "fresh, straightforward", modestly priced American
menu and "cheerful" servers at this "home away from home for East
Side Wasps"; others say "Busby's = boring."

Bussola Bar & Grill 🅂   21 | 18 | 18 | $38
65 Fourth Ave. (bet. 9th & 10th Sts.), 212-254-1940
☑ Fans cite "great food and service", the "best gelato in the city" and
an "affordable wine list" at this East Village Southern Italian; a few
critics report "rushed, rude" and "overpriced."

Butterfield 81 🅂   19 | 18 | 18 | $44
170 E. 81st St. (bet. Lexington & 3rd Aves.), 212-288-2700
■ There's a "very good new chef" at this "clubby, unpretentious", "dark
and cozy" American that's a "tight fit" but "good for eavesdropping";
however, some don't "understand the hoopla" and say it's "overpriced."

Cabana ◗🅂   – | – | – | M
1022 Third Ave. (bet. 60th & 61st Sts.), 212-980-5678
107-10 70th Rd. (bet. Queens Blvd. & Austin St.), Queens, 718-263-3600
Casual, colorful, tropical East Side Caribbean with palm trees a part of
its bright decor; following its Forest Hills parent, this newcomer offers
moderately priced Caribbean fare, plus Cuban and South American.

Cabana Carioca 🅂   16 | 9 | 13 | $24
123 W. 45th St. (bet. 6th & 7th Aves.), 212-581-8088
☑ "Bring your appetite and a sense of humor" to the Theater District's
favorite "zesty, colorful" Brazilian; look for "heroic portions" of "cheap,
tasty food" and "immensely tacky" "voodoo decor", plus lunch buffets
that may be the "best deal in town."

Cafe Asean 🅂⇗   18 | 13 | 17 | $21
117 W. 10th St. (bet. Greenwich & 6th Aves.), 212-633-0348
■ With "fresh, interesting", "affordable" Pan-Asian food and "friendly
service", this "sweet little" West Village "oasis" with a garden is fairly
summed up as a "gem"; but why is it "often empty?"

Cafe Aubette ◐ ▽ 14 | 22 | 15 | $22
119 E. 27th St. (bet. Lexington & Park Aves.), 212-686-5500
■ The "romantic, intimate" setting and "hip attitude" at this new Gramercy American "cafe by day and bar by night" draws a "good-looking" crowd that's "more interested in meeting than dining."

Cafe Beulah [S] 20 | 19 | 18 | $36
39 E. 19th St. (bet. B'way & Park Ave. S.), 212-777-9700
■ "Southern Low Country" fare in a "snazzy", "convivial" yet "relaxed" Flatiron "refuge"; go for a "charming change of pace and style" and "great sides" of "New Age Soul Food."

CAFÉ BOTANICA [S] 22 | 27 | 23 | $45
Essex House, 160 Central Park S. (bet. 6th & 7th Aves.), 212-484-5120
■ Besides having a "splendid view of the Park", this "elegant", garden-themed New American hotel restaurant is "gracious", "civilized" and "family-friendly"; you can plan on "lush", "carefully prepared" food at bargain prix fixe tabs, plus a "sensational brunch."

Cafe Cento Sette ◐[S] 15 | 13 | 14 | $22
107 Third Ave. (13th St.), 212-420-5933
◪ Local fans crowd into this "casual", "good date" Italian East Village "hideaway" for "terrific" pastas and desserts at a "price you can't beat"; however, critics call it "boring" and "cramped."

Cafe Centro 19 | 19 | 18 | $37
MetLife Bldg., 200 Park Ave. (45th St. & Vanderbilt Ave.), 212-818-1222
■ "The glitter is close to glitz and the noise close to crescendo" at this "bustling", "huge" Grand Central French-Mediterranean; it's "perfect for a business lunch" or early commuter dinner with "lots of action" à la Paris' La Coupole.

Cafe Colonial ◐[S] 20 | 21 | 17 | $36
73 E. Houston St. (Elizabeth St.), 212-274-0044
■ You can get "high on the cool atmosphere" at this SoHo "Hollywood set" of French colonial Vietnam; its "clever" Brazilian-American menu comes with slightly "spacey service."

Cafe Con Leche ◐[S] 17 | 11 | 13 | $18
726 Amsterdam Ave. (bet. 95th & 96th Sts.), 212-678-7000
424 Amsterdam Ave. (bet. 80th & 81st Sts.), 212-595-7000
◪ The "authentic, earthy" Cuban-Dominican fare and "fabulous coffee" at these "crowded" West Side "no-frills joints" are "so cheap that even Castro would approve"; it's "a sure bet for a casual, fun meal" even if "getting a waitress is harder than hugging smoke."

Café Crocodile 21 | 18 | 21 | $42
354 E. 74th St. (bet. 1st & 2nd Aves.), 212-249-6619
■ Everyone gets a "warm reception" at this "lovely" East Side townhouse Mediterranean that's "like eating in someone's private dining room", but better because there's a "superb" menu with "excellent specials"; it's "expensive but worth it."

Café de Bruxelles ◐[S] 20 | 17 | 19 | $36
118 Greenwich Ave. (W. 13th St.), 212-206-1830
■ A "homey", "quietly successful" West Village Belgian cafe with "awesome mussels" and "unbeatable Belgian brews"; in sum, it's "très agréable", "almost like being in Belgium."

Café de Paris [S] 18 | 15 | 16 | $36
924 Second Ave. (49th St.), 212-486-1411
◪ Regulars find "reliable" "French comfort food" and brunch at this Midtown "Parisian cafe"; not-so-regulars blame "cramped quarters" and "offhand service" for their "quaint not great" verdict.

CAFÉ DES ARTISTES ⬤🅂   24 | 27 | 23 | $53
1 W. 67th St. (bet. Columbus Ave. & CPW), 212-877-3500
■ 4,500 surveyors say when "you want to feel like Rockefeller", "seduce someone" or "fall in love all over again", nothing's better than this Lincoln Center "timeless classic"; the "lovely" murals of gamboling nymphs and "gorgeous" flowers create an "eternally romantic" backdrop for French food that's "always a treat" even if you "can't afford many visits"; P.S. its $23 "lunch is a true bargain."

Cafe du Pont 🅂   19 | 14 | 19 | $36
1038 First Ave. (bet. 56th & 57th Sts.), 212-223-1133
■ A "pleasant little" Sutton Place storefront "retreat" for "elegant yet casual", "affordable" French-Continental dining; though "cramped", it proves "good things come in small packages."

Cafe Español ⬤🅂   19 | 13 | 18 | $25
63 Carmine St. (7th Ave. S.), 212-675-3312

Cafe Español ⬤🅂   19 | 13 | 16 | $26
172 Bleecker St. (bet. MacDougal & Sullivan Sts.), 212-505-0657
■ There's "garlic mania", "big size" "yummy" paella and "fabulous" "bargain" lobster accompanied by pitchers of sangria in both of these separately owned, "noisy", "tight squeeze", "cheerful" "Spanish Village landmarks"; they're most "fun for a group."

Cafe Europa 🅂   14 | 13 | 13 | $22
205 W. 57th St. (7th Ave.), 212-977-4030 ⬤
1177 Sixth Ave. (46th St.), 212-575-7272
▣ "Lunchtime regulars" and "late-night dessert" lovers find it's "easy eating" "nuevo trendy sandwiches" and "quick bites" at these "casual" ("more Prague than Paris") Continental coffee shops; critics mumble about "tourists", the "McInternational menu" and staff attitude.

Café Fès ⬤🅂   18 | 19 | 16 | $29
246 W. Fourth St. (Charles St.), 212-924-7653
■ "Come to the casbah"; this "dark", "reasonably priced" West Village Moroccan cafe serves "richly flavored" dishes amid "enough exotic tiles to please a sheik"; it's "an authentic experience" right down to "snail's pace service" and "uncomfortable seats."

Cafe Fiorello ⬤🅂   20 | 17 | 18 | $36
1900 Broadway (bet. 63rd & 64th Sts.), 212-595-5330
■ A "consistent" Lincoln Center "favorite" for "quick" pre-theater Italian dining of the pizza, pasta, salad sort and leisure people-watching from outdoor seats; the antipasti bar stars.

Cafe Gitane ⬤🅂⇄   15 | 16 | 12 | $17
242 Mott St. (bet. Houston & Prince Sts.), 212-334-9552
▣ When "in need of caffeine", a "perfect drop-in for a sandwich" or just a place "to hang around", try this "arty" NoLita Eclectic "bastion of black-clad chain smokers"; its mantra, exemplified by "hipper than thou" staff, should be "atmosphere is everything."

Cafe Greco 🅂   17 | 15 | 17 | $29
1390 Second Ave. (bet. 71st & 72nd Sts.), 212-737-4300
■ A Greek-Mediterranean East Side "bargain" "haven" where "mature" diners ("bring Bubbe and Zayde") catch "good value" via what may be the "best early-bird dinner in town"; low prices (e.g. lunch for $9.95) keep it "one big happy, busy place."

Cafe Inferno ⬤🅂   – | – | – | M
165 Eighth Ave. (bet. 18th & 19th Sts.), 212-989-2330
It's definitely hot, as Chelseans (and Joyce habitués) have quickly discovered this new, red-lit Continental-Mediterranean with its wood-burning brick oven and happening bar scene.

F	D	S	C

Cafe Lalo ◐[S]≠ — 19 | 17 | 12 | $15
201 W. 83rd St. (bet. Amsterdam Ave. & B'way), 212-496-6031
◪ "There's no room for claustrophobes" at this "bustling" West Side coffeehouse/cafe that features an "infinite array" of "decadent desserts" and oh "so many coffee drinks."

Café Loup ◐[S] — 19 | 18 | 19 | $36
105 W. 13th St. (bet. 6th & 7th Aves.), 212-255-4746
■ Good service goes with the "well-priced", "honest" French bistro food that Village neighbors swear "can be eaten day after day", but it's the "oodles of charm" that cements this as a place to "spend time and have dinner with friends."

Cafe Luxembourg ◐[S] — 19 | 18 | 17 | $42
200 W. 70th St. (bet. Amsterdam & West End Aves.), 212-873-7411
■ "It's crowded, it's noisy and the waiters usually ignore you", but this "upscale" French bistro near Lincoln Center is as "hip as ever" and "still classy after all these years" thanks to its "ultrareliable" kitchen and the fact that "there's always someone famous to ogle."

Cafe Margaux ◐[S] — ▽ 19 | 17 | 16 | $32
175 Ave. B (11th St.), 212-260-7960
◪ This "innovative" Eclectic-French East Village newcomer "has potential" but "hasn't lived up to it yet"; despite "*Casablanca*" decor, it reportedly is uneven in daily performance.

Cafe Mona Lisa ◐[S] — 17 | 20 | 14 | $17
282 Bleecker St. (bet. Jones St. & 7th Ave. S.), 212-929-1262
■ "You can be master of your own domain" "once you settle into" the "big comfy" armchairs in this Village coffeehouse; "they let you sit for days" over the "most authentically Italian-tasting coffee", "supreme" desserts or just a "simple bite to eat."

Cafe Nicholson — 19 | 23 | 21 | $50
323 E. 58th St. (bet. 1st & 2nd Aves.), 212-355-6769
■ Excellent for private parties and proposing, this "very romantic" art- and antiques-filled East Side Continental is open only when John Nicholson is in the mood, thus this "quirky", "strangely appealing" "hideaway" comes with a "big mystery – is it ever open?"

Cafe Noir ◐[S] — 16 | 17 | 15 | $29
32 Grand St. (Thompson St.), 212-431-7910
◪ If you "ever wonder where shaved head, leather pant–wearing Francophones" go in SoHo, try this Gitane-smoking, "funky, sexy, harem" of a midpriced Mediterranean cafe.

Cafe Nosidam ◐[S] — 17 | 16 | 16 | $37
768 Madison Ave. (66th St.), 212-717-5633
◪ Dyslexics delight in "ton dab nailatl" (not bad Italian) food from Cafe Madison-spelled-backwards while "watching chic shoppers" from "fun sidewalk tables" filled with nosy nibblers; critics say "more than the name is backwards" and it's lucky it's not on Park.

CAFÉ PIERRE [S] — 23 | 24 | 24 | $57
Pierre Hotel, 2 E. 61st St. (bet. 5th & Madison Aves.), 212-940-8185
■ A "staid but elegant", gray satin East Side cafe where "fine" French food, "classy" surroundings and "attentive", "white glove service" are a "throwback to a more gracious time" "despite the hefty tab"; there's a delightful chanteuse pianist, Kathleen Landis, after 8:30 PM.

Cafe Remy ◐ — 21 | 19 | 18 | $38
104 Greenwich St. (Carlisle St.), 212-267-4646
◪ "Fine pastas and sandwiches" plus "good service" make for an "unhurried" meal at this midpriced Downtown Eclectic cafe.

Cafe Riazor ●🅂
16 | 10 | 15 | $25
245 W. 16th St. (bet. 7th & 8th Aves.), 212-727-2132
☑ Face it, this Chelsea Spaniard looks like "the original dive" but what "it lacks in ambiance it makes up for" in "solid value" and "gargantuan portions" of "tasty", "authentic" food.

Cafe S.F.A. 🅂
18 | 17 | 17 | $24
Saks Fifth Ave., 611 Fifth Ave., 8th fl. (bet. 49th & 50th Sts.), 212-940-4080
■ For a shopping or office break, lunch in Saks' "surprisingly good" 8th-floor American "sanctuary" may be tailored to "your size and price"; look for "fresh" salads, sandwiches and soups accessorized with views of St. Patrick's and Rockefeller Center.

Café St. John 🅂
17 | 15 | 16 | $27
500 W. 110th St. (Amsterdam Ave.), 212-932-8420
☑ You "take what you can get" opposite St. John the Divine; plan on "uneven" French fare and "indifferent service" in a "bourgeois" bistro that is "decent and workmanlike but not divine."

Cafe Trevi ●
22 | 19 | 23 | $42
1570 First Ave. (bet. 81st & 82nd Sts.), 212-249-0040
■ "This is what NYC dining is all about": a "small, well-run" Upper East Side favorite for civilized dining, where a "solid" Northern Italian menu, an owner (Primo) who exudes "gracious hospitality" and "stellar" service give you a "satisfied warm glow."

Cafe Un Deux Trois ●🅂
15 | 14 | 15 | $33
123 W. 44th St. (bet. B'way & 6th Ave.), 212-354-4148
☑ "Large, loud" "fast" French brasserie "echo chamber" near Times Square that continues to pack them in; if you "order simply" and have earplugs, "you won't be disappointed."

Café Word of Mouth 🅂
18 | 11 | 15 | $24
1012 Lexington Ave., 2nd fl. (bet. 72nd & 73rd Sts.), 212-249-5351
☑ "Once you get up the steep stairs", you'll discover a "tight squeeze" breakfast and lunch "sleeper" for East Side "private school moms" (dinner served Tuesday–Friday); the "well-prepared but limited" Eclectic menu comes "with an order of snob on the side."

Caffe Bianco 🅂
17 | 15 | 15 | $22
1486 Second Ave. (bet. 77th & 78th Sts.), 212-988-2655
■ Many "love" this "reliable, affordable" East Side coffeehouse as "a Starbucks alternative"; it's "not fancy" but the "soothing" backyard and "clever" Eclectic menu have stood the test of time.

Caffe Biondo ●🅂⊟
▽ 19 | 18 | 17 | $18
141 Mulberry St. (bet. Grand & Hester Sts.), 212-226-9285
■ Surveyors tout this "cool", brick-walled Little Italy coffeehouse as "a delightful place for coffee, a light meal or cake" plus "good people-watching"; it brings back "old-world" Mulberry Street.

Caffé Bondí 🅂
20 | 17 | 19 | $36
7 W. 20th St. (bet. 5th & 6th Aves.), 212-691-8136
■ "Carefully prepared" "esoteric" Sicilian specialties, "simple decor" and "welcoming staff" at this Flatiron cafe draw a full house at lunch; dinner is less crowded and the garden feels "oh-so Italy."

Caffe Buon Gusto ●🅂
16 | 12 | 15 | $22
236 E. 77th St. (bet. 2nd & 3rd Aves.), 212-535-6884 ⊟
1009 Second Ave. (bet. 53rd & 54th Sts.), 212-755-1476
71 W. 71st St. (bet. Columbus Ave. & CPW), 212-875-1512 ⊟
151 Montague St. (bet. Clinton & Henry Sts.), Brooklyn, 718-624-3838
☑ These "low-key" "homes of mix-and-match pasta and sauces" have "tight seating", "slow service" and what some call "stubbornly average food"; still, with prices this cheap, criticism seems unfair.

Caffe Cielo S
18 | 17 | 19 | $34

881 Eighth Ave. (bet. 52nd & 53rd Sts.), 212-246-9555
■ "Reliable if uninspired" Italian food and "hospitable" staff in a "pleasantly decorated" cloud motif room sum up this "inviting" West Midtown cafe; it's "noisy at peak times" but "visually soothing."

Caffe Grazie S
18 | 16 | 18 | $33

26 E. 84th St. (bet. 5th & Madison Aves.), 212-717-4407
☑ Since "it's hard to find a relaxing place to stop" near the Met, this townhouse Italian cafe is often "crowded and noisy"; art lovers and food fans alike are "happy to have this as a neighbor."

Caffé Lure ◑S⇜
20 | 15 | 15 | $28

169 Sullivan St. (bet. Bleecker & Houston Sts.), 212-473-2642
■ Another "real food at real prices" "winner"; whether you "think fish" or "brunch is the thing", this Villager's "creative" French cooking, "simple decor" and "friendly" staff add up to "Village charm."

Caffe Popolo S
17 | 12 | 16 | $21

351 Columbus Ave. (bet. 76th & 77th Sts.), 212-362-1777
☑ Maybe it's a "throwback to the West Side old days", but you still get "nicely priced", "solid" Italian food, from "homemade pastas" to "paper-thin" brick-oven pizzas, at this "low-key winner."

Caffe Rafaella ◑S⇜
17 | 19 | 15 | $19

134 Seventh Ave. S. (bet. Charles & 10th Sts.), 212-929-7247
■ With "fabulous", "cushy" old armchairs and sofas, and waiters "who forget you", this West Village coffeehouse encourages lingering and "people-watching" over delish "devilish desserts."

Caffe Reggio ◑S⇜
15 | 18 | 13 | $15

119 MacDougal St. (bet. Bleecker & W. 3rd Sts.), 212-475-9557
■ Opened in 1927, this Italian may be "the original Village coffeehouse" and still serves first-rate coffee and tea; "baroque", "full of character" and characters plus "local chatter", it's "about as real as NY gets."

Caffe Rosso ◑S
▽ 20 | 20 | 19 | $30

284 W. 12th St. (W. 4th St.), 212-633-9277
■ "Everything is done well" at this reasonably priced, "little" West Village neighborhood Italian; "hip, casual, welcoming and delicioso", it's "a great place to be a regular" or take a date.

Caffé Taci ◑S⇜
– | – | – | I

2841 Broadway (110th St.), 212-678-5345
Upper West Side Italian trattoria with funky brick walls and pseudo-Pompeian decor; the Columbia crowd touts both the student-sensitive prices and no-cover-charge weekend music.

Caffé Torino ◑S
17 | 16 | 17 | $25

139 W. 10th St. (bet. Greenwich Ave. & 7th Ave. S.), 212-675-5554
☑ "Good", "crowded", "noisy" and "cheap" are "the code words" for this "gay-friendly" Village Italian-cum-garden; fans cite "tasty", "family-style" food served by "playful waiters"; foes say "pretentious."

Caffé Vivaldi ◑S⇜
16 | 18 | 15 | $17

32 Jones St. (bet. Bleecker & W. 4th Sts.), 212-929-9384
■ You can "have your cake and eat it too" at this "cute" little Village coffeehouse where you "spend the afternoon" listening to "great classical music"; in the winter, you've got to "love that fireplace."

Cajun S
16 | 14 | 15 | $27

129 Eighth Ave. (bet. 16th & 17th Sts.), 212-691-6174
☑ The "faded" red "bordello" decor at this Chelsea Cajun standby is "irrelevant" to what's really going on: "plentiful servings" of "food as hot" as the Dixieland music is "loud"; try the jazz "brunch-o-rama."

Calidad Latina S
▽ | 18 | 8 | 16 | $18 |
132 Ninth Ave. (18th St.), 212-255-3446
☑ Get "bang for your buck, baby" with "good Cuban food any time of the day" in Chelsea and "better service" than expected; what more do you want – good looks?

California Burrito S
| 12 | 7 | 10 | $10 |
1530 Third Ave. (bet. 86th & 87th Sts.), 212-348-9225
237 Park Ave. (bet. 46th & 47th Sts.), 212-867-7676
2067 Broadway (bet. 71st & 72nd Sts.), 212-579-3939
Port Authority Bus Terminal, 625 Eighth Ave., concourse level (bet. 40th & 41st Sts.), 212-564-6969
750 Seventh Ave. (49th St.), 212-265-4433
172 Seventh Ave. (bet. 20th & 21st Sts.), 212-604-9118
295 Park Ave. S. (bet. 23rd & 24th Sts.), 212-777-7217
4 World Financial Ctr. (250 Vesey St.), 212-233-6800
☑ Despite "no decor" and "brain-dead" staff, "burritos as big as China" "make lunch a screaming deal"; even critics say it's "quick" and will "do in a pinch" so "take the food and run."

California Pizza Kitchen S
| 15 | 11 | 14 | $18 |
201 E. 60th St. (bet. 2nd & 3rd Aves.), 212-755-7773
☑ It's easy to become "addicted" to these "crazy but tasty", wood-oven "California culture" pizzas, and many NYers have succumbed – "where else can you get ham and pineapple pizza?"; critics "hope it gets hit with the big one" or goes "back to Lala Land."

Calla Larga (Queens)
| – | – | – | E |
247-63 Jamaica Ave. (1/4 mi. east of Cross Island Pkwy.), 718-343-2185
Despite Holiday Inn–type decor and an out-of-the-way location, a friendly, tuxedoed staff and good, if pricey, Northern Italian fare reportedly make this Bellerose place worth the schlep; let us know what you think.

Cal's ◑S
| 18 | 18 | 17 | $35 |
55 W. 21st St. (bet. 5th & 6th Aves.), 212-929-0740
■ "Stick with the basics", e.g. "good" burgers, risotto, pasta and pot-au-feu, at this "charming", "friendly" Eclectic-Mediterranean Flatiron loft; the "large, airy room" allows you to enjoy the "satisfying food" in "relative privacy" and at your leisure.

CamaJe ◑S
▽ | 21 | 15 | 21 | $34 |
85 MacDougal St. (bet. Bleecker & Houston Sts.), 212-673-8184
■ Early clients are "impressed" by the "good value" meal served at this petite Village French newcomer; "friendly, attentive" service and the "original" food of chef Patrick Woodside make diners come back.

Cambodian Cuisine (Brooklyn) S ▽
| 19 | 6 | 15 | $14 |
87 S. Elliot Pl. (bet. Fulton St. & Lafayette Ave.), 718-858-3262
■ "BAM's secret is out" – Brooklyn's Cambodian "may be a trek" and "a hole-in-the-wall" with "zip decor", but it "graciously presents" "delicious", "exotic" food for "less than it costs to cook yourself."

Camille's Clover Hill (Brooklyn) S
| 17 | 16 | 16 | $25 |
272 Court St. (bet. DeGraw & Kane Sts.), 718-875-0895
☑ The "no-stress" ambiance helps make this inexpensive Heights "charmer" "a good brunch spot", but "inconsistent" Eclectic food and "kooky service" cause critics to conclude that it's "hit or miss."

Campagna ◑S
| 24 | 21 | 21 | $48 |
24 E. 21st St. (bet. B'way & Park Ave. S.), 212-460-0900
■ A "top of the line" Flatiron Italian that has it all: a "brilliant", "full flavor" menu, the requisite "killer wine list" and a "country ambiance with city attitude"; it's a guaranteed "beautiful people", air kiss "scene."

Campagnola §
1382 First Ave. (bet. 73rd & 74th Sts.), 212-861-1102 — 23 | 19 | 21 | $47

☑ Join the "loyal clientele" and be "welcomed like family" into this always popular, East Side Italian "stargazing spot"; "you pay for" "first-rate" food, but some claim service seems reserved for regulars.

Can ●§
482 W. Broadway (Houston St.), 212-533-6333 — 18 | 18 | 17 | $35

☑ It's really quite simple – you're a Can fan if you like the "cool" SoHo "minimalist decor" and French-Vietnamese fare; "Can nots" seek "tastier food" and feel the "staff should stick to acting."

Canal House ●§
SoHo Grand Hotel, 310 W. Broadway, 2nd fl. (Grand St.), 212-965-3588 — ▽ 19 | 21 | 19 | $39

■ Filling a "dramatic space" in SoHo's new hotel, this yearling American "Yankee" proves "you can be cool and still eat macaroni and cheese"; the bar scene is "hip to the point of exhaustion."

Candela ●§
116 E. 16th St. (bet. Irving Pl. & Park Ave. S.), 212-254-1600 — 20 | 22 | 19 | $35

■ Lit by "tons of candles", this "hot", "tasty" Union Square American can be like dining in a "sexy" "medieval banquet room" ("the vampire Lestat would love it"); even the "affable" if "untrained" staff seems to come "from another time zone."

Candido Pizza ●§≠
1606 First Ave. (bet. 83rd & 84th Sts.), 212-396-9401 — 20 | 9 | 11 | $17

☑ A "simple" East Side pizzeria that produces "one of the top" "brick-oven thin-crust pizzas in NY"; it comes with in-house service "like an *I Love Lucy* routine" or to your house via slow cycle.

Candle Cafe §
1307 Third Ave. (bet. 74th & 75th Sts.), 212-472-0970 — 17 | 12 | 16 | $20

☑ It's "quirky" and needs a decorator, but this East Side Vegetarian is popular with the "granola set" in spite of "slow, mellow service."

Canton §≠
45 Division St. (bet. Bowery & Market St.), 212-226-4441 — 24 | 13 | 20 | $35

■ "Don't be deceived" by the "typical uninspired decor" – here's where you find "top-echelon" Cantonese in "the heart of Chinatown" accompanied by "solicitous", "informative" service and "an attentive" manager (Eileen) on hand – follow her advice when ordering.

Canyon Road §
1470 First Ave. (bet. 76th & 77th Sts.), 212-734-1600 — 20 | 18 | 16 | $29

■ At this East Side "Ralph Laurenish SW beauty", the fajitas and other fare is so good it's "always crowded"; "mucho gusto margaritas" help.

CAPSOUTO FRÈRES §
451 Washington St. (Watts St.), 212-966-4900 — 22 | 23 | 21 | $46

■ "Order a dessert soufflé first" and then settle into this "charming", "satisfying" TriBeCa French dining experience; it's so "far from the maddening crowds" that you need to "bring a compass", but luckily there's convenient free parking; how about brunch?

Captain's Table, The
860 Second Ave. (46th St.), 212-697-9538 — 19 | 15 | 18 | $39

☑ "Talk about old-fashioned", this Turtle Bay veteran is "still good for seafood" at "fair prices", but stuffy waiters and "decor past its prime" "need some rethinking."

Cara Mia §
654 Ninth Ave. (bet. 45th & 46th Sts.), 212-262-6767 — – | – | – | M

Try this fetching new Midtown storefront Italian with low-priced pastas and you're likely to think the name fits; it's handy for a pre-theater meal.

Caravan ☒
▽ 20 | 13 | 17 | $23

741 Eighth Ave. (bet. 46th & 47th Sts.), 212-262-2021

■ "Kebab heaven" in the Theater District with "fawning service" and first-class Afghan food at modest prices; though in a "hectic" area, it's "rarely busy for lunch."

Caravan of Dreams ☒
17 | 13 | 15 | $18

405 E. Sixth St. (bet. Ave. A & 1st Ave.), 212-254-1613

☑ An East Village "Vegetarian with flavor" that offers a "flashback" "page out of the '60s"; "flower children" of the '90s "feel virtuous eating" the "groovy" bread and "abundant", "homemade" food; a "grubby feel" and vegged-out service may be turnoffs.

Caribe ☒
17 | 16 | 14 | $23

117 Perry St. (Greenwich St.), 212-255-9191

■ "Ya mon", "huge servings" of "cheap", "spicy island food" and "killer" frozen drinks will get you Jamaica without "jet lag" in the West Village; "dress tropical" and ignore the "unfriendly staff."

Carino ☒
18 | 11 | 18 | $30

1710 Second Ave. (bet. 88th & 89th Sts.), 212-860-0566

■ "It's always a pleasure to see Mama Carino" in this well-priced East Side "old-fashioned red sauce" Italian "family affair"; you're "guaranteed a good meal" along with "sparse decor."

CARLYLE RESTAURANT ☒
23 | 26 | 24 | $58

Carlyle Hotel, 35 E. 76th St. (Madison Ave.), 212-744-1600

■ It's like "eating in a rich man's drawing room" at this "stately", "quiet", "quintessential NY" restaurant; it exudes "style all the way" from the "calm, polished service" of the fine "classic" French menu to "magnificent flowers" "so tall they graze the ceiling"; sure it's pricey, but none of the well-coiffed and tailored customers complains.

Carmen Pagina Uno ●☒
– | – | – | M

308 E. 49th St. (bet. 1st & 2nd Aves.), 212-935-8433

Boasting a piano bar on weekends, this Midtown Italian newcomer provides the old-fashioned basics with caring service and a solid kitchen; the dreary decor could still stand an overhaul.

CARMINE'S ☒
18 | 14 | 16 | $27

2450 Broadway (bet. 90th & 91st Sts.), 212-362-2200
200 W. 44th St. (bet. B'way & 8th Ave.), 212-221-3800 ●

☑ Boosters "bring all their friends and tell them to bring their friends" to this "crowded, noisy", "family-style" Italian duo, where "bathtubs of pasta" come with "bocce ball–size garlic cloves"; to "avoid the herd", go at off-hours; to avoid overeating, split orders.

CARNEGIE DELI ●☒⇗
20 | 8 | 12 | $20

854 Seventh Ave. (55th St.), 212-757-2245

■ "Loud, crowded and expensive" but "it's NY" so you gotta "love it"; expect "Jurassic-sized sandwiches", "barracks-style dining" and "jaded", "gruff" staff directing lines of tourists and deli-crazed locals.

Carol's Cafe (Staten Island)
▽ 26 | 21 | 21 | $39

1571 Richmond Rd. (bet. Four Corners Rd. & Seaview Ave.), 718-979-5600

■ "Yes, it is worth the drive" to this "shining star in Staten Island" for "superb", "professionally served" Eclectic cuisine; check to see if "Carol is there to make sure everything runs properly."

Casa Brasil ☒
▽ 20 | 17 | 20 | $31

316 E. 53rd St. (bet. 1st & 2nd Aves.), 212-355-5360

■ An authentic East Side Brazilian with "large portions" of "tasty", reasonably priced food served by an "eager to please" staff.

Casa del Pescatore ●🅂
`17` `15` `16` `$32`
957 Second Ave. (bet. 50th & 51st Sts.), 212-980-6978
■ This "friendly, unassuming" Italian Eastsider "makes anything anyway you like it"; it's a reasonable "neighborhood find" for "fresh fish, good pasta" and lots more.

Casa Di Pre 🅂
▽ `18` `14` `19` `$25`
283 W. 12th St. (W. 4th St.), 212-243-7073
■ "Locals" enjoy "decent food and good value" "any time for any reason" at this "casual" West Village Italian-Mediterranean basement; it's been around forever.

Casa La Femme ●🅂
`15` `23` `14` `$39`
150 Wooster St. (bet. Houston & Prince Sts.), 212-505-0005
☑ SoHo's "opulent" Egyptian "Aladdin's love nest" has clients and "gossamer" "tented tables that are so vogue" you may feel like "a sheik", but the food is "uneven" and "service is snooty as ever."

Casa Mia 🅂
▽ `19` `18` `19` `$27`
225 E. 24th St. (bet. 2nd & 3rd Aves.), 212-679-5606
■ "Your privacy is guaranteed" when "tucked away behind the deli" at this Murray Hill "old boys club"; it's an Italian "find" with "delicious homemade pastas and sauces" and "good basic service."

Cascabel
`22` `20` `21` `$46`
218 Lafayette St. (bet. Broome & Spring Sts.), 212-431-7300
■ There may be a "sense of sin" within the "deep red walls" of this "dark", "'50s nightclub"–like SoHo hangout, but the "gutsy", "creative" New American menu and "obliging" service can be heavenly; it's owned by the Zaccaro family, as in Geraldine Ferraro.

Castellano 🅂
`21` `18` `20` `$44`
138 W. 55th St. (bet. 6th & 7th Aves.), 212-664-1975
■ This light wood–paneled Midtown Italian "music industry haunt" across from City Center serves "consistently good" food but "at a price"; a "power lunch" venue, it's quieter and more romantic at night.

Caviar Russe
`–` `–` `–` `E`
538 Madison Ave. (bet. 54th & 55th Sts.), 212-980-5908
Comrades unite over caviar, cigars, cognac and a few other luxury edibles at this mezzanine Midtown Russian; rich and inviting, this Petit Trianon–style newcomer is perfect for tsars and stars alike.

Caviarteria 🅂
`23` `15` `18` `$42`
Delmonico Hotel, 502 Park Ave. (59th St.), 212-759-7410
☑ "Bring money" because this Eastsider is "the place to indulge yourself" with "caviar, blinis and champagne"; so "what's not to love" about their "lighthearted approach to living large" – how about an "awkward", "small space" and "spasmodic service."

CELLAR IN THE SKY
`22` `26` `24` `VE`
1 World Trade Ctr. (bet. Liberty & Vesey Sts.), 212-524-7014
■ "Sky-high prices" for this New American "food experience" may be "aimed at tourists", but delighted locals declare it "worth every penny" since the "matching of wine", food and service is "unparalleled" and "on a clear night you can see forever"; N.B. one seating only for a $125 prix fixe with all wine included.

Cellini
`21` `19` `21` `$40`
65 E. 54th St. (bet. Madison & Park Aves.), 212-751-1555
■ They "treat you like family" at this Midtown "Tuscan farmhouse" that's also a "good business lunch place"; it's an "unlikely location" for such "great spirit" and "fairly priced" Italian "comfy cucina."

Cendrillon [S] — 20 | 17 | 18 | $34
45 Mercer St. (bet. Broome & Grand Sts.), 212-343-9012
■ For the "best fusion of East and West", try this SoHo "Zen garden" where an "imaginative" kitchen sends out "sensational", "aromatic" Filipino food served by a "mellow staff"; it's a "real find."

Cent'Anni [S] — 23 | 16 | 21 | $42
50 Carmine St. (bet. Bedford & Bleecker Sts.), 212-989-9494
■ The "sincere welcome" at this "low-key" "oldie but goodie" Village "storefront" trattoria makes you "feel like a longtime patron"; however, the "wonderful" Tuscan food is "not cheap."

Chadwick's (Brooklyn) [S] — 19 | 18 | 19 | $30
8822 Third Ave. (89th St.), 718-833-9855
■ "You get your money's worth" of "old-time" American dishes at this "inn-like" "classic steakhouse" (with fish and pasta too) on "Bay Ridge's restaurant row"; "their beef Wellington is my Waterloo."

Champagne's ◐[S] — ▽ 19 | 22 | 21 | $53
20 W. 55th St. (bet. 5th & 6th Aves.), 212-639-9460
◪ French-Continental Midtown hideaway that's "so beautifully decorated it will make you cry and if it doesn't, the price of a glass of champagne will"; to some the "elegance" here is simply "tacky."

Chanpen Thai [S] — ▽ 20 | 16 | 20 | $20
761 Ninth Ave. (51st St.), 212-586-6808
■ Combine "mouthwatering", inexpensive Thai classics with an "irresistible" staff "wearing wonderful Thai garb" and you have this "spicy new addition to Ninth Avenue's restaurant explosion."

CHANTERELLE — 27 | 26 | 27 | $71
2 Harrison St. (Hudson St.), 212-966-6960
■ Devotees of David and Karen Waltuck's "oh-so-pure" TriBeCa "paradise regained" find "perfection" in the "austere", "ethereal" room with a "premium-priced" New French menu, "psychic staff" and "widely spaced tables"; dissenters, a small minority, find that the "big white room, big white plates, tiny little portions and big big greenbacks" leave them "kind of cold."

Charlie Mom [S] — 15 | 11 | 15 | $18
1491 First Ave. (bet. 77th & 78th Sts.), 212-439-6363 ◐
404 Sixth Ave. (8th St.), 212-777-6999 ◐
464 Sixth Ave. (bet. 11th & 12th Sts.), 212-807-8585
47 Seventh Ave. S. (bet. Bleecker & Morton Sts.), 212-255-2848 ◐
■ "There are no surprises" in the "cheap", "generic" Chinese fare at these "reliable" "neighborhood standbys"; their "amazing", "fast home delivery" is "perfect for those lazy nights."

Charlotte ◐[S] — 19 | 20 | 19 | $42
Millennium Broadway, 145 W. 44th St. (bet. B'way & 6th Ave.), 212-789-7508
■ A "well-prepared" New American menu is served in this "pretty but pricey" "luxurious spot" for the "all-important pre-theater scene"; the "subdued decor" may be "better than the show you're going to see."

Chat 'n Chew [S] — 16 | 14 | 14 | $19
10 E. 16th St. (bet. 5th Ave. & Union Sq. W.), 212-243-1616
◪ "Garage sale decor" and American comfort food highlight this kinda "cutesy" but "kinda good" Union Square "calorie heaven"; critics "prefer the chat to the chew" and say "send it back to the mall."

Cheetah — ▽ 11 | 19 | 16 | $31
12 W. 21st St. (bet. 5th & 6th Aves.), 212-206-7770
◪ Even hipsters "can't believe how crowded" this new, "upscale" Chelsea New American–Italian "hot spot" lounge can get; they love the look and "great decor" but wonder "do people eat there?"

F | D | S | C

Chef Ho's [S] 18 | 12 | 15 | $21
1720 Second Ave. (bet. 89th & 90th Sts.), 212-348-9444
■ "If you can't make it to Chinatown", this low-budget, low-decor East Side "old faithful" is "the place for dumplings"; plan on a "cut above the usual" Hunan food and fast delivery.

Chelsea Bistro & Bar [S] 22 | 20 | 20 | $41
358 W. 23rd St. (bet. 8th & 9th Aves.), 212-727-2026
■ Chalk it up to being "the pride of Chelsea", but local loyalists brag about the "fab" French bistro fare, "impressive wines" and "attentive" staff at this "sophisticated" outpost; a "cozy" fireplace adds to the "very French" feeling.

Chelsea Feast [S] ▽ 19 | 11 | 15 | $22
505 W. 23rd St. (bet. 10th & 11th Aves.), 212-675-8728
◩ American "home cooking" with "inventive twists" is the draw at this new "kid-friendly" Chelsea cafe; it may be "still finding its voice" and ratings indicate it never found a decorator.

Chelsea Grill ◐[S] 17 | 15 | 16 | $28
135 Eighth Ave. (bet. 16th & 17th Sts.), 212-242-5336
■ "Wear black only" when you join the "mixed", "fun" crowd at Chelsea's Eclectic-American "basic neighborhood joint"; it works best for a "moderately priced", "quick" lunch or brunch; the "garden dining is very hip" – "you never know who you'll see."

Chelsea Ristorante [S] 19 | 17 | 19 | $35
108 Eighth Ave. (bet. 15th & 16th Sts.), 212-924-7786
■ Chelsea's "intelligent choice" for "nonfussy", "affordable" Italian food and "thoughtful service"; regulars enjoy the "cheerful" ambiance and the "scene" at the "well-spaced tables."

Chez Brigitte ⊄ 17 | 9 | 17 | $16
77 Greenwich Ave. (bet. Bank St. & 7th Ave. S.), 212-929-6736
◩ "Blink and you'll miss" this "shoe box–sized" Village lunch counter that fans say is the "best in NY": it has "only 11 seats but it's worth the wait" for "fast", "hearty" French stews and omelets.

Chez Es Saada ◐[S] – | – | – | E
42 E. First St. (bet. 1st & 2nd Aves.), 212-777-5617
The "awesome downstairs caverns" will make "you think you're in Marrakech", but that impression lasts only "until you taste the food" at this sizzling hot new East Village Moroccan-French lounge; stick to the "extensive drink menu" or the "great mint tea", and ogle.

Chez Jacqueline [S] 20 | 17 | 19 | $37
72 MacDougal St. (bet. Bleecker & W. Houston Sts.), 212-505-0727
■ A "friendly" Village "basic bistro" that's "solid" "all-around" from its "good bourgeois" French fare to its "Downtown chic"; "efficient service" helps make this "one of NY's better French roosts."

Chez Josephine ◐ 19 | 20 | 19 | $39
414 W. 42nd St. (bet. 9th & 10th Aves.), 212-594-1925
■ "Appropriately eccentric for the Theater District", this "sexy" "shrine to Josephine Baker" is a "show in itself" and "great for a pre- or post-theater hug, kiss and snack" of "hearty French" fare; owner Jean-Claude "makes you feel he's waited all day just for you."

Chez Le Chef ◐[S] – | – | – | E
127 Lexington Ave. (bet. 28th & 29th Sts.), 212-685-1888
Somewhat hokey, somewhat charming new pastry shop and French bistro; white-whiskered master chef Frédéric Piepenburg looks like a character out of a children's fairy tale.

Chez Ma Tante ◐[S] — 19 | 17 | 18 | $36

189 W. 10th St. (bet. Bleecker & W. 4th Sts.), 212-620-0223

■ For "fine French bistro food in close quarters", this "top-notch" Villager is a real "sleeper value"; besides having "attentive service", it exudes romance and offers a satisfying brunch from sidewalk seats in warm weather.

Chez Michallet [S] — 24 | 21 | 22 | $42

90 Bedford St. (bet. Bleecker & W. 4th Sts.), 212-242-8309

■ "You'd never know it's there, but you should" because this "adorable", "postage stamp–size" West Village French bistro is a "delicious" "little secret" with "serious professional food" and "personal attention"; it may be NY's "best first date restaurant."

Chez Napoléon — 19 | 13 | 20 | $34

365 W. 50th St. (bet. 8th & 9th Aves.), 212-265-6980

■ "Time stands still" at this "family-run" Theater District classic where the "friendly" service and midpriced French bistro food are always "satisfying"; sure it's "dowdy", but "many love this little nook."

Chez Suzette ◐[S] — 18 | 17 | 20 | $32

675B Ninth Ave. (bet. 46th & 47th Sts.), 212-581-9717

■ A "pleasant", "affordable" Theater District "Paris bistro" with "down-home" French fare; the "attentive staff" "knows how to get you out in time for the theater without rushing you."

Chiam ◐[S] — 22 | 20 | 21 | $39

160 E. 48th St. (bet. Lexington & 3rd Aves.), 212-371-2323

■ With its "delicate" "New Age" "mix of flavors", "innovative dim sum" and "high-tech decor", this "pricey" "power crowd" East Midtowner is "not your father's Chinese" – make it yours.

Chianti [S] — 20 | 16 | 17 | $35

1043 Second Ave. (55th St.), 212-980-8686

■ An "underrated" East Midtown "neighborhood" Italian that "gets return business" because its "kitchen produces"; everyone says the early-bird dinner is a "superb" "bargain."

Chianti (Brooklyn) [S] — ▽ 20 | 16 | 19 | $31

8530 Third Ave. (86th St.), 718-921-6300

■ "Brooklyn's answer to Carmine's", this "raucous", "family-style" Bay Ridge "storefront" has "homestyle" platters of "delicious" "if not always pretty" Italian food at "close to low" prices; split portions.

Chikubu — ▽ 22 | 15 | 18 | $42

12 E. 44th St. (bet. 5th & Madison Aves.), 212-818-0715

■ "Outstanding" Grand Central–area traditional Japanese with "fresh and fabulous" food that's "so authentic" that dining here can be "a mystery to Westerners"; the "spare" interior looks as if it might have been "designed by a hospital internist."

Chili Pepper ◐[S] — ▽ 17 | 16 | 17 | $25

245 Park Ave. S. (bet. 19th & 20th Sts.), 212-529-2888

◪ "Still finding its niche", this Thai Flatiron newcomer is drawing an audience with "pleasant service", a "quiet", "comfortable" setting and "interesting" food.

China Fun ◐[S] — 15 | 8 | 12 | $17

1239 Second Ave. (65th St.), 212-752-0810

246 Columbus Ave. (bet. 71st & 72nd Sts.), 212-580-1516

◪ East and West Side "local Chinese" standbys; expect "basic", "cheeeap" food for a "decent" "neighborhood" "fix" but "forget ambiance" – "busy", "noisy" and "brusque", they're "no fun" for some.

F | D | S | C

CHINA GRILL [S] — 23 | 21 | 19 | $41
CBS Bldg., 52 W. 53rd St. (bet. 5th & 6th Aves.), 212-333-7788
■ "Feel the power" when you walk into the "buzzy", "high-energy", high-ceilinged modern space of this outstanding Eclectic Midtowner; it's "a must" "if someone else is paying", and there's a bar scene with a "svelte, leggy", oh "so self-aware" crowd.

Chin Chin ◐[S] — 23 | 20 | 21 | $39
216 E. 49th St. (bet. 2nd & 3rd Aves.), 212-888-4555
■ Be prepared for a "well-heeled crowd as interesting" as the "well-prepared, refined" food at this "civilized" "expense-account Chinese"; "beautifully designed" with "gracious", "impeccable service", it's definitely "top of the line."

Choga ◐[S] — – | – | – | M
145 Bleecker St. (bet. La Guardia Pl. & Thompson St.), 212-598-5946
NYU-area patrons tout this local Asian for its mix of Japanese and Korean dishes ranging from sushi and tempura to bi-bim-bap and kalbi; easy on your wallet, this casual spot has a lot of heart and Seoul.

Choshi [S] — 19 | 12 | 15 | $27
77 Irving Pl. (E. 19th St.), 212-420-1419
◪ "Come on in, the sushi's fine" at this well-priced Gramercy Japanese; "you can't beat" the "fresh", "inventive combinations", and, in good weather, "you can eat outside" to "enjoy Irving Place."

Christer's — 21 | 20 | 20 | $44
145 W. 55th St. (bet. 6th & 7th Aves.), 212-974-7224
■ "Handy to City Center" and Carnegie Hall, this "Scandinavian salmon lover's dream" offers a "provocative menu" served by an "attentive staff"; while most surveyors like the "lodgelike" decor, it reminds a few of the "Adirondacks on acid."

Christina's [S] — 16 | 11 | 14 | $21
606 Second Ave. (bet. 33rd & 34th Sts.), 212-889-5169
◪ "Cheap", "nontrendy" Italian "home cooking" and "slow service" would make for only "standard" Murray Hill "neighborhood" dining, but for the "pleasant outdoor garden" that transports you from NY.

Christine's [S]≠ — 16 | 7 | 13 | $16
208 First Ave. (bet. 12th & 13th Sts.), 212-254-2474
◪ This "nothing fancy" "staple" on the "Ukrainian strip in the East Village" has "hearty, straightforward" "Polish home cooking" with "low-end prices" and "Soviet bloc decor."

Christos Hasapo-Taverna (Queens) ◐[S] — ▽ 23 | 18 | 22 | $32
41-08 23rd Ave. (41st St.), 718-726-5195
■ For "truly Greek" grilled fish and steak "at good prices" plus "homey", "ethnic" ambiance, head to this Astoria taverna; "friendly" servers take the time to "explain everything."

Chumley's [S]≠ — 13 | 17 | 13 | $21
86 Bedford St. (bet. Bleecker St. & 7th Ave. S.), 212-675-4449
◪ Behind the "unmarked wooden door" is an appealing "historic" Village "speakeasy" with a young, casual crowd; though its "pub grub is weak", its beer choices are strong – if you can find it.

Churrascaria Plataforma ◐[S] — 22 | 20 | 21 | $38
Belvedere Hotel, 316 W. 49th St. (bet. 8th & 9th Aves.), 212-245-0505
■ At this "friendly", "noisy" Midtown Brazilian rotisserie, there's an "amazing parade of delectable meats", "a superior salad bar", "friendly service" and the "food just keeps on coming"; but this "carnival" is "not for the faint of heart or appetite"; it raises the question "where isn't the beef?"

Ciao Bella Cafe S⇔
▽ 20 | 15 | 15 | $20

27 E. 92nd St. (bet. 5th & Madison Aves.), 212-831-5555
200 W. 57th St. (7th Ave.), 212-956-5555
■ Try these Carnegie Hill and Midtown "convenient lunch spots" for the "best sorbet and gelati around" – "and the other stuff ain't bad either."

Ciao Europa ◐S
18 | 19 | 18 | $35

Warwick Hotel, 63 W. 54th St. (bet. 5th & 6th Aves.), 212-247-1200
☑ Near Carnegie Hall, this Midtown Italian can be a "positive surprise" with "European ambiance", "devoted" service and "consistent" midpriced food "on the cusp of being really good."

Cibar ◐S
– | – | – | M

The Inn at Irving Place, 56 Irving Pl. (bet. 17th & 18th Sts.), 212-460-5656
Sultry Gramercy newcomer with an elegant lounge and bar mixing up unusual concoctions and serving svelte surveyors with cheeses, caviar, foie gras and other Eclectic bites until the wee hours.

Cibo S
20 | 19 | 20 | $38

767 Second Ave. (bet. 41st & 42nd Sts.), 212-681-1616
■ This "attractive", yet not too expensive, East Midtown Italian is "a standout" with "simple, well-presented" food, "interesting" wines and a "clubby, upbeat feeling" that's "corporate fancy" but "relaxing."

Ciccio & Tony's East
16 | 16 | 15 | $28

561-565 Third Ave. (bet. 37th & 38th Sts.), 212-490-1558
☑ Just "shout louder than the next table" and you'll do fine in this "fraternity row", "generic" East Side Italian newcomer; though it's "quite the scene", the food is "uneven" unless you "stick to basics."

Cinquanta ◐S
18 | 17 | 20 | $40

50 E. 50th St. (bet. Madison & Park Aves.), 212-759-5050
■ Surveyors enjoy the "old-world pleasures" of "fine, authentic Italian" dining and "more than attentive service" at this Midtown "sleeper" – even if it charges "new-world prices."

Cinque Terre S
20 | 16 | 19 | $39

22 E. 38th St. (bet. Madison & Park Aves.), 212-213-0910
■ An "unsung Italian neighborhood favorite" in the dining "no man's land" of Murray Hill; "thoughtful, interesting" Ligurian cuisine and "caring service" at nonoppressive prices make this a local hit.

Ci Piace S
15 | 14 | 18 | $28

1426 Third Ave. (81st St.), 212-794-1810
☑ A place for "down-to-earth Italian served in a quiet setting at your own pace", this Upper Eastsider is also called "run-of-the-mill"; the "nice back garden" could help you decide.

Circa ◐S
19 | 20 | 16 | $34

103 Second Ave. (6th St.), 212-777-4120
☑ "What a concept" – "lots of modely women and fashionable men" against a "beautiful colored glass backdrop" in the East Village where the midpriced Mediterranean menu is "confident", "noise is circus level" and the "insouciant" "staff is somewhere else."

Circo, Osteria del S
22 | 24 | 20 | $48

120 W. 55th St. (bet. 6th & 7th Aves.), 212-265-3636
■ This "playful", "energetic" Midtown offspring of Le Cirque has "hype", "hefty prices", heady Italian food and a "hot and happening" "party atmosphere"; Adam Tihany's "knock your socks off" circus setting is a "must-see" and service, under Sirio's three sons, Mario, Marco and Mauro, is smooth as silk.

Circus S

20 | 19 | 19 | $38

808 Lexington Ave. (bet. 62nd & 63rd Sts.), 212-223-2965

■ With its "modern, lighter version of traditional Brazilian" fare, this Eastsider is a "delightful" "all-around winner" from the "sensible portions" of "potent", "rich, hot flavors" to the "wonderful" staff.

Ciro Trattoria S

▽ 18 | 17 | 16 | $31

813 Eighth St. (49th St.), 212-307-5484

■ "Yet another Theater District trattoria" but one with "good food" in a "relaxing atmosphere" "plus cool lighting" and a "staff that tries"; ardent fans say that the chef at this newcomer "should be sainted."

Cité ●S

21 | 20 | 20 | $47

120 W. 51st St. (bet. 6th & 7th Aves.), 212-956-7100

■ This "elegant" Midtown "business lunch standby" steakhouse may seem like a "Chinese fire drill pre-theater", but after 8 PM the all you can drink prix fixe wine dinner "may be the best deal in town"; it's "a wonderful place for a party", with "excellent well-aged steaks" and "waiters who don't flinch" while pouring "nonstop wine."

Cité Grill ●S

20 | 18 | 19 | $40

120 W. 51st St. (bet. 6th & 7th Aves.), 212-956-7262

■ Posing a "less expensive", "less formal" "alternative" to "big brother" Cité, this attractive steak frites bistro serves "attorney burgers" to "suits galore" at lunch and is also popular pre-theater.

Citrus Bar & Grill ●S

– | – | – | M

320 Amsterdam Ave. (75th St.), 212-595-0500

Brand-new West Side Southwestern with warm, come-hither decor plus hot cuisine at moderate prices and a cool scene.

City Bakery, The

21 | 12 | 13 | $15

22 E. 17th St. (bet. B'way & 5th Ave.), 212-366-1414

◪ Baker "Maury Rubin is a master" of his art, serving "gorgeous", "sinfully good" pastries from breakfast through early evening in his Flatiron bakery; still, as ratings show, customers don't warm to the "minimalist" "anti-decor" decor and service at this "bakery as gallery."

City Crab & Seafood Co. ●S

18 | 15 | 15 | $34

235 Park Ave. S. (19th St.), 212-529-3800

◪ Flatiron seafood house that "holds its own amid its trendsetter neighbors" by offering "decent" "Maryland in Manhattan" seafood in a "decent setting at a decent price"; but watch out, at times it feels like a "huge" "frat party."

City Wine & Cigar Co. ●S

21 | 23 | 20 | $42

62 Laight St. (Greenwich St.), 212-334-2274

■ "Brokers to the right, traders to the left" and "real foodies" all around fill Drew Nieporent's "innovative" American-Eclectic TriBeCa newcomer; the "handsome", clublike interiors and pro staff invite lingering over a good cigar, and a very good meal.

Ci Vediamo S

19 | 17 | 17 | $29

1431 Third Ave. (81st St.), 212-650-0850

■ "Respectable food" "priced right" makes this a standout in the "Upper East Side sea of Italian restaurants"; there's dining "upstairs, downstairs and outside" so you "can have any ambiance" you want.

Clarke's, P.J. ●S

14 | 14 | 13 | $25

915 Third Ave. (55th St.), 212-759-1650

◪ "You can't say you're a NYer until you've had a burger" and brew at this East Side 'teflon' pub; still, some dismiss this "classic" as a "McDonald's for the middle-aged" that's "way past its bedtime."

F	D	S	C

Clementine ◐ [S] — 21 | 20 | 18 | $43

1 Fifth Ave. (8th St.), 212-253-0003

■ If anything "can save this jinxed lower Fifth Avenue space" it will be chef John Schenk's "newest incarnation" featuring "outrageously good" New American food, one of the "coolest", "remarkably attitude-free" bars in the city and "celebrity sightings galore."

Cloister Cafe, The ◐ [S] ≠ — 11 | 21 | 12 | $18

238 E. Ninth St. (bet. 2nd & 3rd Aves.), 212-777-9128

◪ "Concentrate on" the "peaceful" "vine-covered garden" and "stick to dessert and coffee" at this East Village cafe; despite "pathetic service" and Continental food that inspires lines like "I'd rather lick the sidewalk", "that garden is worth any aggravation."

Club Macanudo — 14 | 22 | 17 | $36

26 E. 63rd St. (bet. Madison & Park Aves.), 212-752-8200

■ This "posh" East Side "cigar lover's dream" is made for "hanging out", "puffing stogies" and downing fine cognacs; the Eclectic "food is secondary" to the let's see "who can outstatus each other" games played by "hundreds of Bruce and Demi wanna-bes."

Coco Marina — - | - | - | M

2 World Financial Ctr., Winter Garden (bet. Liberty & Vesey Sts.), 212-385-8080

For a welcome WFC change of pace, this elegant new Italian looking out on the Winter Garden is worth a try; with the East Side's Coco Pazzo as its parent, it clearly has good bloodlines.

Coconut Grill ◐ [S] — 16 | 13 | 14 | $25

1481 Second Ave. (77th St.), 212-772-6262

■ An "old faithful", "straightforward", affordable American that's "packed to the rafters" with pretty young Upper Eastsiders during "stroller-friendly" days and "see and be seen" nights.

Coco Opera [S] — 17 | 17 | 16 | $41

58 W. 65th St. (bet. Columbus Ave. & CPW), 212-873-3700

◪ "Nothing to sing about", Pino Luongo's Lincoln Center Italian newcomer (ex Sfuzzi) is playing to early mixed notices: critics cite "ordinary" food and staff needing a "get over yourself attitude" adjustment, while fans say after a "slow start", it's "getting better."

Coco Pazzo ◐ [S] — 22 | 21 | 20 | $51

23 E. 74th St. (bet. 5th & Madison Aves.), 212-794-0205

■ "Always impressive" with "a style all its own", this Upper East Side "celebrity-focused" "trendfest" is the "ultimate chic" Italian with an "inspired" Tuscan menu at "grandiose prices"; despite "caste system" service, most say it's "a total delight."

Coco Pazzo Teatro ◐ [S] — 19 | 19 | 18 | $44

Paramount Hotel, 235 W. 46th St. (bet. B'way & 8th Ave.), 212-827-4222

◪ "Well-run", "cool" Theater District Italian yearling that's a "cut above its competitors"; however, disappointed diners complain that Pino Luongo's "formula" is "becoming a bit of a bore."

Cody's Bar & Grill ◐ [S] — - | - | - | M

282 Hudson St. (Dominick St.), 212-924-5853

Worth checking out if you're in way West SoHo, this new corner bar features easily affordable American food and a cozy ambiance.

Coffee Shop ◐ [S] — 15 | 13 | 11 | $24

29 Union Sq. W. (16th St.), 212-243-7969

◪ The "miniskirt capital" of Union Square where "you can see models" while eating Brazilian cuisine and other stuff that's "best late at night"; though the "highly attitudinal" staff is too busy "waiting for their close-up", "sometimes you need a little coffee shop in your life."

F | D | S | C

Col Legno ◖🅂   19 | 13 | 15 | $31
231 E. Ninth St. (bet. 2nd & 3rd Aves.), 212-777-4650
■ You'll get "real Italian, not pasta of the week" and "fantastic brick-oven pizza" at this affordable East Village bare-bones "rustic."

Colony 🅂   15 | 16 | 15 | $25
1199 First Ave. (65th St.), 212-249-7878
◪ The "refreshing", SE Asian food at this East Side yearling is "not bad but it's not Vong"; ditto the "neat bamboo" setting; still, with an "ice-cold Saigon beer", it's hard to beat at the price.

Columbus Bakery 🅂   18 | 13 | 11 | $14
957 First Ave. (bet. 52nd & 53rd Sts.), 212-421-0334
474 Columbus Ave. (bet. 82nd & 83rd Sts.), 212-724-6880
■ "A daily tradition" for those who love the "close-to-home-baked goods", prepared foods and "mammoth coffees" at these "compact" "country parlors" on the East and West Sides; but the "confusing setup" and "free-for-all" service are discouraging.

Comfort Diner 🅂   16 | 15 | 15 | $17
214 E. 45th St. (bet. 2nd & 3rd Aves.), 212-867-4555
■ "A diner by any other name is still a diner", but this East Side American "flashback" "from the '50s" with "low" "retro" prices is "comforting for aging baby boomers" and their kids.

Coming or Going   20 | 17 | 19 | $30
38 E. 58th St. (bet. Madison & Park Aves.), 212-980-5858
■ Regulars "hate to let the secret out" because this "cute Midtown hideaway" has "world-class" American "small-town food", "country charm" and "calm service" in this "most urban of cities."

Community Bar & Grill 🅂   17 | 15 | 16 | $28
216 Seventh Ave. (bet. 22nd & 23rd Sts.), 212-242-7900
■ "They work hard" at this "inviting" Chelsea American where "nice people serve you" "good basic food" in "a simple setting"; though "nothing exciting", it's a "bargain" spot to "relax and have a good time."

Contrapunto ◖🅂   17 | 14 | 15 | $32
200 E. 60th St. (3rd Ave.), 212-751-8616
■ "After a hard day at Bloomie's", this East Side "Arizona meets Italy" mezzanine eatery is "convenient" for a "light meal" of "satisfying" pastas and salads with "competent" service; in sum, it's "in and out with pasta in the middle."

Cooking With Jazz (Queens) 🅂   23 | 14 | 21 | $32
12-01 154th St. (12th Ave.), 718-767-6979
■ "You won't regret the visit" to this "real out of the way", "shoe box–sized" Cajun in Whitestone; there's "food with a bang" plus "great" jazz, making for the "hippest, coolest" "taste of New Orleans" that you can get "this side of the Mason-Dixon line."

Copeland's 🅂   ▽ 19 | 13 | 17 | $23
547 W. 145th St. (bet. Amsterdam Ave. & B'way), 212-234-2357
■ "Get thee to Harlem" for a "warm welcome" and sincere Soul Food; the "utilitarian cafeteria setting" may be "nothing to brag about", but there are "hallelujahs" for the "gospel Sunday brunch", "AYCE buffet" and modest prices.

Cornelia Street Cafe ◖🅂   17 | 14 | 15 | $27
29 Cornelia St. (bet. Bleecker & W. 4th Sts.), 212-989-9319
◪ "If you're in the beatnik mood" or want to see the "Village as it used to be", join the "art and literary wanna-bes" at this "pleasant if uninspired" "old shoe" American cafe for "simple" "sustenance" and "careless" "I'm an actress, not a waitress" service.

58

Corner Bistro ❶🅂⇗
331 W. Fourth St. (Jane St.), 212-242-9502
■ For a "smoky, dingy joint" with "disinterested staff", this comfy West Village American bistro sure has a lot of fans; they rank it "best" for its bar, jukebox and "big, fat, sloppy" burgers, and sum it up as "dress down, hunker down, chow down."

| 20 | 11 | 11 | $14 |

Corsica ❶🅂
310 W. Fourth St. (bet. Bank & W. 12th Sts.), 212-691-8541
Drissia and Jean-Roger Rafael have revamped their Village mainstay, L'Auberge du Midi, into this cozy Corsican, offering hearty specials and plenty of caring service in an intimate, rustic setting.

| – | – | – | M |

Cortina ❶🅂
1448 Second Ave. (bet. 75th & 76th Sts.), 212-517-2066
Originally a dessert and coffee specialist, this inexpensive East Side Italian has shifted to a full menu, and at these low prices, they're practically paying you to go.

| – | – | – | I |

Cosí Sandwich Bar
60 E. 56th St. (bet. Madison & Park Aves.), 212-588-0888
165 E. 52nd St. (bet. Lexington & 3rd Aves.), 212-758-7800
38 E. 45th St. (bet. Madison & Vanderbilt Aves.), 212-949-7400
11 W. 42nd St. (bet. 5th & 6th Aves.), 212-398-6660
■ "Lunchtime is more fun" in Midtown now that "sandwiches have been taken to a higher level"; with a "cult-like following" for its "addictive" bread and fillings, this minichain draws "long lines"; in due course, it will probably go public.

| 20 | 13 | 14 | $12 |

Country Café ❶🅂⇗
69 Thompson St. (bet. Broome & Spring Sts.), 212-966-5417
■ Take a "break from SoHo fashion" and "feel whisked away" to the "French countryside" at this "cozy" French-Moroccan bistro with "beautifully prepared" food; the "all cute, all the time" waiters are "as friendly as French gets."

| 22 | 19 | 19 | $32 |

Cowgirl Hall of Fame 🅂
519 Hudson St. (10th St.), 212-633-1133
☑ "Amusing", "kid-friendly" West Village Tex-Mex "foot-stomping country fair" that's home to "authentic tackiness", "redneck" food and a "sassy staff"; most customers "can't resist the fun drinks", "great gift shop" and "ice cream desserts."

| 14 | 17 | 14 | $22 |

C3 ❶🅂
Washington Sq. Hotel, 103 Waverly Pl. (MacDougal St.), 212-254-1200
☑ "Sometimes great, sometimes average" sums up this "cool, quiet", "intimate" Villager with "very good", "homey" American food "at reasonable prices"; regulars tout its brunch and "theme nights", but some notice it can be empty – "if you can C2 people, it's a miracle."

| 20 | 17 | 18 | $27 |

Cub Room ❶🅂
131 Sullivan St. (Prince St.), 212-677-4100

Cub Room Cafe ❶🅂
183 Prince St. (Sullivan St.), 212-777-0030
■ "Uptown meets Downtown in peaceful coexistence" at this "solid" SoHo spot for "adventurous", at times "inspired" American food; there's also a "chic bar scene" and adjacent storefront cafe "comfort zone."

| 21 | 21 | 19 | $39 |

CUCINA (Brooklyn)
256 Fifth Ave. (bet. Carroll St. & Garfield Pl.), 718-230-0711
■ It may be "over the bridge" and "off the beaten path" but "they never let you down" at Michael Ayoub's "comfortable", "always mobbed", "lusty" Italian; satisfied surveyors cite food, staff and prices "that make you smile", and the bonus of valet parking.

| 24 | 21 | 21 | $38 |

Cucina & Co.   16 | 13 | 15 | $22
MetLife Bldg., 200 Park Ave. (45th St.), 212-682-2700
■ "If you can take the noise" and the "Grand Central crowd", you'll get a "nice lunch for a nice price" or on weeknights, "two meals for $20" at this Midtown Mediterranean cafeteria-style "standby"; if not, the takeout is a "great buy" for "busy commuters."

Cucina Della Fontana S   15 | 19 | 16 | $22
368 Bleecker St. (Charles St.), 212-242-0636
☑ This "cheap and cheery" Village Italian has "inconsistent" food and service but fans love the "delightfully tacky" "interior garden"; just "head downstairs" and "forget all about Manhattan."

Cucina della Nonna ◐S   ▽ 19 | 17 | 19 | $31
104 Grand St. (Mercer St.), 212-925-5488
■ For "above-average Italian basics" at below-average tabs, served "without attitude", this "lovely, low-key" SoHo "retreat" is "just as good as grandma's" and an "intimate" "meeting place for singles."

Cucina di Pesce ◐S⇗   18 | 13 | 15 | $22
87 E. Fourth St. (bet. 2nd & 3rd Aves.), 212-260-6800
■ "Packed", "dark, tiny" East Village "pasta of the week place"; "bargain basement seafood", "free mussels at the bar" and "sweet service" are reason enough for our surveyors "to wait hours."

Cucina Stagionale ◐S⇗   17 | 12 | 15 | $21
275 Bleecker St. (bet. 6th & 7th Aves.), 212-924-2707
■ "The food is everything" at this "Village bargain" "standout" for "hefty Italian" fare; it's "cramped but has a certain charm" (like an "Italian mama's kitchen"), so "beat the wait, get there early" and BYO.

Cucina Vivolo   19 | 16 | 17 | $27
138 E. 74th St. (bet. Lexington & Park Aves.), 212-717-4700
■ For inexpensive "quick dining" that's "defiantly not fast food", try this East Side Italian; the "high-quality, low-cost lunch" is "simple but good" and there's "real value" in the "best takeout around."

Cuisine de Saigon S   18 | 11 | 16 | $25
154 W. 13th St. (bet. 6th & 7th Aves.), 212-255-6003
☑ Focus on the "warm service" and "richly flavored food" rather than the decor at this "true Vietnamese" Villager and you'll be happy.

Cupcake Cafe S⇗   21 | 7 | 13 | $13
522 Ninth Ave. (39th St.), 212-465-1530
■ "Calling it a cafe is pushing it" because this cheap Midtowner in the badlands behind the Port Authority terminal "is really a store with a few chairs"; but its lovely cakes, "hearty soups" and "waffles with real maple syrup" outweigh its "Depression-era ambiance."

Cupping Room Café ◐S   16 | 16 | 14 | $23
359 W. Broadway (bet. Broome & Grand Sts.), 212-925-2898
■ "You can feel rushed" by the staff "grouches" and "rather crushed" by the "tourists" at this SoHo brunch headquarters, but for regulars this affordable, "quaint" Eclectic cafe remains a "lasting classic."

Cyclo S   – | – | – | M
203 First Ave. (bet. 12th & 13th Sts.), 212-673-3957
Stylish East Village Vietnamese newcomer with modest prices and a hip staff; it's already so popular you may not be able to get in the door.

Da Ciro S   20 | 15 | 17 | $34
229 Lexington Ave. (bet. 33rd & 34th Sts.), 212-532-1636
■ "Wonderful" Murray Hill "neighborhood Italian" with "great pizza" from a wood-burning oven; though both "charming" and "lively", some diners find it "harried" and "overpriced."

Daily Soup 💳 — 20 | 10 | 15 | $10
134 E. 43rd St. (bet. Lexington & 3rd Aves.), 212-949-7687
21 E. 41st St. (bet. 5th & Madison Aves.), 212-953-7687
325 Park Ave. S. (bet. 24th & 25th Sts.), 212-531-7687
17 E. 17th St. (bet. 5th Ave. & B'way), 212-929-7687
41 John St. (bet. Nassau & William Sts.), 212-791-7687
■ Five locations ladle out "sensational", "hearty" budget-lunch soups; service is "friendly", but plan on "long lines."

Dallas BBQ ◐[S] — 14 | 8 | 12 | $17
1265 Third Ave. (bet. 72nd & 73rd Sts.), 212-772-9393
27 W. 72nd St. (bet. Columbus Ave. & CPW), 212-873-2004
21 University Pl. (8th St.), 212-674-4450
132 Second Ave. (St. Marks Pl.), 212-777-5574
◪ "Texas-size portions" of "good comfort food" at "Rhode Island–size prices" keep this "cheerful" BBQ chain "always hopping"; parents and kids seem to love them despite minimal decor and service.

Da Mario [S] — – | – | – | E
883 First Ave. (bet. 49th & 50th Sts.), 212-750-1804
Chef-owner Mario Napoli (ex Da Umberto) brings a medley of Sicilian flavors to this UN-area trattoria; it's popular with the weekday UN lunch crowd and a "quiet find" for a Saturday night date.

Danal [S] — 21 | 22 | 18 | $29
90 E. 10th St. (bet. 3rd & 4th Aves.), 212-982-6930
◪ "As cozy as it gets", this "romantic", bon marché, Central Village "shabby chic" "country French bistro" is a "great date place" and serves a "fabulous Sunday brunch"; dissenters decry "cramped" quarters, "snippy" service and "ventilation that needs work."

D'Angelo, Osteria — ▽ 20 | 17 | 20 | $32
242 W. 56th St. (bet. B'way & 8th Ave.), 212-307-0700
◪ "Consistently above average", this "busy", modestly priced Theater District Northern Italian yearling is "pleasant but unexciting"; "friendly staff" is a plus, but "sterile surroundings" are a minus.

Da Nico [S] — 20 | 16 | 17 | $27
164 Mulberry St. (bet. Broome & Grand Sts.), 212-343-1212
■ A "delightful, old-fashioned" Little Italy "favorite" with "friendly" waiters serving "real Italian" food at old-fashioned prices to the likes of Al Pacino; check out the "wonderful garden."

DANIEL — 28 | 25 | 25 | $71
Surrey Hotel, 20 E. 76th St. (bet. 5th & Madison Aves.), 212-288-0033
■ "Only a poet could adequately describe the ambrosia" that comes from Daniel Boulud's No. 1–rated East Side Classic French kitchen, but well-heeled diners try – "truly glorious", "divine", "creative", "magnifique"; service may occasionally be "supercilious", the room "cramped" and you may have to "pawn your wife's wedding ring" when you get your check, but overall high ratings confirm that "all is forgiven" over "one of life's memorable meals" prepared by the chef whom cognoscenti see as NY's culinary leader.

Daniella Ristorante [S] — ▽ 23 | 18 | 20 | $40
320 Eighth Ave. (26th St.), 212-807-0977
■ "Modest in size but big in quality" and price, this "friendly", "noisy" Chelsea Italian "neighborhood restaurant" is for some "the only viable choice near Madison Square Garden."

Dan Maxwell's Steakhouse [S] — 18 | 15 | 18 | $33
1708 Second Ave. (bet. 88th & 89th Sts.), 212-426-7688
■ A "traditional", "pub-style" East Side steakhouse with "big portions" of "tasty" food and "attentive" service at fair prices.

Darbar S
21 | 19 | 19 | $36

44 W. 56th St. (bet. 5th & 6th Aves.), 212-432-7227

◪ Diners split as to whether this "classy" Midtown Indian is "reliable", serving some of "the best Indian food in NYC", or "inconsistent" and "overpriced"; to resolve the issue try the $12.95 AYCE buffet lunch.

Da Silvano ◕S
22 | 18 | 19 | $44

260 Sixth Ave. (bet. Bleecker & Houston Sts.), 212-982-2343

■ This "charming", "hip" Greenwich Village Italian is "a survivor" that has a "loyal following" for its "excellent", "fresh" food; "very European" and "indefatigably chic" (with "lots of celebs"), it can get "noisy and crowded" – so "sit outdoors."

Da Tommaso ◕S
20 | 14 | 19 | $37

903 Eighth Ave. (bet. 53rd & 54th Sts.), 212-265-1890

■ "Fine Northern Italian food" and a "hardworking staff" earn this West Midtowner good "word of mouth"; only the decor needs help.

Da Umberto
24 | 19 | 21 | $48

107 W. 17th St. (bet. 6th & 7th Aves.), 212-989-0303

■ Chelsea's "sensationally good", if "expensive", Tuscan "deserves every compliment"; the "chic business crowd" that frequents this "gorgeous place" to gorge on "great Italian food" advises "don't let the noise" or "snob-o-la waiters" bother you.

Da Vittorio
22 | 19 | 22 | $44

43 E. 20th St. (bet. B'way & Park Ave. S.), 212-979-6532

◪ "Like father" Umberto, son Vittorio runs a "consistently good", "charming" Tuscan with "extrafriendly staff"; still, some find it "overpriced" and say "Vittorio has much to learn from papa."

Dawat S
22 | 19 | 20 | $38

210 E. 58th St. (bet. 2nd & 3rd Aves.), 212-355-7555

■ This "fancy" yet "relaxed" East Side Indian under the tutelage of cookbook author Madhur Jaffrey may be "the best Indian outside India"; though "expensive" for Indian, surveyors say it's "dawicious."

Daydream Cafe S
▽ 20 | 17 | 15 | $14

405 W. 51st St. (bet. 9th & 10th Aves.), 212-333-7766

■ "The most creative hangout in West Midtown" is aptly named: "grab an iced decaf cappuccino", an outdoor table and a light, healthy Eclectic bite and "daydream the afternoon away."

Decade ◕
▽ 16 | 20 | 17 | $46

1117 First Ave. (bet. 61st & 62nd Sts.), 212-835-5979

◪ "Dance off your dinner" at this "fun" new East Side "'50s-style supper club" serving "overpriced" and underspiced American and Continental fare; the "friendly singles scene at the bar" and '60s and '70s music attract a slightly "older" second-time-around crowd.

DeGrezia
22 | 21 | 22 | $46

231 E. 50th St. (bet. 2nd & 3rd Aves.), 212-750-5353

■ "Underrated" and "undiscovered" except by the local business crowd, this Midtown Italian with "lovely ambiance" and "gracious service" is "consistently very good", though not a bargain.

Delano Drive S
▽ 17 | 17 | 19 | $27

15 Waterside Plaza (bet. 25th St. & FDR Dr.), 212-683-3001

■ New, "kid-friendly" "local hangout"-cum-piano bar providing "generous servings" of "decent" American and Italian food and a "view of NYC along the East River."

Delegates' Dining Room
| 20 | 21 | 20 | $35 |

UN, 4th fl. (1st Ave. & 46th St.), 212-963-7626
■ In the UN, "overlooking the East River", this "best-kept secret" has diplomat clients and a changing International lunch buffet; it's "worth the security hassle", is "tax-free" and "good for impressing" visitors.

Delia's
▽ | 15 | 20 | 17 | $39 |

197 E. Third St. (bet. Aves. A & B), 212-254-9184
☑ The majority would "skip dinner, just go later to dance" at this "fun", "offbeat" weekend-only East Village supper club; a minority insists that its French-Caribbean kitchen offers "good food" too.

Delphini ⬤🅂
| 20 | 21 | 17 | $37 |

519 Columbus Ave. (85th St.), 212-579-1145
☑ "Completely lit by candles", this "romantic" Westsider produces "surprisingly delicious" Mediterranean fare, but its popularity leads to service that's "hit or miss" and high noise levels.

Demarchelier ⬤🅂
| 17 | 17 | 16 | $39 |

50 E. 86th St. (bet. Madison & Park Aves.), 212-249-6300
☑ Patrons debate whether this "attractive" Upper East Side French bistro (with a "lively bar") is an "inexpensive", "tasty" "oasis" or "pricey", "pretentious" and "disappointing."

Demi 🅂
| 19 | 20 | 19 | $42 |

1316 Madison Ave. (93rd St.), 212-534-3475
■ "Shh – a find": an "older crowd" comes to this "utterly charming townhouse" basement in Carnegie Hill for "romantic" fireplace-side Continental meals that are "East Side chic with prices to match."

Denino's Tavern (Staten Island) ⬤🅂⇥
▽ | 23 | 11 | 17 | $17 |

524 Port Richmond Ave. (bet. Hooker Pl. & Walker St.), 718-442-9401
■ Those seeking the "best pizza on SI and possibly in NY" join the lines at this "lively", family-run pizzeria, a "landmark" since 1937.

Deniz a la Turk ⬤
| 22 | 19 | 20 | $42 |

400 E. 57th St. (bet. 1st Ave. & Sutton Pl.), 212-486-2255
■ "Don't let the name frighten you", this "excellent", "spacious", "friendly" East Midtown Turk has "fish so fresh it feels like a fishing boat is alongside"; "go late and stay for the party."

DeRosa
▽ | 23 | 20 | 22 | $38 |

531 Second Ave. (bet. 29th & 30th Sts.), 212-213-6833
■ "The homemade pasta is to die for" at this "new and wonderful" Kips Bay Neapolitan; expect "fresh, honest cooking", but in "small portions", and for not so small prices.

Destinée
| – | – | – | E |

134 E. 61st St. (bet. Lexington & Park Aves.), 212-888-1220
Highly touted chef Jean-Yves Schillinger, with two Michelin stars to his credit, has recently opened this attractive East Side New French; though it looks good, it's still too soon to predict its destiny; prix fixe lunch is $28, dinner is $42.

Dionysos
▽ | 18 | 17 | 20 | $33 |

75 Fifth Ave. (bet. 15th & 16th Sts.), 212-229-2992
☑ Yea-sayers cite "superb" food and ambiance at this new Union Square Greek, but naysayers counter "I've had better at Greek diners."

Dish of Salt ⬤
| 19 | 20 | 18 | $38 |

133 W. 47th St. (bet. 6th & 7th Aves.), 212-921-4242
☑ "Class" and "impeccable service" define this Theater District "gourmet Chinese"; however, though "very good", some say you can find "better and more reasonable Chinese elsewhere."

Diva ◐[S] — 17 | 18 | 14 | $33
341 W. Broadway (bet. Broome & Grand Sts.), 212-941-9024
◩ "So-so food, bad service, but who cares?" – not the "Eurotrash", "Wall Street traders" or "model wanna-bes" that crowd this "sexy" red SoHo Italian boîte.

Divina Commedia ◐[S] — – | – | – | M
737 Ninth Ave. (50th St.), 212-265-6649
New Hell's Kitchen Italian with a staff that's trying hard with inexpensive lunch specials that are the way to go; it's also handy pre-theater.

Divine Bar ◐[S] — 17 | 21 | 16 | $25
244 E. 51st St. (bet. 2nd & 3rd Aves.), 212-319-WINE
■ "Tasty tapas", "funky decor" and a "cool uptairs lounge" highlight this Eclectic "slice of SoHo in Midtown"; it's a "hit with the after-work crowd", but "avoid it if you don't like noise and smoke."

Divino Ristorante ◐[S] — 18 | 14 | 18 | $35
1556 Second Ave. (bet. 80th & 81st Sts.), 212-861-1096
◩ Surveyors "aren't crazy about" the decor of this "reliable" East Side Italian "neighborhood standby", but most describe it as "casual", "friendly" and "hearty."

Diwan Grill [S] — 21 | 18 | 19 | $30
148 E. 48th St. (bet. Lexington & 3rd Aves.), 212-593-5425
■ "It doesn't get the press of Dawat, but darn good food", especially the $12.95 lunch buffet, plus "attentive service" and "attractive ambiance" pull Midtown lunchtime crowds; the "spacious" room is "quiet" and "relaxing" in the evening.

Docks Oyster Bar [S] — 21 | 16 | 17 | $38
633 Third Ave. (40th St.), 212-986-8080
2427 Broadway (bet. 89th & 90th Sts.), 212-724-5588
◩ Two "large", "classy", often "crowded" "quintessential NY" seafood houses with "fresh, fresh, fresh" fish that most surveyors like; if some find the finny fare "bland", the "smoky singles scene" at the bar after work in Midtown is far from bland.

Dojo ◐[S]⊘ — 14 | 8 | 11 | $13
14 W. Fourth St. (bet. B'way & Mercer St.), 212-505-8934
24-26 St. Marks Pl. (bet. 2nd & 3rd Aves.), 212-674-9821
■ "Cheap eats, no frills, no thrills" Village "McVegans" serving "somewhat healthy" American-Japanese fare to a "young" "NYU crowd"; the "tattoo and body piercing show" is free of charge.

Dok Suni ◐[S]⊘ — 21 | 16 | 14 | $23
119 First Ave. (bet. 7th St. & St. Marks Pl.), 212-477-9506
◩ "Korean food goes hipster" at this "fun and flavorful", "small and smoky" "sweet vibe" East Villager; despite its low prices, Korean cognoscenti say the food is "wimpy" and only "pseudo Korean."

Dolce — 17 | 18 | 18 | $36
60 E. 49th St. (bet. Madison & Park Aves.), 212-692-9292
◩ It's too soon to tell whether chef Greg Waters will give this "boring" but "serviceable" Midtown Italian the "kick in the pants" that many think it needs; even so, some like its "pleasant" feel.

Domingo ◐ — 16 | 18 | 16 | $42
209 E. 49th St. (bet. 2nd & 3rd Aves.), 212-826-8269
◩ Placido Domingo's Midtown Spaniard draws mixed reviews: from "class act" and "solid paella" to "bland" and "uneven"; put musically, it has "many flats, few sharps"; still, the upstairs dining room and terrace are enticing.

Dominick's (Bronx) 🅂≠
2335 Arthur Ave. (187th St.), 718-733-2807

22	9	15	$29

■ "Long waits, communal tables, no menu, no written check, no credit cards", but the "quintessence of Italian cooking" makes this a "convivial" "Bronx treasure"; the advice is to "eat what the waiters tell you" and come early or late to avoid the wait.

Don Giovanni Ristorante ◑🅂
358 W. 44th St. (bet. 8th & 9th Aves.), 212-581-4939
214 10th Ave. (bet. 22nd & 23rd Sts.), 212-242-9054

17	12	13	$21

☑ "A cheap little place" for brick-oven thin-crust pizza and "decent pasta", this Theater District and Chelsea Italian duo has minimal decor and service ("just try to find a waiter"), but most don't mind.

Downtown ◑🅂
376 W. Broadway (Broome St.), 212-343-0999

17	18	15	$49

☑ "Park your Porsche on West Broadway" and "see and be seen" downstairs or in the "roof garden" of Giuseppe Cipriani's "costly" SoHo Italian; some think the food is "surprisingly good", but critics assert it's a "rip-off."

Drip ◑🅂
489 Amsterdam Ave. (bet. 83rd & 84th Sts.), 212-875-1032

14	17	14	$11

■ The "coffee and pastry are good" but aren't the main course at this cheap, West Side "community kaffeeklatsch" with *Brady Bunch* decor" that's "packed with Gen Xers looking through ring binders for a mate"; if you get a drip, they're not responsible.

Drovers Tap Room ◑🅂
9 Jones St. (bet. Bleecker & W. 4th Sts.), 212-627-1233

19	18	18	$33

■ You'll find "homey, hearty" "comfort food at its finest" at David Page's "friendly" new "Midwestern-style cafe"; surveyors find it as refreshing as a trip to Wisconsin.

Druids ◑🅂
736 10th Ave. (bet. 50th & 51st Sts.), 212-307-6410

▽ 18	16	18	$27

■ The "upscale menu" of Eclectic cuisine surprises many visitors to this "warm and friendly" pub in Hell's Kitchen; there's a garden too.

DT•UT ◑🅂≠
1626 Second Ave. (bet. 84th & 85th Sts.), 212-327-1327

17	21	14	$12

■ "Welcome to *Friends*": frugal but friendly Eastsiders enjoy "wine and fondue" or coffee, cake and light bites at this "groovy" lounge; most come to socialize on open mike, movie and bingo nights.

Duane Park Cafe
157 Duane St. (bet. Hudson St. & W. B'way), 212-732-5555

23	20	21	$42

■ This "unexpected little treasure" in TriBeCa is an "unsung hero" to admirers who applaud its "outstanding, inventive", fairly priced New American menu and "quiet", "cozy" ambiance; check it out for yourself.

Due ◑🅂
1396 Third Ave. (bet. 79th & 80th Sts.), 212-772-3331

19	16	17	$34

☑ A "cute little" Upper East Side "neighborhood" Italian offering "consistent", "well-priced, well-served" food; however, while "always a favorite" for some, others feel it's "lost its touch."

E & O ◑🅂
100 W. Houston St. (bet. La Guardia Pl. & Thompson St.), 212-254-7000

16	18	14	$33

☑ "Wear black" to this SoHo Pan-Asian celebrity center; fans like seeing "beautiful people paired with good food", while skeptics say it's "a typical Nell Campbell place – haute, hot and high priced."

Ear Inn ⦿S

| 14 | 15 | 14 | $19 |

326 Spring St. (bet. Greenwich & Washington Sts.), 212-226-9060

■ There's "decent" "grub" at this "moderately priced", "friendly", "smoky and somewhat gritty" 1817 vintage "classic NY pub"; it's "a great dive" with "salty charm" and "poetic burgers."

East S

| 17 | 12 | 14 | $24 |

1420 Third Ave. (bet. 80th & 81st Sts.), 212-472-3975
354 E. 66th St. (bet. 1st & 2nd Aves.), 212-734-5270
210 E. 44th St. (bet. 2nd & 3rd Aves.), 212-687-5075
251 W. 55th St. (bet. B'way & 8th Ave.), 212-581-2240
9 E. 38th St. (bet. 5th & Madison Aves.), 212-685-5205
366 Third Ave. (bet. 26th & 27th Sts.), 212-889-2326
9 Barrow St. (bet. 7th Ave. S. & W. 4th St.), 212-929-3353 ⦿

☑ "Unpretentious" and "reasonable" describes the "Bennigan's of sushi" – a "fast", "kid-friendly" Japanese chain with "picture menus for the gaijin"; P.S. try the bento box lunch.

Eastern Villa ⦿S

▽ | 23 | 11 | 16 | $25 |

66 Mott St. (bet. Bayard & Canal Sts.), 212-226-4675

■ You get a lot of "bang for your buck" at this "simple", "clean" Chinese that's among "Chinatown's best choices for fresh fish"; no reserving except for big groups means there's "often a frustrating wait."

East Lake (Queens) ⦿S⌷

▽ | 21 | 9 | 13 | $21 |

42-33 Main St. (Franklin Ave.), 718-539-8532

■ "The queen of dim sum" is this "inexpensive", "jammed" Flushing "glitz diner"; "Chinese families congregate" for the "authentic" (eel lips anyone?) "fresh seafood" taken live from the tanks and cooked to order.

East of Eighth ⦿S

▽ | 17 | 19 | 17 | $24 |

254 W. 23rd St. (bet. 7th & 8th Aves.), 212-352-0075

☑ Chelseaites "welcome" this "new", "reasonable" American-Eclectic; the "airy setting", "gorgeous garden" and brunch all get praise, but it's not unanimous – "uninspired", "so-so."

East River Cafe S

| 19 | 18 | 19 | $34 |

1111 First Ave. (61st St.), 212-980-3144

■ "You get a good meal for a good price" ($9.95 for brunch, $19.95 pre-theater) at this "friendly", "cozy" East Side Italian; it's "very pleasant" with few disappointments.

E.A.T. S

| 19 | 11 | 13 | $31 |

1064 Madison Ave. (bet. 80th & 81st Sts.), 212-772-0022

■ Diners "hate to admit it" but Eli Zabar's "shamelessly overpriced" Upper East Side "pumped-up coffee shop" has "great wholesome" soups, sandwiches and snacks, albeit with "shoddy service."

Eat & Drink S

| 18 | 17 | 16 | $27 |

148 Mercer St. (bet. Houston & Prince Sts.), 212-925-2477

☑ "Comfy" and "mellow", this "loungey, minimalist", "hip SoHo" Pan-Asian has fans who find its food "imaginative" and "visually polished", but critics are "exceedingly underwhelmed."

Ecco

| 21 | 17 | 19 | $38 |

124 Chambers St. (bet. Church St. & W. B'way), 212-227-7074

☑ "The old NY setting" is appealing at this "white tablecloth" Wall Street–area Italian; though "a bit pricey", reviewers keep returning for the "wonderful" "homestyle" food and "warm" ambiance.

Ecco-La ⦿S

| 18 | 14 | 15 | $21 |

1660 Third Ave. (93rd St.), 212-860-5609

☑ Despite "cramped quarters", this "festive" Upper East Side Italian has "very good, cheap pasta"; just "ask to be seated in the back" and "watch all the couples on first dates."

Edgar's Cafe ◐🅂⇄
17 | 17 | 14 | $16

255 W. 84th St. (bet. B'way & West End Ave.), 212-496-6126

■ "Atmospheric" West Side "salad and dessert" cafe with "slow" service but "truly dreamy desserts" and Edgar Allan "Poe–inspired decor"; in sum, it's "a place you can linger with friends."

Edison Cafe 🅂⇄
15 | 9 | 13 | $17

Hotel Edison, 228 W. 47th St. (bet. B'way & 8th Ave.), 212-840-5000

☑ This "theatrical hangout", "a real greasy spoon" "that time forgot", is "perfect if you miss your Jewish grandma" and is a "last vestige of old Times Square before Disneyfication."

Ed Sullivan's
17 | 20 | 17 | $36

1697 Broadway (bet. 53rd & 54th Sts.), 212-541-1697

☑ Walking into this "swanky" deco Theater District "magnet under the *Late Show* marquee" is "like stepping back in time"; it offers "surprisingly good" New American food but is "not a really big show."

Eighteenth & Eighth ◐🅂
18 | 14 | 17 | $21

159 Eighth Ave. (18th St.), 212-242-5000

■ "You may go for the beefcake, but the burgers and brunch are good too" at this "cheap", "cheery", "cramped" Chelsea "gay diner"; "service comes with a smile, and a wink."

85 Down ◐🅂
▽ 20 | 16 | 19 | $27

85 Ave. A (bet. 5th & 6th Sts.), 212-673-8073

■ An "older East Village crowd" comes to this "cozy", "charismatic" American newcomer for its "attentive service" and "imaginatively prepared" "comfort food"; they "really want to do well" and it shows.

Eisenberg Sandwich Shop ⇄
17 | 10 | 14 | $11

174 Fifth Ave. (bet. 22nd & 23rd Sts.), 212-675-5096

■ Opened in 1929, this cheap, "classic" coffee shop "still serves egg creams" as well as "the top tuna salad in NY"; it's "down and dirty but definitely delicious", and has "the best casting since *Seinfeld*."

EJ'S LUNCHEONETTE 🅂
16 | 12 | 14 | $17

1271 Third Ave. (73rd St.), 212-472-0600 ⇄
447 Amsterdam Ave. (bet. 81st & 82nd Sts.), 212-873-3444 ⇄
432 Sixth Ave. (bet. 9th & 10th Sts.), 212-473-5555

☑ "Good but not great" "Norman Rockwell luncheonettes" serving "hearty" American diner food; they're "fun for kids" and weekend brunch "if you don't mind waiting" and mobs.

Elaine's ◐🅂
12 | 13 | 13 | $39

1703 Second Ave. (bet. 88th & 89th Sts.), 212-534-8103

☑ "Everyone's too busy people-watching to notice the mediocre food" at this atmospheric Upper East Side Italian celebrity watering hole; "if you're not a Who's Who, don't bother."

El Charro Español ◐🅂
21 | 15 | 19 | $30

4 Charles St. (bet. Greenwich Ave. & 7th Ave. S.), 212-242-9547

☑ This "classic" reasonable West Village Spaniard is "muy bueno" and very "festive, especially if you drink" the "killer margaritas"; but it can also be "dark, dated" and "claustrophobic."

El Cid 🅂
22 | 13 | 18 | $30

322 W. 15th St. (bet. 8th & 9th Aves.), 212-929-9332

■ "The best tapas outside Madrid", "at the right price", can be found at this "tiny" "honky-tonk" Chelsea Spaniard; "bring friends."

Elephant, The ◐🅂
– | – | – | M

58 E. First St. (bet. 1st & 2nd Aves.), 212-505-7739

An exotic East Village Thai bistro offering scrumptious eats and curt service to local hipsters; N.B. Tiger Woods is said to be an investor.

Elephant & Castle ◐⧓   16 | 13 | 14 | $21
68 Greenwich Ave. (bet. 7th Ave. & 11th St.), 212-243-1400
■ "Go for breakfast, brunch or lunch" at this "simple", "cheap and collegiate-feeling" Village American "old friend"; "it hasn't changed in years and that's what's so good about it."

El Faro ◐⧓   21 | 12 | 17 | $30
823 Greenwich St. (Horatio St.), 212-929-8210
■ Feel the "true vibe of the old Village" at this "shabby" Spaniard that packs them in for "garlicky paella and green sauce dishes"; "intimate on weekdays", it's almost "impenetrable" on weekends.

Elias Corner (Queens) ◐⧓⊟⇗   23 | 9 | 15 | $27
24-02 31st St. (24th Ave.), 718-932-1510
■ "Simple but sublime", this "crowded" Astoria Greek-cum-garden is "like being in Greece without the jet lag" or the tab for tickets; surveyors ask "why pay for decor and service with fish this good?"

Elio's ◐⧓   22 | 17 | 19 | $47
1621 Second Ave. (bet. 84th & 85th Sts.), 212-772-2242
■ "The epitome of the East Side" describes this "see-and-be-seen Italian" with "celebs and prices to match"; this "clubby" "hot spot" serves "consistent, excellent food" but can be "overbooked" – "don't even think of eating here on a Sunday night."

El Parador Cafe ⧓   19 | 16 | 19 | $33
325 E. 34th St. (bet. 1st & 2nd Aves.), 212-679-6812
◪ "Like no other Mexican", this Murray Hill "hideaway" "is holding its own" "in a tough area to find good food"; however, critics insist "it ain't what it used to be" and "needs a face-lift."

El Pollo ⧓   19 | 10 | 14 | $16
1746 First Ave. (bet. 90th & 91st Sts.), 212-996-7810
482 Broome St. (Wooster St.), 212-431-5666
■ "You'll go loco over the pollo" and "unique side dishes" at these "inexpensive" Peruvian chicken "joints"; the "tiny" Uptown location "inspires one to take out", Downtown is for lingering.

El Pote Español   19 | 12 | 18 | $30
718 Second Ave. (bet. 38th & 39th Sts.), 212-889-6680
◪ "Well-known to locals and well-loved", this "welcoming" Murray Hill Spaniard serves "very good, homey food"; but diners are less impressed by its "dark and boring" space.

El Quijote ◐⧓   19 | 14 | 16 | $30
226 W. 23rd St. (bet. 7th & 8th Aves.), 212-929-1855
■ "The best lobster for the price" is found at this somewhat "frayed" "throwback to the '40s" Chelsea Spaniard; it works "with a big group."

El Rio Grande ◐⧓   16 | 15 | 14 | $26
160 E. 38th St. (3rd Ave.), 212-867-0922
◪ B&T "twentysomethings line up for the happy hour" "meet market" on the "great outside patio" at this margarita-fueled "festive Mexican"; some are "so drunk" they "don't notice" the "generic" grub.

El Teddy's ◐⧓   17 | 19 | 15 | $31
219 W. Broadway (bet. Franklin & White Sts.), 212-941-7070
◪ "Always hopping" with "all kinds of people", this midpriced TriBeCa "New Wave Mexican" has a "happening bar scene" and "funky" decor; after a few of their "dangerous margaritas", all faults fade away.

Emack & Bolio's ⧓⇗   22 | 10 | 16 | $10
389 Amsterdam Ave. (bet. 78th & 79th Sts.), 212-362-2747
■ "Chocolate addicts" love this "charming" West Side ice cream shop; fans say it "rivals Ben & Jerry's" and "blows Häagen Dazs away."

Embers (Brooklyn) 🄢⌀
22 | 14 | 17 | $32

9519 Third Ave. (bet. 95th & 96th Sts.), 718-745-3700

■ "You get a helluva steak for the price" at this old but "good" Bay Ridge steakhouse; the somewhat "depressing" space "could be a movie set" with the "gold chain and poofy hair" crowd as "extras."

Emerald Planet 🄢
18 | 13 | 15 | $11

2 Great Jones St. (bet. B'way & Lafayette St.), 212-353-9727

☑ "Finally someone got the wrap right" is the word on this new, "cheap", "quick and tasty" East Villager whose use of "diverse ingredients" and "tasty fruit shakes" are out of this world.

Emilios
19 | 16 | 19 | $42

167 E. 33rd St. (bet. Lexington & 3rd Aves.), 212-684-3223

■ Though it's "sometimes uneven", "they try so hard to please" at this "quiet", "old-fashioned" Murray Hill Italian-cum-piano bar.

Emily's Restaurant 🄢
∇ 20 | 14 | 17 | $23

1325 Fifth Ave. (bet. 111th & 112th Sts.), 212-996-1212

■ "You're made to feel very welcome" at this "bright light in Harlem" that serves affordable "Southern food with style and sweetness."

Empire Diner ◐🄢
14 | 15 | 13 | $21

210 10th Ave. (22nd St.), 212-243-2736

■ Though "a little expensive for a diner", if you "stick to the classics" this "hip", 24-hour, chrome and glass Chelsea "art deco" icon can be "fun", and "for late-night drag queen–watching" it has no equal; their refusal to serve artificial sweeteners, skim milk or diet drinks says a lot.

Empire Korea ◐🄢
19 | 16 | 17 | $27

6 E. 32nd St. (bet. 5th & Madison Aves.), 212-725-1333

■ "Very good" Korean "banquet-style dining", with "quality meats and seafood" at fair prices, is the hallmark of this "gymnasium-sized restaurant"; "don't let the glitzy *Wheel of Fortune* decor deter you."

Empire Szechuan ◐🄢
15 | 9 | 13 | $18

4041 Broadway (170th St.), 212-568-1600
2642 Broadway (100th St.), 212-662-9404
2574 Broadway (97th St.), 212-663-6005
251 W. 72nd St. (bet. B'way & West End Ave.), 212-496-8460
193 Columbus Ave. (bet. 68th & 69th Sts.), 212-496-8778
381 Third Ave. (bet. 27th & 28th Sts.), 212-685-6215
15 Greenwich Ave. (bet. 6th Ave. & W. 10th St.), 212-691-1535
173 Seventh Ave. S. (bet. 11th & Perry Sts.), 212-243-6046

☑ "The menu is like a phone book" at this "quick, cheap, reliable" "if not exciting" McChinese chain that every NYer has ordered from; some locations also serve Japanese, Thai and dim sum.

Ennio and Michael 🄢
21 | 18 | 21 | $35

539 La Guardia Pl. (bet. Bleecker & W. 3rd Sts.), 212-677-8577

■ "Epitomizing a good neighborhood restaurant", this child-friendly NYU-area spot is "like an Italian *Cheers*" – "always steady", "friendly" and "tasty", with spacious seating indoors and out.

Epices du Traiteur 🄢
∇ 17 | 14 | 18 | $26

103 W. 70th St. (bet. B'way & Columbus Ave.), 212-579-5904

☑ "The jury is still out" on this new, "very cheap, very small" Mediterranean that some think is a "tremendous addition" to the West Side; others say it "has potential but is slightly amateurish."

Erizo ◐🄢
22 | 18 | 18 | $37

422 W. Broadway (bet. Prince & Spring Sts.), 212-941-5811

■ Try this well-run "electric" SoHo Nuevo Latino for an "adventure of the palate"; it's "pricey" and a little "cramped" but has a wide range of grills, tapas and seviche "that you don't make at home."

Erminia
23 | 23 | 23 | $47

250 E. 83rd St. (bet. 2nd & 3rd Aves.), 212-879-4284
■ If not "the city's most romantic restaurant", this "enchanting", "tiny" candlelit Upper East Side Italian comes close; "amazing food" and "wonderful service" add to the charm.

Ernie's ●S
16 | 15 | 15 | $28

2150 Broadway (bet. 75th & 76th Sts.), 212-496-1588
■ You get "good portions" of "decent" pizza, pasta, etc. for "good prices" at this "hopping", "cavernous", "kid-friendly" Italian Westsider; "bustling and cheerful" can also mean "too noisy."

Eros ●
17 | 21 | 15 | $38

1076 First Ave. (bet. 58th & 59th Sts.), 212-223-2322
☑ Though some find it "overpriced" with "snobby service", this Sutton Place Greek offers a "dark and sultry", "made for lovers" interior that's enough for surveyors seeking Eros.

Ess-a-Bagel S
22 | 7 | 12 | $10

831 Third Ave. (bet. 50th & 51st Sts.), 212-980-1010
359 First Ave. (21st St.), 212-260-2252
☑ "God bless Ess-a-Bagel": the "Texas-sized", "hot 'n' chewy", "warm and fluffy" bagels and their slavered toppings have NYers ready to face "long lines", "hectic" ambiance and "surly" service.

Est! Est!! Est!!!
22 | 19 | 21 | $37

64 Carmine St. (bet. Bedford St. & 7th Ave. S.), 212-255-6294
■ There are "several unique dishes" at this "surprisingly good and satisfying" midpriced Village Italian; "personal service" from "simple nice folks" has diners saying "yes, yes, yes."

Estihana S
– | – | – | M

221 W. 79th St. (bet. B'way & Amsterdam Ave.), 212-501-0393
A blend of Asian, Japanese and kosher fare is found at this casual new Westsider; it offers an interesting mix of cultures at a modest cost.

Etats-Unis S
23 | 15 | 21 | $48

242 E. 81st St. (bet. 2nd & 3rd Aves.), 212-517-8826
■ "The father-son team makes you feel like a regular, even if it's your first time" ordering their "innovative" Eclectic cuisine from a "limited menu"; this Eastsider is "small" and "expensive but worth it", that is, if you can get a reservation.

Evelyn, The ●S
– | – | – | M

380 Columbus Ave. (78th St.), 212-724-2363
Named after the notorious Evelyn Nesbit (read *Ragtime*), this midpriced Westsider is too new to call for its upstairs American food and service, but its downstairs jazz lounge is already a pulsating late-night scene.

Evergreen, Cafe ●S
17 | 14 | 18 | $24

1288 First Ave. (bet. 69th & 70th Sts.), 212-744-3266
☑ Some surveyors say you can get "great dim sum" and "gourmet Chinese" at "easy prices" at this "clean, calm and comfortable", "kid-friendly" Far Eastsider; but critics say it's "nothing special."

Excellent Dumpling House S⊅
18 | 5 | 11 | $13

111 Lafayette St. (bet. Canal & Walker Sts.), 212-219-0212
☑ "One good thing about jury duty" is this "cheap" "dive" in Chinatown; its food "lives up to its name", but, as ratings show, "that's all."

Factory Cafe ●S⊅
▽ 14 | 18 | 15 | $17

104 Christopher St. (bet. Bleecker & Hudson Sts.), 212-807-6900
☑ "The tin ceiling is extraordinary" and the "supersize" lattes and muffins please many at this affordable new Village New American; however, it's "none too gourmet" and service can be latte.

Fado ●⬛
—|—|—| M

504 Canal St. (bet. Greenwich & Washington Sts.), 212-941-9878
It may be off the beaten path, but this TriBeCa Portuguese aims to
please with unhurried, Mediterranean-style service and a variety of
seafood dishes; prices please too.

Fanelli ●⬛
13 | 16 | 13 | $20

94 Prince St. (Mercer St.), 212-226-9412
☑ The "sole survivor of old SoHo", this 1872 vintage "locals' bar" is
home to "hipsters", "artists", "gallery shoppers", "wanna-bes" and
those who simply appreciate a good "beer and burger"; it's "crowded,
dark and smoky", but that's all part of its appeal.

Fantino ⬛
▽ 22 | 25 | 23 | $53

Ritz-Carlton, 112 Central Park S. (bet. 6th & 7th Aves.), 212-664-7700
☑ The "civilized", "quiet", "luxurious" ambiance and "excellent"
Italian-Continental food win praise, but there are reasons that it's
"never crowded" – "predictable", "stuffy", "overpriced."

Farfalle Trattoria ●⬛
18 | 16 | 17 | $28

680 Columbus Ave. (93rd St.), 212-666-2431
■ Westsiders welcome this "pleasant", family-friendly trattoria,
praising its "warm" service and "good pasta" at "moderate rates."

Fashion Cafe ●⬛
9 | 14 | 11 | $26

51 Rockefeller Plaza, 51st St. (bet. 5th & 6th Aves.), 212-765-3131
☑ "The joke is on you" at this "all hype", "not even chic" fashion-theme
cafe that's "all dressed up with no place to go"; filled with Kansans
and "13-year-old model wanna-bes", it proves why models are thin.

FELIDIA
25 | 22 | 23 | $55

243 E. 58th St. (bet. 2nd & 3rd Aves.), 212-758-1479
■ "Anything Lidia Bastianich touches turns to gold" at her "authentic",
Trieste-style restaurant that many consider "the best Italian in NY"
with "one of the best wine lists"; "seamless" service and "swanky"
brick and wood-paneled decor also win high marks.

Félix ●⬛
17 | 17 | 14 | $36

340 W. Broadway (Grand St.), 212-431-0021
☑ Good for soaking up the SoHo scene and sun at its outdoor tables,
this casual French bistro looks "like Paris", but its attitude is all NY;
critics cite "loud music", "snotty" service and an "uneven" kitchen.

Ferdinando's Focacceria
(Brooklyn) ⊄
▽ 20 | 12 | 17 | $18

151 Union St. (bet. Columbia & Hicks Sts.), 718-855-1545
■ You step into a "time warp" at this vintage 1904 blue-collar joint
where they serve Sicilian specialties "as good as grandma's"; but for
the decor, this place makes many "glad to live in" Carroll Gardens.

Ferrara ⬛
18 | 13 | 12 | $14

195 Grand St. (bet. Mott & Mulberry Sts.), 212-226-6150 ●
1700 Broadway (bet. 53rd & 54th Sts.), 212-581-3335 ●
201 W. 42nd St. (7th Ave.), 212-398-6064 ●
3 Greenwich Ave. (Christopher St.), 212-367-7500
☑ In business since 1892, this Little Italy landmark is where the tourist
buses stop for coffee and pastries; still, some say "you pay for the
name" and the new branches are not up to snuff.

Ferrier ●⬛
18 | 16 | 14 | $40

29 E. 65th St. (bet. Madison & Park Aves.), 212-772-9000
☑ A Euro-accented "pickup scene", this "noisy", "smoky", "seductive"
East Side French bistro with sidewalk seating has good food but is more
about how pretty you are and how big your limo is.

71

Fez at Time Cafe ◐[S] — 16 | 20 | 13 | $24
380 Lafayette St. (Great Jones St.), 212-533-3000
◪ "Funky, dark" Moroccan decor and a "harem" feel, plus live music and "cool" crowds, make this NoHo American cafe/bar "the place to be"; but some find it "boorish" with attitude as thick as the smoke.

Fiamma [S] — – | – | – | I
1481 First Ave. (bet. 77th & 78th Sts.), 212-717-5131
Colorful little East Side storefront Italo-Brazilian with specialties all under $10; though too new to rate, it has casual, low-cost appeal.

FIFTY-SEVEN FIFTY-SEVEN [S] — 23 | 25 | 23 | $54
Four Seasons Hotel, 57 E. 57th St. (bet. Madison & Park Aves.), 212-758-5757
■ They treat you "like royalty" at this I.M. Pei–designed "modern masterpiece" where the American food is "outstanding" if arguably "overpriced"; those who find it "like eating in Grant's Tomb" are easily outvoted: "gorgeous room, gorgeous food."

F.illi Ponte — 21 | 23 | 20 | $50
39 Desbrosses St. (West Side Hwy.), 212-226-4621
■ This out-of-the-way waterfront Italian with live jazz and a "great Hudson view" has "finally come into its own"; the "big hair" crowd, joined by mobile yuppies and brokers, all shout "abbondanza."

Fine & Schapiro [S] — 15 | 7 | 11 | $19
138 W. 72nd St. (bet. B'way & Columbus Ave.), 212-877-2874
◪ West Side Jewish deli with traditional "cranky staff" and "good", affordable kosher fare; critics find it "not so fine" and "overpriced."

Fino [S] — 19 | 17 | 19 | $40
4 E. 36th St. (bet. 5th & Madison Aves.), 212-689-8040
◪ Widely said to be "the best Murray Hill Italian" with "good food" and "warm service"; this business lunch specialist has a "pretty room" with "gorgeous flowers", but to some it's "tacky" "like the *Love Boat*."

Fiorentino's (Brooklyn) [S] — 20 | 12 | 17 | $24
311 Ave. U (bet. McDonald Ave. & West St.), 718-372-1445
◪ "You can't beat the prices for quality food" at this "authentic", family-run Bensonhurst red sauce Italian; but you can easily beat the "noisy, cramped and crowded" "Italian kitsch setting."

FIREBIRD [S] — 20 | 27 | 22 | $48
365 W. 46th St. (bet 8th & 9th Aves.), 212-586-0244
◪ An "exquisite jewel box–like series of dining rooms" makes this Theater District Russian newcomer "a great replacement for the Russian Tea Room"; the "caviar, blinis and zakuski" are very good, and the $19.50 pre-theater dinner is an easy way to go.

Firenze ◐[S] — 21 | 17 | 21 | $40
1594 Second Ave. (bet. 82nd & 83rd Sts.), 212-861-9368
■ "Standing out among Upper East Side Italians", this "cozy" storefront features an "unbeatable combination" of "excellent", "fresh" food, "attentive, caring service" and "good value."

First ◐[S] — 21 | 19 | 18 | $36
87 First Ave. (bet. 5th & 6th Sts.), 212-674-3823
■ This "East Village chic" seasonal American with big comfy booths offers "excellent fare at a fair price"; however, the "so hip it hurts" scene is "loud" and "dark" enough to scare away any over-40s.

First Wok ◐[S] — 15 | 8 | 14 | $17
1570 Third Ave. (88th St.), 212-410-7747
1374 Third Ave. (78th St.), 212-861-2600
◪ "Reliable" and "cheap for the East Side", this "no- frills" Chinese duo is famed for fast delivery; the food is "generic", but "fresh" and "tasty."

Fish [S] 17 | 13 | 16 | $26
2799 Broadway (108th St.), 212-864-5000
◪ Despite "zero decor" and clueless staff, "fresh", "inventive" seafood at a "reasonable" price makes for "a star" in the Columbia area.

Fishin Eddie ◐[S] 19 | 16 | 17 | $37
73 W. 71st St. (bet. Columbus Ave. & CPW), 212-874-3474
◪ Though "a bit pricey", the "simple", "zesty" seafood served at this "cozy" Westsider satisfies most surveyors; if some say it "needs new lines or better bait", most find it "reliable" and "consistent."

Fish Market [S] – | – | – | M
1429 Second Ave. (bet. 74th & 75th Sts.), 212-585-2100
Elemental East Side seafood house, with enough Greek and Italian accents to qualify as Mediterranean; it's too new to call but well priced.

Fitzers [S] – | – | – | M
Fitzpatrick Manhattan Hotel, 687 Lexington Ave. (bet. 56th & 57th Sts.), 212-355-0100
Better than average, cozy Irish Eastsider that draws diners from beyond the built-in audience of Fitzpatrick Hotel guests; fortunately the kitchen accommodates those who prefer something that's not fried or boiled; the PM tea is pleasant post-Bloomie's.

Flea Market Cafe ◐[S]⊘ – | – | – | M
131 Ave. A (bet. St. Marks Pl. & 9th St.), 212-358-9282
Casual and inviting with slightly zany decor (an old ironing board used as shelf space) sums up this appealing new East Village French bistro; though recently opened, it's already crowded.

Flor de Mayo ◐[S] 20 | 8 | 15 | $16
2651 Broadway (bet. 100th & 101st Sts.), 212-595-2525
■ This "bare-bones", "best value" Peruvian-Chinese has a fervent following only for the Latin side of its menu; "juicy roast chicken", grilled pork and sweet plantains, plus the $6 specials, all get praise.

Flor de Sol ◐ ▽ 17 | 20 | 17 | $32
361 Greenwich St. (bet. Franklin & Harrison Sts.), 212-334-6411
◪ "Authentic tapas", "great sangria" and a handsome "Gothic" interior along with "open-air seating" win olés for this high-energy TriBeCa Spanish newcomer; critics cry "high" as in noise, salt and prices.

Florent ◐[S]⊘ 18 | 15 | 15 | $26
69 Gansevoort St. (bet. Greenwich & Washington Sts.), 212-989-5779
■ "Permanently cool", this ever-"popular", "film noir" eclectic French bistro/diner caters to "club kids", "butchers, bikers and drag queens" with "good, honest food" at "moderate prices" plus "sweet staff."

Flower Drum [S] 18 | 16 | 18 | $29
856 Second Ave. (bet. 45th & 46th Sts.), 212-697-4280
◪ Reviews are mixed for this "old-fashioned" East Midtown Chinese: some tout "first-rate" food in a "beautiful interior"; others "beat the drum slowly" over "suburban Chinese" fare and "'50s decor."

Flowers [S] 18 | 19 | 15 | $37
21 W. 17th St. (bet. 5th & 6th Aves.), 212-691-8888
◪ The "relaxing" rooftop garden is a "beautiful people hangout" at this Flatiron duplex New American; some find the food "delicious and inventive", while others sniff "too much show, not enough substance."

Flute ◐[S] – | – | – | M
205 W. 54th St., downstairs (bet. B'way & 7th Ave.), 212-265-5169
Romantic Midtown champagne lounge with elegant light bites; back in the 1920s it was Texas Guinan's speakeasy, Club Intime, and 'intime' it is; after 10 PM, it's most bubbly.

Focacceria 🅂
| – | – | – | I |

87 MacDougal St. (bet. Bleecker & Houston Sts.), 212-253-8049
Small, modest yet airy sums up this cheap West Village focacceria,
which serves up a variety of yummy pastas, salads and sandwiches.

Foley's Fish House ◑🅂
| 21 | 22 | 20 | $41 |

Renaissance NY Hotel, 714 Seventh Ave. (bet. 47th & 48th Sts.), 212-261-5200
☑ This yearling offers "surprisingly good" fish and a "spectacular"
view down Times Square, so "reserve now for New Year's Eve 2000";
critics call it "pay-per-view dining" with "members of the AARP."

Follonico 🅂
| 22 | 20 | 21 | $44 |

6 W. 24th St. (bet. 5th & 6th Aves.), 212-691-6359
■ A "casually elegant" Flatiron Tuscan with "beautiful brick decor"
and a wood-burning oven, serving a seasonal menu that, though
"pricey", "always has fantastic finds in it"; service also wins kudos,
though it can be "a little slow" at the publishing crowd "lunch rush."

Fontana di Trevi 🅂
| 18 | 16 | 19 | $35 |

151 W. 57th St. (bet. 6th & 7th Aves.), 212-247-5683
☑ This Northern Italian preconcert standby near Carnegie Hall gets
mixed but generally affectionate reviews: "good food in a drab setting"
at "reasonable prices" is the majority verdict.

Fortune Garden 🅂
| 18 | 15 | 18 | $25 |

845 Second Ave. (bet. 45th & 46th Sts.), 212-687-7471
■ A "nice neighborhood Chinese" in the East 40s that offers "solid"
fare and "polite service" at moderate prices; an $8.50 lunch and a
"lively" after-work bar are bonuses, but some still sigh "ho hum."

44 🅂
| 20 | 23 | 16 | $44 |

Royalton Hotel, 44 W. 44th St. (bet. 5th & 6th Aves.), 212-944-8844
☑ The "busboys are in Armani", the celebs "in black" and the Condé
Nast brass are in force at this "very good" Midtown New American
power lunch scene; while service is "snooty" and prices high, diners
tout the "*Star Trek*" decor" and bathrooms at "the original fashion cafe."

FOUR SEASONS
| 26 | 27 | 26 | $65 |

99 E. 52nd St. (bet. Lexington & Park Aves.), 212-754-9494
■ Though possibly a bit "dated", the granddaddy of NY's world-class
restaurants is still going strong, boasting "the most gorgeous rooms in
NYC"; it's a modernist icon that's "a temple of power [in the Grill Room
at lunch] and of good taste [in the Pool Room at night]" with creative
Continental cuisine that "keeps pace"; prices may be stratospheric,
but the $43.50 pre-theater menu is "a best buy."

Francisco's Centro Vasco ◑🅂
| 21 | 11 | 16 | $34 |

159 W. 23rd St. (bet. 6th & 7th Aves.), 212-645-6224
☑ "Best lobster in the city" at "super prices" is the verdict for this
"festive" Chelsea "Spanish dive"; incidentally there's also "delicious
paella"; but "the wait can be torture" unless Madonna is on line.

Frankie & Johnnie's
| 21 | 14 | 19 | $41 |

269 W. 45th St. (bet. B'way & 8th Ave.), 212-997-9494 ◑
194-05 Northern Blvd. (194th St.), Queens, 718-357-2444 🅂
☑ "A classic NY steakhouse", this celeb-frequented Theater District
institution (with a Queens branch) is known for "huge" midpriced steaks
and chops; critics claim it's "living on past glories."

Franklin Station Cafe 🅂
| 18 | 14 | 16 | $20 |

222 W. Broadway (Franklin St.), 212-274-8525
☑ "An artistic blend of French and Malaysian fare" with "delectable
noodle soups and curries" and "luscious fruit tarts" at modest prices
pleases most comers at this plain BYO TriBeCa "staple"; still, some
find the service "so attentive it's annoying."

Frank's Restaurant ⬛
20	15	19	$42

85 Tenth Ave. (15th St.), 212-243-1349

⬛ This "large", "comfortable" West Chelsea steakhouse standby is not just a "manly place" but "a carnivorous woman's dream – my dish was at the next table in a suit"; besides offering "good meat and service", there are rooms for cigar smokers and party givers.

Fraunces Tavern
14	21	17	$36

54 Pearl St. (Broad St.), 212-269-0144

◩ In business since the 1760s, this Downtown American, where George Washington bid farewell to his officers is both a tourist stop and "Wall Street power lunch (and breakfast) scene"; critics say the food tastes like "leftovers from the Revolutionary era."

Freddie & Pepper's ◐⬛⊄
17	4	11	$9

303 Amsterdam Ave. (bet. 74th & 75th Sts.), 212-799-2378

⬛ "Small, hot", divey, "but the best" cheap slice on the West Side if you like thick cheese, whole wheat crust and "innovative" variations.

Fred's ◐⬛
–	–	–	M

476 Amsterdam Ave. (83rd St.), 212-572-3076

Brand-new, semi-underground West Side American that's so popular it's turning would-be patrons away; named after Fred the Dog whose pictures adorn the walls, it has a red brick interior and pleasant bar.

Fred's at Barneys NY ⬛
19	18	16	$36

10 E. 61st St. (bet. 5th & Madison Aves.), 212-833-2200

◩ Mark Straussman's "robust" Barneys-based Tuscan gets mixed reviews, ranging from "animated", "stylish and surprisingly good" to "overrated", "overpriced" and "only for the Random House breakfast."

Fred's Beauty
–	–	–	M

4 W. 22nd St. (bet. 5th & 6th Aves.), 212-463-0888

Energetic new Chelsea loft with a Persian-Asian tapas menu including kebabs, samosas, ribs and rolls; it's a nonstop party.

French Roast Cafe ◐⬛
14	13	10	$19

2340 Broadway (85th St.), 212-799-1533
458 Sixth Ave. (11th St.), 212-533-2233

◩ At these 24-hour French cafes, the coffee may be "cold", food just "decent" and service "snobby", but low prices and hip atmosphere draw a "funky crowd" for brunch and people-watching.

Fresco by Scotto
22	20	21	$46

34 E. 52nd St. (bet. Madison & Park Aves.), 212-935-3434

⬛ "The Scotto family has a hit" at this "bustling" Midtown "Italian hot spot" where a "well-heeled" crowd, including many "famous faces", enjoys "amazing thin pizza", "really good pasta" and potent martinis.

Fresco Tortilla Grill ⬛⊄
16	4	12	$8

36 Lexington Ave. (bet. 23rd & 24th Sts.), 212-475-7380

Fresco Tortillas ⬛
980 Second Ave. (bet. 51st & 52nd Sts.), 212-688-0718
719 Second Ave. (bet. 38th & 39th Sts.), 212-972-7648 ⊄
858 10th Ave. (bet. 56th & 57th Sts.), 212-489-5007 ⊄
98 Chambers St. (bet. B'way & Church St.), 212-227-5151 ⊄
536 Ninth Ave. (bet. 39th & 40th Sts.), 212-465-8898 ⊄
766 Ninth Ave. (bet. 51st & 52nd Sts.), 212-489-5301 ⊄
546 Third Ave. (bet. 36th & 37th Sts.), 212-685-3886 ⊄
125 W. 42nd St. (bet. B'way & 6th Ave.), 212-221-5849 ⊄

Fresco Tortilla Taco ⬛⊄
215 W. 14th St. (bet. 7th & 8th Aves.), 212-352-0686
(Continues)

Fresco Tortilla Taco (Cont.)
253 Eighth Ave. (bet. 22nd & 23rd Sts.), 212-463-8877
769 Sixth Ave. (bet. 25th & 26th Sts.), 212-691-5588
◪ "The Chinese owners make a mean tortilla" as well as other "fast, fresh" Mexican fare at "amazingly cheap prices" at these "bare-bones fluorescent-lit" joints; takeout is the way to go.

Frico [S] — 17 | 15 | 15 | $29
402 W. 43rd St. (9th Ave.), 212-564-7272
■ "The frico's the thing" at Joe Bastianich's "friendly", "casual" Theater District Italian, but "good", well-priced pasta, pizza, salads and tapas all find enough fans to make it "noisy" and "rushed."

Friend of a Farmer [S] — 16 | 17 | 15 | $23
77 Irving Pl. (bet. 18th & 19th Sts.), 212-477-2188
◪ "Faux Martha Stewart" Vermont-style Gramercy New American with "great" pot pie, baked goods, etc. that help you "pretend you're not in NY"; critics call it "cutesy" and "bland", but brunch is a scene.

Frontière — 22 | 20 | 21 | $42
199 Prince St. (bet. MacDougal & Sullivan Sts.), 212-387-0898
■ The French-Italian border cuisine at this "charming SoHo bistro" consists of "earthy food" enhanced by "warm, pro service"; the interior is "intimate" to some, "minuscule" and "claustrophobic" to others.

Frutti di Mare ◐[S]≠ — 18 | 13 | 15 | $22
84 E. Fourth St. (2nd Ave.), 212-979-2034
◪ "Dark", "crowded" East Village Italian seafooder offering "the best value for this quality", assuming you don't mind "sardine" seating; for a starter, try the $9.95 prix fixe special.

F•stop ◐ — 16 | 18 | 15 | $33
28 W. 20th St. (bet. 5th & 6th Aves.), 212-627-STOP
◪ "Great photos on the wall", live jazz and "beautiful people" are the main draws at this "dark, moody" Flatiron Continental-cum-photo gallery, but by most accounts "the food is not so special" and service "sloppy" – "guess we weren't young enough."

Fujii ◐[S] — ▽ 23 | 16 | 21 | $32
62 Greenwich Ave. (bet. 7th Ave. & 11th St.), 212-675-6195
■ What it lacks in ambiance, it makes up for in superfresh "good sushi" and "pleasant service" at this West Village Japanese.

Fujiyama Mama ◐[S] — 20 | 19 | 16 | $34
467 Columbus Ave. (bet. 82nd & 83rd Sts.), 212-769-1144
■ You "feel like you're part of a music video" at this "hip West Side sushi place" where a DJ maintains a high-decibel disco beat; though the sushi is "fresh and flavorful", service "could be friendlier."

Fuleen Seafood ◐[S] — – | – | – | M
11 Division St. (E. B'way), 212-941-6888
"You'd have to swim to China for fresher, more authentic Chinese" seafood, and the raw bar is a prime place to "meet and greet"; in sum, this cheap Chinatown newcomer looks like a winner.

Fu's House ◐[S] — 19 | 14 | 17 | $29
972 Second Ave. (bet. 51st & 52nd Sts.), 212-421-2322
◪ Though "calm and comfortable" with "good quality" "seasonal and regional menus", this midpriced Midtown Chinese "lacks ambiance."

Gabriela's [S] — 20 | 12 | 17 | $22
685 Amsterdam Ave. (93rd St.), 212-961-0574
■ "Like a visit to Mexico without Montezuma's revenge", this "madhouse" Mexican coffee shop on the West Side is "big" on portions, quality, service and crowds, but happily low on price.

F | D | S | C

Gabriel's — 21 | 17 | 20 | $44

11 W. 60th St. (bet. B'way & Columbus Ave.), 212-956-4600

■ Gabriel Aiello's Lincoln Center Tuscan is "stylish" and media "star filled" with the likes of Herbert Allen, Michael Eisner and Peter Jennings; it's an odds-on choice for "superfriendly" service and "marvelous" food even if you "can't afford it daily."

Gage & Tollner (Brooklyn) — 21 | 23 | 21 | $41

372 Fulton St. (Jay St.), 718-875-5181

◪ It's "worth crossing the bridge" to check out Brooklyn's vintage 1879 American steak and seafood house, an "elegant" "landmark" space where local pols and BAM-goers gather for "superior", "crusty" service and chef Rad Matmati's "really good" food; still, some say it's "not the same since it reopened" last year.

Galaxy, The ◐[S] — 17 | 16 | 14 | $21

15 Irving Pl. (15th St.), 212-777-3631

◪ Go "global" at this "funky", "smoky" Irving Place Eclectic; young diners like the "creative" menu that's "tasty and cheap", but some wonder "what's hemp?" – a favorite ingredient here.

Gallagher's Steak House ◐[S] — 20 | 16 | 17 | $45

228 W. 52nd St. (bet. B'way & 8th Ave.), 212-245-5336

◪ Slabs of aging prime beef greet diners at this landmark Theater District steakhouse that carnivores call "steak heaven"; despite lots of "testosterone" and waiters old enough to have served "the Last Supper", as an "old-style NY steakhouse", it's "one of the best."

Garage Restaurant ◐[S] — 17 | 17 | 16 | $26

99 Seventh Ave. S. (bet. Barrow & Grove Sts.), 212-645-0600

■ Park and enjoy the new high-speed bar scene at this low-meter West Village American; it's a good pit stop to "people-watch" over a "juicy" burger or brunch, especially outdoors.

Garden Cafe [S] — ▽ 20 | 22 | 20 | $35

Kitano Hotel, 40 E. 38th St. (Park Ave.), 212-885-7123

■ A "hard to find" "oasis" in Murray Hill, but once discovered, the "serene" setting and "terrific" midpriced Euro-Japanese food are a "pleasant surprise."

Garden Cafe (Brooklyn) — ▽ 24 | 18 | 23 | $33

620 Vanderbilt Ave. (Prospect Pl.), 718-857-8863

■ Heights diners plead "don't tell anyone" about this "best-kept secret", a "tiny" storefront "treasure" for New American food cooked to "perfection" and servers who "make you feel at home."

Gargiulo's (Brooklyn) [S] — 20 | 16 | 18 | $34

2911 W. 15th St. (bet. Mermaid & Surf Aves.), 718-266-4891

◪ Aficionados say this huge Coney Island Southern Italian has "been here forever" yet the prices and food are still "good"; others sum it up as "same old, same old."

Gascogne [S] — 22 | 20 | 19 | $42

158 Eighth Ave. (bet. 17th & 18th Sts.), 212-675-6564

■ "Cozy" Chelsea French bistro offering a "wonderful all-around dining experience" (especially in the lovely back garden) that "keeps getting better"; it's "*très français*, but *trop cher*" for some.

Gemelli — – | – | – | E

1 World Trade Ctr. (Church & Dey Sts.), 212-488-2100

Tony May brings his top-drawer Italian stamp to the World Trade Center in this classy newcomer facing the Plaza fountain with comfortable outdoor seating, an open kitchen and friendly staff.

Gene's 🅂
73 W. 11th St. (bet. 5th & 6th Aves.), 212-675-2048   18 | 13 | 20 | $30
■ When you need a fix of "old-fashioned" Italian, head to this West Village "old school, but good school" "landmark" where "50-year-olds feel young"; it's "a little seedy" but "reasonably" priced.

Gennaro 🅂⊅
665 Amsterdam Ave. (bet. 92nd & 93rd Sts.), 212-665-5348   23 | 9 | 16 | $30
■ They should "clone the chef" at this new West Side storefront that serves the kind of "marvelous", midpriced Italian food you'd normally look for in Little Italy; with about 25 seats and no reserving, it's often "impossibly crowded"; specials may be more expensive, but worth it.

Gertrude's ◗🅂
33 E. 61st St. (bet. Madison & Park Aves.), 212-888-9127   – | – | – | E
Whether dining romantically upstairs or living it up in the jazz room downstairs, this posh newcomer targets East Side sophisticates with the Gascogne specialties of chef Laurent Manrique; once reservation kinks are worked out, it may become a major player.

Giambelli ◗🅂
46 E. 50th St. (bet. Madison & Park Aves.), 212-688-2760   20 | 18 | 20 | $48
☑ An Italian where high quality is matched by high prices, this Midtown "warhorse" still serves its signature clientele "divine" Northern Italian food accompanied by a fine wine list custom-made for "expense accounts"; critics counter "boring", "too dark", "a bit over the hill."

Giando on the Water (Brooklyn) 🅂
400 Kent Ave. (B'way), 718-387-7000   15 | 23 | 18 | $40
☑ The East River and Manhattan skyline view from this Williamsburg Italian is "hard to beat", but the decor and midpriced food are middling.

Gigino 🅂
323 Greenwich St. (bet. Duane & Reade Sts.), 212-431-1112   21 | 21 | 19 | $33
■ "You feel like you're in Tuscany" at this "consistently good" TriBeCa Italian that "always delivers" its pasta, pizza and seafood "far above expectations" in a "warm", theatrical barnlike setting.

Gills 🅂
1568 First Ave. (bet. 81st & 82nd Sts.), 212-396-3208   ▽ 19 | 14 | 16 | $34
☑ "What should be" a welcome newcomer in the seafood-short East Side gets mixed reactions: "fabulous", "creative", "great start-up" vs. "ordinary", "expensive", "why go back?"

Ginger House 🅂
330 Seventh Ave. (bet. 28th & 29th Sts.), 212-760-2661   ▽ 17 | 16 | 16 | $22
☑ For flavorful "cheap" Chinese near Madison Square Garden, this wood-paneled place with a waterfall in the back room is a "go."

Gino 🅂⊅
780 Lexington Ave. (bet. 60th & 61st Sts.), 212-758-4466   19 | 12 | 18 | $37
☑ A clubby "East Side fixture" where an "old NYC crowd" enjoys "hearty" Italian fare amidst drab digs; "regulars get the best tables."

Giorgio's of Gramercy 🅂
27 E. 21st St. (bet. B'way & Park Ave. S.), 212-477-0007   20 | 18 | 18 | $26
■ Though "tough to find", this "sexy" Flatiron Mediterranean is "worth" the search, especially given the "reasonable check."

Giovanni 🅂
47 W. 55th St. (bet. 5th & 6th Aves.), 212-262-2828   21 | 19 | 20 | $42
☑ "Personable staff", an "elegant look" and "top of the line" Italian food make this a "favorite" pre–Carnegie Hall choice; "uninspired" and "expensive" may explain "why it isn't more popular."

Giovanni Venti Cinque 🇸   ▽ 18 | 17 | 19 | $44
25 E. 83rd St. (bet. 5th & Madison Aves.), 212-988-7300
☒ While some find this East Side Italian a "fine neighborhood place" where one feels "comfortable" and leaves "well fed", others say it's "overpriced" and undercooked.

Girasole ●🇸   20 | 17 | 19 | $45
151 E. 82nd St. (bet. Lexington & 3rd Aves.), 212-772-6690
☒ "Refined" Italian in a "cozy" Upper East Side brownstone featuring "surprisingly good" fare served by a "warm, friendly" staff; the unimpressed deem it "average" and "overpriced."

Global 33 ●🇸   17 | 20 | 14 | $28
93 Second Ave. (bet. 5th & 6th Sts.), 212-477-8427
☒ "Bring your earplugs", mambo shoes and buddies to this "I am chic-er than thou", "dark, sexy", *Jetsons*-style" East Village tapas bar; though the tapas are "tasty", this place is "best if you're under 25."

Globe, The ●🇸   – | – | – | M
373 Park Ave. S. (bet. 26th & 27th Sts.), 212-545-8800
So hip it hurts, this huge new cafeteria-influenced American-Eclectic has a wide-ranging midpriced menu and offers everything from breakfast to a raw bar, pizza, kebabs and sundaes; the banquettes are just right for your own private party.

Golden Monkey 🇸   ▽ 20 | 10 | 15 | $21
133-47 Roosevelt Ave. (Prince St.), Queens, 718-762-2664 ⇔
1367 First Ave. (bet. 73rd & 74th Sts.), 212-535-7530
☒ Some say it's "worth a subway ride" to Flushing for the "only real Szechuan" in NYC, but others say you "have to know what to order" and call it "not so golden" anymore; N.B. a too-new-to-rate branch just opened on the Upper East Side.

Golden Pot ●🇸   – | – | – | M
89 Greenwich Ave. (bet. 12th & Bank Sts.), 212-807-6688
A casual West Village fondue newcomer; those who don't do fondue can sample Swiss specialties or stick to basic salads and pastas.

Golden Unicorn 🇸   20 | 11 | 13 | $23
18 E. Broadway (Catherine St.), 212-941-0911
■ "Dim sum heaven" three floors up in Chinatown, but "get there early" or "beware of the wait"; besides being a good substitute for a "visit to Hong Kong", it's well set up for private parties.

Good Enough to Eat 🇸   19 | 15 | 15 | $21
483 Amsterdam Ave. (bet. 83rd & 84th Sts.), 212-496-0163
■ The affordable American food and brunch at this popular "New Englandy" Westsider is "better than home" and, like home, you can get three-squares a day; the only thing "missing is mom"; re the name, one surveyor wonders "why do they have to tell us that?"

Goodfella's Brick Oven Pizza 🇸   19 | 11 | 15 | $17
96-06 Third Ave. (bet. 96th & 97th Sts.), Brooklyn, 718-833-6200
1718 Hylan Blvd. (Seaview Ave.), Staten Island, 718-987-2422
☒ For many, it's "worth the trip" to either bustling locale for the award-winning, "mouthwatering" vodka pizza and tiramisu; others call it "ordinary" and say the topping "tastes fake", as if "from a jar."

Goody's (Queens) 🇸⇔   21 | 7 | 15 | $20
94-03B 63rd Dr. (bet. Booth & Saunders Sts.), 718-896-7159
83-34 Broadway (83rd St.), 718-803-9484 ●
■ There's "something for everyone" at this Shanghai-inspired duo, especially "ethereal dumplings" and "heaven on earth soup"; it's "dark and dingy", but so cheap, who's looking?

F | D | S | C

GOTHAM BAR & GRILL [S] 27 | 24 | 25 | $55

12 E. 12th St. (bet. 5th Ave. & University Pl.), 212-620-4020

■ "Absolutely decadent", Alfred Portale's "vertical" New American dishes are "architecture on a plate", and when more than 3,500 surveyors rate it "one of NY's best", you know it's a "special spot"; the "glamorous", spacious Village setting and "attentive" staff add to the lure, as does its bargain $19.98 lunch.

Grabstein's Deli (Brooklyn) [S] 18 | 8 | 13 | $19

1845 Rockaway Pkwy. (Ave. M), 718-251-2280

■ This "old-fashioned", "low-budget" "Yiddish delight" in Canarsie may be the "last of a dying breed", but it's nirvana for those seeking Dr. Brown's sodas and big "fatty" sandwiches with no frills and a schmear of "old times."

Grace's Trattoria [S] – | – | – | M

201 E. 71st St. (bet. 2nd & 3rd Aves.), 212-452-2323

New East Side AM coffee bar, PM Italian trattoria that provides shoppers with a cheerful respite for brick-oven pizza; though pastas and other entrees can be pricey, BYO makes it an affordable dinner choice.

GRAMERCY TAVERN [S] 26 | 26 | 25 | $58

42 E. 20th St. (bet. B'way & Park Ave. S.), 212-477-0777

■ Danny Meyer's "class act" American neo-tavern boasts chef Tom Colicchio's "superb" food, a winning wine list, a "romantic" New England setting and "civilized", "friendly" service that together place it "solidly in the running" for one of NYC's best; dinner may be "pricey", but for less-expensive "impromptu" dining, try the upfront Tavern Room.

Grand Ticino [S] 19 | 16 | 19 | $35

228 Thompson St. (bet. Bleecker & W. 3rd Sts.), 212-777-5922

◪ "Cozy", "quintessential" Village Italian that was featured in *Moonstruck*; regulars say it's "always a pleasure" and "Cher knew what she was doing"; however, some insist the "food's not great."

Grange Hall ◐[S] 20 | 20 | 18 | $31

50 Commerce St. (Barrow St.), 212-924-5246

■ "Loosen that belt" and bring on the Midwestern comfort food at this Village hideaway; "terrific" food, a "standout brunch", "charming Depression-era" decor and fair prices attract a "hip" clientele.

Grano Trattoria ◐[S]💳 – | – | – | M

21 Greenwich Ave. (W. 10th St.), 212-645-2121

West Village offshoot of the popular Borgo Antico, this casual, lively corner Italian is a godsend to locals and tourists alike, with bargain prices for pastas, fish and the owners' signature game dishes.

Granville Restaurant/Lounge ◐[S] 18 | 20 | 18 | $40

40 E. 20th St. (bet. B'way & Park Ave. S.), 212-253-9088

◪ "Cigar-trendy", "babe-loaded" Flatiron American yearling; fans say it serves the "first good Creole" food in NYC and is a "cool" place to "model-gaze"; others say it's still "searching for an identity."

Gray's Papaya ◐[S]💳 17 | 4 | 11 | $8

2090 Broadway (72nd St.), 212-799-0243
402 Sixth Ave. (8th St.), 212-260-3532

■ "Hot doggie, dog", these 24-hour "dirt cheap" stands "aren't pretty", but where else can you get two dogs and a tropical drink for two bucks?

Graziella [S] ▽ 18 | 11 | 18 | $25

41 Greenwich Ave. (bet. Charles & Perry Sts.), 212-255-5972

◪ A Village "favorite" for "neighborhood" Italian dining; though many find the "basement" setting "homely" and "claustrophobic", they still say it's "reliable", "friendly" and a "good value."

Great Jones Cafe ◐🖺≠
18 | 13 | 15 | $20

54 Great Jones St. (bet. Bowery & Lafayette St.), 212-674-9304
■ Appealing to the "blue jean college crowd", this "grungy", "tiny" NoHo bar/cafe is the "place to be" for "finger-lickin'" Cajun "grub", "killer Bloody Marys" and the "best [as in loud] jukebox in town."

Great Shanghai 🖺
20 | 12 | 15 | $23

27 Division St. (Bowery), 212-966-7663
■ NYers and tourists rub elbows waiting in line at this nondescript Chinatown mainstay; "go with a group and treat yourself" to a "bargain" "banquet" and be sure to sample the Peking duck.

Greek Captain (Queens) 🖺≠
▽ 19 | 8 | 14 | $22

56-27 Van Doren St. (108th St.), 718-760-5984
32-10 36th Ave. (32nd St.), 718-786-6015 ◑
40-34 82nd St. (bet. Baxter St. & Roosevelt Ave.), 718-651-4640
☑ "Fresh" seafood that's "tasty" and "well priced" is the bait at these Greeks; but many wish they'd spiff up these "dingy", "smoky" places.

Green Field (Queens) 🖺
19 | 14 | 18 | $26

108-01 Northern Blvd. (108th St.), 718-672-5202
■ If ready for an "all you can eat meat orgy" head to Corona for this "football stadium–sized" Brazilian rotisserie; it's a "real fun place" to go with a group, complete with "good" service and a "cheap" tab.

Grey Dog's Coffee ◐🖺≠
▽ 19 | 19 | 19 | $13

33 Carmine St. (bet. Bleecker & Bedford Sts.), 212-462-0041
■ This "simple" West Village coffee shop is the "happiest spot on the block", serving "coffee better than Starbucks", "first-class breakfast" plus good sandwiches, soups and burgers, all at real low prices.

Grifone
23 | 19 | 23 | $47

244 E. 46th St. (bet. 2nd & 3rd Aves.), 212-490-7275
■ "An old reliable", "elegant" East Side Northern Italian with "never fail" food and service; the "steep" tab makes it most popular with "big-spending clientele" or for "special occasions."

Grill Room, The
– | – | – | E

World Financial Ctr., 225 Liberty St. (West St.), 212-945-9400
Handsome, wood-paneled grill in the World Financial Center where one has a good view of the Hudson while enjoying renowned chef Larry Forgione's take on American steak 'n' chop grill cooking.

Grove 🖺
20 | 19 | 18 | $31

314 Bleecker St. (Grove St.), 212-675-9463
■ A West Village "jewel", this French-American bistro glows brightest in warm weather for garden dining that's "très romantic"; it's well priced and "reliable" for brunch and starlight dining.

Grove St. Brasserie ◐🖺
– | – | – | M

53 Grove St. (bet. Bleecker St. & 7th Ave. S.), 212-924-8299
A new, comfy, modestly priced Village American brasserie catering to smokers and nonsmokers alike while boasting a garden out back; the big news is the presence of talented chef Bruce Barnes.

Guh Ho
– | – | – | E

22 W. 46th St. (bet. 5th & 6th Aves.), 212-719-2557
Few surveyors know this new three-story Midtown Korean, but first reports say not only is the cuisine "royal", but so, too, are the prices.

Gus' Place ◐🖺
20 | 19 | 20 | $34

149 Waverly Pl. (bet. Christopher St. & 6th Ave.), 212-645-8511
■ "Dependable" Mediterranean offering "style" and "service with a smile", and Gus' "sweetness" makes the "food even better"; it's *the* place to "eat and linger" in the Village.

Haikara Grill 🅂 ▽ | 21 | 21 | 20 | $39 |
1016 Second Ave. (bet. 53rd & 54th Sts.), 212-355-7000
■ "Kudos" go to this "elegant" East Midtown kosher Japanese, which you "don't have to be kosher to enjoy"; though pricey, it's a "must-try" for "very fresh", "authentic" food.

Hakata ◑🅂 | 17 | 11 | 15 | $25 |
224 W. 47th St. (bet. B'way & 8th Ave.), 212-730-6863
230 W. 48th St. (bet. B'way & 8th Ave.), 212-245-1020
☑ Theater District locations make this "reasonable" Japanese duo a "fine stop" pre-show for the "basics"; despite "bare", "depressing" decor, they're "clean", "quick" and "polite."

Halcyon ◑🅂 | 22 | 24 | 22 | $47 |
Rihga Royal Hotel, 151 W. 54th St. (bet. 6th & 7th Aves.), 212-468-8888
☑ "Very good" New American food and "attentive" service draw in the pre-theater, brunch and lunch crowds to this "stately", "conversation-friendly" Midtown dining room; although "the $19.98 lunch is a steal", some surveyors just can't warm up to the "chilly ambiance."

Hale & Hearty Soups ⊄ | 20 | 9 | 13 | $11 |
849 Lexington Ave. (bet. 64th & 65th Sts.), 212-517-7600
55 W. 56th St. (bet. 5th & 6th Aves.), 212-245-9200 🅂
Chelsea Market, 75 Ninth Ave. (bet. 15th & 16th Sts.), 212-255-2400 🅂
■ You can "depend on" this minichain's "exceptionally well prepared", "fresh" soups that offer big "meals in a bowl" for relatively little; the only thing lacking is some *Seinfeld* PR.

Hallo Berlin 🅂⊄ | 18 | 8 | 13 | $16 |
402 W. 51st St. (bet. 9th & 10th Aves.), 212-541-6248
☑ You "gotta love the good brat" and "old-country wurst and kraut" at this Hell's Kitchen indoor/outdoor beer garden "hole-in-the-wall"; it's "finally catching on" with NYers despite "wurst service."

Hamachi ◑ | 20 | 12 | 15 | $29 |
34 E. 20th St. (bet. B'way & Park Ave. S.), 212-420-8608
☑ The "amazing selection" of sushi at this Flatiron Japanese has even "turned meat lovers onto sushi"; even "sterile" decor, long lines and service that some call "inept" don't turn them off.

HANGAWI 🅂 | 24 | 26 | 24 | $38 |
12 E. 32nd St. (bet. 5th & Madison Aves.), 212-213-0077
■ "Exquisite highbrow" Midtown Korean-Vegetarian that's "so Zen" and "sensual" it's nearly a "religious" experience; "exotic" tastes, "caring" staff and "ethereal" ambiance leave surveyors smiling; wear clean socks since you take off your shoes and sit on the floor.

Han Sung 🅂 ▽ | 21 | 16 | 18 | $26 |
42 W. 35th St. (bet. 5th & 6th Aves.), 212-563-1285
■ This "unusual", "authentic" eatery "stands out" among its "Koreatown peers" for quality and price; although the place is "too noisy" for some, the staff is "energetic" without rushing you.

Harbour Lights ◑🅂 | 17 | 22 | 17 | $38 |
South St. Seaport, Pier 17, 3rd fl. (Fulton & South Sts.), 212-227-2800
☑ Overlooking the harbor, this slightly "pricey" South Street Seaport New American is a "great place to take out-of-towners"; the "formula" seafood "doesn't match the view", but that's not a criticism.

Hard Rock Cafe ◑🅂 | 12 | 19 | 13 | $24 |
221 W. 57th St. (bet. B'way & 7th Ave.), 212-489-6565
☑ Kids "love it", while adults dis the "noise" and "long lines", but "everyone should come once" to this "granddaddy of theme restaurants"; "it's hard to knock" their burgers and "rock 'n' roll museum" motif, but some do: "oh, puh-leeze", "enough already."

Harley Davidson Cafe ●🄢
11 | 17 | 13 | $24
1370 Sixth Ave. (56th St.), 212-245-6000
☑ Just "another theme restaurant" with "deafening noise", wanna-be bikers, tourists and "plain Jane" "pub grub"; it's "fun for kids" or "if you like leather jackets and leathery food."

Harry Cipriani 🄢
22 | 20 | 20 | $58
Sherry Netherland, 781 Fifth Ave. (bet. 59th & 60th Sts.), 212-753-5566
☑ Midtown's "ultimate see and be seen" scene ("royalty welcome") is "almost Venice"; surveyors go for the "celeb sightings", "authentic" Venetian food and "exquisite Bellinis", but not for the "silly" prices, "crowded" seating at short-legged tables and "major attitude."

Harry's at Hanover Square
16 | 15 | 17 | $35
1 Hanover Sq. (bet. Pearl & Stone Sts.), 212-425-3412
☑ Wood-paneled "Wall Street boys club" with private party rooms and relatively inexpensive "good" Continental food and wine; "bulls and bears are the house specialties"; pretty women cause stampedes.

Haru ●🄢
23 | 17 | 17 | $31
433 Amsterdam Ave. (bet. 80th & 81st Sts.), 212-579-5655
☑ This Japanese newcomer is "just what the West Side needed", serving "maximum" sushi, in both quantity and quality, in stylish, "minimalist" digs; it's "not cheap" but "good" enough to be "crowded."

HASAKI ●🄢
25 | 15 | 18 | $32
210 E. Ninth St. (bet. 2nd & 3rd Aves.), 212-473-3327
■ Due to no-reserving and "small space", you must "expect long lines" at this East Village Japanese; but it's "worth" waiting for the "perfect" sushi even if it would be "less time-consuming to go fishing."

Hatsuhana
24 | 17 | 20 | $42
17 E. 48th St. (bet. 5th & Madison Aves.), 212-355-3345
237 Park Ave. (46th St.), 212-661-3400
■ Veteran Midtown twins that are for "serious sushi eaters"; though they're "not much on decor" and the bill may induce "sticker shock", they remain perennially popular.

Hatsune
▽ 20 | 13 | 18 | $34
401 E. 73rd St. (1st Ave.), 212-744-9743
☑ Fans say this "mom and pop" East Side Japanese has the "best sushi in the 'hood" plus good service; fortunately, it's too dark to see the decor.

Havana Chelsea 🄢⇄
▽ 20 | 6 | 13 | $17
188 Eighth Ave. (bet. 19th & 20th Sts.), 212-243-9421
■ An elemental Cuban "luncheonette" with the "best" sandwiches, rice and beans and yuca in garlic, all "very cheap."

Havana Tea Room/ Cigar House ●🄢
▽ 16 | 22 | 18 | $21
265 E. 78th St. (bet. 2nd & 3rd Aves.), 212-327-2012
☑ This Eastsider's "Cuban veranda" decor offers an appealing setting for "afternoon tea" or a "late-night port and cigar"; the Cuban cuisine is "uneven" but won't "break the bank."

Haveli ●🄢
21 | 18 | 19 | $24
100 Second Ave. (bet. 5th & 6th Sts.), 212-982-0533
■ "Curry Row's perennial favorite" is best known for its "outstanding" "rare" dishes served with "style and dignity"; though a "little pricier" than its neighbors, it's "well worth it."

Heartland Brewery 🄢
13 | 14 | 13 | $22
35 Union Sq. W. (bet. 16th & 17th Sts.), 212-645-3400
☑ Pub grub with an "occasional twist" and a "dictionary of beers" draw the "hip and trendy" to this "noisy", "crowded" Union Square brewery.

Heidelberg [S] — 17 | 14 | 16 | $26
1648 Second Ave. (bet. 85th & 86th Sts.), 212-628-2332
■ Nostalgia buffs "hope we never lose" "one of the last German joints in Yorktown" where the inexpensive wursts, schnitzel and potato pancakes "fill you up" and "never let you down."

Heights Cafe (Brooklyn) ◐[S] — 16 | 17 | 15 | $25
84 Montague St. (Hicks St.), 718-625-5555
◪ An affordable Brooklyn Heights "neighborhood hangout" that offers "tasty" New American food and "upbeat" service; still, some suggest "it tries too hard" and "simpler would be better."

Helena's ◐[S] — - | - | - | M
432 Lafayette St. (bet. Astor Pl. & 4th St.), 212-677-5151
Offering a casual midpriced tapas formula, plus a spacious urban garden, this cheery red and yellow Village newcomer is one to try.

Helianthus Vegetarian [S] — ▽ 19 | 14 | 19 | $21
48 MacDougal St. (bet. Houston & Prince Sts.), 212-598-0387
◪ A "swell" SoHo Vegetarian that makes its "diverse" Asian veggie fare "taste like real food" with "textures" so dense you "really don't miss meat"; still, others say it's "vaguely depressing" and "dull."

Henry's End (Brooklyn) [S] — 23 | 14 | 21 | $34
44 Henry St. (Cranberry St.), 718-834-1776
■ "Where else can you eat antelope and lion" other than at this "cheerful" Brooklyn Heights New American with servers who are always "warm" and "friendly"; it's worth crossing the bridge.

Herban Kitchen [S] — - | - | - | M
290 Hudson St. (Spring St.), 212-627-2257
Surveyors tout this midpriced SoHo "organic" for its "tasty" health food; besides vegan items, it offers organic fish, poultry and beef dishes.

Hog Pit ◐[S]≠ — ▽ 14 | 11 | 13 | $19
22 Ninth Ave. (13th St.), 212-604-0092
◪ "Brassy as the name sounds" and "with a loud jukebox", this "down 'n' dirty" BBQ is "as close to North Carolina as you can get in NY"; it's "like dining with the *Beverly Hillbillies.*"

Holy Basil ◐[S] — ▽ 22 | 18 | 18 | $27
149 Second Ave. (bet. 9th & 10th Sts.), 212-460-5557
■ A "shrine to Thai cooking" producing "outstanding", "wonderfully spiced" cuisine and bringing "new elegance" to the East Village; this moderately priced place "keeps customers coming back – often."

Home [S] — 22 | 17 | 19 | $33
20 Cornelia St. (bet. Bleecker & W. 4th Sts.), 212-243-9579
■ An "appropriately named", "cozy" narrow Village storefront and backyard garden with "solid", "fresh" American home cooking ("mom never cooked this good") and "friendly" staff.

HONMURA AN [S] — 25 | 23 | 23 | $44
170 Mercer St. (bet. Houston & Prince Sts.), 212-334-5253
■ "Treat" yourself to a "spiritual noodle experience" at this "elegant" SoHo soba shop; though "expensive", it's "Zen-like" enough to leave you with a "return to Japan feeling"; "calling this a noodle house is like calling Peter Luger a burger joint."

Hooters ◐[S] — - | - | - | I
211 W. 56th St. (bet. 7th Ave. & B'way), 212-581-5656
You wouldn't want to meet your boss at this new Midtown branch of the national wings-and-beer chain, famous (or infamous) for its well-endowed waitresses in under-endowed outfits; while we'll keep abreast of surveyor response, only time will tell if it proves titillating or falls flat.

Hosteria Fiorella ◐[S] 19 | 17 | 18 | $38
1081 Third Ave. (bet. 63rd & 64th Sts.), 212-838-7570
■ East Side Italian with "consistently good" seafood and antipasti; though a bit "pricey", "family-fun" crowds advise "become a regular."

Hotel Galvez [S] ▽ 19 | 17 | 18 | $23
103 Ave. B (bet. 6th & 7th Sts.), 212-358-9683
◩ It may feel like "a Sam Shepard down 'n' out dive in the wastelands", but fans want this East Village Mexican-Southwestern with "creative", "cheap" eats to be their "secret"; P.S. there's "live music" too.

Hot Tomato ◐[S] 16 | 13 | 14 | $23
676 Sixth Ave. (21st St.), 212-691-3535
◩ The mood is "festive" and the food "hearty" at this Chelsea American newcomer that's "frequented by the gay and art crowds"; still, some remain cool, calling it "more hype than bite."

Hourglass Tavern ◐[S] 18 | 16 | 18 | $24
373 W. 46th St. (bet. 8th & 9th Aves.), 212-265-2060
■ In less than an hour "you're out, in time for the theater" at this "tiny", "bargain" Restaurant Row American "home-cooking" specialist; but you can also linger after 8 PM and enjoy food that's "just like mama's."

Houston's [S] – | – | – | M
CitiCorp Ctr., 153 E. 53rd St. (bet. Lexington & 3rd Aves.), 212-888-3828
"Eager staff", intimate booths and good American food "inspire zealousness" for this new Midtowner; it's hard to believe it's a chain.

HSF ◐[S] 18 | 10 | 12 | $22
46 Bowery (bet. Bayard & Canal Sts.), 212-374-1319
◩ "Crowded" Chinatown dim sum standby that's big on "variety" and "value", small on decor and bathrooms; it's "fun" for groups.

Hudson Corner Cafe [S] 17 | 15 | 16 | $21
570 Hudson St. (W. 11th St.), 212-229-2727
◩ "Decently priced" Village New American cafe where most report "everything is done right"; dissenters call it a "monument to mediocrity" and are "baffled" by the crowds.

Hudson Grill 17 | 16 | 16 | $30
350 Hudson St. (King St.), 212-691-9060
◩ A "pleasant" TriBeCa American "hangout" that's the perfect place to "pop in for lunch" or a pre-theater bite; still, it's "no big deal."

HUDSON RIVER CLUB [S] 24 | 26 | 23 | $54
4 World Financial Ctr., 250 Vesey St. (West St.), 212-786-1500
■ "Power and elegance" combine at this WFC "first choice" for Hudson River Valley fare that offers a beautiful view of the harbor (especially at sunset) and seamless service; new chef Jim Porteus gets kudos – "change hasn't affected quality."

Hué [S] 16 | 10 | 14 | $19
210 E. 23rd St. (bet. 2nd & 3rd Aves.), 212-696-4779
◩ Locals "pass the word" that this "interesting" Vietnamese is "dependable", "cheap" and good for takeout, but some find it "inconsistent", with "small" portions and "basement-like" decor.

Hunan Balcony ◐[S] 16 | 10 | 15 | $20
1417 Second Ave. (74th St.), 212-517-2088
2596 Broadway (98th St.), 212-865-0400
◩ Crosstown Chinese twins with "inexpensive" fare that's "better than most"; critics grouse the food is "watered down", service is "perfunctory" and the "free wine [is meant] to help forget the meal."

Hunan Park ●S
18 | 11 | 15 | $19

721 Columbus Ave. (95th St.), 212-222-6511
235 Columbus Ave. (bet. 70th & 71st Sts.), 212-724-4411
◪ There's "no atmosphere" at these "family" eateries, but the Chinese food earns votes as the West Side's "best", with "fast" service and "fair" prices; foes find them "indistinguishable from the pack."

Hunters ●S
15 | 14 | 15 | $27

1387 Third Ave. (bet. 78th & 79th Sts.), 212-734-6008
◪ "Inexpensive" Eastsider with "home-cooked" American pub-type food that "mom would have made"; though it has a "cozy fireplace", it leaves some cold: "nothing original", "weird."

Hurley's ●S
18 | 16 | 19 | $33

1240 Sixth Ave. (49th St.), 212-765-8981
◪ Besides owner Adrien Barbey, who may be "the best host in NYC", this Rock Center "media hangout" with American fare has "character, history" and "worldly bartenders"; it feels "like a Johnny Carson rerun."

Hurricane Island S
16 | 11 | 15 | $34

1303 Third Ave. (bet. 74th & 75th Sts.), 212-717-6600
◪ Some locals love the seafood, lobsters and simple "New England town" setting, while others call this "plain" Eastsider "stormy at best."

Hyotan Nippon S
▽ 20 | 13 | 18 | $34

119 E. 59th St. (bet. Lexington & Park Aves.), 212-751-7690
◪ East Side neighborhood Japanese featuring a "simple" menu of "really good" sushi and soba noodles, but many report it's "time for a spruce up" and claim "portions become smaller" as "prices go up."

Ici S
20 | 18 | 17 | $48

19 E. 69th St. (bet. Madison & Park Aves.), 212-794-6419
◪ "Euros and the ladies who lunch" keep this tiny, pricey East Side French "gem" "crowded"; but many decry the staff's "snobbery" and warn "don't go if you don't like smoking."

Ikeno Hana S
▽ 21 | 14 | 18 | $29

1016 Lexington Ave. (bet. 72nd & 73rd Sts.), 212-737-6639
■ "Large pieces of fresh fish" come at "moderate prices" at this East Side Japanese; it's "crowded and social", with "warm, friendly" service.

Il Bagatto ●S⊅
23 | 17 | 16 | $26

192 E. Second St. (bet. Aves. A & B), 212-228-0977
◪ An "insanely popular", inexpensive East Village Italian that fans say "should be cloned"; they "treat you like family" and cook "Italian food like in Rome", "simple" and "as authentic as it gets"; critics cite "very dark" digs, "rude servers" and "long waits."

Il Boschetto (Bronx) S
20 | 16 | 19 | $35

1660 E. Gun Hill Rd. (Tiemann Ave.), 718-379-9335
◪ It's "worth the ride" to this "reliable" Bronx Italian old-timer for "big portions" of "excellent food" in an "old-style" setting; still, some say it's "not bad, but you can do better" for less.

Il Buco ●S⊅
21 | 24 | 17 | $37

47 Bond St. (bet. Bowery & Lafayette St.), 212-533-1932
◪ "Order and share" "ebullient tapas" and "homemade desserts" at this "quaint" Village Mediterranean "antique-o-rama"; it's a fine "first date place", but skeptics find it "understaffed" and "deceptively" pricey.

Il Cantinori ●S
22 | 21 | 20 | $49

32 E. 10th St. (bet. B'way & University Pl.), 212-673-6044
◪ "Welcome to Tuscany"; for years now this classy, pricey Village Italian in a "graceful" space has served "sophisticated food", including "perfect pastas", to a stylish crowd; "save it for that special evening."

Il Corallo ◐ [S] — 20 | 13 | 17 | $23

172-176 Prince St. (bet. Sullivan & Thompson Sts.), 212-941-7119

■ The "infinite pasta combos" and "strong entrees" at this SoHo Italian come "cheap", so don't be surprised to "wait in the street."

Il Cortile ◐ [S] — 22 | 20 | 19 | $40

125 Mulberry St. (bet. Canal & Hester Sts.), 212-226-6060

■ This "cornerstone of Little Italy" is known for "huge portions of tasty, fresh food" served in a "lovely" "indoor garden setting"; it would be even better if the waiters took "a crash course in smiling."

Il Faro — ▽ 19 | 14 | 18 | $32

45 W. 39th St. (bet. 5th & 6th Aves.), 212-382-3061

◪ Still "undiscovered", this Southern Italian "Garment District winner" has "above-average food and service" but below-average decor.

Il Fornaio [S] — ▽ 19 | 13 | 17 | $24

132A Mulberry St. (bet. Grand & Hester Sts.), 212-226-8306

■ The "honest Italian food" is "so cheap you feel guilty" at this Little Italy vet; it's "homier than its neighbors" with "nice outdoor seating."

Il Gabbiano [S] — 20 | 17 | 20 | $40

232 E. 58th St. (bet. 2nd & 3rd Aves.), 212-754-1033

◪ This "good" East Side Italian has "one of the best pre-theater values in town" and is "a favorite" for "fast service", but some call it "ordinary."

IL GIGLIO — 25 | 19 | 22 | $49

81 Warren St. (bet. Greenwich St. & W. B'way), 212-571-5555

■ "Robust Italian food" and homemade desserts, though pricey, make this "lovely", "more civilized" sister to Il Mulino a Downtown star; even the sometimes criticized "waiters are great once you get them going."

Il Menestrello — 22 | 20 | 22 | $47

14 E. 52nd St. (bet. 5th & Madison Aves.), 212-421-7588

■ With "great" pastas and veal and perhaps "the best Dover sole in NY", this "elegant" Midtown Italian draws a well-heeled crowd; "warm and welcoming", it's "expensive but worth it."

Il Monello [S] — 23 | 20 | 21 | $49

1460 Second Ave. (bet. 76th & 77th Sts.), 212-535-9310

■ "They'll make anything you ask for" at this "expensive" but "dependable" East Side Italian "doing service and food the way it should be" in a "relaxed setting" for an "older sedate crowd"; "don't eat the day before" so you'll have room for all the good food.

IL MULINO ◐ — 27 | 19 | 23 | $56

86 W. Third St. (bet. Sullivan & Thompson Sts.), 212-673-3783

■ Rated NYC's No. 1 Italian for the 15th year in a row; "they treat you like a big shot" at this "crowded" "Italiano perfecto" Village "pinnacle of garlicdom" and "big portions"; patrons "dream of going back" and swear they "didn't know food could be this amazing"; since you may have to wait up to "one hour even with reservations" at night, consider going at lunch when it's "less hectic."

Il Nido — 24 | 20 | 22 | $53

251 E. 53rd St. (bet. 2nd & 3rd Aves.), 212-753-8450

■ "Like dinner in Milan", this "extravagantly good" Midtown Northern Italian is "the real deal", with "knowledgeable waiters" and "awesome pasta"; it can be "cramped" and its classy clients say "bring lots of lire."

Il Palazzo ◐ [S] — ▽ 23 | 19 | 22 | $36

151 Mulberry St. (bet. Grand & Hester Sts.), 212-343-7000

■ "Sit in the romantic garden" at this "challenger to Il Cortile as the class of Little Italy"; the few surveyors who know it rate it highly and suggest "going off the menu" to eat exactly what you want.

	F	D	S	C
Il Pellicano [S]	17	16	17	$33

401 E. 62nd St. (bet. 1st & York Aves.), 212-223-1040

◪ For "abbondanza" dining, this "intimate" East Side Italian offers a "good casual meal" and "excellent house wines"; it's "a well-kept secret" "across from the movieplex", but some find it "very uneven."

	F	D	S	C
Il Postino ◐[S]	20	17	18	$54

337 E. 49th St. (bet. 1st & 2nd Aves.), 212-688-0033

◪ The "huge portions" of "tasty food" served by "real Italian waiters with great accents" at this East Midtowner include an "awesome mushroom risotto"; but some feel the recitation of "the laundry list of specials is ridiculous" and suggest "stick to the movie, it's cheaper."

	F	D	S	C
Il Tinello	23	20	23	$50

16 W. 56th St. (bet. 5th & 6th Aves.), 212-245-4388

■ With an array of "imaginatively prepared dishes" and "attentive staff", this "sophisticated", pricey Midtown Northern Italian "never falters", offering "gracious pampered dining" "good for a special occasion" or "expense-account lunch."

	F	D	S	C
Il Toscanaccio	20	20	19	$45

7 E. 59th St. (bet. 5th & Madison Aves.), 212-935-3535

■ "Elegant food" with "a terrific use of herbs" in a "lovely setting" make this "quality Italian" near Central Park "always a pleasure"; "the antipasti table is great", but be sure to "save room for dessert."

	F	D	S	C
Il Vagabondo ◐[S]	16	13	16	$31

351 E. 62nd St. (bet. 1st & 2nd Aves.), 212-832-9221

◪ "Indoor bocce", veal parmigiana and "family-style" pasta are hallmarks of this "earthy", "hustle-bustle" East Side "red sauce" Italian; it's "fun with a group" or for weekend dinner "with kids."

	F	D	S	C
Il Valentino [S] ▽	19	21	20	$41

Sutton Hotel, 330 E. 56th St. (bet. 1st & 2nd Aves.), 212-355-0001

■ "Hospitable" if "unexciting" Sutton Place "neighborhood" Piedmontese with "quietly competent" staff serving "a really good meal" in "relaxed" surroundings; "try the garden in summer."

	F	D	S	C
Inagiku [S]	22	21	21	$49

Waldorf-Astoria, 111 E. 49th St. (bet. Lexington & Park Aves.), 212-355-0440

■ "From sushi to soba", even "Japanese friends are impressed" by the "delicate, delicious" food and "elegant lunch box" at this "renovated" Midtowner; it's best if you're "not in a hurry" or price-sensitive.

	F	D	S	C
Independent, The ◐[S]	19	18	17	$41

179 W. Broadway (bet. Leonard & Worth Sts.), 212-219-2010

◪ This "urbane", "happening" TriBeCa duplex newcomer has made a "good start" with surprisingly "well-prepared" American home cookin' (like you wish mama made) for the "gossip column set" (JFK, Jr., Michael Jordan); outvoted critics say "you can't eat Page Six."

	F	D	S	C
India Grill [S] ▽	20	17	20	$28

240 E. 81st St. (bet. 2nd & 3rd Aves.), 212-988-4646

■ "Some of the best Indian food north of Sixth Street" is at this "extremely friendly", "quiet and roomy" Upper East Side "sleeper"; "flavorful" cooking at "good prices" makes it "a keeper."

	F	D	S	C
Indigo [S]	21	18	18	$35

142 W. 10th St. (bet. Greenwich Ave. & Waverly Pl.), 212-691-7757

■ Scott Bryan's West Village American-Eclectic is "first-rate all the way" and "a good value" for "inventive, satisfying combos" and "flavorful spicing"; "packed with a young in-crowd by 10 PM", "this Indigo will not make you blue."

Indochine ●🅂
20 | 20 | 17 | $41 |

430 Lafayette St. (bet. Astor Pl. & 4th St.), 212-505-5111

■ "The fusion of tastes makes for adventure" at this "unique", "imaginative", pricey Vietnamese-French "comeback" opposite the Public Theater in the Village; it's "still sexy after all these years", so "wear the uniform black turtleneck, wire-rim glasses and beret."

In Padella ●🅂
15 | 14 | 13 | $22 |

145 Second Ave. (9th St.), 212-598-9800

☑ An "inexpensive" East Village Italian "catering to 20s and 30s" "pierced clientele" that's great for "a quick bite" or to "share a bottle of red" over "a decent plate of pasta"; foes cite "out to lunch waitrons."

Ipanema 🅂
17 | 13 | 18 | $30 |

13 W. 46th St. (bet. 5th & 6th Aves.), 212-730-5848

■ "Just like Rio", this brio Midtown "change of pace" offers "hearty Brazilian fare" at "fair prices" served by "welcoming" waiters with "bedroom eyes"; diners like it despite the "sterile" interior.

Iridium Jazz ●🅂
15 | 20 | 15 | $38 |

Radisson Empire Hotel, 48 W. 63rd St. (bet. B'way & Columbus Ave.), 212-582-2121

☑ Although the French-American food, service and prices "strike a sour note", this "cool" jazz joint handily located opposite Lincoln Center remains popular; "Freud would have had a field day" with the "hallucinogenic" *Alice in Wonderland* decor.

Isabella's ●🅂
19 | 18 | 16 | $31 |

359 Columbus Ave. (77th St.), 212-724-2100

☑ With "tasty food", "trendy" people-watching, "adorable waiters" and a "lovely sidewalk cafe", this energized West Side Mediterranean is a "happy surprise" and "a best deal"; though "great for brunch" or "sunset dinner", detractors say it's "the epitome of yuppieville."

Island ●🅂
15 | 15 | 15 | $34 |

1305 Madison Ave. (bet. 92nd & 93rd Sts.), 212-996-1200

☑ It "would be nice to be stranded" with the "good" American food at this "bustling", Hamptons-esque Carnegie Hill bistro; expect a "clubby", "preppy den" that's often "noisy" and "crowded."

Island Burgers & Shakes 🅂🍴
19 | 11 | 15 | $13 |

766 Ninth Ave. (bet. 51st & 52nd Sts.), 212-307-7934

■ "Like a spartan Hardee's but 10 times as good", this "nice addition to Ninth Avenue" offers "amazing malteds" and megaburgers; but "it's a closet" and you must expect a "wait" even for takeout.

Island Spice
19 | 13 | 15 | $24 |

402 W. 44th St. (bet. 9th & 10th Aves.), 212-765-1737

■ "The spice is right", ditto the price, at this "informal" Theater District "jerk" Caribbean; though "a bit cramped" and "confused", you can't beat the "bargain lunch" with "ginger beer" – "ya mon."

Isle of Capri
16 | 15 | 18 | $36 |

1028 Third Ave. (61st St.), 212-223-9430

☑ A "throwback in time", this "sweet" East Side Italian boasts a "solid, dependable menu" and "friendly, caring waiters"; yet some think it's "so old it creaks" and is "more like the Isle of Staten."

ISO ●
25 | 14 | 16 | $33 |

175 Second Ave. (11th St.), 212-777-0361

☑ "Bliss" in the East Village is "excellent value" sushi "so good you think you've died and gone to Japan"; "Isoooo good!", "the only way to get fresher fish is to catch it yourself"; the downside is "long lines", "wacky waiters" and "crowded", "hard banquette" seating.

F D S C

Isola ◐ [S] — 16 | 13 | 15 | $28
485 Columbus Ave. (bet. 83rd & 84th Sts.), 212-362-7400
◪ "Decent Italian fare" of the pasta/pizza ilk makes this West Side "yuppie hangout" a "good choice for a casual outing"; but to critics it's "unremarkable" and "too loud to even taste the food."

Istanbul [S] — 17 | 14 | 19 | $29
413 Amsterdam Ave. (bet. 79th & 80th Sts.), 212-799-6363
◪ "Every taste transports you" at this "cheap", "authentic", "robust" West Side Turk; though "the staff tries hard", the "sparse setting" is "a bit dreary."

Ithaka ◐ [S] — 22 | 21 | 21 | $34
48 Barrow St. (bet. Bedford & Bleecker Sts.), 212-727-8886
■ "Better than a trip to Athens (or Queens)" and "a re-education for anyone who thinks that Greek is diner food", this cheerful Villager is "transporting and scrumptious" with a "warm, efficient" staff; "try the garden in the back."

I Tre Merli ◐ [S] — 16 | 17 | 14 | $36
463 W. Broadway (bet. Houston & Prince Sts.), 212-254-8699
◪ "Sip the wine" at this "see and be seen" SoHo cafe-cum-bar that's "rock steady" for "Italian food"; still, to some it's a "pretentious Eurotrash dive" with "dead from the neck up" "model waitresses."

I Trulli — 23 | 22 | 21 | $45
122 E. 27th St. (bet. Lexington Ave. & Park Ave. S.), 212-481-7372
■ "A rising star", this "wonderful" but "pricey" Gramercy Italian offers "scrumptious", "authentic" Italian "cuisine and "outstanding wines"; the "engaging waiters", "enchanting garden" and "roaring fireplace" have fans singing "I love you Trulli."

It's a Wrap [S] 🚫 — 15 | 11 | 13 | $12
2012 Broadway (bet. 68th & 69th Sts.), 212-362-7922
◪ The "cheap", "creative combos" of "healthy California cuisine" and "very filling", "addictive sandwiches" at this Westsider are "a great concept"; but many blast "bland", "tasteless" execution.

Jackson Diner (Queens) [S] 🚫 — 24 | 7 | 16 | $16
37-03 74th St. (bet. Roosevelt & 37th Aves.), 718-672-1232
■ "Devotees make pilgrimages" to Jackson Heights to eat at the *Survey*'s highest-rated and lowest-priced Indian; though the decor is "as charming as a prison mess hall", the food is "absolute nirvana."

Jackson Hole [S] — 15 | 9 | 13 | $17
1270 Madison Ave. (91st St.), 212-427-2820
1611 Second Ave. (bet. 83rd & 84th Sts.), 212-737-8788 ◐
232 E. 64th St. (bet. 2nd & 3rd Aves.), 212-371-7187 ◐
517 Columbus Ave. (85th St.), 212-362-5177 ◐
521 Third Ave. (35th St.), 212-679-3264 ◐
69-35 Astoria Blvd. (70th St.), Queens, 718-204-7070 ◐
◪ "Burgers as big as Wyoming" are the stock-in-trade of these low-budget "beefed-up diners"; they're "almost too much to handle."

Jacques' Bistro [S] — ▽ 18 | 15 | 17 | $26
204 E. 85th St. (3rd Ave.), 212-327-2272
■ "A pleasant find" with a "real French bistro" feel, this Eastsider is a "great brunch place" serving "good crêpes" "without beating up your wallet"; post-renovation, it "has potential."

Jade Plaza (Brooklyn) [S] — ▽ 22 | 16 | 17 | $21
6022 Eighth Ave. (bet. 60th & 61st Sts.), 718-492-6888
■ It's "definitely worth the trip" to this Sunset Park Chinese "for great seafood and dim sum"; with "lovely ambiance" and "large tables", it's quite "affordable for this quality."

Jai-Ya Thai ◐[S] 21 | 10 | 14 | $23
396 Third Ave. (bet. 28th & 29th Sts.), 212-889-1330
81-11 Broadway (bet. 81st & 82nd Sts.), Queens, 718-651-1330
◪ "They know how to do it" "fiery hot" at this "authentic" Murray Hill Thai tongue teaser; still, some say if they have to deal with "cramped quarters" and "rude" staff, they'd prefer to do it at the Queens original.

Jake's Steakhouse ◐[S] 13 | 13 | 13 | $36
1155 Third Ave. (bet. 67th & 68th Sts.), 212-879-9888
◪ There's praise for the prime rib and "wonderful lunch" at this "spacious new" East Side steakhouse; but even at the popular $12.95 early bird, "service is a crapshoot and so is the food."

Janine's ◐[S] 16 | 12 | 15 | $24
302 Columbus Ave. (bet. 74th & 75th Sts.), 212-501-7500
◪ "You can bring the kids and still feel cool" eating the well-priced American comfort food in the "red Naugahyde booths" at this West Side two-year-old; surprisingly, it's often "half empty."

Japas 47 ◐[S] – | – | – | M
137 E. 47th St. (bet. Lexington & 3rd Aves.), 212-980-7909
Formerly the Japanese restaurant East, this Midtowner has switched to a combination of Mediterranean tapas (over 60 kinds) and pasta.

Japonica [S] 23 | 16 | 18 | $34
100 University Pl. (12th St.), 212-243-7752
■ "They welcome you with open arms" at this "upscale" Village Japanese where possibly "the best" and "most" sushi "for the price" draws crowds; to avoid "interminable waits", "go at off hours."

Jean Claude ◐[S]🚫 21 | 14 | 16 | $35
137 Sullivan St. (bet. Houston & Prince Sts.), 212-475-9232
◪ This "very Parisian Left Bank" bistro in SoHo ("home of the air kiss") has "stylish French food" at "reasonable prices"; detractors cite noise and attitude (too much) and space (too little).

JEAN GEORGES 28 | 25 | 26 | $73
Trump Int'l Hotel, 1 Central Park West (bet. 60th & 61st Sts.), 212-299-3900
■ At 1997's "best newcomer", rated No. 5 in NYC for its New French food, "you'll taste flavors you never knew existed" and are likely to be "dazzled" by chef Jean-Georges Vongerichten's culinary "wizardry"; add in understated Adam Tihany decor and seamless service and you have what most customers call a "delectable dining experience"; would-be surveyors say "get me in and I'll let you know"; N.B. there are three dining areas: a formal room, a more casual cafe and a terrace.

Jean Lafitte ◐[S] 18 | 18 | 18 | $42
68 W. 58th St. (6th Ave.), 212-751-2323
◪ The "romantic setting" and daily specials give this convenient Midtown French-Cajun a "real Paris bistro feel"; but some "wish they were more consistent" and dis the "French hauteur."

Jekyll & Hyde ◐[S] 11 | 22 | 14 | $24
1409 Sixth Ave. (bet. 57th & 58th Sts.), 212-541-9505
91 Seventh Ave. S. (bet. Barrow & Grove Sts.), 212-989-7701
◪ "No 11-year-old should miss" Midtown's "haunted house" "theme park" American-Eclectic cafe (the Village original is simpler) with "ghoulish servers" and "tons of stuff to keep one entertained"; "go for the beer and music", but "Hyde from the food."

Jerry's ◐[S] 17 | 13 | 14 | $26
101 Prince St. (bet. Greene & Mercer Sts.), 212-966-9464
◪ "SoHo's interpretation of a diner" offers "decent value" for "down-to-earth" American fare; though it's "buzzing with gallery owners and models", some see it "showing scenes of wear."

F	D	S	C

Jewel of India [S] — 21 | 20 | 20 | $31
15 W. 44th St. (bet. 5th & 6th Aves.), 212-869-5544
■ For "good, spicy" Indian food, try the pre-theater "early-bird bargain" or the "savory buffet" lunch at this "peaceful Midtown oasis"; with "gracious, helpful staff" and "decor verging on elegance", it's a "quantum leap" over all but a few NYC Indians.

JEZEBEL — 20 | 25 | 19 | $41
630 Ninth Ave. (45th St.), 212-582-1045
■ "Tara's got nothing on this" "sinfully sexy" Theater District Soul Food specialist; while you "sit in a swing and eat like a pig", the "bordello ambiance" will "transport you" to the sly "Old South."

J.G. Melon ◐[S]⊘ — 16 | 12 | 14 | $23
1291 Third Ave. (74th St.), 212-744-0585
◪ This "homey", low-budget East Side "hangout" pub "hasn't changed in 20 years" and remains a "great place" for a super burger, chile and beer; regulars say "the watermelon decor grows on you."

Jimmy Sung's [S] — 20 | 20 | 21 | $32
219 E. 44th St. (bet. 2nd & 3rd Aves.), 212-682-5678
■ Jimmy sets the tone as "the perfect host" in his "elegant" yet inexpensive East Midtown Chinese; surveyors tout his "very good" food, private rooms for parties and "charming service."

Jing Fong [S] — 19 | 12 | 10 | $19
20 Elizabeth St. (bet. Bayard & Canal Sts.), 212-964-5256
◪ "Very Hong Kong" and "as authentic as it gets", this "cavernous" Chinatown "football field" "with 1,100 seats" is "dim sum paradise", but "prepare to wait" and face "the worst service in the city."

Jo-An Japanese [S] — 20 | 13 | 19 | $25
2707 Broadway (bet. 103rd & 104th Sts.), 212-678-2103
◪ A "small quiet nook" serving "fresh", "supersized sushi" to price-conscious Westsiders; though "a fun place to eat", some say it's "not as good as before" its recent renovation.

Joanna's [S] — ▽ 20 | 18 | 20 | $37
30 E. 92nd St. (bet. 5th & Madison Aves.), 212-360-1103
◪ Some size up this Italian as a "delightful addition to the Upper East Side", citing "unpretentious" food, "excellent prix fixes" and "superb wines"; critics say it's "noisy", "pricey" and "has a long way to go."

Joe Allen ◐[S] — 16 | 15 | 16 | $32
326 W. 46th St. (bet. 8th & 9th Aves.), 212-581-6464
■ The "quintessential Restaurant Row theater choice" is as American as its "fab" burgers, and its other standards are "tasty" too; drawing stars, chorus liners and gawkers, it defines "showbiz."

Joe Jr.'s ◐[S]⊘ — 16 | 9 | 17 | $14
482 Sixth Ave. (bet. 11th & 12th Sts.), 212-924-5220
■ "God bless the hometown diner feel" and low prices at this "popular" Village Greek-American coffee shop, a "no-nonsense joint" with "the best $5 breakfast around."

Joe's Pizza ◐[S]⊘ — 23 | 7 | 14 | $18
7 Carmine St. (Bleecker St.), 212-255-3946
233 Bleecker St. (Carmine St.), 212-366-1182
■ This Village duo wins pizza fans with what may be the "best thin crust in town" and mozzarella "smoother than Billy Dee Williams"; remember, pizza places aren't supposed to have much decor or service, and hey, you can "go there till 4 AM."

Joe's Shanghai 🅂⇗   23 | 8 | 14 | $20
9 Pell St. (bet. Bowery & Mott St.), 212-233-8888 ◐
136-21 37th Ave. (bet. Main & Union Sts.), Queens, 718-539-3838
■ For "delicious noodles", "addictive steamed buns" and especially the signature "soup dumplings", "Shanghai your friends and go, go, go" to Joe's; both the Chinatown and Flushing locations have "zero atmosphere" and "lines getting long" but are "well worth any wait."

Johnny Tejano's 🅂   – | – | – | M
1662 Third Ave. (93rd St.), 212-426-5422
East Side cowpeople welcome this festive 'as Tex-Mex as it gits' newcomer to the neighborhood; where else nearby can you round up the gang for happy-hour marg specials and enchilada combos the size of Texas?

John's of 12th Street 🅂⇗   19 | 12 | 16 | $24
302 E. 12th St. (2nd Ave.), 212-475-9531
■ A "romantic", candlelit, vintage 1908 East Village "hideaway" with "reliable" red sauce cuisine, "old-fashioned Southern Italian charm and red-checked tablecloths"; it's "great for first dates."

John's Pizzeria ◐🅂   21 | 11 | 14 | $17
278 Bleecker St. (bet. 6th Ave. & 7th Ave S.), 212-243-1680 ⇗
408 E. 64th St. (bet. 1st & York Aves.), 212-935-2895
48 W. 65th St. (bet. Columbus Ave. & CPW), 212-721-7001
260 W. 44th St. (bet. B'way & 8th Ave.), 212-391-7560
■ "The crowds can't be wrong" – "the upper crust of pizzerias" has "delicious thin-crust pies served fast" plus Frank Sinatra and "Dion on the jukebox"; the charmingly "run-down decor [at the original Bleecker Street location] makes the pizza taste even better."

JO JO   25 | 21 | 21 | $52
160 E. 64th St. (bet. Lexington & 3rd Aves.), 212-223-5656
■ "Highly inventive", "gorgeously presented" and "healthily prepared" dishes plus "personalized service" in a "charming townhouse" make this East Side French bistro justifiably popular; "tables are tight", but some think this is "Vongerichten's best" and "most affordable", especially at the $25 lunch.

Josephina ◐🅂   18 | 16 | 17 | $32
1900 Broadway (bet. 63rd & 64th Sts.), 212-799-1000
■ "Perfect pre– or post–Lincoln Center", this "friendly" but "plain" Eclectic is a "solid choice" for "affordable" "gourmet health food" and "delicious, frothy" drinks; it's "quieter after 8 PM" or at lunch.

Joseph's   ▽ 20 | 17 | 18 | $38
3 Hanover Sq. (bet. Pearl & Water Sts.), 212-747-1300
■ In "food-starved" Downtown, this "highbrow Italian" offers "very tasty", slightly pricey fare that's "good for a business lunch"; however, it's a no go "if you're in a hurry."

Josie's ◐🅂   21 | 16 | 16 | $28
300 Amsterdam Ave. (74th St.), 212-769-1212
☑ "Proof that healthy can be yummy", this "casual" PC Westsider is "perhaps the best organic restaurant in NYC" and a solid "bang for your buck"; as a result, crowds are a problem.

J. Sung Dynasty 🅂   20 | 19 | 19 | $35
Hotel Lexington, 511 Lexington Ave. (48th St.), 212-355-1200
☑ The shark's fin and other soups are "fabulous" at this "totally underrated" mezzanine Midtown Chinese; it's a "lunchtime treat" with "accommodating service" and "great for large parties"; former clients feel "it's not the same without Jimmy Sung."

Jubilee 🟦　21 | 17 | 18 | $37
347 E. 54th St. (bet. 1st & 2nd Aves.), 212-888-3569

■ "Les moules rule" at this "very French" Sutton Place bistro; there are also steak frites, salads and jubilee brunch to enjoy, but the "usually low-key" setting can be "noisy and crowded."

JUdson Grill　21 | 20 | 19 | $44
152 W. 52nd St. (bet. 6th & 7th Aves.), 212-582-5252

☑ "Spacious", "elegant", "bustling" Midtown American brasserie that's "excellent for business lunch", pre-theater dinner or after work for drinks; most surveyors "leave in a better mood", but skeptics say it's like "a date whose name you can't remember a year later."

Jules ◑🟦　19 | 19 | 15 | $30
65 St. Marks Pl. (bet. 1st & 2nd Aves.), 212-477-5560

■ "Refreshingly unpretentious", this "authentic French bistro" where "you can hear your friends speak" is "Euro without the trash"; "brunch is a bargain" ditto the steak frites and mussels.

Julian's ◑🟦　18 | 18 | 17 | $29
802 Ninth Ave. (bet. 53rd & 54th Sts.), 212-262-4800

■ "Lively" Hell's Kitchen Mediterranean ("Polygram" cafe) with "flair", "value" and "welcoming staff"; besides "great side-alley outdoor dining", it's "good for pre-theater."

Junior's (Brooklyn) ◑🟦　17 | 10 | 14 | $19
386 Flatbush Ave. Ext. (DeKalb Ave.), 718-852-5257

☑ For "the sweetest, creamiest cheesecake" and "good food across the menu", try this "orange vinyl" Downtown Brooklyn deli landmark where "everything is mammoth"; pre-BAM, it's "quick and cheap" with typecast "surly" deli waiters.

Justin's ◑　 _ | _ | _ | M
31 W. 21st St. (bet. 5th & 6th Aves.), 212-352-0599

A Caribbean–Soul Food happening with Sean Combs (aka Puff Daddy) as managing partner, this handsome, red-awning Chelsea newcomer next to Tramps music club is one to watch for its Southern food and music industry clients; buppies love it.

Kabul Cafe 🟦　▽ 19 | 13 | 17 | $22
265 W. 54th St. (bet. B'way & 8th Ave.), 212-757-2037

■ "A nice change of pace", this "minuscule" Theater District Afghan offers "large portions for little money" including good kebabs and vegetarian entrees; "dark and nearly decorless", it's rarely crowded.

Kalio (Brooklyn) 🟦　19 | 17 | 18 | $29
254 Court St. (bet. Butler & Kane Sts.), 718-625-1295

■ A "home away from home" in a "lovely room" in Cobble Hill, this "reasonable", "hip", "up-and-coming" Eclectic-American is already a "favorite neighborhood place" where "regulars are recognized and newcomers made welcome"; still, a few say "pretends to be more than it is."

Kam Chueh ◑🟦⌿　▽ 21 | 6 | 12 | $23
40 Bowery (Bayard St.), 212-791-6868

☑ "Seafood connoisseurs" tout this cheap Chinatowner to "take eight or 10 people" and "sample many species of seafood"; however, "dreadful decor" and "indifferent service" are drawbacks.

Kang Suh ◑🟦　21 | 9 | 12 | $24
1250 Broadway (32nd St.), 212-564-6845

☑ You "cook your own food", so you can't complain at this "good" Garment District Korean BBQ where "lots of spicy sides" and the smell of smoke may "last for days"; on the downside, there's "drab decor" and "short-shrift" service unless you speak Korean.

Kan Pai ●🄢
17 | 13 | 15 | $26
1482 Second Ave. (bet. 77th & 78th Sts.), 212-772-9560
☑ "Fresh" sushi and "interesting specials" are pluses at this affordable Japanese Eastsider; a "large TV" and blue neon decor are minuses.

Kaplan's at the Delmonico 🄢
15 | 6 | 12 | $20
59 E. 59th St. (bet. Madison & Park Aves.), 212-755-5959
☑ For a corned beef or pastrami "fix", this '50s-style, kosher-style Jewish is all you've got in this East Side area; but surveyors say it's "ugly", "rushed" and "about what you'd expect" for the price.

Karahi 🄢
– | – | – | M
508 Broome St. (bet. W. B'way & Thompson St.), 212-965-1515
"Calcutta Jewish" cuisine is "a most interesting idea pulled off wisely" at this "brand-new good value" in SoHo; there's a "terrific inexpensive lunch buffet" and "it's nice to be recognized" by the staff.

Karyatis (Queens) ●🄢
21 | 17 | 18 | $32
35-03 Broadway (bet. 35th & 36th Sts.), 718-204-0666
■ This "fine", "upscale" Astoria Greek comes with "great prices compared to Manhattan"; the "romantic setting" and "live music are pluses" that help make it "worth the N train ride."

Katch ●🄢
– | – | – | M
339 E. 75th St. (bet. 1st & 2nd Aves.), 212-396-4434
New, midpriced East Side neighborhood American with Pacific Rim accents and a staff that's trying hard; the attractive candlelit setting is a soothing backdrop for a drink or quiet, late dinner.

Katsuhama 🄢
▽ 20 | 12 | 16 | $27
11 E. 47th St. (bet. 5th & Madison Aves.), 212-758-5909
■ Though "the acoustics [and decor] are not great", this modestly priced Midtowner is NY's "best for a quick tonkatsu lunch" and, with "clientele almost 100 percent Japanese", you can bet it's "authentic."

Katz's Deli 🄢
18 | 8 | 10 | $16
205 E. Houston St. (Ludlow St.), 212-254-2246
☑ "It's still there, still real", an 1888 "avatar of the Jewish Lower East Side" where the "brisket rivals mother's", and "how about that pastrami?"; sure it's "noisy" and "crowded", but for hot dogs, sandwiches and celery seltzer, this is "deli as it should be"; P.S. "I'll have what she's having."

K.B. Garden (Queens) 🄢
▽ 21 | 12 | 14 | $21
136-28 39th Ave. (bet. Main & Union Sts.), 718-961-9088
☑ It's "worth the schlep" for the "best dim sum brunch in Queens" at this stadium-sized but diminutively priced Flushing Cantonese; tip: "try everything" or "go with 10 people and order a banquet."

Keens Steakhouse
20 | 20 | 18 | $43
72 W. 36th St. (bet. 5th & 6th Aves.), 212-947-3636
■ A "heaven for meat-eating, scotch-drinking, cigar-smoking" types, this Garment District American would also make a good museum of 19th-century NY; be sure to take a tour.

Keewah Yen ●🄢
20 | 17 | 20 | $31
50 W. 56th St. (bet. 5th & 6th Aves.), 212-246-0770
☑ "Like an old friend", this Midtown Chinese is "dependable and classy" enough for local business people to bring clients; however, regulars report it "needs a face-lift" and may be "a bit bland."

Kelley & Ping 🄢
17 | 16 | 13 | $21
127 Greene St. (bet. Houston & Prince Sts.), 212-228-1212
☑ A "hip" noodle shop, tearoom and store, this SoHo Pan-Asian is best "for a quick lunch"; it's "a great date place", but for "attitude."

F | D | S | C

Khyber Pass ◐ [S] — 19 | 15 | 16 | $21

34 St. Marks Pl. (bet. 2nd & 3rd Aves.), 212-473-0989

■ "A special, only in NY experience", this "cozy little" "affordable" East Village Afghan has "nice, tender lamb" and noodles that are "a must"; in sum, it's top Afghan pre-Taliban.

Kiev ◐ [S] ⊘ — 17 | 6 | 12 | $15

117 Second Ave. (7th St.), 212-674-4040

◪ The blintzes, pierogi, potato pancakes and other "cheap Slavic grub" at this 24-hour East Village "dump" are so good they're "just like bubbe used to make", despite "unfriendly" staff and "no ambiance", when "it's 2 AM, where else are you gonna go for kielbasa and eggs?"

Kiiroi-Hana [S] — 20 | 11 | 15 | $30

23 W. 56th St. (bet. 5th & 6th Aves.), 212-582-7499

■ This "long-running" Midtown Japanese is "convenient" and "reasonably priced" for "fresh sushi" and warming "noodle soups"; "decor needs a lift", but you "can't miss" with a meal here.

Killmeyer's (Staten Island) [S] — – | – | – | M

4254 Arthur Hill Rd. (Sharrotts Rd.), 718-984-1202

Beer memorabilia adorns the walls of this casual Bavarian where the colorfully garbed staff serves heavy fare to a middle-aged crowd.

KING COLE BAR & LOUNGE ◐ [S] — 19 | 26 | 22 | $37

St. Regis Hotel, 2 E. 55th St. (bet. 5th & Madison Aves.), 212-339-6721

■ St. Regis "class and opulence", "Maxfield Parrish" decor and "friendly bartenders" make this landmark room a prime "place to meet people", have a "nightcap" or "enjoy a light [American] meal."

King Crab ◐ [S] — 17 | 13 | 16 | $27

871 Eighth Ave. (52nd St.), 212-765-4393

◪ The crab cakes and other "cheap seafood" are good bets at this Theater District storefront; however, a "Davy Jones' locker setting" and "unconcerned staff" drown surveyor enthusiasm.

KINGS' CARRIAGE HOUSE [S] — 21 | 26 | 22 | $44

251 E. 82nd St. (bet. 2nd & 3rd Aves.), 212-734-5490

■ "The cooking is royally good" at this "beautifully lit", "romantic brownstone" Continental that's like "slipping away to England for a couple of hours"; with "pretty, small rooms" and "attentive service", it's an ideal "place to celebrate" or just have tea.

Kings Plaza Diner (Brooklyn) ◐ [S] — 17 | 13 | 16 | $18

4124 Ave. U (bet. Coleman & Hendrickson Sts.), 718-951-6700

◪ "The epitome of Brooklyn", this busy diner serves "huge" portions at "unbelievably low prices"; still, some say: "not as good as advertised."

Kin Khao ◐ [S] — 20 | 17 | 14 | $30

171 Spring St. (bet. Thompson St. & W. B'way), 212-966-3939

■ The name "means 'eat rice', but you'll eat a lot more at this splendid" SoHo Thai; it's a "white-hot scene" but also "good for a get-together with friends"; only the "Downtown staff attitude is tiresome."

Kiosk, The ◐ [S] — 16 | 16 | 15 | $35

1007 Lexington Ave. (bet. 72nd & 73rd Sts.), 212-535-6000

◪ A "cute little" "almost hip" East Side hangout filled with "beautiful people" and serving a "limited but good" midpriced French menu; dissenters call it "mediocre", "dreary" and "overpriced."

Kitaro [S] — ▽ 21 | 16 | 20 | $35

1164 First Ave. (bet. 63rd & 64th Sts.), 212-317-9892

■ "Definitely on the rise", this East Side Japanese yearling offers "very creative", "extremely fresh sushi" and "great deals when you order for two"; "cozy" with "lots of privacy", it's a real sleeper.

Kitchen Club 🅂
21 | 16 | 20 | $37

30 Prince St. (Mott St.), 212-274-0025

☑ The Japanese-French "fusion cooking" at this petite, Zen-like SoHo spot "never fails to satisfy"; though a few find the ambiance "odd", most enjoy dining while talking to Dutch chef-hostess Marja Samm in her open kitchen.

Kitchenette 🅂
20 | 13 | 14 | $16

80 W. Broadway (Warren St.), 212-267-6740

☑ "Reason enough to live Downtown", this "cute" TriBeCa American is "better now" in "expanded quarters"; it's "fun" for a good, quick breakfast, brunch or lunch despite "uncomfortable seats" and service that can be "grumpy."

Knickerbocker Bar & Grill ❶🅂
18 | 18 | 17 | $33

33 University Pl. (9th St.), 212-228-8490

■ "Great steak" and "old-fashioned American food" at moderate tabs "enhanced by first-class jazz" make this "swanky" Village "time capsule" "a nice place to be any night", and that's where many are.

Kokachin ❶🅂
22 | 20 | 20 | $58

Omni Berkshire Pl. Hotel, 21 E. 52nd St. (bet. 5th & Madison Aves.), 212-355-9300

☑ "Not appreciated enough", this "calm and gracious", hotel-based Midtown French-Asian "can be brilliant"; however, it sure is "pricey" and perhaps "isn't what it was" "since Elka Gilmore left as chef."

Korea Palace 🅂
18 | 15 | 16 | $31

127 E. 54th St. (bet. Lexington & Park Aves.), 212-832-2350

☑ The "only bright, nonsmoky Korean in NY" also is surprisingly "authentic" given its Midtown location; it strikes some as "expensive", but "maybe you're paying for the waiters' ability to speak English."

Krispy Kreme 🅂⇗
22 | 7 | 12 | $8

280 W. 125th St. (Frederick Douglass Blvd.), 212-531-0111
265 W. 23rd St. (bet. 7th & 8th Aves.), 212-620-0111 ❶

■ "Calories be damned", these "addictive", "supersweet" doughnuts "give sex a run for the money"; myriad fans say "you will never eat" other doughnuts again and wish they'd "open more" shops.

Kum Gang San (Queens) ❶🅂
▽ 24 | 20 | 18 | $25

138-28 Northern Blvd. (bet. Main & Union Sts.), 718-461-0909

■ "Worth the trip" to Flushing, this huge, "reliably good Korean" would be a "bargain" in Manhattan; add 24-hour "service with a smile" and free parking and surveyors are all smiles.

Kum Kau Kitchen (Brooklyn) 🅂
– | – | – | I

465 Myrtle Ave. (Washington Ave.), 718-638-1850

This mostly takeout Clinton Hill Chinese has to be seen to be believed; it's so good and so cheap that 25 chefs have trouble keeping up with the orders; now, they've added a simple side dining room.

Kuruma Zushi
▽ 25 | 16 | 21 | $63

7 E. 47th St., 2nd fl. (bet. 5th & Madison Aves.), 212-317-2802

■ "Amazing sushi" "for the real connoisseur" and smooth service are the hallmarks of this "excellent", "très cher" Midtown mezzanine Japanese; you'll "love to take people there when they pay."

La Baraka (Queens) 🅂
21 | 18 | 23 | $33

255-09 Northern Blvd. (Little Neck Pkwy.), 718-428-1461

■ You're "made to feel special" by the "personalized" service at this "consistently good", "cozy" Little Neck French-Tunisian; besides having NY's "best couscous", it's a "wonderful value."

F | D | S | C

La Belle Epoque ◐[S] ▽ 17 | 24 | 17 | $32

827 Broadway (bet. 12th & 13th Sts.), 212-254-6436

■ "Gorgeous" art nouveau decor, "live music", a "sumptous Sunday buffet" and weekly changing menu, in that order, make this Village French-Creole a "delightful escapist experience."

La Boheme ◐[S] 17 | 16 | 16 | $35

24 Minetta Ln. (bet. Bleecker & W. 3rd Sts.), 212-473-6447

◪ A "warm, reliable" Village bistro that serves "amazing", "moderately priced" pizzas and "good" Provençal fare in a "tight" but "quaint" space; the garlic mashed potatoes bring down the house.

La Boite en Bois [S]≠ 21 | 18 | 20 | $43

75 W. 68th St. (bet. Columbus Ave. & CPW), 212-874-2705

■ "Don't take your tall friends" to this "charming", "shoe box"–size French bistro near Lincoln Center where you can stretch and touch all four walls; smaller surveyors savor the "authentic" "country" food and "courteous" service despite prices that are not so little.

La Bonne Soupe ◐[S] 15 | 12 | 13 | $22

48 W. 55th St. (bet. 5th & 6th Aves.), 212-586-7650

◪ "Convenient" for a "fast", "cheap and satisfying" Midtown lunch or "a light dinner" of soup, salad and fondue but "not much else", this French "bargain basement" bistro is "ok a pinch."

La Bouillabaisse (Brooklyn) [S]≠ 23 | 11 | 18 | $28

145 Atlantic Ave. (bet. Clinton & Henry Sts.), 718-522-8275

■ "There's always a line" so go early to this no-reservations, "good for the money", cash-only Brooklyn Heights French seafooder that's "cramped" but "cozy", "simple" but "super."

La Boulangere [S]≠ 19 | 10 | 12 | $17

49 E 21st St. (bet. B'way & Park Ave. S.), 212-475-8772

495 Broadway (bet. Broome & Spring Sts.), 212-334-4600

◪ At these Flatiron and SoHo bakery/cafes, "light" French-American meals satisfy cash-starved, self-serve surveyors; but "rude" staff and "factory-like" decor reduce ratings.

L'Absinthe [S] 22 | 22 | 20 | $50

227 E. 67th St. (bet. 2nd & 3rd Aves.), 212-794-4950

■ A "chic", "beautiful" East Side classic Parisian bistro where chef-owner Jean-Michel Bergougnoux creates "near flawless" "very French" fare; "you pay for it", but "c'est magnifique."

L'Acajou ◐[S] 19 | 13 | 17 | $36

53 W. 19th St. (bet. 5th & 6th Aves.), 212-645-1706

◪ For a "funky time" with "great wine", the "best french fries" and "lively" ambiance, head to this "quirky" but "good" Flatiron Alsatian bistro; it's a "bargain at lunch", but "don't look at the room."

LA CARAVELLE 26 | 25 | 26 | $64

Shoreham Hotel, 33 W. 55th St. (bet. 5th & 6th Aves.), 212-586-4252

■ The "Rolls-Royce of French restaurants", this "elegant" "old classic" offers the "delightful" Contemporary French fare of Cyril Renaud (ex Bouley) in an ambiance that's "understated perfection"; André and Rita Jammet's "sublime" "special treat" comes complete with surprisingly un-French "warm", inclusive service.

La Caridad 78 ◐[S]≠ 18 | 6 | 11 | $14

2197-2199 Broadway (78th St.), 212-874-2780

◪ "Amazing", "robust" Cuban-Chinese food at "rock-bottom prices" fuels fans frantic for the "best cheap eats around"; though service is shaky at this taxi-favored "food dispatchery", continued crowds post-makeover prove the adage: "if you expand, they will come."

La Cigale ●S
▽ 19 | 20 | 16 | $38

231 Mott St. (bet. Prince & Spring Sts.), 212-334-4331

■ A "charming" back garden, "fresh" Continental food with "not a bad thing on the menu" and good service make this "hidden", "romantic" NoLita yearling a "trendy" must-try when in the 'hood.

La Cocina S
17 | 13 | 15 | $21

2608 Broadway (bet. 98th & 99th Sts.), 212-865-7333
217 W. 85th St. (bet. Amsterdam Ave. & B'way), 212-874-0770 ●
762 Eighth Ave. (bet. 46th & 47th Sts.), 212-730-1860

☑ "Surprisingly tasty" Mexican treats are found at this "bargain" trio with "the best frozen margaritas"; low decor scores suggest takeout.

La Collina S
▽ 18 | 14 | 19 | $35

1402 Lexington Ave. (92nd St.), 212-860-1218

■ Offering "reliable", reasonably priced Northern Italian fare near the 92nd Street Y, this "tiny" but "cozy" "archetypal neighborhood cafe" draws customers from beyond its neighborhood.

La Colombe d'Or S
21 | 20 | 20 | $46

134 E. 26th St. (bet. Lexington & 3rd Aves.), 212-689-0666

■ New-old owners George and Helen Studley oversee this "sweet and romantic" Gramercy Provençal and reviewers report it's "back in good hands again"; for best results, go for a "quiet", "intimate" dinner with friends and dream of the French countryside.

LA CÔTE BASQUE S
27 | 26 | 26 | $66

60 W. 55th St. (bet. 5th & 6th Aves.), 212-688-6525

■ It may be in "new digs", but chef Jean-Jacques Rachou's "elegant" Classic French "grand dame" is still a "tried and true" Midtown "favorite"; "sublime", "better than ever" food, "faultless" service and "enchanting" murals of the Basque coast combine to make the experience totally "top drawer"; N.B. it's most affordably enjoyed at the $33 prix fixe lunch.

La Crêpe de Bretagne S
▽ 21 | 16 | 19 | $25

46 W. 56th St. (bet. 5th & 6th Aves.), 212-245-4565

■ "Finally crêpes are back" exclaim surveyors surprised by this "fine" Midtown newcomer with "very good" signature treats and frites; at these prices, it looks like a keeper.

Lady Mendl's S
▽ 21 | 26 | 24 | $30

Inn at Irving Place, 56 Irving Pl. (bet. 17th & 18th Sts.), 212-533-4466

■ For a Henry Jamesian spot of tea with the "ladies who wear hats", "travel back in time" to this "lovely" Gramercy inn tearoom; it's a bit pricey, but the tea is "superlative" and service "civilized."

Lafayette Grill & Bar
▽ 20 | 17 | 18 | $35

54 Franklin St. (bet. B'way & Lafayette St.), 212-732-4449

☑ This midpriced Mediterranean Downtown newcomer "is good to know about when on jury duty but not worth a special trip" for its well-rated though "uneven" fare.

La Fenice ●S
▽ 16 | 14 | 15 | $24

2014 Broadway (bet. 68th & 69th Sts.), 212-579-1337

☑ It's "new on the block", but the Lincoln Square crowd already treats this "moderately priced" Italian cafe as "a great place to hang out" over "zippy salads", "antipasto snacks" and "spectacular desserts."

La Focaccia ●S
20 | 17 | 18 | $30

51 Bank St. (W. 4th St.), 212-675-3754

■ "Warm, lush, romantic . . . and that's just the bread" say addicts of this West Village Italian whose oven-baked pizzas and other affordable fare can draw crowds; late-night look for a "chic" clientele basking in "intimate candlelight" and humming "abbondanza."

La Folie 🅂

16 18 16 $39

1422 Third Ave. (bet. 80th & 81st Sts.), 212-744-6327

◾ A "relaxing" Eastsider with a "romantic", "fin de siècle" setting, live music and just "above-average" French fare; though some say it's "uneven", it's still good for a neighborhood night out.

La Fontana 🅂

▽ 21 20 20 $36

309 E. 83rd St. (bet. 1st & 2nd Aves.), 212-734-6343

◾ "Excellent preparation" is the hallmark of this East Side glatt kosher Italian with "mouthwatering" homemade pastas; it's "as good as kosher gets" but typically a bit pricey.

La Giara 🅂

▽ 22 20 23 $32

50 Third Ave. (bet. 33rd & 34th Sts.), 212-726-9855

◾ "They aim to please" and, per high ratings, obviously succeed at this "popularly priced" Murray Hill Italian newcomer; though a few feel it's "too soon to tell", most are ready to declare it "a winner."

La Gioconda

▽ 21 17 20 $29

226 E. 53rd St. (bet. 2nd & 3rd Aves.), 212-371-3536

◾ A "good", "unpretentious", "red brick–walled" "neighborhood Italian" "well-kept secret" in Midtown serving "authentic", "fresh" dishes at "reasonable" prices; it's "cozy" with "try-hard" "hunky" servers and the "feel of Italy" – "speak Italian and they love you."

La Goulue ◑🅂

18 19 17 $46

746 Madison Ave. (bet. 64th & 65th Sts.), 212-988-8169

◾ "See and be seen", kiss and be kissed are the themes at this wood-paneled East Side French bistro catering to the "Euroset", "the Barneys crowd" and just plain "celebs"; it may be "chaotic" and "expensive", but it's "as close to Paris as you get" in NY.

La Granita ◑🅂

16 14 14 $26

1470 Second Ave. (77th St.), 212-717-5500

◾ Favored for affordable pasta and brick-oven pizza, this Eastsider offers a summer sidewalk cafe and an upstairs fireplace in winter; the unimpressed yawn – "just another pasta place, seen 'em all."

LA GRENOUILLE ◑

27 28 27 $71

3 E. 52nd St. (bet. 5th & Madison Aves.), 212-752-1495

◾ For a "flawless" "Francophile heaven" that's an "epicurean feast for both eyes and palate", this "classic" haute French where the powerful and beautiful come to dine is "worth the splurge" for "sublime food and service to match" in a flower-filled "Garden of Eden"; "this is where to spend your afterlife"; N.B. prix fixe only.

La Jumelle ◑🅂

18 16 15 $29

55 Grand St. (bet. W. B'way & Wooster St.), 212-941-9651

◾ A "funky" SoHo "boîte" with "superb" fries, beef and copious "red wine" at fair prices, this "late-night" French steak bistro may be "trendy", but it's also "unpretentious" "fun."

Lake Cafe (Staten Island) 🅂

▽ 15 22 15 $41

1150 Clove Rd. (Victory Blvd.), 718-442-7451

◾ For a "romantic", "peaceful escape" with a "breathtaking view of the lake", head to this Staten Island American; but beware, many find it pricey for "below-average food."

Lakruwana 🅂

▽ 17 16 18 $24

358 W. 44th St. (bet. 8th & 9th Aves.), 212-957-4480

◾ "Every lover of ethnic food must try this" "exotic", cheap BYO Sri Lankan with "garage-sale colonial decor" and "attentive" service; it's a "truly original", "spicy" Theater District choice.

La Lanterna di Vittorio ●⬤S⇗   ▽ 19 | 24 | 15 | $17
129 MacDougal St. (bet. W. 3rd & 4th Sts.), 212-529-5945
■ "The coziest cafe in Gotham" is a "romantic", "tranquil" Village Italian dessert specialist with fireplace; "excellent" sweets, coffee and easily "affordable" checks also light up customers.

La Lunchonette ●S   21 | 15 | 18 | $34
130 Tenth Ave. (18th St.), 212-675-0342
◪ An "oasis" in the West Chelsea "wasteland", this "funky", "low-key" French bistro serves "delicious", "moderately priced" "comfort" food in "warm and cozy" (some say "dark, bizarre") digs.

La Maison Japonaise   19 | 18 | 18 | $35
125 E. 39th St. (bet. Lexington & Park Aves.), 212-682-7375
■ "Imaginative" French-Japanese cuisine in a "lovely" townhouse makes this Midtown standby an "unusual" treat; a few find it "tired", but most maintain it's "still fresh" and "lovely in every way."

La Mangeoire S   18 | 19 | 18 | $39
1008 Second Ave. (bet. 53rd & 54th Sts.), 212-759-7086
■ A "longtime" East Midtown "favorite" with fairly priced, "satisfying" Provençal bistro fare and a "charming" "flower-filled" ambiance; it's "not world-class", but you really "can't go wrong here."

Lamarca ⇗   18 | 8 | 14 | $16
161 E. 22nd St. (3rd Ave.), 212-674-6363
■ "Good for a quick bite", this "no decor" Gramercy BYO Southern Italian offers pastas, soups and sauces to NYers on the go; it's "not fancy", but "fresh and delicious" as well as "cheap."

La Mediterranée S   18 | 17 | 18 | $38
947 Second Ave. (bet. 50th & 51st Sts.), 212-755-4155
■ A "cute" "good buy" Midtown bistro that's "very" French and very "enjoyable" though "nothing exciting"; if you need something "steady" where even the piano music is "civilized", this is the place.

La Mela S   19 | 11 | 17 | $30
167 Mulberry St. (bet. Broome & Grand Sts.), 212-431-9493
◪ "The food just keeps coming 'til you say stop" at this "slightly bawdy", no-menu, family-style Little Italy "party place" that's best "for a large group"; some feel "force fed" and call it "touristy."

La Metairie S   22 | 20 | 19 | $43
189 W. 10th St. (W. 4th St.), 212-989-0343
◪ "Cozy" vs. "cramped" Village Provençal with "delicious" "country" dishes and "warm" service; for "cheek to cheek" romancing, this "lovely", "rustic" place is "just what Village dining should be."

La Mirabelle S   21 | 18 | 22 | $40
333 W. 86th St. (bet. Riverside Dr. & West End Ave.), 212-496-0458
■ "Everyone feels welcome" at this "charming" if dowdy West Side French bistro that serves "home cooking – if home were in Paris"; "cheerful" service and "fair prices" make it a "local favorite."

Lan ●S   ▽ 19 | 19 | 22 | $25
56 Third Ave. (bet. 10th & 11th Sts.), 212-254-1959
■ East Villagers give a "wholehearted welcome" to this new Japanese; besides being "affordable" and "attentive", it offers "large amounts of good food" from its sushi and grill bars.

Landmark Tavern S   15 | 18 | 16 | $29
626 11th Ave. (46th St.), 212-757-8595
◪ Exuding "old-world charm, decor and service", this "historic" 1868 tavern "right out of Eugene O'Neill" proves "good English-Irish cuisine" isn't an oxymoron, at least after a brew or two.

F D S C

La Nouvelle Justine ◐ [S] — – – – M
206 W. 23rd St. (bet. 7th & 8th Aves.), 212-727-8642
If you want to be shackled and insulted, make your way to this campy S&M Chelsea newcomer specializing in abuse and French fare; its dark, red-light interior is either a fantasy world or a living hell.

Lansky Lounge ◐ [S] — ▽ 16 20 14 $25
104 Norfolk St. (bet. Delancey & Rivington Sts.), 212-677-9489
■ The Eclectic fare ("they have food?") takes a back seat to the martinis, "spectacular" paintings and bar scene at this "dark, cozy" Lower East Side newcomer; it's "a trip – if you can find it."

Lanza Restaurant [S] — 17 13 17 $26
168 First Ave. (bet. 10th & 11th Sts.), 212-674-7014
◪ "Garlic lovers unite" at this "classic" 1904 East Village Italian that dishes out "great value" in "vintage" digs and a "nice, quiet garden"; dissenters say it's "nothing special" but "ok if you live nearby."

La Paella ◐ [S] — 19 17 15 $26
557 Hudson St. (bet. Perry & W. 11th Sts.), 212-627-3092
214 E. Ninth St. (bet. 2nd & 3rd Aves.), 212-598-4321
◪ Though the namesake dish gets mixed reviews, "tasty tapas" and "super sangria" get olés at these "festive" Village Spaniards; "loud, cramped" but "fun", they're an easy "way to spend an evening."

La Petite Auberge [S] — 20 17 19 $38
116 Lexington Ave. (bet. 27th & 28th Sts.), 212-689-5003
■ "Always good" country French fare, especially the "killer soufflés", are why this "charming" "old-fashioned" Gramercy bistro has been a "neighborhood treat" for over 20 years; though some regret it's "not what it used to be", for most it remains a "warm, inviting" place.

La Pizza Fresca [S] — ▽ 20 15 16 $26
31 E. 20th St. (bet. Park Ave. S. & B'way), 212-598-0141
■ "A good addition" to the Flatiron District, this Italian newcomer is "a little inexperienced as yet", but with "amazing" brick-oven pizza as well as pastas and salads, it "feels like you're in Italy."

La Primavera — 18 18 18 $38
234 W. 48th St. (bet. B'way & 8th Ave.), 212-586-2233
◪ "Better than average", this Theater District Northern Italian is a B'way-convenient "attractive choice" that gets you to the show on time; still, it's "nothing to write [fan letters] about."

L'Ardoise [S] — 20 12 18 $35
1207 First Ave. (bet. 65th & 66th Sts.), 212-744-4752
■ "Quirky", "narrow", "crowded" East Side French bistro that's touted for "fantastic food at moderate prices" and for its "zany" host-owner as the "entertainment"; "bring your sense of humor."

La Reserve — 24 24 24 $58
4 W. 49th St. (bet. 5th & 6th Aves.), 212-247-2993
■ "A class act in all respects", Jean-Louis Missud's "old-world", "elegant" French Midtowner is ideal "to impress a client" or "take your favorite companion"; from the "first-rate" food to the "gorgeous" room and "superb service", "what more could you ask for?"

La Ripaille [S] — 19 18 18 $40
605 Hudson St. (bet. Bethune & W. 12th Sts.), 212-255-4406
■ "Flavorful French food", "friendly service" and "romantic", "snug" ambiance ensure a following for this standby West Village bistro; most call it a "real winner", but a few counter "slipped", "overpriced."

La Rivista ◐ 19 | 16 | 19 | $40
313 W. 46th St. (bet. 8th & 9th Aves.), 212-245-1707
■ "One of the better pre-theater spots", this Restaurant Row Italian is "a tad overpriced" but offers "good food", "free parking" and "accommodating" staff that makes sure "you're in your seat on time."

La Rosita [S] ▽ 19 | 7 | 13 | $14
2809 Broadway (bet. 108th & 109th Sts.), 212-663-7804
◪ This Columbia-area "hole-in-the-wall" tenders "delicious" Cuban cuisine that makes it "cheaper than cooking at home" and a "student's dream" come true.

La Taza de Oro ⊭ 19 | 6 | 14 | $14
96 Eighth Ave. (bet. 14th & 15th Sts.), 212-243-9946
■ It has "no decor to speak of, but excellent, simple" meals can be had for a song at this Chelsea "real Latino" coffee shop; it also serves "the best cafe con leche" in this Starbucks-riddled town.

La Traviata [S] ▽ 19 | 16 | 19 | $31
461 W. 23rd St. (bet. 9th & 10th Aves.), 212-243-5497
■ Though "Verdi would not write an aria about it", this Chelsea Italian is a "great neighborhood place" with a "homey" feel, "moderate prices" and weekend piano.

Lattanzi ◐ 21 | 19 | 20 | $42
361 W. 46th St. (bet. 8th & 9th Aves.), 212-315-0980
■ "Delectable" Italian (with "fine Roman-Jewish dishes" after 8 PM) can be found at this Restaurant Row "charmer"; the "artichokes are sublime", the garden "lovely" and service "welcoming."

La Vela [S] – | – | – | M
373 Amsterdam Ave. (bet. 77th & 78th Sts.), 212-877-7818
Surveyors write in to tell us that this "family-friendly" West Side Italian yearling has won a local following for its "attentive service", "good pastas" and "people-watching."

Layla [S] 20 | 22 | 19 | $43
211 W. Broadway (Franklin St.), 212-431-0700
◪ The De Niro–Nieporent team "scores again" with "melt in your mouth" Mediterranean–Middle Eastern fare, "funky", dark, "Arabian Nights" decor and "exotic" post–9 PM belly dancing at this "fanciful" "TriBeCa winner"; it's "pricey" but "fun for a change."

Le Bar Bat ◐[S] 13 | 18 | 13 | $30
311 W. 57th St. (bet. 8th & 9th Aves.), 212-307-7228
◪ "It's Halloween every night" at this "Lycra meets pasta" singles scene West Midtowner where the "gothic" bat cave theme decor overshadows the "uninspiring" New American food; young BATs (bridge and tunnelers) hang here and "dance until dawn."

Le Beaujolais 19 | 14 | 20 | $34
364 W. 46th St. (bet. 8th & 9th Aves.), 212-974-7464
■ Though the decor could use some "sprucing up", the rest of this Theater District French "oozes charm" with "classic bistro fare", "friendly service" and "unbelievable" value; it's a "tiny gem, find it."

LE BERNARDIN 28 | 27 | 27 | $71
155 W. 51st St. (bet. 6th & 7th Aves.), 212-489-1515
■ "Manhattan's ultimate *poisson* palace" is "in a school by itself" with "exquisite" prix fixe ($42 at lunch, $70 for dinner) seafood, a "spectacular room" and "flawless service"; siren owner Maguy LeCoze and Neptunologist chef Eric Ripert continue to reel in happy fish lovers to this Midtown "temple of elegance" that wins surveyors' No. 2 food ranking; fish lovers say "everything goes swimmingly" and if you "go once, you're hooked."

F	D	S	C

Le Biarritz [S] — 18 | 15 | 17 | $36

325 W. 57th St. (bet. 8th & 9th Aves.), 212-757-2390

◪ Though "innovations would be desirable", this "reliable" "classic" West Midtown French bistro "hasn't changed"; nonetheless, it "doesn't disappoint" its local fans.

Le Bilboquet [S] — 20 | 18 | 16 | $41

25 E. 63rd St. (bet. Madison & Park Aves.), 212-751-3036

◪ "Very good", "oh so chic", "Euro-crowd" East Side French bistro; some query "how can a place so tiny have such gigantic attitude?"

Le Bistrot de Maxim's [S] — 19 | 21 | 18 | $42

680 Madison Ave. (bet. 61st & 62nd Sts.), 212-751-5111

◪ An East Side French-style bistro providing "very fine" if pricey food, "winning ambiance" and nightly cabaret, but it "doesn't have its act together" causing some to brand it "pleasant, not exceptional."

Le Boeuf à la Mode [S] — 21 | 19 | 21 | $42

539 E. 81st St. (bet. East End & York Aves.), 212-249-1473

■ "Every neighborhood should have one" brag locals who have no beefs with this "bit of Paris on the East Side"; "quiet with lots of space between tables", it's a "wonderful refuge" for "quality" French fare.

Le Bouchon [S] — ▽ 19 | 15 | 18 | $33

319 W. 51st St. (bet. 8th & 9th Aves.), 212-765-6463

◪ "On the edge of the Theater District", "value" can be uncorked at this sleeper serving "very homey French fare"; though the decor is "too back room–like", "surprisingly good food" makes it worth a visit.

LE CHANTILLY [S] — 23 | 23 | 22 | $58

106 E. 57th St. (bet. Lexington & Park Aves.), 212-751-2931

■ "Your spirits will rise with the soufflé" at this "solid" haute French Eastsider that still delights with "sumptuous" meals, "bargain prix fixe lunch", "gracious service" and "elegance from another era"; though a little "stuffy" and "expensive", it's good "for special evenings."

LE CIRQUE 2000 [S] — 25 | 23 | 23 | $75

NY Palace Hotel, 455 Madison Ave. (bet. 50th & 51st Sts.), 212-794-9292

◪ "Dazzling" to some, deeply "disappointing" to others, Sirio Maccioni's recently relocated and enlarged Midtown French legend in the Villard Houses has dropped a point or two in its early ratings, but scores remain high and reservations hard to get for longtime chefs Sottha Khunn and Jacques Torres' cooking; while still perfect for "rubbernecking", more than a few surveyors debate Adam Tihany's over-the-top "*Jetsons* meet Buckingham Palace decor" and complain that service inevitably suffers when Sirio is in another room.

L'Ecole — 22 | 18 | 20 | $36

French Culinary Institute, 462 Broadway (Grand St.), 212-219-3300

■ The FCI should award "straight As" to the student chefs at this "remarkable" "bargain" SoHo restaurant; of course, it helps to have renowned chefs Pépin, Sailhac, Soltner and Torres on the faculty.

Le Colonial ◐[S] — 22 | 23 | 18 | $44

149 E. 57th St. (bet. Lexington & 3rd Aves.), 212-752-0808

■ Dining at this "chic" French colonial-style East Side Vietnamese is like being on "a movie set" ("James Bond goes to Saigon") complete with "inventive", "flavorful" food and a "sophisticated, beautiful" cast; don't miss the "chic", "hip" upstairs bar/lounge.

Le Figaro Cafe ◐[S]⊭ — 15 | 14 | 13 | $18

184 Bleecker St. (MacDougal St.), 212-677-1100

◪ "Still a good place to sip and people-watch", especially at brunch, this "quintessential" Village "bohemian" coffeehouse has "uninspired" Eclectic fare but always appealing "rich desserts."

Le Gamin ◖🅂≠
17 | 15 | 11 | $18

183 Ninth Ave. (21st St.), 212-243-8864
50 MacDougal St. (bet. Houston & Prince Sts.), 212-254-4678

☑ You can "sit all day with a cafe au lait" in a "big, steaming bowl" at these "very French" "slacker meccas"; the "nice, homey feel" will "transport you to Paris", but "secondhand smoke", "cramped quarters" and "frustrating" service will pull you back to reality.

Le Gigot 🅂
20 | 17 | 17 | $40

18 Cornelia St. (bet. W. 4th & Bleecker Sts.), 212-627-3737

☑ Le gigot and other "hearty" meats are the "specialty" at this new, "very French" West Village bistro; it's popular with "local professionals" despite being "cramped" and "rushed."

Le Grenadin 🅂
21 | 19 | 21 | $48

13 E. 37th St. (bet. 5th & Madison Aves.), 212-725-0560

☑ "Formal" but "hospitable" Murray Hill Classic French with a "very good" kitchen; the "older crowd" enjoys it as a "place to linger" and "unite with friends."

Le Jardin Bistro ◖🅂
20 | 19 | 17 | $34

25 Cleveland Pl. (bet. Kenmare & Spring Sts.), 212-343-9599

■ "Affordable", "honest", "tasty" SoHo French bistro that's "an instant trip to France" with a "beautiful" tent-covered garden and decor from "NJ tag sales"; it's "unpretentious and likable" but "slow."

Le Madeleine 🅂
18 | 19 | 18 | $36

403 W. 43rd St. (bet. 9th & 10th Aves.), 212-246-2993

■ "Ask for a garden seat" at this "cute", "moderately priced" Theater District French staple; with "steady" food and service and "bargain" pre/post-show menus, it offers remembrance of things past.

Le Madri ◖🅂
22 | 22 | 20 | $48

168 W. 18th St. (7th Ave.), 212-727-8022

■ "Vibrant", "highbrow", "pricey" Chelsea Italian in a "stylish" "soaring" setting; local book publishers, celebrities and the Joyce Theater crowd tout its "robust" Tuscan dishes and "efficient" staff.

Le Marais ◖🅂
19 | 15 | 16 | $39

150 W. 46th St. (bet. 6th & 7th Aves.), 212-869-0900

■ "You don't have to be Jewish to love" this "crowded and noisy", "fairly priced" Times Square glatt kosher French steakhouse whose "zesty steaks" taste "surprisingly good" "even to a nonbeliever."

Le Max 🅂
16 | 15 | 17 | $32

147 W. 43rd St. (bet. B'way & 6th Ave.), 212-764-3705

☑ "High ceilings" and "ersatz Versailles decor" set the stage for the theater crowd that frequents this "large" Times Square bistro; aside from the "bargain" pre-theater menu, it's "nothing exceptional."

Lemongrass Grill 🅂
18 | 12 | 14 | $20

2534 Broadway (bet. 94th & 95th Sts.), 212-666-0888 ◑
494 Amsterdam Ave. (84th St.), 212-579-0344
80 University Pl. (11th St.), 212-604-9870 ◑
37 Barrow St. (7th Ave. S.), 212-242-0606 ◑
61A Seventh Ave. (bet. Berkeley & Lincoln Pls.), Brooklyn, 718-399-7100

☑ "Quick", "cheap", "tasty but greasy" Thais with some locations better than others; despite "cramped" settings and "frustrating" service, they remain popular, especially for takeout.

Lemon Tree Cafe 🅂
16 | 10 | 14 | $18

769 Ninth Ave. (bet. 51st & 52nd Sts.), 212-245-0818

☑ A "standard", "never too crowded", "down 'n' dirty" Hell's Kitchen Middle Eastern offering "oily" hummus and "falafel on an actor's budget"; it's "fast and cheap" enough to be a "welcome" neighbor.

F	D	S	C

Lenge §   17 | 11 | 15 | $26

1465 Third Ave. (bet. 82nd & 83rd Sts.), 212-535-9661
200 Columbus Ave. (69th St.), 212-799-9188 ◑
☑ "Cheap", "crowded" crosstown Japanese duo with "uninspiring" but "dependable", "workmanlike" sushi, "dismal" NFL ("not for lingering") atmosphere and "quick" service.

Lenox Hill Grill §   – | – | – | M

1105 Lexington Ave. (bet. 77th & 78th Sts.), 212-879-9520
Pure BATH – as in Better Alternative to Home – this just-upgraded East Side American coffee shop has a little of everything at low prices and is casual enough to be relaxing after work.

Lenox Room §   22 | 20 | 21 | $50

1278 Third Ave. (bet. 73rd & 74th Sts.), 212-772-0404
■ "Tony" – as in Fortuna – "clubby", "comfortable" Eastsider packed daily with finely turned-out, necessarily well-heeled "upper-crust" types dining on "impressive", "inventive" New American food; for a start, try brunch.

Lento's (Brooklyn) §   19 | 10 | 15 | $20

7003 Third Ave. (Ovington Ave.), 718-745-9197 ⌐
833 Union St. (bet. 6th & 7th Aves.), 718-399-8782 ◑
☑ Bar-like Bay Ridge and Park Slope Italian joints prized for their legendary "thin-crust" pies; the "rest of the menu [is] so-so."

L'Entrecote   19 | 15 | 20 | $39

1057 First Ave. (bet. 57th & 58th Sts.), 212-755-0080
■ A "cozy" Sutton Place French bistro with a much-touted eponymous entree, a "wonderful" owner and "attentive staff"; "watch out for the smoke" and "not so petite" tabs.

Leopard, The   22 | 22 | 23 | $53

253 E. 50th St. (bet. 2nd & 3rd Aves.), 212-759-3735
☑ "Elegant" "time warp" East Midtown French-Continental townhouse party site where the $55 prix fixe dinner with unlimited wine receives nearly universal praise; those who find it "pompous" and "faded" say you may "feel like Norma Desmond."

Le Pain Quotidien §≠   21 | 18 | 17 | $21

1131 Madison Ave. (bet. 84th & 85th Sts.), 212-327-4900
■ "A welcome Belgian import", this "rustic" East Side coffeehouse produces "wonderful" breakfasts, desserts and coffees at modest tabs; the communal table is a lonely hearts magnet.

Le Perigord §   24 | 23 | 24 | $60

405 E. 52nd St. (bet. 1st Ave. & FDR Dr.), 212-755-6244
■ This "perfect classic French" restaurant in East Midtown recalls the "John Lindsay era"; it's "an old reliable" "preserver of traditional formality" that also manages to be "friendly" thanks to the warmth of owner Georges Briguet; some find it a bit "dowdy", but the vast majority swears by its "better than ever" haute cuisine.

Le Pescadou ◑§   20 | 16 | 17 | $42

18 King St. (6th Ave.), 212-924-3434
■ A "cozy, romantic", "Left Bank"–like SoHo French "local hangout" bistro with "fresh", "inventive" seafood that "makes it special"; "the owner is on stage all the time."

Le Petit Hulot §   18 | 17 | 18 | $40

973 Lexington Ave. (bet. 70th & 71st Sts.), 212-794-9800
☑ "Welcoming service" and a "lovely garden" support the "good standard bistro fare" at this "cozy" East Side French neighbor; if prices are on the high side, the prix fixe dinner is a buy.

Le Quercy S
20 | 15 | 19 | $36

52 W. 55th St. (bet. 5th & 6th Aves.), 212-265-8141

■ "Arthur Schwartz is right again, this sincere French bistro is a good value"; a "solid", "friendly", "busy" place, it has become a Midtown "home away from home" "defining competence."

Le Refuge S
22 | 22 | 21 | $47

166 E. 82nd St. (bet. Lexington & 3rd Aves.), 212-861-4505

■ Serving "satisfying" "country French" fare, this "charming" East Side side-street refuge-cum-garden is ever popular; if the bill is "more than expected", that can be prix-fixed with best-buy brunch, lunch and pre-theater menus.

Le Refuge Inn (Bronx) S
▽ 25 | 23 | 21 | $57

Le Refuge Inn, 620 City Island Ave. (Sutherland St.), 718-885-2478

■ "Pierre treats you like family" at this City Island inn that offers "excellent" updated French fare in an "unexpectedly lovely setting"; it's "like a B&B on Cape Cod" where "you may want to spend the night."

LE RÉGENCE S
25 | 28 | 26 | $64

Hotel Plaza Athénée, 37 E. 64th St. (bet. Madison & Park Aves.), 212-606-4647

☑ Like "dining in Versailles" or "the inside of a Faberge egg", this "old school" French restaurant can also produce "exceptional cuisine" and has service so attentive that you half expect the waiter "to give you a massage"; nonetheless, "hefty prices" and "stuffy" ambiance often leave this throne room eerily empty.

Le Relais S
17 | 17 | 16 | $43

712 Madison Ave. (63rd St.), 212-751-5108

☑ "If you do lunch" and enjoy chic "people-watching", try to get a Madison-side seat at this "crowded", hip French perennial; critics say it's just "average" with "high prices" "basically paying the rent."

Le Rivage S
20 | 16 | 19 | $37

340 W. 46th St. (bet. 8th & 9th Aves.), 212-765-7374

■ By most accounts, the "best Theater District French bistro" offers "hearty" "selections on its three-course prix fixe lunch and dinner" and a "low-key", "homey" setting; better yet, it's "reasonably priced", "family" friendly and "gets you to the show on time."

L'Ermitage S
21 | 21 | 21 | $46

40 W. 56th St. (bet. 5th & 6th Aves.), 212-581-0777

☑ "Tasty" Midtown Franco-Russian food served "with French finesse and Russian gusto" in a "beautiful" townhouse; despite prix fixe "steals", this "trip to St. Petersburg for cab fare" is often "empty."

LES CÉLÉBRITÉS
27 | 28 | 27 | $77

Essex House, 155 W. 58th St. (bet. 6th & 7th Aves.), 212-484-5113

■ Rated No. 2 for its overall average of food, decor and service, this Midtown haute French under star chef Christian Delouvrier features an "exquisite room, food to match", celebrity paintings on the walls and service that "makes patrons feel like celebrities"; though "you may have to mortgage your house" to foot the bill, it's "worth every penny" for what many call "the ultimate formal NY dining experience."

Les Deux Gamins ●S
20 | 18 | 12 | $26

170 Waverly Pl. (Grove St.), 212-807-7357

☑ Plan to put up with "obnoxious service" and "long waits" for the "excellent French bistro food" at this "smoky" Village brasserie that "transports one to Europe"; celeb-spotting and good prices are pluses.

Les Deux Lapins ●⌿
– | – | – | I

536 E. Fifth St. (bet. Aves. A & B), 212-387-8484

Superfriendly new Caribbean East Villager with warm ambiance and even warmer spicy food; fortunately, the prices are cool.

F | D | S | C

Les Halles ◐[S] 20 | 15 | 16 | $38
411 Park Ave. S. (bet. 28th & 29th Sts.), 212-679-4111
◪ This butcher shop/bistro is "a slice of Paris" that packs business lunch and social dinner crowds in elbow-to-elbow for "great steaks" accompanied by "attitude avec noise."

Le Singe Vert ◐[S] ▽ 19 | 20 | 20 | $42
160 Seventh Ave. (bet. 19th & 20th Sts.), 212-366-4100
■ "Property values went up when Georges Forgeois opened" his "instant hit" French bistro; it's a jumping "neighborhood place" where the Left Bank meets Chelsea.

LESPINASSE 28 | 28 | 28 | $78
St. Regis Hotel, 2 E. 55th St. (bet. 5th & Madison Aves.), 212-339-6719
■ Surveyors, "kings and presidents can find no fault" with Gray Kunz's "sumptuous", overall top-rated Asian-accented French Midtown jewel where "every bite is a delight"; rated No. 3 for food and No. 1 for both decor and service, it has a spacious Louis XVI setting that's "deliciously opulent" and service that's "formal" but not stiff; while the bill can be overpowering, so is the consensus: "heaven, thy name is Lespinasse."

Les Pyrénées ◐[S] 18 | 16 | 18 | $39
251 W. 51st St. (bet. B'way & 8th Ave.), 212-246-0044
◪ The food gets mixed reviews ("good but fattening" vs. "ok at best") at this "pleasant", "old reliable" Theater District French bistro; look for an "ample" pre-theater prix fixe and service "without pretense."

Les Routiers [S] 19 | 16 | 19 | $38
568 Amsterdam Ave. (bet. 87th & 88th Sts.), 212-874-2742
■ "Authentic French" at fair prices "endears" this West Side bistro to locals; the "cozy setting" "defies the truck stop" allusions of the name.

Les Sans Culottes ◐[S] 16 | 14 | 16 | $31
1085 Second Ave. (bet. 57th & 58th Sts.), 212-838-6660
329 W. 51st St. (bet. 8th & 9th Aves.), 212-581-1283
347 W. 46th St. (bet. 8th & 9th Aves.), 212-247-4284
◪ "High fat, low prices" and "good portions" create a "carnival" ambiance at this trio of "very friendly French bistros"; however, "on a quiet night, you can hear your arteries harden" here.

Le Taxi [S] 17 | 16 | 16 | $41
37 E. 60th St. (bet. Madison & Park Aves.), 212-832-5500
◪ To some, this East Side French bistro is a "fun place with decent food" that "looks like a bistro should – snappy and brassy"; others have a bumpier ride, citing "overpriced", "ordinary" food and service that "makes you feel like hailing a taxi."

Letizia ◐[S] 20 | 17 | 20 | $42
1352 First Ave. (bet. 72nd & 73rd Sts.), 212-517-2244
■ Even if a few find it "a tad pricey", "good food and service" and "warm atmosphere" augmented by nightly piano music have won Eastsiders over to this family-friendly Italian; it "seldom disappoints."

Levana [S] 21 | 17 | 19 | $45
141 W. 69th St. (bet. B'way & Columbus Ave.), 212-877-8457
■ By many accounts "the best [glatt] kosher in Manhattan", this West Side New American is "unmatched for kosher creativity" well served in "a really comfortable room"; some find it "expensive", but its prix fixe meals are "a real bargain."

Le Veau D'Or 17 | 13 | 17 | $41
129 E. 60th St. (bet. Lexington & Park Aves.), 212-838-8133
◪ Opened in 1937, this old-school East Side French bistro has decor, staff and menu that have changed little over the decades; "pleasantly old-fashioned" to its fans, critics slam it as "tired" and "outdated."

| | **F** | **D** | **S** | **C** |

L'Express ●S
249 Park Ave. S. (20th St.), 212-254-5858   16 | 16 | 13 | $25
☑ Open 24 hours a day, this low-cost, high-speed Flatiron "Left Bank" bistro with "good, light" fare is "charming" if sometimes feckless, with a staff composed largely of "unemployed models."

Le Zoo S
314 W. 11th St. (Greenwich St.), 212-620-0393   21 | 16 | 18 | $33
■ "It's all happening at Le Zoo" thanks to this West Village bistro's "smart French food", "reasonable prices", "fun, attentive staff" led by "saucy owners" and "casual" ambiance enjoyed by a young crowd.

Liam S
170 Thompson St. (bet. Bleecker & Houston Sts.), 212-387-0666   – | – | – | M
An inviting, brick-walled Village newcomer offering flavorful New American fare with zest at moderate prices; the warm interior and friendly staff make you feel at home.

Library, The ●S
Regency Hotel, 540 Park Ave. (61st St.), 212-339-4050   ▽ 19 | 24 | 20 | $40
■ "A cozy place to eat and read on a rainy day", "just as one's own library should be", this East Side New American is "great for light (or late) snacks"; now power breakfasting can be a family affair.

Life Cafe ●S
343 E. 10th St. (Ave. B), 212-477-8791   15 | 14 | 13 | $18
☑ "Immortalized by *Rent* as the bastion of bohemia", this Eclectic "crypto healthy", hassle-free East Village '80s pioneer remains a "good grunge cafe – cheap, plentiful" and "smoke-filled"; though "the food is weak" and service "slooow", it's still a "local favorite."

Limoncello S
Michelangelo Hotel, 777 Seventh Ave. (bet. 50th & 51st Sts.), 212-582-7932   20 | 19 | 20 | $43
☑ Opened last year, this "civilized" Theater District Italian offers a "pleasant" well-lighted space with good food that seems to be best enjoyed for "business lunches"; though pricey, it has lots of potential.

Lincoln Tavern ●S
51 W. 64th St. (bet. B'way & CPW), 212-721-8271   15 | 14 | 15 | $29
☑ "Pleasant and comfortable" with "cozy big booths", this Lincoln Center New American is "as good as most" places in the area; still, scores suggest you may want another emancipation address.

Lips ●S
2 Bank St. (Greenwich Ave.), 212-675-7710   – | – | – | M
"My, Jennifer, what a low voice you have" say unsuspecting diners at this kitschy Village drag dive; though "Oscar-winning" lip-synching queens lure diners in, "surprisingly good" Eclectic food at "decent prices" makes this "gimmick" plausible.

Lipstick Cafe
Lipstick Bldg., 885 Third Ave. (bet. 53rd & 54th Sts.), 212-486-8664   17 | 13 | 14 | $21
☑ "Creative" salads, sandwiches and desserts at "reasonable prices" make this East Midtown New American a popular hangout for "cute lawyers" and other local office folk.

Little Italy Pizza
65 Vanderbilt Ave. (bet. 45th & 46th Sts.), 212-687-3660   ▽ 22 | 7 | 13 | $10
72 W. 45th St. (6th Ave.), 212-730-7575
182A Varick St. (bet. Charlton & King Sts.), 212-366-5566 S
11 Park Pl. (bet. B'way & Church Sts.), 212-227-7077
■ "The lunch lines are insane" and there's "barely room to breathe" inside, but it's all worth it for "memorable toppings" on "thick, hearty slices" of "the best pizza" in Midtown.

F	D	S	C

Little Jezebel [S] 🚫 ▽ 19 | 21 | 16 | $25

529 Columbus Ave. (86th St.), 212-579-4952

◪ It "feels like the Old South" at this "minuscule" Upper West Side Soul specialist; despite strong support for its "brothel-like" setting and standout Southern dishes, it's not unanimously acclaimed.

Little Saigon [S] 🚫 – | – | – | I

374 W. 46th St. (bet. 8th & 9th Aves.), 212-956-0639

Little in size, decor and price, but big in flavor, this tiny nondescript Vietnamese coffee shop is one to try on Restaurant Row.

Little Szechuan [S] ▽ 24 | 7 | 17 | $17

5 E. Broadway (in front of Chatham Sq.), 212-732-0796

◪ Loyalists consider this Chinatown denizen to be "absolutely the best Szechuan" in NY for the price; its "patient", "pleasant" service helps make up for the bare-bones decor at its new East B'way shop.

Little Village (Queens) ◐ [S] 🚫 – | – | – | I

25-60 Steinway St. (bet. 25th & 28th Aves.), 718-728-5560

Inexpensive, no-decor Astoria Moroccan with friendly, 'here-try-this' service, where everyone seems to know one another and English is the second language; try the b'steeya and chicken makali.

Live Bait ◐ 14 | 11 | 12 | $21

14 E. 23rd St. (bet. B'way & Madison Ave.), 212-353-2400

◪ "Maybe they should call it jailbait"; "young", "long-legged Kate Moss wanna-be" waitresses, a "lively bar scene", low prices and "trailer park decor" keep this Flatiron Southern dive going strong.

Lobster Box (Bronx) [S] 17 | 15 | 16 | $36

34 City Island Ave. (bet. Belden & Rochelle Sts.), 718-885-1952

◪ "A City Island mainstay" with "pretty views from window tables" serving "good lobsters" and other seafood that gets mixed reviews; it can be fun, but many deem it "past its prime" and "expensive."

Lobster Club [S] 21 | 19 | 20 | $48

24 E. 80th St. (bet. 5th & Madison Aves.), 212-249-6500

◪ Fans savor the signature lobster club sandwich and other "creative" comfort food at this attractive, "club-like" East Side townhouse American; however, critics complain that it's "inconsistent" and "not up to Anne Rosenzweig's capabilities."

Lola ◐ [S] 19 | 20 | 18 | $39

30 W. 22nd St. (bet. 5th & 6th Aves.), 212-675-6700

■ Both the food and scene are "vibrant and exciting" (read "noisy") at this "jazzy" Flatiron Eclectic-Southern where a "multicultural crowd" swings to live music; don't miss the Sunday gospel brunch.

Lombardi's [S] 🚫 24 | 11 | 16 | $19

32 Spring St. (bet. Mott & Mulberry Sts.), 212-941-7994

■ SoHo's candidate for the "best pizza in NY" – vintage thin-crust brick-oven pies with "the freshest" in toppings; "family atmosphere" and an outdoor patio add to the pleasure.

London Lennie's (Queens) [S] 21 | 15 | 18 | $31

63-88 Woodhaven Blvd. (63rd Dr.), 718-894-8084

■ "Fish so fresh it swims to the plate" plus regular "surprises on the menu" keep 'em coming to this "plain", "always jammed" Rego Park "madhouse"; no reserving and low prices often mean long waits.

Lotfi's Moroccan 19 | 14 | 17 | $28

358 W. 46th St. (bet. 8th & 9th Aves.), 212-582-5850

■ Moroccan decor, "good ethnic food", "decent prices" and a "friendly", "helpful staff" make this Restaurant Row Moroccan not just an appealing pre-theater choice, but almost "a miracle."

Louie's Westside Cafe ◑ [S] — 17 | 14 | 16 | $27
441 Amsterdam Ave. (81st St.), 212-877-1900
◩ A "homey" West Side "American standard" that's good for breakfast through "family dinner"; the unimpressed ask "what's the deal?"

Loui Loui ◑ [S] — 16 | 15 | 15 | $30
1311 Third Ave. (75th St.), 212-717-4500
◩ "Dependable Italian fare", outdoor tables, "kid friendly" and "pretty cheap", by East Side standards, is the formula for success at this Eastsider; still, some are not won over: "nothing special."

Louisiana Community Bar/Grill [S] — 17 | 18 | 16 | $27
622 Broadway (bet. Bleecker & Houston Sts.), 212-460-9633
◩ "Don't be afraid to order the 'gator" at this "real Cajun" LoBro yuppie hangout; you can expect "a good ole time" with a "huge bar" "pickup scene", live jazz "as spicy as the food" and "fab swing dancing."

Lucky Cheng's ◑ [S] — 12 | 17 | 16 | $30
24 First Ave. (bet. 1st & 2nd Sts.), 212-473-0516
■ At this East Village Asian-Eclectic transvestite "campfest", the main dish is drag cabaret; the food is simply a drag.

Lucky Strike ◑ [S] — 16 | 15 | 13 | $27
59 Grand St. (bet. W. B'way & Wooster St.), 212-941-0479
◩ "Old-style SoHo" better-late-than-ever bistro (open till 4 AM) that's "a good steak frites kind of place" with a "smoky" who's hot, who's not ambiance; critics say its "luck has run out."

Luke's Bar and Grill ◑ [S] ⊘ — 15 | 13 | 15 | $22
1394 Third Ave. (bet. 79th & 80th Sts.), 212-249-7070
■ Locals laud this "watering hole" "bastion of low-key in the sea of East Side posh" for its brew, burgers and value; with "fraternity-type" ambiance, it bridges the gap between "yuppies" and "cycle gangs."

L'Ulivo ◑ [S] ⊘ — ▽ 19 | 16 | 17 | $27
184 Spring St. (bet. Sullivan & Thompson Sts.), 212-343-1445
■ "Authentic thin-crust pizza", "fresh pasta" and "friendly" service in a "simple room" are the winning combo at this moderately priced SoHo Italian yearling; if "generic", it's nonetheless "pleasant."

Luma [S] — 24 | 18 | 21 | $44
200 Ninth Ave. (bet. 22nd & 23rd Sts.), 212-633-8033
■ "Refreshing, playful seasonings" make "even the simplest dishes flavorful" at this "superior" Chelsea New French; though a few find the experience "drab" and "expensive", the vast majority "keeps going back" because it's "always good."

Lumi ◑ [S] — 20 | 19 | 18 | $43
963 Lexington Ave. (70th St.), 212-570-2335
■ "An excellent entrant to the East Side Italian set", this "quiet", "family-oriented" "neighborhood club" offers "above-average" food in a "lovely" "old townhouse setting."

Lundy Bros. (Brooklyn) [S] — 15 | 16 | 14 | $35
1901 Emmons Ave. (Ocean Ave.), 718-743-0022
◩ A reincarnated "Brooklyn institution", this "cavernous" 800-seat seafooder overlooking Sheepshead Bay proves that "you can't go home again"; though praised for "fresh" fish and "beautiful decor", it's also bashed as a "factory" that's "a far cry from the original."

Lupe's East L.A. Kitchen ◑ [S] ⊘ — 17 | 11 | 14 | $17
110 Sixth Ave. (Watts St.), 212-966-1326
■ "Cheap and cheery", this "wonderfully dumpy" Mexican may serve the "cheapest good food in SoHo"; some find the "cheesy, beany" fare "bland", but most enjoy this "bueno bang for the buck."

Lusardi's ●S
22 | 18 | 21 | $46

1494 Second Ave. (bet. 77th & 78th Sts.), 212-249-2020

■ Heartfelt praise is all but unanimous for this "always crowded" East Side Italian; it's loved as much for "one of the nicest staffs in town" as for its "reliable, delicious" food; yes, prices are high, but they're quite acceptable to the "heavy hitter" clientele.

LUTÈCE
26 | 24 | 25 | $70

249 E. 50th St. (bet. 2nd & 3rd Aves.), 212-752-2225

■ Since its transfer from André Soltner to Eberhard Mueller in 1995, diners have wondered whether this East Midtown haute French icon would be the same; happily, Mueller's more modern French food is not the same, but, many agree, even "better"; dining here is still an "exquisite" "three-hour experience" with "the best food, service and presentation" and "beautifully reborn" decor; since the prix fixe $65 dinner is a bargain in its league, it's time to revisit this old friend.

Luxia ●S
19 | 18 | 20 | $35

315 W. 48th St. (bet. 8th & 9th Aves.), 212-957-0800

■ "A lovely back garden" lends "tucked-away charm" to this midpriced Theater District American-Italian sophomore; "excellent" steaks, lobster and fruit martinis are served by staff with "so much heart, you feel like passing around digitalis."

Luzia's S
18 | 13 | 17 | $26

429 Amsterdam Ave. (bet. 80th & 81st Sts.), 212-595-2000

■ With few Portuguese options, this "delightful", "inexpensive" Iberian "home-cooking" specialist has won over enough Westsiders to be often "crowded", though recently expanded quarters offer some relief.

Mad Fish S
20 | 17 | 17 | $38

2182 Broadway (bet. 77th & 78th Sts.), 212-787-0202

☑ This Hamptons-on-Broadway "madhouse with above-average seafood" is "near enough to Lincoln Center and the Sony theaters" to be taken seriously, despite complaints about "maddening prices."

Madison Bistro S
18 | 15 | 17 | $35

238 Madison Ave. (bet. 37th & 38th Sts.), 212-447-1919

■ A "relaxing" edge of Murray Hill "lunch spot" (dinner too) with "solid" Gallic bistro food served with a "very French" flair; it seems "a bit snooty" to Francophobes, but most of its neighbors vote oui.

Magic Carpet S
19 | 12 | 18 | $21

54 Carmine St. (bet. 6th Ave. & 7th Ave. S.), 212-627-9019

☑ Middle Eastern mavens "look past" this "accommodating" Village eatery's lack of decor to plates piled high with "tasty", "wholesome", "well-priced" specialties; for a good intro order the "magic combo."

Main Street S
16 | 15 | 16 | $27

446 Columbus Ave. (bet. 81st & 82nd Sts.), 212-873-5025

■ The affordable meat loaf and mashed potatoes American fare dished up family-style in this lofty Westsider solves the riddle where do you take "16 people who won't eat anything they can't pronounce?"

Malaga S
19 | 9 | 17 | $29

406 E. 73rd St. (bet. 1st & York Aves.), 212-737-7659

■ A Spanish local filled with dressed-down Eastsiders plainly enjoying the "close your eyes atmosphere" as much as the sangria, paella and seafood; those who expect service should avoid Saturday night.

Malayboo S
19 | 13 | 17 | $25

378 Third Ave. (bet. 27th & 28th Sts.), 212-532-4500

☑ In Murray Hill, Silk's more affordable Malaysian successor "conjures up memories of Kuala Lumpur" with "spicy", "flavorful" food and tropical color; it also offers a "great bar" (with "no scene").

Malika [S] ▽ 18 | 15 | 16 | $28
210 E. 43rd St. (bet. 2nd & 3rd Aves.), 212-681-6775
◪ Per its supporters (a majority), this little known East Side Indian has "excellently prepared" food and solid service at good prices, most notably a "generous" $10.95 lunch buffet.

Maloney & Porcelli ◐[S] 21 | 20 | 20 | $51
37 E. 50th St. (bet. Madison & Park Aves.), 212-750-2233
■ "Dynamic and energetic", with "gargantuan" steaks and seafood platters plus a major bar/cigar scene, this handsome high-ceilinged Midtown "deal-maker place" has food and service that "really are good"; sure, it's "male-oriented", "homogenized" and high priced, but, named after owner Alan Stillman's lawyers, it's improving the reputation of the legal profession.

Mama Buddha ◐[S] 19 | 13 | 20 | $18
578 Hudson St. (W. 11th St.), 212-924-2762
■ Hailed as a vegetarian's "dream come true" ("never seen fresher vegetables"), this "clean", "cheap", "attentive" West Villager is one of the best of the "spartan Chinese"; try it for "outdoor dining."

Mamá Mexico ◐[S] - | - | - | M
2672 Broadway (bet. 101st & 102nd Sts.), 212-864-2323
Bright lights, colorful murals, mean margaritas and a mariachi singer set the tone at this small, too-new-to-rate Upper West Side Mexican.

Mama's Food Shop ⊘ ▽ 20 | 11 | 14 | $12
200 E. Third St. (bet. Aves. A & B), 212-777-4425
◪ "White trash luncheonette decor" and "fend for yourself" seating are just what you'd expect at an East Village comfort food station; its "good", "fresh", "homey and cheap" dineresque eats will "keep you alive on the day before payday."

Mandarin Court [S] 20 | 8 | 13 | $19
61 Mott St. (bet. Bayard & Canal Sts.), 212-608-3838
■ Expect "terrific dim sum", "not so terrific waits", "decorless" surroundings and a "language barrier"; but don't miss the dumplings or "sticky rice in a banana leaf with roasted buried treasures" at this Chinatown lunch "bargain."

M & R Bar – Dining Room ◐[S] 16 | 17 | 15 | $25
264 Elizabeth St. (bet. Houston & Prince Sts.), 212-226-0559
■ A "cool", low-cost SoHo East New American that works "best for hard drinks in retro splendor" in the crowded "bar part"; there's a "quiet and romantic" garden out back, "sorry" service throughout.

Manducatis (Queens) [S] 21 | 12 | 18 | $33
13-27 Jackson Ave. (21st St. & 47th Ave.), 718-729-4602
■ For family-style Italian ("like Sunday dinner at Aunt Teresa's") take the subway to this Long Island City icon, "let the waiter order", "have some wine" and "roll" with the program.

Manganaro's Hero-Boy 18 | 7 | 12 | $14
492 Ninth Ave. (bet. 37th & 38th Sts.), 212-947-7325
◪ "The hero of the hero"; its "mile-high", six-foot sub is a "NY institution", as is the "no-class", "cafeteria setup" and "crusty" help.

Mangez Avec Moi - | - | - | I
71 W. Broadway (bet. Warren & Murray Sts.), 212-385-0008
Quirky TriBeCa BYO Thai-Vietnamese-Laotian storefront with a wide-ranging menu that's so cheap you can't afford not to try it.

Mangia   21 | 13 | 14 | $19
16 E. 48th St. (bet. 5th & Madison Aves.), 212-754-0637
50 W. 57th St. (bet. 5th & 6th Aves.), 212-582-5554
Marketplace at Macy's, 151 W. 34th St. (Herald Sq.), 212-494-5654 S
☑ Choosing from the "delicious" gourmet sandwiches, antipasti and
pastas at these upscale Midtown Med-Italian commissaries is a "kid
in a candy store experience"; given the crowds, some opt for delivery.

Mangia e Bevi ◐S   17 | 13 | 15 | $25
800 Ninth Ave. (53rd St.), 212-956-3976
■ "Tambourine-slamming", "dancing on chairs" and getting down on
garlic keep this Hell's Kitchen Italian rocking with twentysomething
birthday and bachelorette bashes; here, the waiters entertain and the
cheap pasta "does what it should – absorbs alcohol."

Manhattan Bistro ◐S   17 | 16 | 16 | $31
129 Spring St. (bet. Greene & Wooster Sts.), 212-966-3459
☑ Recently "revamped with a new menu", this Paris-in-SoHo bistro
is "still not great but much improved"; affordable steak frites and
"relaxed" lunches are its trademarks.

Manhattan Grille S   22 | 21 | 21 | $48
1161 First Ave. (bet. 63rd & 64th Sts.), 212-888-6556
■ "Great steaks and seafood" in a "splendid Diamond Jim Brady"
setting, backed by "polite" help cause surveyors to wonder why this
Eastsider isn't "better known"; perhaps new improvements, including
floor-to-ceiling mahogany windows and doors, will help.

MANHATTAN OCEAN CLUB ◐S   25 | 22 | 22 | $56
57 W. 58th St. (bet. 5th & 6th Aves.), 212-371-7777
■ Epitomizing "high dining Manhattan-style", this duplex seafood
house just south of Central Park offers some of the best and freshest
fish in the city, "elegant" service and the feeling of dining on a "classy
yacht"; there's the added fillip of "few calories and no guilt" – that is,
if you resist dessert and go easy on the fab wines.

Man Ray S   15 | 15 | 14 | $29
169 Eighth Ave. (bet. 18th & 19th Sts.), 212-627-4220
☑ Way "too casual" (service-wise), Joyce Theater New American
staple chugging along on a "few good dishes" and "twilight zone" chic;
it's "ok, but there are better joints along the Chelsea strip."

Maple Garden Beijing   ▽ 21 | 15 | 20 | $32
Duck House S
236 E. 53rd St. (bet. 2nd & 3rd Aves.), 212-759-8260
■ "Masterful" midpriced Peking duck is the main reason for booking
this business-class Midtown Chinese; however, there are a host of
other "unique" offerings worth trying.

Mappamondo ◐S   16 | 13 | 13 | $22
114 MacDougal St. (bet. Bleecker & W. 3rd Sts.), 212-674-8900
581 Hudson St. (Bank St.), 212-675-7474 ⊟
11 Abingdon Sq. (8th Ave.), 212-675-3100 ⊟
☑ "Bargain pasta joints" with "dark and crowded" "bohemian"
ambiance and outdoor seats; after a "predictably good meal", patient
young twentysomethings "leave here with a full tummy and wallet."

MARCH ◐S   26 | 25 | 26 | $71
405 E. 58th St. (bet. 1st Ave. & Sutton Pl.), 212-754-6272
■ "Romantic" and "refined", this "lovely Sutton Place hideaway"
showcases chef Wayne Nish's "adventurous" New American cuisine
(available prix fixe, dinner only) and "quality wines"; one of his
"incredible" menus, enhanced by "impeccable" service, comes as
close as you can get to a surefire "special evening."

Marchi's 20 | 19 | 21 | $43
251 E. 31st St. (bet. 2nd & 3rd Aves.), 212-679-2494
■ "A crowd-pleaser", and why not, since the Marchi family have "been working on the same meal for 50 years"; this "home-like" Italian near Bellevue serves more food on its $34.75 set price menu than one can ever eat.

Marco Polo (Brooklyn) [S] 21 | 18 | 20 | $34
345 Court St. (Union St.), 718-852-5015
◪ A better than "typical Brooklyn Italian" in Carroll Gardens that appeals to nostalgic fans of "old-country" cooking, "dress-up" dining, "'70s" decor and piano playing; ask for the "black pasta with seafood (not on the menu, but great)."

Mardi Gras (Queens) [S] ▽ 20 | 19 | 19 | $26
70-20 Austin St. (70th Rd.), 718-261-8555
■ "Pass the remoulade" – there's a "taste of New Orleans on Austin Street" where "decent value" Cajun-Creole eats, "kid-friendly" folks and live music keep this "joint jumpin'"; it's "fun" even if "franchisey."

Marguery Grill [S] 22 | 21 | 20 | $50
133 E. 65th St. (bet. Lexington & Park Aves.), 212-744-2533
■ "Perfect" for its tony East 60s nabe, this "pretty" Contemporary American "opens like a flower" as you step inside; with "original food", "coolly elegant decor" and "caring" service, it can "bowl you over", especially at their $19.98 lunch.

Maria Elena [S] ▽ 16 | 16 | 17 | $38
133 W. 13th St. (bet. 6th & 7th Aves.), 212-741-3663
■ There's "a warm welcome for regulars" at this "lively" Italian, where a "lovely garden" and "roaring fireplace" provide "comfy settings" for "classic" cooking; still, some snipe at non-Villagey prices.

Marichu 22 | 19 | 21 | $40
342 E. 46th St. (bet. 1st & 2nd Aves.), 212-370-1866
■ "Delicious Basque food", "charming" hosts and a "wonderful" setting with garden keep this UN-area "sleeper" (for most NYers) "mobbed with UN types"; check when "baby eels are in season."

Marina Cafe (Staten Island) [S] ▽ 17 | 23 | 18 | $34
154 Mansion Ave. (bet. Hillside Terr. & Hylan Blvd.), 718-967-3077
◪ Its waterside setting is fine for boat-watching and meeting friends, but dining is less of a sure thing at this Staten Island seafooder.

Marinella [S] ▽ 21 | 15 | 17 | $34
49 Carmine St. (Bedford St.), 212-807-7472
■ This neighborhood Italian does its best to "make you feel like you are in Italy" with "authentic" pasta, "fresh fish" and "relaxing" ways; it's the "best-known well-kept secret in the Village."

Marion's Continental ◐ [S] 15 | 18 | 16 | $27
354 Bowery (bet. Great Jones & 4th Sts.), 212-475-7621
◪ "Morticia Addams meets Elvis" at this "superkitschy" East Village martini lounge-cum-Continental restaurant where "socializing" and people-watching are the main events; given "rather be elsewhere" servers, dinner is "leisurely."

Mario's (Bronx) [S] 20 | 13 | 18 | $31
2342 Arthur Ave. (bet. 184th & 186th Sts.), 718-584-1188
◪ "Somewhat fancier" than Dominick's (across the street), this Italo-American "landmark" makes "some of the best pizza in the Bronx" and a few good pasta and seafood dishes; however, critics say it has gotten "touristy" and is "past its time."

MARK'S 🄢
23 | 25 | 23 | $53

The Mark, 25 E. 77th St. (Madison Ave.), 212-879-1864
■ Celebs and royalty take "refuge from the outside world" at this "elegant", "Edwardian" East Side dining room with "excellent" French and American cuisine; prix fixe "bargains" (notably a $19.98 lunch) and an "Anglophile's" tea make it accessible to the rest of us.

Marti 🄞🄢
▽ 18 | 12 | 17 | $30

1269 First Ave. (bet. 68th & 69th Sts.), 212-737-6104
238 E. 24th St. (bet. 2nd & 3rd Aves.), 212-545-0602
■ "Solid", "family-run" Ottomans, whose good "price/quality" ratio is improved by BYO at the Downtown site, but not by "train compartment" seating; Uptown there's enough space to "bring on the belly dancers."

Martini's 🄞🄢
14 | 14 | 14 | $32

810 Seventh Ave. (53rd St.), 212-767-1717
☑ A "massive" "martini for any mood", year-round street scenery and a handy location are reasons to suffer "auditioning" staff at this Midtown Cal-Ital; reviewers go both ways on chef Richard Krause's trendy pasta, pizza and grilled seafood menu.

Mary Ann's 🄢
16 | 12 | 14 | $20

1503 Second Ave. (bet. 78th & 79th Sts.), 212-249-6165
2452 Broadway (91st St.), 212-877-0132
116 Eighth Ave. (16th St.), 212-633-0877
80 Second Ave. (5th St.), 212-475-5939
☑ "Cheap, greasy" and "way too crowded", these Tex-Mexers draw fire across the board, yet remain "inexplicably popular" for margaritas, "endless" chips 'n' salsa and cheesy, piled-up plates – they're to Mexican food what the Monkees are "to the Beatles."

Marylou's 🄞🄢
19 | 18 | 18 | $38

21 W. Ninth St. (bet. 5th & 6th Aves.), 212-533-0012
☑ Known for its "cozy" ambiance, "people-watching", fish and brunch, this "aging" Village Continental hosts a clubby bar and private party scene; still, some prescribe "a pep pill."

Mary's 🄞🄢
18 | 19 | 19 | $39

42 Bedford St. (bet. Carmine & Leroy Sts.), 212-741-3387
■ "Mostly gay" West Village American whose bower-like tribute to Angie Dickinson is the "perfect private" party room; as a restaurant, it's "longer on atmosphere than food", but there's "always something outrageous happening here."

Massimo Al Ponte Vecchio 🄢
▽ 22 | 17 | 20 | $31

206 Thompson St. (bet. Bleecker & W. 3rd Sts.), 212-228-7701
☑ "The city's hardest-working owner" offers everything from "family-sized portions" to ambitious game dinners and wines to make this Village Italian better known; ratings show he's succeeding.

Master Grill International
(Queens) 🄢
– | – | – | M

34-09 College Point Blvd. (bet. 34th & 35th Aves.), 718-762-0300
The salad bar is as diverse as the clientele at this glitzy, bright 1,000-seat Flushing AYCE churrascaria ($18.95 for dinner, $12.95 for lunch); there are long waits and you'll hear the roar of the crowd, but you can gorge yourself.

Match 🄞🄢
18 | 17 | 15 | $35

160 Mercer St. (bet. Houston & Prince Sts.), 212-343-0020
☑ A "sexy" mix of "model types", American-Eclectic "grazing" and "Downtown attitude" powers this SoHo scene past competition from newer hot spots; go late "to be seen", or for "better service", do lunch.

Match Uptown ◐[S]
19 | 19 | 16 | $41
33 E. 60th St. (bet. Madison & Park Aves.), 212-906-9177
■ Good-looking Euro types (and "bored waiters") make this "pricey", "hip" East Side "scene" to enjoy "surprisingly good" American-Eclectic dining and "after-dinner browsing" (power lunching is also in vogue); no need to take a date, you'll find one there.

Matthew's [S]
21 | 21 | 19 | $45
1030 Third Ave. (61st St.), 212-838-4343
■ This "lovely, airy" Eastsider, with an "escape" to Casablanca feel, is a "relaxing, romantic" backdrop for the prolific Matthew Kenney's (Monzù, Mezze) "original" Mediterranean cuisine; "classy" and cosmopolitan, it works for everything from a drink to a client meal.

Mavalli Palace [S]
21 | 15 | 17 | $24
46 E. 29th St. (bet. Madison Ave. & Park Ave. S.), 212-679-5535
■ "As in Madras", this "excellent" Curry Hill exemplar of Southern India's complex vegetarian cuisine sets off flavor "explosions" with every bargain bite; less of a marvel are its "modern" setting and staffers who "meditate more than serve."

Max & Moritz (Brooklyn) **[S]**
21 | 16 | 16 | $31
426A Seventh Ave. (14th St.), 718-499-5557
◪ At this understated New American–French bistro in Park Slope, the "inventive", "affordable" cooking will "knock you out", but the "offhand service" may wear you out; it probably has the area's "best food", but naysayers tell us that "doesn't take much to do."

Maxwell's [S]
– | – | – | M
1269 Lexington Ave. (bet. 85th & 86th Sts.), 212-828-1616
With the shell steak topping the menu at $16.95, this modestly priced, seven-day-a-week Eclectic newcomer shows promise as a casual home away from home for East Side locals.

Maya [S]
▽ 22 | 22 | 17 | $45
1191 First Ave. (bet. 64th & 65th Sts.), 212-585-1818
■ "High-end" Mexican newcomer with hard-to-pronounce dishes in attractive East Side surroundings; though service needs "smoothing out", this "fascinating twist on the Mexican theme" is "on the way up."

Mayfair ◐[S]
15 | 12 | 18 | $29
964 First Ave. (53rd St.), 212-421-6216
◪ A Sutton Place "neighborhood" haunt with "gay pride and grey pride", "inexpensive" German-American "mommy food" and "warmhearted" help; most leave feeling "well fed and treated."

Mayrose ◐[S]
14 | 12 | 12 | $19
920 Broadway (21st St.), 212-533-3663
◪ More "trendy" "studio set" ("Julia Roberts spotted here") than diner, this "reasonably priced" Flatiron corner is "best at breakfast" and a "prime target for weekend brunch"; but given "hit or miss" service and retro cooking, it's hard to understand the "lines to get in."

Maz Mezcal [S]
20 | 16 | 19 | $30
316 E. 86th St. (bet. 1st & 2nd Aves.), 212-472-1599
■ Cooked-to-order paella, notable margaritas and a "refreshingly unhysterical" ambiance make for a "great combo of cuisine and neighborhood feel" at this midpriced East 80s Mexican – holy mole!

Mazzei [S]
22 | 18 | 21 | $44
1564 Second Ave. (bet. 81st & 82nd Sts.), 212-628-3131
◪ The brick oven turns out "amazing" appetizers, fish and breads at this "down-to-earth", "accommodating" East Side Italian; while hardly flawless ("noisy" "crowded", "pricey"), it's generally well liked.

F	D	S	C

McSorley's Old Ale House ◐[S]⊄ — 11 | 17 | 13 | $18

15 E. Seventh St. (bet. 2nd & 3rd Aves.), 212-473-9148

◩ This "landmark" 1854 vintage East Village "swill house", with its "cranky" waiters and "drinking with the boys" atmosphere, is "living" history; come "smell the tradition" and "check out the dust", but "forget the [saloon] food."

Mediterraneo ◐[S] — 17 | 15 | 15 | $31

1260 Second Ave. (66th St.), 212-734-7407

◩ "Cramped quarters" make for "great eavesdropping" at this East Side movie-handy pasta place whose homemade noodles and "Euro" clientele give it "like Florence" credibility.

Medusa ◐[S] — ▽ 20 | 20 | 18 | $38

239 Park Ave. S. (bet. 19th & 20th Sts.), 212-477-1500

■ A "vampire red bar lures night crawlers" to this new Mediterranean "hot spot" in the Flatiron-Gramercy feeding grounds; "instantly trendy", it's a pretty place, as in "pretty cafe, pretty staff and pretty expensive."

Mee Noodle Shop [S] — 17 | 6 | 12 | $13

922 Second Ave. (49th St.), 212-888-0027
795 Ninth Ave. (53rd St.), 212-765-2929 ◐
547 Second Ave. (30th St.), 212-779-1596
219 First Ave. (13th St.), 212-995-0333

■ "Cheap", "no-frills" Chinese noodle house chainlet that's "reliably good down to the number of scallions floating in the soup"; however, noise and "mop under your feet" service discourage lingering.

Mekka ◐[S] — 17 | 14 | 15 | $24

14 Ave. A (bet. Houston & 2nd Sts.), 212-475-8500

◩ An "animated" mix of "hip-hop" and budget "yuppie soul food" fuels this "dress your best" East Village scene; while the Caribe-Southern calories have takers, they're a "diversion" from the live DJ (on weekends) and "sexy" crowd.

MeKong [S] — 20 | 14 | 15 | $24

44 Prince St. (bet. Mott & Mulberry Sts.), 212-343-8169

■ In SoHo East, this "soothing", well-priced Vietnamese-lite supplies "sweet" servers, "delicious" outdoor dining and "neighborly" vibes.

Meli Melo — ▽ 19 | 17 | 16 | $32

110 Madison Ave. (bet. 29th & 30th Sts.), 212-686-5551

◩ "Anything is welcome" in this restaurant-poor locale, doubly so this "intimate" modern Eclectic, featuring chef Bernard Ros' unusual, pan-global food; despite kinks, it's "one of the better newcomers."

Meltemi [S] — 20 | 17 | 18 | $34

905 First Ave. (51st St.), 212-355-4040

■ When the Sutton Place set "can't get to Astoria", they drop by this cheerful "white and blue" Greek taverna for "fresh" charcoal-grilled fish; it's a "bit more civilized" (and expensive) than most.

Melting Pot (Queens) [S] — ▽ 17 | 15 | 18 | $34

1 Station Sq. (bet. Burns St. & Continental Ave.), 718-261-6993

◩ Although this "unique" Forest Hills fondue specialist can be "fattening" family or dating fun (especially the chocolate fondue dessert), it's not for everyone – "high hopes melted in a boiling pot."

Menchanko-tei — 19 | 10 | 14 | $20

131 E. 45th St. (bet. Lexington & 3rd Aves.), 212-986-6805 ◐[S]
43-45 W. 55th St. (bet. 5th & 6th Aves.), 212-247-1585 ◐[S]
5 World Trade Ctr. Concourse, 212-432-4210

■ These Japanese noodle shops are the "genuine article: cheap, fast, healthy, tasty" and patronized by Japanese; their "flavorful" "hot noodle soups" and sake hit the spot on a "cold, wet day."

Mercantile Grill
▽ 17 | 18 | 15 | $25

126 Pearl St. (bet. Hanover Sq. & Wall St.), 212-482-1221

◪ Only two years old, this "old-fashioned"–looking Wall Street American hangout already "feels like home"; overall, it's "good", even if a few think it "should be better."

Merchants, N.Y. ◐S
15 | 17 | 13 | $26

1125 First Ave. (62nd St.), 212-832-1551
521 Columbus Ave. (bet. 85th & 86th Sts.), 212-721-3689
112 Seventh Ave. (bet. 16th & 17th Sts.), 212-366-7267

◪ With wine bars, cigar and martini lounges, sidewalk cafes and sink-into-a-sofa living rooms plus trendy New American light fare, these "appealing", scenic gathering spots are often jammed; but watch out for Madonna wanna-bes at the East Side branch.

Meridiana ◐S
16 | 17 | 15 | $30

2756 Broadway (bet. 105th & 106th Sts.), 212-222-4453

◪ The lack of "date places" in Morningside Heights causes lovelorn locals to look kindly upon this Pompeii ruin–style Italian for its "tasty" pasta and "friendly" (if slow) service; P.S. check out the lovely garden.

Meriken ◐S
18 | 14 | 16 | $29

189 Seventh Ave. (21st St.), 212-620-9684

◪ A seemingly "timeless" Chelsea Japanese with "reliable", "fresh" fish, some "wonderful cooked dishes" and "*Miami Vice* deco" decor; most like the "low-key" ambiance, but a few call for "redecoration."

Merlot Bar & Grill ◐S
17 | 19 | 15 | $38

48 W. 63rd St. (bet. B'way & Columbus Ave.), 212-363-7568

◪ Faced with hundreds of wines (over 80 Merlots) and surreal Willy Wonka surroundings, it's hard to focus on the often "quite good" French-American food at this Lincoln Center spot.

Mesa City S
19 | 16 | 16 | $33

1059 Third Ave. (bet. 62nd & 63rd Sts.), 212-207-1919

◪ "Brassy" Southwestern Eastsider featuring scaled-down (price- and portion-wise) versions of media chef Bobby Flay's explosive cooking modeled on his Mesa Grill; given the noise, young after-work drinking crowds and "limited menu", many prefer the "original."

MESA GRILL S
24 | 21 | 21 | $43

102 Fifth Ave. (bet. 15th & 16th Sts.), 212-807-7400

■ A "must go"; Bobby Flay's "always good", hugely successful Southwestern near Union Square serves some of the "most inventive food" in the city; its high-energy, lofty space is a "must-see" but can be so crowded that regulars don't even "try to talk."

Meskerem S
▽ 20 | 12 | 16 | $18

682 Eleventh Ave. (49th St.), 212-541-7858
468 W. 47th St. (bet. 9th & 10th Aves.), 212-664-0520 ◐

■ On the far West Side, African food aficionados "fight with cab drivers for the few seats" in two of NYC's "most authentic" Ethiopians; the highly spiced, lowly priced stews are an "escape from the ordinary."

Messina Cafe S
▽ 21 | 16 | 19 | $31

566 Third Ave. (bet. 37th & 38th Sts.), 212-557-0055

■ While scoping the "sidewalk bustle", locals enjoy "moderately priced" "hearty Mediterranean" dishes and "friendly service" at this "promising" Murray Hill newcomer.

Métisse S
21 | 17 | 20 | $35

239 W. 105th St. (bet. Amsterdam Ave. & B'way), 212-666-8825

■ "Tucked away" in "SoCo" (south of Columbia U), this "offbeat", reasonably priced French bistro earns "kudos for effort, enthusiasm" and "good" food; thereabouts, it's pretty much it for "gracious" dining.

	F	D	S	C

Metronome ◐ ▽ | 17 | 20 | 16 | $37

915 Broadway (21st St.), 212-505-7400

◪ With "couches, candles, high ceilings and great live music", this "reborn", "elegant", art deco Flatiron supper club sets the scene well, even if its Mediterranean food and service are "hit or miss."

Metropolitan Cafe ◐[S] | 15 | 16 | 16 | $30

959 First Ave. (bet. 52nd & 53rd Sts.), 212-759-5600

◪ "Outdoor summer dining" and brunch highlight this "serviceable" Sutton Place American; its bright, sprawling digs and "predictable" "decent" fare define basic dining.

Mezzaluna ◐[S] | 18 | 14 | 16 | $34

1295 Third Ave. (bet. 74th & 75th Sts.), 212-535-9600

◪ An East Side "closet" serving some of NY's "best, overpriced" pizza and pasta to "trendy", fashionable clients who celebrate "new chairs" that fit "American seats."

Mezzanotte (Queens) [S] ▽ | 20 | 17 | 18 | $28

32-11 Broadway (bet. 32nd & 33rd Sts.), 718-274-6611

■ Brick-oven pizzas "packed full of punch" and some of the "best marinara in Queens" inspire visits to this "glitzy" Astoria Southern Italian; allow time to explore the area's old-country groceries and cafes.

Mezze | 20 | 15 | 16 | $23

10 E. 44th St. (bet. 5th & Madison Aves.), 212-697-6644

■ "Matthew Kenney strikes again" with "terrific" Mediterranean and Moroccan fare at this "stylish" Midtown location; his appetizers, flatbread pizza, soups and wraps give lunch a "delicious" "different point of view"; delivery and catering are "nicely done" too.

Mezzogiorno ◐[S] | 19 | 16 | 15 | $38

195 Spring St. (Sullivan St.), 212-334-2112

◪ Fans love to sit by this SoHo Italian's French doors and enjoy "delightful" pasta, pizza and salads while scoping the street scene; critics call it "pricey", "pushy" and, worst of all, "boring."

Michael's | 22 | 21 | 20 | $48

24 W. 55th St. (bet. 5th & 6th Aves.), 212-767-0555

■ "Ever so civilized", with "first-class" contemporary art, food and service, Michael McCarty's celebrity-lined Californian is "quite the publishing/entertainment scene at lunch", and also a major breakfast club; critics fault the "turnaround time" (long) and expense account mentality, but it's "a damn good place even if it's from Santa Monica."

Mickey Mantle's ◐[S] | 13 | 17 | 15 | $29

42 Central Park S. (bet. 5th & 6th Aves.), 212-688-7777

■ "No. 7 shrine" with "a great name and location" (off Central Park) plus sports memorabilia, game-watching TVs and affordable, edible burgers, ribs and waffle fries; dads and sons "love it."

Mi Cocina [S] | 22 | 15 | 17 | $31

57 Jane St. (Hudson St.), 212-627-8273

■ This West Village kitchen proves that "Mexican cuisine is not an oxymoron"; "so what if it's crowded and noisy", its regulars are happy to wait for "real" south of the border food and prices.

Mid City Grill ▽ | 19 | 16 | 19 | $35

575 Fifth Ave. (47th St.), 212-682-1000

■ Rusty Staub's "worthy successor" tenders "imaginative", not too costly American food with "attentive" service in a "perfect" Midtown "business lunch" locale; try the steak or ribs.

Mike & Tony's (Brooklyn) S
23 | 21 | 21 | $43

239 Fifth Ave. (Carroll St.), 718-857-2800
■ "Pay your respects to a great porterhouse" at Cucina-owner Michael Ayoub's "wonderful" Park Slope American grill; here, everything from the "olde NY" saloon setting to the "excellent" food and service is done with "flair."

Mike's American Bar & Grill ●S
17 | 15 | 17 | $24

650 Tenth Ave. (bet. 45th & 46th Sts.), 212-246-4115
☑ In "no man's land" (Hell's Kitchen), "quirky" theme changes, "abundant" American chow and "easygoing" manners earn this "inexpensive" "old-timer" pre-theater applause.

Mill Korean Restaurant S
▽ 18 | 13 | 14 | $17

2895 Broadway (bet. 112th & 113th Sts.), 212-666-7653
☑ Though no substitute for Koreatown, this student-priced, "spunky", "bare-bones", Columbia-area Korean is "nose-running spicy and good"; "believe it or not, they make egg creams."

Milos
– | – | – | VE

125 W. 55th St. (bet. 6th & 7th Aves.), 212-245-7400
Some of the world's freshest fish are cast in starring roles at this recently opened, handsome, high-ceilinged modern Midtown Greek; its major drawback is that it's deceptively expensive ordering fish by the pound, but we suspect Ulysses would have rushed home for this.

Minetta Tavern ●S
17 | 16 | 17 | $33

113 MacDougal St. (bet. Bleecker & W. 3rd Sts.), 212-475-3850
■ It takes a "big stomach" and sense of history to appreciate this '30s-era Village Italian; its "sturdy", midpriced food, like its service, is grounded in "old recipes and old values" – just "step back in time and relax."

Mingala Burmese S
17 | 11 | 15 | $21

21-23 E. Seventh St. (bet. 2nd & 3rd Aves.), 212-529-3656
☑ Early-bird specials ($5.50) make this unprepossessing East Village Burmese an "incredible" bargain; its "flavorful", "exotic" food, though "a bit greasy" and "slow" in arriving, is "very appealing."

Mingala West S
18 | 13 | 16 | $22

325 Amsterdam Ave. (bet. 75th & 76th Sts.), 212-873-0787
■ "When your group is arguing Chinese vs. Indian vs. Thai", this "simple" West Side Burmese may well be the compromise "solution"; it's "a tasty break" with "lots of interesting dishes."

Mi Nidito ●S
17 | 9 | 15 | $20

852 Eighth Ave. (bet. 51st & 52nd Sts.), 212-265-0022
■ This West Side storefront is "ready to please" with a "rainbow" of margarita flavors and a "healthy Mex" menu with vegetarian options, all cheap enough to make choosing risk-free.

Miracle Grill ●S
20 | 16 | 16 | $29

112 First Ave. (bet. 6th & 7th Sts.), 212-254-2353
415 Bleecker St. (bet. Bank & W. 11th Sts.), 212-924-1900
■ With one of the city's best backyards and "wonderful SW food at a price you can't beat", this East Village miracle epitomizes what NYers are "living here for"; to avoid waits at the original site, try the new indoor-only Bleecker location.

Mirezi S
23 | 22 | 20 | $41

59 Fifth Ave. (bet. 12th & 13th Sts.), 212-242-9709
■ This "high-style" Village Asian fuses Anita Lo's (ex Bouley) "original" takes on Korean, Japanese and Indochinese fare with an "ultracool" modern setting; neophytes can rely on the "knowledgeable" staff for advice, but must plan to pay for "luxury."

Mishima [S] ▽ 21 | 12 | 18 | $28
164 Lexington Ave. (bet. 30th & 31st Sts.), 212-532-9596
■ "Best value for sushi" contender, this Murray Hill Japanese is "cramped but efficient", with "top-notch sushi" at "bargain" rates; it's a "great place" for lunch if decor isn't important to you.

Miss Saigon [S] 18 | 12 | 16 | $23
1425 Third Ave. (bet. 80th & 81st Sts.), 212-988-8828
473 Columbus Ave. (bet. 82nd & 83rd Sts.), 212-595-8919
◪ Modern, fast-food (in a good way) crosstown Vietnamese duo whose "spicy", "cheap", vegetable-laden dishes are a "welcome addition to pasta city"; they're often "crowded and cramped."

Mitali East/West ◐[S] 20 | 14 | 17 | $24
296 Bleecker St. (7th Ave. S.), 212-989-1367
334 E. Sixth St. (bet. 1st & 2nd Aves.), 212-533-2508
■ "Dependable", "modestly priced" Indians known for rich curries and "warm smiles" in two Village locations – "East is better for food, the reverse for decor"; both are deservedly popular.

Mme. Romaine de Lyon [S] 16 | 13 | 16 | $30
132 E. 61st St. (bet. Lexington & Park Aves.), 212-758-2422
◪ Omelets-R-Us is the byword for this East Side "ladies lunch delight" featuring over 500 choices plus eggstra specials; its "bright" premises, prices and the nonegg dishes mostly draw clucks.

Mocca Hungarian [S]⊘ 17 | 10 | 16 | $23
1588 Second Ave. (bet. 82nd & 83rd Sts.), 212-734-6470
◪ For Mittel European "mothering", Hungarian soul food and people-watching, this Yorkville "old", as in "old", standby has no peer – where else can you get a three-course lunch for under $7?

Molyvos ◐[S] – | – | – | E
871 Seventh Ave. (bet. 55th & 56th Sts.), 212-582-7500
Riding a media blitz, this "sophisticated" Greek has become an overnight success near Carnegie Hall thanks to its adventurous menu and comfy attractive setting; only high prices upset diners' enthusiasm.

Momoyama [S] – | – | – | M
1572 Second Ave. (bet. 81st & 82nd Sts.), 212-988-1188
You can sit up front and watch studious Japanese chefs prepare sushi, or head to the back to Zen out by the soothing waterfall at this informal, clean East Side newcomer; it's still too new to call.

Monkey Bar [S] 21 | 23 | 20 | $48
Hotel Elysée, 60 E. 54th St. (bet. Madison & Park Aves.), 212-838-2600
◪ Bankers and baby boomers "feel like movie stars" in the "jazz age" glamour of this Midtown dining room; its "teeming bar scene" and stylish Contemporary American food make it a "must-go."

Monsoon ◐[S] 18 | 11 | 14 | $22
2850 Broadway (bet. 110th & 111th Sts.), 212-665-2700
435 Amsterdam Ave. (81st St.), 212-580-8686
◪ Westsiders storm these "sterile", "elbow fest" Asians for "tasty", low-cost Vietnamese food; fans say they'll "blow you away."

Monster Sushi – | – | – | M
158 W. 23rd St. (bet. 6th & 7th Aves.), 212-620-9131
Inviting blond wood and a hospitable staff greet Chelsea diners in need of a sushi fix; convenience and modest prices are added draws.

Mont Blanc 17 | 14 | 19 | $31
306 W. 48th St. (bet. 8th & 9th Aves.), 212-582-9648
◪ "Homey" Theater District Continental with "solid" virtues and few flaws; go for a filling meal at a fair price, but don't expect more.

Montebello
21 | 19 | 22 | $44

120 E. 56th St. (bet. Lexington & Park Aves.), 212-753-1447
☑ "Gracious Italian hospitality" adds distinction to this "civilized" Midtowner's "pricey" fish and pasta; it's basically a "neighborhood place", but worth visiting even if it's not in your neighborhood.

Monte's Italian Restaurant
(Brooklyn) S
− | − | − | M

451 Carroll St. (bet. 3rd Ave. & Nevins St.), 718-624-8984
Opened in 1906 and still going strong, this midpriced Carroll Gardens red sauce Italian is one of the few places for a good, old-fashioned scaloppine or parmigiana; it's the real thing, including the old-world digs.

MONTRACHET S
26 | 21 | 24 | $57

239 W. Broadway (bet. Walker & White Sts.), 212-219-2777
■ For "world-class" wining and dining, Drew Nieporent's first TriBeCa restaurant – an "understated", slightly "spartan" French bistro with "masterful" service and a "superb" kitchen and cellar – is his "best"; it's a sure thing on any night, but may be most fun if you go for the $19.98 Friday prix fixe lunch and splurge on a fine burgundy.

Monzù ◗S
▽ 21 | 22 | 18 | $42

142 Mercer St. (Prince St.), 212-343-0333
■ "Decorated in gorgeous Mediterranean style", this "SoHo cave" (beneath the Downtown Guggenheim) "spotlights" Matthew Kenney's "sophisticated" take on Sicilian cuisine; despite start-up "kinks", it's already one of the hottest food destinations in town.

Moran's Chelsea S
17 | 17 | 17 | $32

146 Tenth Ave. (19th St.), 212-627-3030
☑ A "no blarney" Chelsea pub where young financiers and B&T hopefuls "hoist a few" in "dark", firelit surroundings; its "Irish country charm" and "hearty" steak and seafood fare are survivors.

Moreno S
20 | 18 | 20 | $39

65 Irving Pl. (18th St.), 212-673-3939
■ "Romantic in winter", with "lovely" alfresco dining in summer and "very good" regional Italian food year-round, this "Irving Place charmer" spells "ambiance" with a capital "A"; let owner Moreno Maltagliati, "the consummate host", handle your next party.

MORGAN COURT CAFE S
16 | 25 | 16 | $23

Pierpont-Morgan Library, 29 E. 36th St. (Madison Ave.), 212-685-0008
■ Lunching in this "spectacular", sun-splashed museum atrium is "better than Prozac for your mood"; weight-watchers report its "easy" salad and sandwich menu won't tempt you off your diet.

Mortimer's ◗S
15 | 14 | 14 | $45

1057 Lexington Ave. (75th St.), 212-517-6400
☑ East Side "club" where they "invented attitude"; as for the "dowdy" American food, the "geriatric Wasp" socialite crowd "likes it that way."

Morton's of Chicago S
23 | 20 | 21 | $53

551 Fifth Ave. (45th St.), 212-972-3315 ◗
90 West St. (bet. Albany & Cedar Sts.), 212-732-5665
☑ For "steak as it should be – thick, juicy, delicious and plenty of it" plus heavy cosseting, it's hard to beat this chain; though ranked with "Luger and Sparks" (no small achievement), its "clichéd" wood-paneled decor, high prices and Saran-wrapped raw meat "presentation" draw fire.

Motown Cafe ◗S
13 | 19 | 14 | $25

104 W. 57th St. (bet. 6th & 7th Aves.), 212-581-8030
☑ "Talented live performers" and memorabilia make this Midtown Motown shrine "entertaining" "fun", but less than supreme service and Soul Food cause some to "stay home and put on a CD instead."

	F	D	S	C

Mottsu S
| | − | − | − | M |

285 Mott St. (bet. Houston & Prince Sts.), 212-343-8017

Boxy, small Japanese sprinkling a dash of fresh, wallet-friendly sushi onto Little Italy's Mott Street; chatty staffers keep things informal while the sushi chefs work with military precision.

Moustache ◐S⇗
| | 22 | 12 | 15 | $17 |

265 E. 10th St. (bet. Ave. A & 1st Ave.), 212-228-2022
90 Bedford St. (bet. Barrow & Grove Sts.), 212-229-2220

Moustache Pitza (Brooklyn) S⇗
405 Atlantic Ave. (bet. Bond & Nevins Sts.), 718-852-5555

■ "Wonderful" ("Allah smiled") Middle Eastern cheap eats generate "brutal" waits at these simple cafes (Brooklyn is separately owned); their distinctive pitzas (pita-based pizza) "spoil you for any other kind."

Mr. Chow ◐S
| | 22 | 22 | 20 | $51 |

324 E. 57th St. (bet. 1st & 2nd Aves.), 212-751-9030

☑ Stargazing and Peking duck are major attractions at this "elegant" high-"glam", high-priced East Side Chinese; it's sure to "impress someone", although "pretensions are laid on a bit heavily."

Mr. Soup ⇗
| | 19 | 6 | 12 | $13 |

120 W. 44th St. (bet. B'way & 6th Ave.), 212-921-1812
108 E. 23rd St. (bet. Lexington Ave. & Park Ave. S.), 212-533-6513

☑ These lunchtime soup kitchens prove the axiom "a good soup makes a good lunch"; however, some counter that they're "souper expensive" for such low-rent surroundings.

Mr. Tang S
| | 17 | 15 | 16 | $25 |

50 Mott St. (Bayard St.), 212-233-8898
7523 Third Ave. (76th St.), Brooklyn, 718-748-0400
1884 86th St. (19th Ave.), Brooklyn, 718-256-2100 ⇗
2650 Coney Island Ave. (Ave. X), Brooklyn, 718-769-9444 ⇗

☑ With "surprisingly good" seafood but "lacking" in decor, this Chinese minidynasty is on a par with other neighborhood Chinese.

Mueng Thai S
| | ▽ 21 | 9 | 19 | $19 |

23 Pell St. (bet. Mott St. & Bowery), 212-406-4259

■ The "bargain lunch" at this "accommodating" Chinatown juror's delight is a spoiler for other Thais; especially noteworthy are its whole grilled fish, spring rolls and soft broad noodle dishes.

Muggs S
| | − | − | − | I |

406 E. 64th St. (bet. 1st & York Aves.), 212-371-2020

Expect baseball memorabilia and cheap American beer and burger eats at this East Side newcomer; the outdoor garden is a plus.

Mughlai ◐S
| | 19 | 14 | 16 | $27 |

320 Columbus Ave. (75th St.), 212-724-6363

☑ Probably the "best" West Side Indian, serving fairly priced, spicy food in "pleasant" digs ("not bad" but not great); critics split on service: "helpful" vs. "condescending."

Museum Cafe ◐S
| | 15 | 14 | 14 | $26 |

366 Columbus Ave. (77th St.), 212-799-0150

☑ "Reliable" for an "inexpensive" brunch and people-watching, this West Side "something for everyone", American diner-like cafe owes its "longevity" to the nearby Museum of Natural History.

Nadaman Hakubai S
| | ▽ 24 | 17 | 25 | $81 |

Kitano Hotel, 66 Park Ave. (38th St.), 212-885-7111

☑ "Beautiful" kaiseki dinners in an "antiseptic" room at "unreal prices" cause some to praise this "exquisite" Japanese but not pay frequent visits; it's small consolation that in Japan such dining is more expensive.

	F	D	S	C

Nadine's ◐ [S] — 18 | 17 | 18 | $28

99 Bank St. (Greenwich St.), 212-924-3165

■ Brunch at this "artsy" West Village Eclectic can "put sunshine into a rainy day"; "Dear Mom, Nadine treats me better than you so I won't be home for dinner."

Nakagawa — 19 | 14 | 17 | $33

7 W. 44th St. (bet. 5th & 6th Aves.), 212-869-8077

◪ Handy for pre-theater, this "conservative" Midtown Japanese has "very fresh fish" and good noodle dishes; but it also has "sterile" decor and staid service that "can make a meal boring."

Nam Phuong [S] — ▽ 18 | 9 | 14 | $19

19 Sixth Ave. (bet. Walker & White Sts.), 212-431-7715

■ "Fast, inexpensive" Vietnamese, like this very plain TriBeCan, threaten to "replace Thai as the 'in' Asian dining experience"; cognoscenti say this one's "terrific bargain" food is "the real thing."

Nanni Il Valletto ◐ — 22 | 19 | 21 | $54

133 E. 61st St. (bet. Lexington & Park Aves.), 212-838-3939

■ The myriad advantages of "being a regular" at this "warm and welcoming", East Side Northern Italian don't come cheap; however, well-heeled regulars don't mind shelling out for some of NY's "best pasta", seamlessly served in quiet, elegant quarters.

Nanni's — 23 | 16 | 21 | $46

146 E. 46th St. (bet. Lexington & 3rd Aves.), 212-697-4161

■ "Nothing too new but all done well and served with grace" at this business-oriented Midtown Northern Italian; here, "meticulously prepared" classics and "old-fashioned", "Italian your way" service demonstrate their staying power (even if it's "a little boring" to some).

Naples 45 — 18 | 16 | 15 | $26

200 Park Ave. (45th St., bet. Lexington & Vanderbilt Aves.), 212-972-7001

◪ "Top-notch" Neapolitan pizza (by the meter) and many other "authentic" Italian choices are offered in this spacious eat-in or take-out setting; critics say it "feels like a cafeteria, charges like a restaurant" and at lunch is "noisier than Grand Central."

Neary's ◐ [S] — 17 | 14 | 20 | $34

358 E. 57th St. (bet. 1st & 2nd Aves.), 212-751-1434

■ Jimmy Neary, NYC's "host of hosts", keeps his Sutton Place Irish pub "a great neighborhood place for a steak and good stiff drink"; being greeted by Jimmy alone is worth the price of a meal.

Negril ◐ [S] — 17 | 16 | 15 | $26

362 W. 23rd St. (bet. 8th & 9th Aves.), 212-807-6411

■ With its "carnival" feel and jerk chicken, this cheap Chelsea Caribbean has "everything but the ocean breeze to transport you to Jamaica."

Nello ◐ [S] — 18 | 16 | 15 | $42

696 Madison Ave. (bet. 62nd & 63rd Sts.), 212-980-9099

◪ "Chic and buzzing", this East Side Italian offers good, "pricey pasta"; however, people-watching from the street-side seats is the main draw.

New Chao Chow [S] 💳̸ — ▽ 19 | 5 | 11 | $15

111 Mott St. (bet. Canal & Hester Sts.), 212-226-2590

◪ "Cheap even for Chinatown", this "dismal"-looking noodle shop does good things, especially if you "use your arms to communicate."

New City Cafe (Brooklyn) [S] — 24 | 20 | 21 | $42

246 DeKalb Ave. (Vanderbilt Ave.), 718-622-5607

■ This "romantic" BAM-area brownstone with a "quaint" backyard is a "congenial" backdrop for "inventive" New American food; service can be slow, but that's easily forgiven as the food is so good.

	F	D	S	C
New Pasteur [S] 🚫💳	19	6	13	$15

85 Baxter St. (bet. Bayard & Canal Sts.), 212-608-3656
◪ "Only in Saigon" can you get a "better deal" on "good, fast", low-cost Vietnamese food (or a tastier "lemongrass pork chop"); its Chinatown digs are "ugly as sin", but convenient for "jury duty."

	F	D	S	C
New Prospect Cafe (Brooklyn) [S]	20	13	17	$26

393 Flatbush Ave. (bet. Plaza St. & Sterling Pl.), 718-638-2148
■ This "tiny New Age" American-Eclectic with its "emphasis on natural ingredients", good wines and "casual" manners more than suits its Park Slope neighbors; to prospect for yourself, try brunch.

	F	D	S	C
New World Coffee	14	11	12	$9

1595 Third Ave. (bet. 89th & 90th Sts.), 212-426-9595 [S]
1246 Lexington Ave. (84th St.), 212-772-1422 [S]
1159 Third Ave. (bet. 67th & 68th Sts.), 212-472-1598 [S]
1046 Third Ave. (bet. 61st & 62nd Sts.), 212-980-2180 [S]
135 E. 57th St. (Lexington Ave.), 212-751-4027 [S]
830 Third Ave. (51st St.), 212-980-1748
400 Madison Ave. (bet. 47th & 48th Sts.), 212-838-2854
342 Madison Ave. (bet. 43rd & 44th Sts.), 212-557-5077
723 Third Ave. (45th St.), 212-599-4142
Columbia University, 2929 Broadway (114th St.), 212-932-0300 [S]
416 Columbus Ave. (80th St.), 212-874-1936 [S]
2151 Broadway (bet. 75th & 76th Sts.), 212-496-0300 [S]
159 Columbus Ave. (67th St.), 212-362-0100 [S]
Olympic Tower, 645 Fifth Ave. (51st St.), 212-980-9230
525 Seventh Ave. (bet. 34th & 35th Sts.), 212-719-4526
488 Sixth Ave. (12th St.), 212-675-0779 [S]
449 Sixth Ave. (bet. 11th & 12th Sts.), 212-633-1966 [S]
100 Wall St. (Water St.), 212-514-5011
412 W. Broadway (bet. Prince & Spring Sts.), 212-431-1015 [S]
1 New York Plaza (South Ferry), 212-785-8345
1 Broadway (Battery Pl.), 212-248-6250 🚫💳
125 Seventh Ave. (Carroll St.), Brooklyn, 718-638-9633 [S]
107-24 Continental Ave. (bet. Austin St. & Queens Blvd.), Queens, 718-261-0238 [S]
◪ Sleek bean bars with coffees, sandwiches and treats to rival Starbucks; amenities vary by location with some offering good people-watching, seating space and service, and others not.

	F	D	S	C
New World Grill [S]	18	16	16	$28

Worldwide Plaza, 329 W. 49th St. (bet. 8th & 9th Aves.), 212-957-4745
■ In nice weather, a "hidden" courtyard provides the ambiance this Hell's Kitchen New American's small interior lacks; but year-round, its "imaginative" kitchen provides inexpensive snacks and grills that are "perfect" for lunch or paired with a movie.

	F	D	S	C
New York Noodle Town ◐ [S] 🚫💳	21	5	12	$17

28 ½ Bowery (Bayard St.), 212-349-0923
■ You can't go wrong with any of the soups, salt-baked seafood, BBQs or noodle dishes at this "excellent" Chinatown Cantonese, which is lucky since you can't communicate with the help; happily, it's also too "crowded" for diners to notice the lack of decor.

	F	D	S	C
Nha Trang [S] 🚫💳	21	6	13	$16

87 Baxter St. (bet. Bayard & Canal Sts.), 212-233-5948
■ Join the "mix of Chinatown locals, tourists, hipsters" and jurors who find this "down and dirty" Vietnamese "guilty of wonderful food at low prices"; you won't find any "faux phos" here.

Nica's ◐[S] ▽ 18 | 20 | 18 | $42
Stanhope Hotel, 995 Fifth Ave. (bet. 80th & 81st Sts.), 212-717-0303
■ With the ubiquitous Matthew Kenney guiding the kitchen, look for some of NYC's best people-watching and Mediterranean eating at this latest revision of a posh hotel cafe.

Nice Restaurant [S] 19 | 11 | 13 | $23
35 E. Broadway (bet. Catherine & Market Sts.), 212-406-9510
◪ It's best to visit this "fast flying", "consistently good" Chinatown dim sum hall "with someone who can order in Chinese"; be prepared for less than lovely decor and din.

Nick & Toni's Cafe ◐[S] – | – | – | E
100 W. 67th St. (bet. B'way & Columbus Ave.), 212-496-4000
The up-and-coming Lincoln Center restaurant scene now has a casual but special French-Italian with an outstanding pedigree (Jonathan Waxman, ex Jams, consulting and Darren McRonald, ex Chez Panisse, behind the stove); consider it for a fast informal meal.

NICK'S PIZZA (Queens) **[S]≠** 25 | 14 | 19 | $17
108-26 Ascan Ave. (bet. Austin & Burns Sts.), 718-263-1126
■ There's "pizza for kings in Queens" (Forest Hills to be precise), where the brick-oven pies, calzones and cannoli plus friendliness draw raves.

Nicola Paone 20 | 18 | 19 | $46
207 E. 34th St. (bet. 2nd & 3rd Aves.), 212-889-3239
◪ A Murray Hill Italian standby featuring "vintage wine and menu"; it does well by its regulars who are willing to pay "new-world prices" for "old-world charm" and quality; critics say "way past its prime."

Nicola's ◐[S] 21 | 16 | 19 | $45
146 E. 84th St. (bet. Lexington & 3rd Aves.), 212-249-9850
◪ "Charter members" of this "Sunday night" Upper East Side pasta "club" swear by its noodles and chops; the rest swear at its "snooty" attitude, "predictable" menu and initiation fee ambiance.

Night Gallery ◐[S] 11 | 18 | 13 | $23
117 Seventh Ave. S. (bet. W. 10th & Christopher Sts.), 212-675-5244
◪ "Rod Serling meets MTV" at this "eerie" Village theme pub; "the look is cool" but touristy and the American food and service are "average."

Niko's Mediterranean Grill ◐[S] 19 | 12 | 15 | $23
2161 Broadway (76th St.), 212-873-7000
◪ Fast-forward through this "price-is-right" Westsider's "vast menu" to the Greek specialties and the place "will transport you"; N.B. it's as "uncomfortable as a crowded Athens cafe."

Nino's ◐[S] 22 | 20 | 21 | $45
1354 First Ave. (bet. 72nd & 73rd Sts.), 212-988-0002
■ Nino, the "charming" host of this old-fashioned East Side Northern Italian, spreads the "best welcome mat in NY", while low lighting, piano music and classical cooking give his place "the comfortable familiarity" his moneyed clientele seeks.

Nippon 22 | 18 | 20 | $45
155 E. 52nd St. (bet. Lexington & 3rd Aves.), 212-758-0226
◪ This Japanese fixture for "serene, solid sushi" in Bloomie's country has many admirers; yet others find better surroundings, service and as good or better sushi "elsewhere" for less.

NIRVANA ◐[S] 17 | 25 | 18 | $42
40 Central Park S. (bet. 5th & 6th Aves.), 212-486-5700
■ "Sunset views of Central Park" in a "sumptuous", "dream" setting overwhelm the "typical" Indian food at this lofty perch; exotic and romantic, it's "a tourist trap" where everyone is happy to be trapped.

NOBU 🅂
27 | 24 | 24 | $61

105 Hudson St. (Franklin St.), 212-219-0500

■ Nobu Matsuhisa's celeb-studded Nouvelle Japanese with Peruvian accents continues to justify its hype and high prices; fans insist each dish is a "culinary miracle", the setting "witty" and the operation run by well-drilled pros; the main complaint: "it's impossible" to get in.

NoHo Star ◐🅂
17 | 15 | 15 | $25

330 Lafayette St. (Bleecker St.), 212-925-0070

☑ In NoHo, this Asian-influenced Eclectic provides breakfast to midnight sustenance for neighborhood types and "preppy" hangers-on; "sometimes it's a no-no, sometimes a star."

Nola ◐🅂
– | – | – | M

428 Amsterdam Ave. (bet. 80th & 81st Sts.), 212-501-7515

Promising new West Side American with a warm open kitchen and lively, 30 wanna-be crowd; there's a big choice of tequilas plus 50¢ oysters and $2 martinis at the bar (Monday–Saturday, 5–8 PM).

Noodle Pudding (Brooklyn) 🅂⇸
20 | 16 | 18 | $28

38 Henry St. (bet. Cranberry & Middagh Sts.), 718-625-3737

■ This Brooklyn Heights Italian's "rustic" home cooking "speaks for itself", as does its "unpretentious" storefront setting and "caring" manners; only a few get a different message: "inconsistent."

Noodles on 28 ◐🅂
18 | 9 | 14 | $16

394 Third Ave. (28th St.), 212-679-2888

■ Watching "good", "cheap" Chinese "grub" made in the window is this Murray Hill noodle shop's only "visible decor", but who needs "atmosphere with such tasty food" (and such fast delivery).

Northside Cafe (Brooklyn) 🅂
– | – | – | M

119 Kent Ave. (N. 7th St.), 718-388-9000

An economical two-tier pricing system (for individuals vs. family-style), a wide choice of Italian dishes, comfy quarters and a large garden make this newcomer north of the Williamsburg Bridge a good bet.

Notaro 🅂
19 | 16 | 18 | $34

635 Second Ave. (bet. 34th & 35th Sts.), 212-686-3400

☑ "Tuscanissimo" is the word coined by fans to describe this Italian's "wonderful breads and pastas", "tasteful" decor and "hospitable" vibes; however, some find it "unexciting."

Nova Grill 🅂
18 | 18 | 16 | $30

2330 Broadway (85th St.), 212-579-5100

☑ Opinions on this "dramatic" West Side Neo-American staffed by "model/actor types" vary from "a strong first showing" (the majority) to "fizzled fast" (minority); for best results, "sit upstairs" where it's "roomy" and less noisy and stick to pizza and salad.

Novecento ◐🅂
▽ 17 | 15 | 15 | $28

343 W. Broadway (bet. Broome & Grand Sts.), 212-925-4706

■ This newly redecorated, easily affordable Euro-Argentinean is a "fun place to eat and party" without the "snooty" attitudes of other SoHo places; few mind if the staff sometimes seems "overwhelmed."

Novitá 🅂
22 | 19 | 20 | $42

102 E. 22nd St. (Park Ave. S.), 212-677-2222

■ "Great seafood", "handmade ravioli" and "charming waiters" in quiet surroundings – no wonder Flatiron denizens are impressed with this Italian hideaway; indeed, its "magical food" has made it a "model heaven" (could it be calorie-free?).

Ñ 33 Crosby ⬤🄢↪
18 | 19 | 14 | $22

33 Crosby St. (bet. Broome & Grand Sts.), 212-219-8856

■ An "easygoing" SoHo watering hole that "pumps out sangria and flamenco music" along with Spanish tapas; space is "tight", the decor "cool" and portions "small" at this "mob scene."

Nyonya ⬤🄢↪
▽ 22 | 14 | 13 | $18

194 Grand St. (Mulberry St.), 212-334-3669

◪ Sample Asian "street food" (the "original fusion cuisine") at this big, "bargain" Malaysian Chinatown yearling; it's spicy and "delicious", but be ready for "unfamiliar" tastes, crowds and language barriers.

Oak Room 🄢
19 | 24 | 20 | $49

Plaza Hotel, 768 Fifth Ave. (Central Park S.), 212-546-5330

◪ "You won't see Cary Grant types" anymore, but this "dignified" oak-paneled American is still "good for a quiet dinner" "for people who lack real clubs"; still, to some it's an "overpriced" "ship that's sailed."

Oaks, The 🄢
▽ 19 | 19 | 17 | $37

49 Grove St. (Bleecker St.), 212-243-8885

■ "Everybody sings" at the piano bar in this "beautifully redone" Village American; there's "good food", but it's more "fun for drinks" and music.

OCEANA
26 | 24 | 24 | $57

55 E. 54th St. (bet. Madison & Park Aves.), 212-759-5941

■ "As fine a fish place as exists anywhere", this "impeccable", "top-drawer" Midtowner has cruise-ship elegant decor and "celestial" seafood for comparable prices; check out the private "wine-cellar dining room" and "true value" "prix fixe lunch."

Ocean Grill ⬤🄢
23 | 21 | 20 | $42

384 Columbus Ave. (bet. 78th & 79th Sts.), 212-579-2300

■ "Desperately needed on the Upper West Side", Steve Hanson's "excellent newcomer" has "delicious grilled fish" and a "wonderful raw bar"; add "gracious" service and a "comfortable" setting and it's no wonder it's packed and often has "horrendous noise levels."

Ocean Palace (Brooklyn) ⬤🄢
20 | 12 | 15 | $21

5423 Eighth Ave. (55th St.), 718-871-8080
1418 Ave. U (bet. 14th & 15th Sts.) 718-376-3838

◪ "Children stare" as fish "swim from the tank onto your dish" at these Brooklyn Chinese "ocean shack"–style "dim sum heavens"; besides a "cheap", "large selection" of "terrific food" there's parking, too; for best results go with a group that isn't afraid to get down and dirty.

Odeon ⬤🄢
19 | 18 | 17 | $36

145 W. Broadway (Thomas St.), 212-233-0507

◪ A "legendary" "old friend" that "still has energy", this TriBeCa American "gets the stars and star-watchers" and, put simply, is "a great place to unwind"; it's "open conveniently late" with reliable "bistro-style food at affordable prices", so "long waits" are common.

Odessa ⬤🄢
15 | 9 | 13 | $17

119 Ave. A (bet. 7th St. & St. Marks Pl.), 212-253-1470

◪ "You can't beat the price, the portions" or the "waitresses' accents" at this "funky reverse chic" East Village Eastern European coffee shop that's both a "place to quell those late-night munchies" and a "favorite breakfast spot"; though "spruced up", it's "still a hole."

Official All Star Cafe ⬤🄢
10 | 19 | 13 | $23

1540 Broadway (45th St.), 212-840-8326

◪ "If you're into sports, burgers and beer", this Times Square themery filled with TV screens and memorabilia may thrill you; it's "great for kids", but poor sports label it "a step down from McD's" and "think Gretzky made the matzo ball soup" possibly by boiling pucks.

129

F	D	S	C

O.G. 🅂
22 | 15 | 18 | $27
507 E. Sixth St. (bet. Aves. A & B), 212-477-4649
■ This "intimate", "inventive" Pan-Asian is like "China Grill but at East Village prices"; it's a "good" "little hideaway" for "something different", with a "dark, casual setting" and "so kind" staff.

Oikawa ◐
▽ **20 | 18 | 18 | $38**
805 Third Ave., 2nd fl. (50th St.), 212-980-1400
■ Such "sophisticated, innovative Japanese cuisine" and "sublime quietude" are "rare" in Midtown; thus, fans wonder "why more people haven't discovered" this "beautiful, modern" midpriced place.

Old Bermuda Inn
(Staten Island) 🅂
▽ **17 | 23 | 18 | $39**
2512 Arthur Kill Rd. (Bloomingdale Rd. & Rossville Ave.), 718-948-7600
■ "Go see the antique decor" at this "lovely" 1716 house, now an "ok" Continental eatery; its "cozy, intimate dining rooms" are "a must for romantics" and make you "forget you're in a restaurant."

Old Devil Moon 🅂
17 | 16 | 15 | $19
511 E. 12th St. (bet. Aves. A & B), 212-475-4357
☑ "Funky", "freaky" East Village Southern "hole-in-the-wall" serving huge portions of "kitschy cheap food" (e.g. "catfish sandwiches", "chicken-fried chicken") to "people who don't own combs."

Old Homestead 🅂
21 | 15 | 18 | $48
56 Ninth Ave. (bet. 14th & 15th Sts.), 212-242-9040
☑ "Meat plain and simple, no-frills" is the tale of this 1868 West Village steakhouse standby where massive helpings – "looks like the cow died on the plate" – of fine beef and lobster keep regulars coming; for others it's "drab", "overpriced" and "medium quality."

Old San Juan 🅂
18 | 12 | 16 | $21
765 Ninth Ave. (bet. 51st & 52nd Sts.), 212-262-6761
☑ A "welcome addition to the ethnic eating scene", this "authentic" West Midtown newcomer "transports you to Puerto Rico"; it's "perfect for sharing", with "excellent" gumbo, mofongo, etc., but "zero atmosphere" and "s-l-o-o-w" service.

Old Town Bar ◐🅂
14 | 17 | 15 | $19
45 E. 18th St. (bet. B'way & Park Ave. S.), 212-529-6732
☑ "If you squint, you can see the ghost of Boss Tweed" at this 1892 "landmark" Flatiron saloon "right out of a Mickey Spillane novel"; "great burgers" for low prices earn praise, but drink comes first.

Olé 🅂
17 | 13 | 17 | $32
434 Second Ave. (bet. 24th & 25th Sts.), 212-725-1953
☑ "Lively and bustling with Spanish singers", this "festive" Gramercy Park "old standard" has lobster as its "main attraction"; critics call it "tacky", "cramped" and dangerous to the hearing.

Ollie's ◐🅂
16 | 9 | 12 | $18
2957 Broadway (116th St.), 212-932-3300
2315 Broadway (84th St.), 212-362-3712
1991 Broadway (67th St.), 212-595-8181
200B W. 44th St. (bet. B'way & 8th Ave.), 212-921-5988
☑ "Soups are meals in themselves" and there's other "tasty", "cheap" Chinese fare at these "mob scenes"; but critics can be harsh: "I'd rather be fried with an egg roll through my heart than eat here."

Omen 🅂
22 | 19 | 19 | $40
113 Thompson St. (bet. Prince & Spring Sts.), 212-925-8923
■ Though "romantic", it "can get expensive" at this "authentic" Kyoto-style SoHo Japanese; it's a "a spot of tranquility" where you'll enjoy "refreshingly polite" service and "beautiful" steak, noodles and sushi.

O'Neals' ◐[S] — 15 | 15 | 16 | $32
49 W. 64th St. (bet. B'way & CPW), 212-787-4663
◪ You'll find good "everyday food" at this "attractive", pubby Lincoln Center Continental "old favorite"; knowing owner Mike O'Neal is half the fun, but critics say "fare is fair."

147 ◐[S] — – | – | – | M
147 W. 15th St. (bet. 6th & 7th Aves.), 212-929-5000
Superhot Chelsea newcomer built into a former firehouse that includes a dining area-cum-jazz club, with a lounge and cigar bar to come; early reports indicate that the New American food and the hip ambiance are lighting a five-alarm blaze.

ONE IF BY LAND, TIBS ◐[S] — 25 | 27 | 24 | $57
17 Barrow St. (bet. 7th Ave. S. & W. 4th St.), 212-228-0822
■ This "most romantic" 1726 Village "townhouse", once owned by Aaron Burr, is a favorite "place to propose" with lilting piano music and firelight as a backdrop; it also has "sumptuous" Continental cuisine (try the signature beef Wellington); "starting an affair?, patching up after a fight?, keeping the flame burning? – this is the place."

101 (Brooklyn) **◐[S]** — 17 | 14 | 15 | $28
10018 Fourth Ave. (101st St.), 718-833-1313
◪ "*Saturday Night Fever* eats out" at this Bay Ridge Italian with a "variety of pasta and fish specials" to go with a "busy bar" scene; for some it's merely "mezza mezza", "overcrowded" and overwrought.

107 West [S] — 17 | 12 | 16 | $25
2787 Broadway (bet. 107th & 108th Sts.), 212-864-1555
◪ "Dependable Cajun and Tex-Mex dishes" mark this "affordable Columbia U hangout"; it's a "good standby", but some feel "quality and service vary."

Onieals Grand St. ◐[S] — ▽ 19 | 22 | 19 | $37
174 Grand St. (bet. Centre & Mulberry Sts.), 212-941-9119
■ With "stunning", "dark wood walls", a "cool bar area" and a cigar lounge, this "speakeasy-feeling" Little Italy American is "a refreshing change" that seems like "a private club."

Onigashima ◐[S] — ▽ 19 | 14 | 12 | $32
43-45 W. 55th St. (bet. 5th & 6th Aves.), 212-541-7145
■ Possibly "the best-kept secret in Midtown", this Japanese with chef Tadashi Ono (ex La Caravelle) in the kitchen puts a slight Western accent on its "well-priced" food; its deficits are "ill-organized" service and bland decor that make some wonder why Ono left his prior job.

Opaline ◐[S] — 18 | 20 | 17 | $34
85 Ave. A (bet. 5th & 6th Sts.), 212-475-5050
◪ There's no "hipper spot" than this East Village basement French bistro that's so "sexy", some call it "foreplay"; it's a "high-energy" yearling with "creative cuisine", "wicked drinks" and a super lounge; still, a few find it "mediocre", "loud" and "priced high for Avenue A."

Orienta ◐[S] — 19 | 16 | 17 | $39
205 E. 75th St. (bet. 2nd & 3rd Aves.), 212-517-7509
◪ "Tiny" East Side Pan-Asian (Thai/Vietnamese/Chinese) "haunt" offering "excellent", "imaginative" food and wine; "early is fine", then it gets "too noisy" and "you need a shoehorn to fit."

Oriental Garden ◐[S] — ▽ 23 | 11 | 15 | $26
14 Elizabeth St. (bet. Bayard & Canal Sts.), 212-619-0085
■ Inexpensive, "wonderful seafood" live out of their tanks and superfresh vegetables make this white Formica Chinatown joint an ethnic standout; "go early because this place [justifiably] gets packed."

Original California Taqueria [S]≠▽ 17 | 7 | 13 | $11
525 Hudson St. (bet. Charles & W. 10th Sts.), 212-924-4119
8 Bergen St. (bet. Court & Smith Sts.), Brooklyn, 718-624-7498
341 Seventh Ave. (bet. 9th & 10th Sts.), Brooklyn, 718-965-0006
◪ "You get your money's worth" at this Cal-Mex chain where "jumbo burritos" and clever quesadillas come "fast", "fresh" and "delicious"; apart from that, ratings nose-dive.

Orleans [S] 15 | 14 | 14 | $29
1438 Third Ave. (bet. 81st & 82nd Sts.), 212-794-1509
◪ "It's not New Orleans" but for "nouveau Cajun-Creole", this "decent", inexpensive East Side "neighborhood place" is "a refreshing change" from the unrelenting area Italians; however, "MIA staff" and what some call "lackluster fare" cost points.

Orologio ◐[S]≠ 18 | 16 | 16 | $23
162 Ave. A (bet. 10th & 11th Sts.), 212-228-6900
◪ NY needs "more places like this" "funky, cool" East Village Italian that "makes for a great date" with "cheap, filling", "good food", outdoor seating and "fun staff."

Orso ◐[S] 22 | 18 | 20 | $41
322 W. 46th St. (bet. 8th & 9th Aves.), 212-489-7212
■ The "perfect complement to a Broadway show", this "popular", "best on Restaurant Row" Italian serves up "dependably tasty" pizza and "unusual pastas" along with super stargazing; but it may "suffer from success" since it's a "big hassle to get a reservation."

Osso Buco [S] 17 | 15 | 16 | $28
88 University Pl. (bet. 11th & 12th Sts.), 212-645-4525
◪ "Go with a lot of friends" for "family-style portions" at this Village Italian that's "a Downtown Carmine's"; critics point to "tacky decor" and warn "quantity is not quality."

Osteria al Doge ◐[S] 19 | 17 | 18 | $36
142 W. 44th St. (bet. B'way & 6th Ave.), 212-944-3643
◪ "Venice in NY", this midpriced Midtown Italian is good both as a "business lunch place" and for pre-theater; dissenters counter that it's "hit and miss" and can be "cramped."

Osteria Fiorentina ◐[S] ▽ 20 | 17 | 18 | $31
281 Bleecker St. (Jones St.), 212-633-2941
◪ "Bring the family for huge pastas and other Italian goodies" and enjoy the "fireplace, piano and violin" at this "charming" Villager; if the noise gets to you, sit outside for prime people-watching.

Otabe [S] 24 | 22 | 22 | $50
68 E. 56th St. (bet. Madison & Park Aves.), 212-223-7575
■ The "Zen serenity" and "sweet waitresses" at this "elegant" Midtown "expense-account Japanese" make it like eating in a fancy Japanese home; there are "terrific teppanyaki grills in back."

Our Place [S] 21 | 15 | 20 | $31
1444 Third Ave. (82nd St.), 212-288-4888
■ "It's nice to have a 'non-fast-food' Chinese" on the Upper East Side, especially an "elegant" one where you become "part of a warm family" that "will pamper you"; locals say it's "a treat" and "way above average", perhaps "the best" "north of Shun Lee."

Oven, The ◐[S] ▽ 24 | 20 | 23 | $20
65 Second Ave. (bet. 3rd & 4th Sts.), 212-353-1444
■ For "pizza the way nature intended it, individually sized with fresh natural ingredients" and "without a soggy crust", "go on an empty stomach" to this East Village brick-oven specialist.

F	D	S	C

Owen Thai [S] 19 | 12 | 16 | $26
(fka Bangkok House)
1485 First Ave. (bet. 77th & 78th Sts.), 212-249-5700
◪ "Dingy" digs but "bright, flavorsome food" is the verdict on this "cheap" East Side "formula Thai" with "lots of umbrella drinks"; surveyors tout takeout since inside is "too dark."

OYSTER BAR 22 | 16 | 16 | $38
Grand Central, lower level (42nd St. & Vanderbilt Ave.), 212-490-6650
■ Despite construction work in Grand Central Station and rebuilding after a recent fire, this "quintessential NY" seafooder continues to draw schools of diners for its splendid "fresh fish", stews and pan roasts, plus "the best oysters around" and "great white wines"; with all this activity under its barrel-vaulted tiled ceiling, it's often "noisy."

Oznot's Dish (Brooklyn) ◐[S]≠ ▽ 21 | 19 | 17 | $21
79 Berry St. (N. 9th St.), 718-599-6596
■ A "real find in Williamsburg", this Med–Middle Eastern has a cheap, "creative menu" with "good vegetarian choices" and seafood; it's "where the real artists break for lunch" in a "nice outdoor patio" with service by "slacker waiters."

Pacifica [S] ▽ 20 | 12 | 16 | $26
Holiday Inn, 138 Lafayette St. (bet. Canal & Howard Sts.), 212-941-4168
◪ "An undiscovered gem" removed from the commotion of Chinatown streets, this Hong Kong–style place on the second floor of the Holiday Inn Downtown serves "surprisingly" "civilized dim sum."

Pacifico [S] 19 | 16 | 17 | $31
1484 Second Ave. (bet. 77th & 78th Sts.), 212-717-2204
■ "A lovely addition" to the East Side, this seafooder lures diners with its "reasonably priced", "creative" "fresh fish" and decidedly "casual", "simple" ambiance.

Pageant 14 | 17 | 14 | $29
109 E. Ninth St. (bet. 3rd & 4th Aves.), 212-529-5333
◪ The "cool upstairs lounge" draws a "swank" after-work crowd and spiked-hair types to this East Village Eclectic; it's a "vibrant", "hey, baby" scene that's "great for a drink" if not for dining.

PALIO 22 | 25 | 21 | $57
151 W. 51st St. (bet. 6th & 7th Aves.), 212-245-4850
■ A "breathtaking" Sandro Chia mural surrounds the "stunning" downstairs bar area and upstairs there's an "elegant", "spacious" setting for "top-grade" Northern Italian food; "expensive but worth it" is surveyors' satisfied consensus.

PALM 25 | 15 | 19 | $52
837 Second Ave. (bet. 44th & 45th Sts.), 212-687-2953
Palm Too [S]
840 Second Ave. (bet. 44th & 45th Sts.), 212-697-5198
◪ As always, this Midtown sawdust-on-the-floor, caricatures-on-the-walls "NY institution" rates highly for its "best"/"biggest" steak/lobster specialties, but it's "a man's world", where "surly" service is part of the "expensive" shtick; try the $19.98 lunch.

PALM COURT, THE ◐[S] 20 | 24 | 20 | $45
Plaza Hotel, 768 Fifth Ave. (59th St. & Central Park S.), 212-546-5350
■ A "throwback to a more elegant" NY and "every tourist's delight", the legendary Plaza Hotel lobby continues to host breakfasts, light lunches, "exquisite" afternoon teas and a "lavish" Sunday brunch under real palm trees in an "oasis of charm"; Midwest relatives love it.

Pamir S — 20 | 17 | 19 | $31
1437 Second Ave. (bet. 74th & 75th Sts.), 212-734-3791
1065 First Ave. (58th St.), 212-644-9258
■ "Evocative", "exotic" settings at this pair of "authentic", "friendly" East Side Afghans serve as backdrops for modestly priced shish kebabs and "interesting pumpkin-based food."

Panarella's S — 17 | 19 | 16 | $30
513 Columbus Ave. (bet. 84th & 85th Sts.), 212-799-5784
◪ There's a "labyrinth" of "charming", if "a bit dusty", dining spaces at this "quirky" West Side Italian where street-side seats secure scoping success; the food is "above average" and "reasonably priced", but service is "spotty."

Pão! S — 20 | 16 | 19 | $33
322 Spring St. (Greenwich St.), 212-334-5464
■ "Off the beaten path" in West SoHo, this "far out Portuguese" packs "a pow of flavor in every bite" of its "good value" food; though "tiny", "warm service" prevents claustrophobia.

Paola's S — 22 | 18 | 20 | $41
343 E. 85th St. (bet. 1st & 2nd Aves.), 212-794-1890
■ The "secret's out" on this "cozy", "romantic", "narrow" East Side Italian storefront where hostess-owner Paola "makes you feel at home"; it's a "favorite" of those who know it.

Papaya King ◐ S ≠ — 18 | 5 | 10 | $9
179 E. 86th St. (3rd Ave.), 212-369-0648
■ NYers head to this East Side "top dog" stand for "delicious" franks and fruit drinks that "hit the spot" "when you need a fix"; where else does "$3 buy you a good meal you can eat in five minutes?"

Paper Moon Express S — - | - | - | M
54 E. 59th St. (bet. Madison & Park Aves.), 212-688-5500
More casual and inexpensive than its parent around the block, this new East Side Italian is handy for lunch and now serves dinner too; modern decor and low couch-like seats add to its charm.

Paper Moon Milano — 18 | 16 | 16 | $39
39 E. 58th St. (bet. Madison & Park Aves.), 212-758-8600
◪ Popular with the "Midtown financial set" and Bloomie's shoppers, this "semistylish" Italian with "good pizza" and pasta is "fine for lunch" "if you can get over the noise" and the elevated price; it's more low-key, languorous and "Euro-chic" at night.

Pappardella ◐ S — 16 | 15 | 16 | $29
316 Columbus Ave. (75th St.), 212-595-7996
■ The sidewalk seating option makes for good "Columbus people-watching" as you dine on "affordable", "straight Italian food."

Parioli Romanissimo — 23 | 23 | 22 | $66
24 E. 81st St. (bet. 5th & Madison Aves.), 212-288-2391
◪ Elegantly set in an East Side townhouse, this "formal" Italian garners praise for its "excellent" cuisine and "top-drawer service"; however, some scoff at "Tiffany prices" for the "same old food" and warn "it has run out of steam."

Paris Commune S — 18 | 17 | 17 | $28
411 Bleecker St. (bet. Bank & W. 11th Sts.), 212-929-0509
■ A "sweet" West Village "haunt" whose "simple" American fare is best as a "delectable brunch"; "faux country" or not, the fireplace and resident cat ensure a mood that's fuzzy and "warm."

Park, The ◐ ▽ 21 | 24 | 21 | $52
Lombardy Hotel, 109 E. 56th St. (bet. Lexington & Park Aves.), 212-750-5656
■ With "beautifully prepared" American fare, "polished service", posh decor and dynamic Scotto family management , this "ornate" Midtown newcomer promises "to be a winner"; sure it's a bit pricey, but it's an ideal bull-market place.

Park Avalon ◐ⓢ 20 | 20 | 17 | $35
225 Park Ave. S. (bet. 18th & 19th Sts.), 212-533-2500
■ Still a "trendy" "people-watching scene", this sprawling Flatiron New American serves "consistently good" food under "gothic candlelight" or at a "fancy bargain brunch" with live jazz; "high noise levels" and "long lines" are par for the course.

PARK AVENUE CAFE ⓢ 25 | 23 | 23 | $54
100 E. 63rd St. (bet. Lexington & Park Aves.), 212-644-1900
■ Star chef David Burke "continues to innovate" with "mouthwatering" New American cuisine and "dreamy desserts" at this "stylish" yet "casual" East Side cafe; with its folk art motif decor, classy "people-watching", "special" kitchen room and new private dining area, it practically shouts 'come.'

Park Bistro ⓢ 22 | 17 | 19 | $43
414 Park Ave. S. (bet. 28th & 29th Sts.), 212-689-1360
☑ "Spirited", "charming" bistro that's "just like Paris", from its "savory", "solid" French food to its "crowded", "tuck in your elbows and knees" seating – even the prices seem Parisian.

Park Side Restaurant (Queens) ◐ⓢ 23 | 18 | 20 | $38
107-01 Corona Ave. (51st Ave.), 718-271-9276
■ For a taste of la "dolce vita" and the "best red sauce outside of Rome", it's "worth the trip" to this Corona Italian where "delicious" "family food" comes with "great service" and "not bad" prices.

Parma ◐ⓢ 20 | 14 | 19 | $45
1404 Third Ave. (bet. 79th & 80th Sts.), 212-535-3520
■ With "traditional", "good home-cooked" meals, this "casual" East Side Italian standby is "what a neighborhood restaurant should be"; charmingly redecorated, it continues to please clients who treat it as their home away from home.

Parsonage, The (Staten Island) ⓢ ▽ 20 | 23 | 20 | $38
74 Arthur Kill Rd. (Clarke Ave.), 718-351-7879
■ "Far from the hustle and bustle", this "delightful" "renovated colonial- era mansion" in historic Richmond Town offers a "charming ambiance" for "serious" if "pricey" Continental dining.

Pascalou ⓢ 21 | 16 | 19 | $35
1308 Madison Ave. (bet. 92nd & 93rd Sts.), 212-534-7522
☑ "Regulars are regular" at this "adorable" little – as in tight – Carnegie Hill French bistro; it's lauded for "excellent" Eclectic-French food, a "great early-bird deal" and "amiable service."

Pasha ⓢ ▽ 22 | 21 | 22 | $33
70 W. 71st St. (bet. Columbus Ave. & CPW), 212-579-8751
■ A new West Side "upscale Turk" that's praised for "delicious", "authentic" food, an "eager to please" staff and "comfortable", ruddy quarters, all at moderate prices; go before it's discovered.

Pasqua Coffee Bar 14 | 10 | 11 | $10
55 E. 53rd St. (bet. Madison & Park Aves.), 212-750-7140
909 Third Ave. (bet. 54th & 55th Sts.), 212-735-9910
335 Madison Ave. (bet. 43rd & 44th Sts.), 212-370-3510
450 Lexington Ave. (bet. 44th & 45th Sts.), 212-661-5459
(Continues)

Pasqua Coffee Bar (Cont.)
1290 Sixth Ave. (bet. 51st & 52nd Sts.), 212-977-4861
1345 Sixth Ave. (bet. 54th & 55th Sts.), 212-265-8610
51 Astor Pl. (3rd Ave.), 212-677-6447 ●🅂
WFC, 250 Vesey St. (AmEx Tower concourse), 212-587-9512 🅂
100 Church St. (bet. Barclay St. & Park Pl.), 212-513-1006
Liberty Plaza, 165 Broadway (Liberty St.), 212-608-6481
La Guardia Airport, USAir Shuttle Terminal, Queens, 718-779-8261
☑ "Better than average" java, "good salads" and big muffins are found at this coffee chain; but for some bean buffs, there's no brew ha ha here.

Passage to India ●🅂 | 17 | 14 | 15 | $20 |
306-308 E. Sixth St. (2nd Ave.), 212-529-5770
■ Possibly the "best Indian on the block", this "classic of the Sixth Street crew" has "good, cheap curry" and even if "seating is tight", at least it's "not decked out in Christmas lights" like its neighbors.

Pasta Lovers 🅂 | 14 | 11 | 14 | $22 |
158 W. 58th St. (bet. 6th & 7th Aves.), 212-582-1355
142 W. 49th St. (bet. 6th & 7th Aves.), 212-819-1155
☑ The "generous portions" of pasta "fill ya" at these "mediocre", "low-budget", Formica Midtown Italians, but "bland" taste raises suspicions that "Chef Boyardee is in the kitchen."

Pastrami King (Queens) 🅂 | 18 | 8 | 12 | $18 |
124-24 Queens Blvd. (82nd Ave.), 718-263-1717
☑ Fans say that the "peppery pastrami" and corned beef at this "classic", "no atmosphere" Queens deli "make all others taste like Spam"; that said, many claim it "used to be better."

PATRÍA 🅂 | 25 | 22 | 21 | $47 |
250 Park Ave. S. (20th St.), 212-777-6211
■ "Adventurous", "zesty" flavors produce a "fiesta for the taste buds" at this pricey, attractive, multitiered Flatiron Nuevo Latino where chef Douglas Rodriguez's "interpretation of Latin food" is said to be "pure genius"; "crowds", "noise" and even some "attitude" are all part of its "unique", "festive" flair.

Patrissy's 🅂 | 20 | 15 | 19 | $36 |
98 Kenmare St. (bet. Centre & Mulberry Sts.), 212-226-2888
■ Avoid the crowds on Mulberry Street at this "perennial Little Italy institution" where the "old-fashioned" Italian cuisine and prices are "consistently pleasing", particularly "if you're in the family."

Patroon | 21 | 21 | 19 | $61 |
160 E. 46th St. (bet. Lexington & 3rd Aves.), 212-883-7373
☑ Celebs flock to Ken Aretsky's "glamorous", "clamorous" new Midtown American to feast on the "professional" kitchen's "great steaks" and lounge in the "clubby" cigar rooms upstairs; while the "handsome" decor is "conservative", "outrageous" prices are not; inevitably, it's compared to the "21" Club which Aretsky used to run.

PATSY GRIMALDI'S (Brooklyn) 🅂≠ | 25 | 12 | 16 | $18 |
(nka Grimaldi's)
19 Old Fulton St. (bet. Front & Water Sts.), 718-858-4300
■ The "hands-down" "best brick-oven pizza" baking "under the Brooklyn Bridge" boasts "fresh ingredients" and a "crispy" thin crust at low prices that warrant "difficult parking" and "long waits."

Patsy's 🅂 | 20 | 14 | 17 | $31 |
236 W. 56th St. (bet B'way & 8th Ave.), 212-247-3491
☑ "A good old standby" for pasta and other "classic Neapolitan" fare, this Midtown Italian is most "fun with friends"; its age shows in its dated menu and "wilting" decor, but don't tell its many old celebrity clients.

Patsy's Pizza [S] ⊅ — 20 | 13 | 14 | $19
2287-91 First Ave. (bet. 117th & 118th Sts.), 212-534-9783 ◐
1312 Second Ave. (69th St.), 212-639-1000
61 W. 74th St. (bet. Columbus Ave. & CPW), 212-579-3000
509 Third Ave. (bet. 34th & 35th Sts.), 212-689-7500
67 University Pl. (bet. 10th & 11th Sts.), 212-533-3500
■ This growing group is a "safe bet" for "delicious, light" thin-crust pizza and "giant salads"; the Harlem original remains a contender for "Manhattan's best pie", but why don't these joints deliver?

Paul & Jimmy's [S] — 18 | 16 | 19 | $36
123 E. 18th St. (bet. Irving Pl. & Park Ave. S.), 212-475-9540
◪ A "small", "comfortable" Gramercy Park "neighborhood" place that adds "local color" to its mix of "good" Italian food and "courteous" service; critics say "pedestrian – not even Transmedia can get us back."

Payard Pâtisserie [S] — - | - | - | E
1032 Lexington Ave. (bet. 73rd & 74th Sts.), 212-717-5252
What Schrafft's would have liked to have been, this Daniel spin-off offers François Payard's top-quality French pastries in the front and Philippe Bertineau's comfortable bistro menu in back; though just opened, East Side foodies are already flocking here.

Peacock Alley [S] — 20 | 23 | 21 | $51
Waldorf-Astoria, 301 Park Ave. (50th St.), 212-872-4895
■ An "old favorite" for "business breakfast", brunch or PM tea, this "dignified" Waldorf-Astoria French cafe for over-40s spreads its wings with "service as it was meant to be"; the question is whether chef Laurent Manrique's departure (to open Gertrude's) will trim its feathers.

Pearl Oyster Bar [S] — - | - | - | M
18 Cornelia St. (bet. Bleecker & W. 4th Sts.), 212-691-8211
New West Village seafooder that's reeling in crowds with reasonably priced, savory fish and nightly specials; though the tiny quarters can be cramped, you won't want this newcomer to get away.

Pearl Room (Brooklyn) [S] — ▽ 18 | 15 | 17 | $34
8203 Third Ave. (bet. 82nd & 83rd Sts.), 718-833-6666
■ New, but already "noisy", Bay Ridge seafooder that's making waves with "interesting" shellfish and grilled fish dishes at a "moderate price."

Pearson's Texas Barbecue (Queens) ⊅ — ▽ 23 | 5 | 11 | $16
5-16 51st Ave. (bet. Vernon Blvd. & East River), 718-937-3030
■ Ribs that taste like "the real thing" and "blazing hot" sauce keep this LI City taste of Texas smoking with some of "the best BBQ in NY."

Peking Duck House [S] — 21 | 8 | 14 | $24
22 Mott St. (bet. Bowery & Pell St.), 212-227-1810
◪ There's little doubt that the "eponymous", "crisp and delicious" duck is "unsurpassed" at this cheap Chinatown "dump"; however, your mantra should be: "duck it all but the duck."

Peking Park [S] — 16 | 15 | 16 | $28
100 Park Ave. (40th St.), 212-725-5570
■ Not for epicures, but this "adequate", "reasonably priced" Midtown Chinese's private rooms work well "for banquets", and local business people find its well-spaced tables profitable for lunch.

Pellegrino's ◐ [S] — ▽ 22 | 16 | 22 | $33
138 Mulberry St. (bet. Grand & Hester Sts.), 212-226-3177
■ With "excellent homemade pastas", "great specials", "super service" and moderate prices, it's no wonder this Little Italy Italian "tourist heaven" is forgiven for its "cheesy" decor.

Pen & Pencil 🆂
20 | 18 | 20 | $47

205 E. 45th St. (3rd Ave.), 212-682-8660

🔳 A "solid standby" "if you like steak", this Midtown steakhouse "maintains its integrity" with "old-guard service" in "traditional" "oak-paneled surroundings"; critics say it's "a little long in the tooth."

Penang
20 | 18 | 16 | $27

1596 Second Ave. (83rd St.), 212-585-3838
109 Spring St. (bet. Greene & Mercer Sts.), 212-274-8883
240 Columbus Ave. (71st St.), 212-769-3988
38-04 Prince St. (Main St.), Queens, 718-321-2078

Penang Bar & Grill ◐🆂
64 Third Ave. (11th St.), 212-228-7888

◼ The "flavorful food" at these bargain Malaysian "hot spots" suits the "kitschy", "tiki hut" setting; however, the "crowded" "jungle" scene can cause service lapses and waits; the Bar & Grill is separately owned.

PERIYALI
24 | 21 | 23 | $46

35 W. 20th St. (bet. 5th & 6th Aves.), 212-463-7890

◼ It's "not a Greek myth" that this "civilized", "classy", "upscale" Flatiron Greek restaurant delivers "outstanding" food and especially "marvelous fish"; the "open, airy setting" and "warm and welcoming" service cap off an epic "Mediterranean experience" that many voters rate No. 1 among NYC's Greeks.

Perry Bistro ◐🆂
▽ 19 | 16 | 18 | $31

551 Hudson St. (Perry St.), 212-989-6833

🔳 A new, "stylish" yet "casual" Village French bistro with midpriced "classic" dishes; if "not great", it's a "fun place" to "go for dinner."

Persepolis 🆂
19 | 15 | 17 | $28

1423 Second Ave. (bet. 74th & 75th Sts.), 212-535-1100

◼ "Right on beat for an offbeat cuisine", this "safely exotic" East Side Persian wins good ratings for "tasty kebabs" and "sour cherry rice"; despite the "limited menu", King "Darius would be thrilled."

Pescatore ◐🆂
18 | 15 | 16 | $32

955 Second Ave. (bet. 50th & 51st Sts.), 212-752-7151

🔳 This East Side Italian with "well-priced", "fine fresh seafood" enjoys a "real neighborhood following"; "the sidewalk tables are nice in summer" but to avoid "crowds", "sit upstairs."

Pesce & Pasta Trattoria ◐🆂
20 | 13 | 17 | $27

1562 Third Ave. (bet. 87th & 88th Sts.), 212-987-4696
1079 First Ave. (59th St.), 212-888-7884
262 Bleecker St. (bet. 6th Ave. & 7th Ave. S.), 212-645-2993

◼ "Simple", "friendly", "informal" Italian trattorias that stay "crowded" for their "well-prepared seafood" and "ample portions" of "homestyle" pasta and antipasta at "fair prices."

Petaluma ◐🆂
18 | 16 | 17 | $36

1356 First Ave. (73rd St.), 212-772-8800

◼ A "busy" East Side Italian that's "dependable" for "crispy" pizzas and "predictable" pasta; the "large, airy space" lets Sotheby's-goers "relax" and "family" "crowds" park their "baby carriages" at lunch.

PETER LUGER STEAK HOUSE
(Brooklyn) 🆂⇗
27 | 15 | 20 | $53

178 Broadway (Driggs Ave.), 718-387-7400

◼ Clearly "best" of its breed (rated NY's No. 1 steakhouse for 14 years in a row), this "supreme" Williamsburg beef house has built its "reputation" with "unbeatable", aged porterhouse steaks plus all the fixings; despite "gruff old waiters" and a "Scorsese movie" "beer hall" setting, "a steer would give his life to be served here."

Pete's Downtown (Brooklyn) S | 19 | 17 | 19 | $28
1 Old Fulton St. (Water St.), 718-858-3510
■ The Italian fare is "good" as are the "reasonable prices", but they pale in contrast with this Brooklyn Heights spot's main asset: a "spectacular" "skyline view" of Downtown NYC.

Pete's Tavern ●S | 13 | 15 | 14 | $25
129 E. 18th St. (Irving Pl.), 212-473-7676
☑ This "dark", "smoky", "old" Gramercy Park "watering hole" and former "O'Henry haunt" (he wrote *The Gift of the Magi* here) has enough 19th-century charm to draw crowds; but its Italian-American food is really little better than "pub grub."

Petite Abeille | – | – | – | M
466 Hudson St. (Barrow St.), 212-741-6479 S
107 W. 18th St. (bet. 6th & 7th Aves.), 212-604-9350 S
400 W. 14th St. (9th Ave.), 212-727-1505 ●
Small but charming Belgian trio with tasty traditional fare and moderate prices that would make Monsieur Poirot proud.

Petite Crevette (Brooklyn) S | – | – | – | M
127 Atlantic Ave. (bet. Henry & Clinton Sts.), 718-858-6660 ⊟
168 Seventh Ave. (1st St.), 718-832-9575
This Brooklyn Heights and Park Slope duo, Neil Ganic's spin-off of his La Bouillabaisse, is already winning over locals with creative French bistro fare; the average decor is not offputting since the price is right.

PETROSSIAN ●S | 24 | 24 | 23 | $61
182 W. 58th St. (7th Ave.), 212-245-2214
■ For "caviar nights and champagne days", it's "well worth the splurge" at this "classy" Carnegie Hall–area Russian-Continental; the "beautiful interior" and service are "fit for a czar", while the proletariat finds the prix fixe lunch a "real deal."

Pho Bang S | 17 | 9 | 13 | $18
102 W. 86th St. (bet. Columbus & Amsterdam Aves.), 212-579-9696
6 Chatham Sq. (Mott St.), 212-587-0870
117 Mott St. (bet. Canal & Hester Sts.), 212-966-3797 ⊟
3 Pike St. (bet. Canal & Division Sts.), 212-233-3947 ⊟
82-90 Broadway (Elmhurst Ave.), Queens, 718-205-1500 ⊟
41-07 Kissena Blvd. (Main St.), Queens, 718-939-5520 ⊟
■ This "quick", "no-frills" Vietnamese chain quells hunger and "cures hangovers" with a "big bowl" of "noodles and broth"; though "service fumbles", you still get a big "bang pho your buck."

Phoenix Garden S⊟ | 21 | 10 | 14 | $26
242 E. 40th St. (bet. 2nd & 3rd Aves.), 212-983-6666
☑ Undiscovered Tudor City Cantonese whose cuisine "soars above the competition" in quality and price, but not in decor or service; old-timers say it "just isn't the same since leaving Chinatown."

Pho Tu Do S | ▽ 18 | 7 | 14 | $15
119 Bowery (Grand St.), 212-966-2666
☑ The "zesty Vietnamese" food is "authentic", "fresh" and "cheap" at this Bowery "dive"; "service varies", but you can count on the strange glow of "fluorescent" and "Christmas tree" lights.

Pho Viet Huong S | ▽ 21 | 11 | 13 | $18
73 Mulberry St. (Canal St.), 212-233-8988
☑ "Superb" dishes from a "menu like a Vietnamese encyclopedia" make this "inexpensive" Chinatown destination "outstanding", in spite of a lack of atmosphere and "confused" staff.

139

Picasso Cafe ◐[S]≠ 18 | 16 | 14 | $19
359 Bleecker St. (Charles St.), 212-929-6232
■ Go for the "tasty", "quality" thin-crust pizzas and "fresh focaccia" at this "casual" West Village Italian cafe; find a seat in the outdoor garden and get "comfy", because "service can be slow."

PICCOLA VENEZIA (Queens) [S] 25 | 17 | 22 | $42
42-01 28th Ave. (42nd St.), 718-721-8470
■ "If you can park", this "amiable", "old-world" Astoria Italian standby offers "fabulous" fish and pasta accompanied by "excellent wine" and "warm" "family service", right down to cooking your order "any way you like it."

Piccolino ▽ 20 | 17 | 18 | $28
8 E. 36th St. (bet. 5th & Madison Aves.), 212-683-6444
◪ Recommended as a "pleasant" "lunch spot" with "excellent" pasta and pizza and "polite", "helpful" staff at "affordable prices", this Italian newcomer in Murray Hill is also called "generic."

Piccolo Angolo [S] 23 | 12 | 19 | $26
621 Hudson St. (Jane St.), 212-229-9177
■ "It's always packed" and "noisy" at this "homey", good value West Village "hole-in-the-wall", where the owner's "entertaining" quick-pace recitation of the menu (some like to talk to Renato, some don't, but you won't have a choice) is as delectable as his "hearty, rustic Italian food"; every neighborhood should have one.

PICHOLINE ◐[S] 25 | 22 | 23 | $56
35 W. 64th St. (bet. B'way & CPW), 212-724-8585
■ Ratings keep improving at this Lincoln Center Mediterranean led by chef-owner Terrance Brennan's "inspired" cooking and backed by a "comfortable" setting and "impressive service"; on top of all this, there's a "superb cheese cart", a bargain prix fixe lunch and a tiny but wonderful private wine room that's ideal for intimate parties.

Pierino ▽ 21 | 19 | 21 | $40
107 Reade St. (bet. Church St. & W. B'way), 212-513-0610
■ With its combination of "consistently good", "traditional" Southern Italian food and "wonderful service", it's unlikely that this "welcoming", midpriced TriBeCan will stay "undiscovered" long.

Pierre au Tunnel 20 | 16 | 20 | $38
250 W. 47th St. (bet. B'way & 8th Ave.), 212-575-1220
■ An "old reliable for theatergoers" seeking "robust" French "country food" at "unpretentious prices"; the "1950s" decor may be "dingy", but the "smooth" service "gets you to the play on time."

Pier 25A (Queens) [S] 16 | 14 | 16 | $31
215-16 Northern Blvd. (bet. 215th & 216th Sts.), 718-423-6395
◪ There are "generous portions" of "fresh fish" at this "glorified" "seafood diner" in Bayside; but decor resembling "the *Jaws* ride at Universal Studios" and an uneven kitchen can be turnoffs.

Pietrasanta [S] 20 | 14 | 18 | $28
683 Ninth Ave. (47th St.), 212-265-9471
■ "Original", "flavorful" pastas keep this "cozy", "bargain" Theater District Italian "packed" and "noisy" right up to the first act; if you go "after 8 PM" or for lunch, there's "no hassle."

Pietro's 23 | 14 | 20 | $49
232 E. 43rd St. (2nd Ave.), 212-682-9760
■ A "quintessential" "old-guard" Midtown steakhouse that's famed for "terrific steaks" and Caesar salads as well as "worthwhile" seafood and Italian dishes; having been in business since 1932, it must be doing some things right.

F | D | S | C

Pig Heaven ◐[S] 17 | 12 | 15 | $25
1540 Second Ave. (bet. 80th & 81st Sts.), 212-744-4333
◪ "A cut above" "the normal takeout" spot, this East Side Chinese has "yummy" "ribs and dumplings" if "inconsistent service"; though the "goofy" "pig" motif appeals to kids, parents find it "a bit much."

Pink Tea Cup ◐[S]≠ 18 | 13 | 15 | $19
42 Grove St. (bet. Bedford & Bleecker Sts.), 212-807-6755
■ The "down-home" Southern cooking at this "shoe box"–sized West Villager includes "heavy on the grease" pork chops, biscuits and grits; but for your cardiologist's bill, it's a "bargain."

Pintaile's Pizza [S] 19 | 7 | 12 | $13
26 E. 91st St. (bet. 5th & Madison Aves.), 212-722-1967
1577 York Ave. (bet. 83rd & 84th Sts.), 212-396-3479
1443 York Ave. (bet. 76th & 77th Sts.), 212-717-4990
◪ "Terrific" "gourmet" pizzas with extra-"thin" crusts and "healthy" toppings at low prices are the plus side of these East Side joints; critics "take it to go" given the "cramped" space and "slow delivery."

Pisces ◐[S] 21 | 16 | 17 | $30
95 Ave. A (6th St.), 212-260-6660
■ A "popular", "comfortable" East Village duplex seafood house whose "super", "unusual fish dishes" have a "trendy", "hip" Downtown meets Uptown crowd hooked; though service is "a little amateurish", early-bird dinner is a "great bargain."

Pitchoune [S] 21 | 15 | 17 | $35
226 Third Ave. (19th St.), 212-614-8641
◪ "Delicious", "authentic" Provençal fare that "won't break the bank" and "warm" ambiance keep this Gramercy French bistro "crowded" (some say "cramped"); most consider it "a find."

Pizzeria Uno Chicago ◐[S] 13 | 11 | 12 | $17
220 E. 86th St. (bet. 2nd & 3rd Aves.), 212-472-5656
432 Columbus Ave. (81st St.), 212-595-4700
391 Sixth Ave. (bet. 8th St. & Waverly Pl.), 212-242-5230
55 Third Ave. (bet. 10th & 11th Sts.), 212-995-9668
South St. Seaport, 89 South St. (Pier 17), 212-791-7999
9201 Fourth Ave. (92nd St.), Brooklyn, 718-748-8667
107-16 70th Rd. (bet. Austin St. & Queens Blvd.), Queens, 718-793-6700
39-02 Bell Blvd. (bet. 39th & 40th Sts.), Queens, 718-279-4900
◪ Chicago-originated deep-dish pizza chain that can "affront" thin-crust NYers who describe it as "Domino's meets Houlihan's staffed by Pizza Hut"; however, many still go for the "cheap", "dependable" pies.

Plan Eat Thailand (Brooklyn) ◐[S]≠ 24 | 11 | 13 | $17
184 Bedford Ave. (N. 7th St.), 718-599-5758
■ The "fantastic", "fiery" Thai food at this "cheap" Williamsburg joint draws a steady "local" "artist crowd" despite "no-frills atmosphere"; it's often "packed", so "prepare to wait at peak times."

Planet Hollywood ◐[S] 12 | 19 | 13 | $25
140 W. 57th St. (bet. 6th & 7th Aves.), 212-333-7827
◪ Both the Eclectic-American food and service need help, but the fab memorabilia at this movie-themed Midtowner generates lines that "stretch to Hollywood"; Arnie, Bruce and Sly won't have to worry about their investment until the last teen tourist from Timbuktu grows up.

Plaza Oyster Bar ◐[S] 19 | 18 | 17 | $41
Plaza Hotel, 768 Fifth Ave. (59th St.), 212-546-5340
◪ This "posh" hotel bar is good for cocktails with a "bucket of steamers", oysters or clam chowder; however, some find the dark setting "dungeon-esque" and service "inefficient."

PÓ 🅂   24 17 20 $39
31 Cornelia St. (bet. Bleecker & W. 4th Sts.), 212-645-2189
■ Many sing the praises of chef Mario Batali's "zesty", "innovative"
Italian dishes and the tasting menu "deal" at this "quaint" Village
"hideaway", but with all the buzz, you'd best "reserve in advance."

Poisson ◑   – – – M
108 W. 44th St. (bet. 6th & 7th Aves.), 212-789-1060
Strikingly designed offspring of Cafe Un Deux Trois; this new French
bistro offers a light, midpriced menu that attracts crowds at lunch, but
as of yet it's light at night; the outdoor terrace is touted for pre-theater.

Pomaire 🅂   18 15 17 $25
371 W. 46th St. (bet. 8th & 9th Aves.), 212-956-3056
■ With "hearty", "well-prepared" food and "helpful staff", this simple
Restaurant Row Chilean is an "interesting" pre-theater choice; with
minimal pretense and low cost, dining here is risk-free.

Pommes Frites 🅂⇗   21 10 15 $14
123 Second Ave. (bet. 7th St. & St. Marks Pl.), 212-674-1234
■ NYC's first Belgian (not French) friterie is set in a "tiny" East Village
"hole-in-the-wall", boasting "unrelenting lines" for its "twice-fried"
potatoes and "delicious" dips; given poor ventilation, you may feel
you've been dipped and fried too.

Pomodori 🅂   18 14 16 $24
1425 Second Ave. (bet. 74th & 75th Sts.), 212-472-5225

Piccolo Pomodoro 🅂
1742 Second Ave. (bet. 90th & 91st Sts.), 212-831-8167

Tre Pomodori 🅂
210 E. 34th St. (bet. 2nd & 3rd Aves.), 212-545-7266
■ These "simple", "friendly" East Side trattoria siblings offer "good",
"basic" Italian fare at "reasonable prices"; they're "nothing special",
but at least there's "no attitude."

Pomodoro Rosso 🅂   19 15 18 $30
229 Columbus Ave. (bet. 70th & 71st Sts.), 212-721-3009
■ A "cheerful" West Side Italian "neighborhood favorite" that "gets
quite crowded" – "understandably so" given the high quality of its
"homemade pasta" and "efficient staff."

Pongsri Thai 🅂   21 12 16 $22
244 W. 48th St. (bet. B'way & 8th Ave.), 212-582-3392 ◑
311 Second Ave. (18th St.), 212-477-4100
■ "Delicious", "spicy" food and "efficient", "fast" service place these
Gramercy and Theater District eateries among NY's "better Thais";
"gentle prices" compensate for their "dreary" settings.

Pop Heaven & Hell ◑🅂   ▽ 15 22 15 $11
304 Eighth Ave. (bet. 25th & 26th Sts.), 212-647-8826
▣ This cheap new Chelsea "spin on a NY coffee shop" serves juices,
coffee and desserts amidst "strange" pearly gates meets Hades decor.

Popover Cafe 🅂   18 15 16 $21
551 Amsterdam Ave. (bet. 86th & 87th Sts.), 212-595-8555
▣ Brunch-seeking Westsiders line up at this teddy bear–decorated
Eclectic "comfort" food cafe to "bliss out" on the "fluffiest popovers"
with "strawberry butter"; but the "cutesy" ambiance may wear thin.

Portobello 🅂   21 16 19 $29
208 Thompson St. (bet. Bleecker & W. 3rd Sts.), 212-473-7794
■ A "casual" Village Italian with "surprisingly good" "traditional
dishes" and possibly the "best" grilled portobello mushrooms; "friendly
service" in a "warm". "intimate" milieu makes it "a find."

Post House S
24 | 20 | 21 | $55
Lowell Hotel, 28 E. 63rd St. (bet. Madison & Park Aves.), 212-935-2888
■ "Stately", Americana-filled East Side steakhouse that's a "mainstay" for "perfectly seared steak" and "excellent seafood"; the "well-lit", "airy" setting and "gracious service" inspire a "civilized" "power scene" that appeals to women as well as men.

Poti Vegetarian (Queens) S
– | – | – | M
41-42 Main St. (bet. Sanford Ave. & 41st Rd.), 718-886-5377
"Otherworldly" describes this Flushing Vegetarian's creations, but as "innovative" as they may be, some say the "only palatable foods are the real vegetables" – unless you like "imitation meat."

Pravda ●S
16 | 22 | 14 | $37
281 Lafayette St. (bet. Houston & Prince Sts.), 212-226-4696
■ The "ultrahip" descend on this "swanky", "smoky" underground SoHo "vodka bar" for "potent martinis", "expensive" Russian "snacks" (e.g. caviar) and to watch the "chic" celebrity-strewn scene unfold; for best results go "late" at night and eat beforehand.

Primavera ●S
23 | 21 | 21 | $56
1598 First Ave. (82nd St.), 212-861-8608
■ This "upscale" Upper East Side Northern Italian is feted for its "outstanding cuisine" and "first-rate" black-tie service in an "elegant", wood-paneled room with a who's who clientele; owner Nicola Civetta is one of NY's best hosts – if he suggests a dish, you can bank on it.

Primola ●S
21 | 16 | 18 | $47
1226 Second Ave. (bet. 64th & 65th Sts.), 212-758-1775
■ "Superior" Italian fare and an "exhilarating" ambiance keep well-cosseted "regulars" coming to this "congenial" East Side address; service is "fine", but the "chaotic" space may be "noisy."

Provence ●S
22 | 22 | 19 | $44
38 MacDougal St. (Prince St.), 212-475-7500
■ "Charming" SoHo Provençal bistro whose "classic" fare, "relaxing", "unpretentious" ambiance and "pleasant" back garden satisfy "cravings" for the "French countryside."

Provi, Provi S
18 | 17 | 18 | $34
228 W. 72nd St. (bet. B'way & West End Ave.), 212-875-9020
☑ For a kosher dairy Italian meal of better than average pasta and fish, this "friendly" Westsider is usually "fine" but may be uneven; some think "even for kosher" it's "overpriced", but most say 'try it.'

Puccini ●S
19 | 16 | 18 | $25
475 Columbus Ave. (83rd St.), 212-875-9532
■ Upper West Side Italian with "mix and match" pastas and sauces at "affordable prices" plus "cheery service"; inside it's "cramped" but "quaint"; outside there's "popular" "people-watching."

Puket ●S
17 | 13 | 15 | $27
945 Second Ave. (50th St.), 212-759-6339
☑ "Solid Thai" food comes with "mild prices" at this "quiet", "friendly" East Midtowner; it's best for lunch if you can handle the "cheesy" decor and don't mind small portions.

Puttanesca S
21 | 15 | 18 | $29
859 Ninth Ave. (56th St.), 212-581-4177
■ An "up-and-coming" Hell's Kitchen Italian praised for "remarkable" "homemade pasta" and "interesting specials" at "affordable" prices; it recently tripled in size.

Q, a Thai Bistro (Queens) S ▽ 21 18 20 $28
108-25 Ascan Ave. (bet. Austin & Burns Sts.), 718-261-6599
■ This "popular" Thai can get "noisy" and "cramped", but "delicately flavored" food, "cool decor" and "eager staff" make it a Forest Hills fave.

Quantum Leap S 19 11 16 $17
88 W. Third St. (bet. Sullivan & Thompson Sts.), 212-677-8050
65-64 Fresh Meadow Ln. (67th Ave.), Queens, 718-461-1307
◪ "Friendly", "funky", "budget Vegetarian", with West Village and Queens branches; fans cite "tried and true" food that "makes you feel righteous"; critics counter "bland", "gives vegetables a bad name."

Quatorze Bis ◐S 21 18 19 $43
323 E. 79th St. (bet. 1st & 2nd Aves.), 212-535-1414
◪ A "charming", "elegant" East Side "neighborhood" zinc-bar French bistro that's "always a favorite" with style-setting locals who come so often it "feels like a club"; "the $14 lunch special" can't be beat.

Quattro Gatti S 19 18 19 $37
205 E. 81st St. (bet. 2nd & 3rd Aves.), 212-570-1073
◪ They "treat you like family" at this "warm" Upper East Side Italian; though "it can be very good", a few say "ordinary", "overpriced."

Queen (Brooklyn) S⊅ 23 14 19 $34
84 Court St. (bet. Livingston & Schermerhorn Sts.), 718-596-5955
■ Run by chefs Pasquino and Vincent Vitiello, it's *Big Night for real* at this "unassuming", "antitrendy" "old Brooklyn" Italian that's also "a Court Street power" scene.

Quilty's S 24 20 21 $46
177 Prince St. (bet. Sullivan & Thompson Sts.), 212-254-1260
◪ Pricey SoHo Contemporary American yearling with "cheerful service", "simple, striking decor" and Katy Sparks, who is touted as the "best new chef in the city"; however, a few dissenters report it's "underwhelming" and does not live up to "all the hype."

Rachel's American Bistro ◐S 19 16 17 $29
608 Ninth Ave. (bet. 43rd & 44th Sts.), 212-957-9050
■ "A charmer for pre-theater", this "informal", "crowded" Midtown American is "worth the squeeze" for its "always good" "home cooking" and $8.95 brunch; still, some call it "just another" place.

Rafaella Ristorante S 20 21 19 $33
381 Bleecker St. (bet. Charles & Perry Sts.), 212-229-9885
■ "For that ever-so-important first date", this "busy" but "romantic" Village Italian dishes out "hearty, tasty" food in a "lovely" setting with high ceilings and candlelight; it's "everyone's secret."

Raffaele ◐S ▽ 20 15 19 $41
1055 First Ave. (bet. 57th & 58th Sts.), 212-750-3232
■ For "a welcome change", try this tiny East Side Italian; though the ambiance "leaves much to be desired" and the food is "a bit pricey", "if they know you, you're treated like royalty."

Rafina S 21 16 19 $31
1481 York Ave. (bet. 78th & 79th Sts.), 212-327-0950
■ "You can almost feel the sea breeze" at this "cheery", modestly priced East Side Greek taverna where surveyors return "again and again" for "fresher than fresh seafood", "grilled to perfection."

Rain S 21 21 19 $33
100 W. 82nd St. (bet. Amsterdam & Columbus Aves.), 212-501-0776
■ At this "popular" Westsider, the "young", "the beautiful" and "yuppie marrieds" mix to dine on "unique" Vietnamese and Thai dishes "without going bankrupt"; a "hopping bar" adds to the "cool" scene.

RAINBOW ROOM ◐[S] 21 | 28 | 23 | $64
GE Bldg., 30 Rockefeller Plaza, 65th fl. (bet. 49th & 50th Sts.), 212-632-5000
■ For a "quintessential NY" experience with "breathtaking" views, you can't do better than this "expensive" but "glorious", "romantic" art deco 65th-floor ballroom where you half expect "Fred and Ginger" to waltz in and chef Waldy Malouf's American cuisine is "a pleasant surprise"; extra bonuses are the adjoining Rainbow & Stars cabaret and the more informal and affordable Promenade Lounge.

RAO'S ⊄ 24 | 14 | 21 | $53
455 E. 114th St. (Pleasant Ave.), 212-722-6709
■ "If you don't know Frank, fuhgedaboutit" since this "East Harlem landmark" Italian is NY's toughest ticket; if you're lucky enough to get a reservation, it's an experience out of *The Godfather* with guys and dolls, celebs and pols wolfing down "very satisfying", "whaddaya like" "home cooking."

Raoul's ◐[S] 22 | 19 | 18 | $44
180 Prince St. (bet. Sullivan & Thompson Sts.), 212-966-3518
■ A "mix of Wall Streeters and Euros" must pass an "attitude test before entering" this "dark", "hip" SoHo French bistro; besides "hearty", "mouthwatering" fare and "amazing" wines, it offers a "beautiful garden", comfy booths, late hours and Uma sightings.

Raphaël 23 | 23 | 23 | $56
33 W. 54th St. (bet. 5th & 6th Aves.), 212-582-8993
◪ "Without any hype", this Midtown French standby continues to serve "tasty" haute bistro food brought to the table by "caring staff" in a "romantic" townhouse; some say it's "boring" and "expensive", but if "you can't get to Paris, this will do."

Rasputin (Brooklyn) **◐[S]** ▽ 17 | 19 | 17 | $54
2670 Coney Island Ave. (Ave. X), 718-332-8111
◪ "The spot among Russians" for "decadence at its best"; "bring your appetite" and earplugs to this Brighton Beach Franco-Russian for "hearty" food and lots of "ice-cold Absolut", and then enjoy a "loud" "Las Vegas–like" floor show and dancing; it's "definitely an experience."

Ratners [S] 17 | 8 | 12 | $22
138 Delancey St. (bet. Norfolk & Suffolk Sts.), 212-677-5588
■ Despite "surly waiters" and Formica decor, this "cheap" Lower East Side kosher dairy offers a nostalgia trip; cheese blintzes, knishes and "chicken soup that will cure anything short of amputations" make it a NY "cultural institution."

Raymond's Cafe [S] ▽ 18 | 16 | 20 | $28
88 Seventh Ave. (bet. 15th & 16th Sts.), 212-929-1778
■ "Perfect after shopping at Loehmann's", this Chelsea Continental is "good all-around" – a "comfortable" "neighborhood" "workhorse", but not a thoroughbred.

Rectangles ◐[S] 17 | 9 | 14 | $21
159 Second Ave. (10th St.), 212-677-8410
◪ This East Village Israeli-Yemenite provides "sustenance" to young locals at "great prices"; given its coffee shop digs, some call it "square."

Redeye Grill ◐[S] 20 | 21 | 18 | $40
890 Seventh Ave. (56th St.), 212-541-9000
■ "An instant favorite", this "cavernous yet chic" American yearling near Carnegie Hall offers an "impressive bar" (and raw bar), a 200-seat cafe and pretty private rooms; the "attractive clientele" reports "terrific", "fresh" seafood and wicked desserts.

Red Light Bistro ◐🅂
∇ 18 | 14 | 16 | $30

50 Ninth Ave. (bet. 14th & 15th Sts.), 212-675-2400
☑ A "pleasant surprise in the Meat Packing District", this bistro yearling has "very good", "light", reasonably priced French-Mediterranean fare; critics flash the "red light" at "decor that needs work."

Red Tulip 🅂
17 | 17 | 18 | $34

439 E. 75th St. (bet. 1st & York Aves.), 212-734-4893
■ "Step inside and 3,000 miles away from NY" at this "romantic", "old-world" East Side Hungarian with "good", "authentic food" and music.

Regency (aka 540 Park) 🅂
20 | 22 | 21 | $51

Regency Hotel, 540 Park Ave. (61st St.), 212-339-4050
■ Best known for its "ultimate power breakfast", but also "a safe bet" for a "quiet conversation" lunch and dinner, this "elegant" Park Avenue dining room offers "simple and good" American cuisine; with Tisches presiding at breakfast, NY's daily agenda is set by 8 AM.

Regional Thai Taste 🅂
19 | 14 | 15 | $23

208 Seventh Ave. (22nd St.), 212-807-9872
■ "Deliciously different" Chelsea Thai with "unique flavors" and "great drinks" at "bargain" prices; it's "a step up from your average Thai."

Remi 🅂
23 | 23 | 21 | $48

145 W. 53rd St. (bet. 6th & 7th Aves.), 212-581-4242
■ A Northern Italian "with panache", Adam Tihany's trompe l'oeil Venetian is ideal for Midtown "business lunches" or social dinners thanks to its "beautiful murals", "attentive" staff and "innovative menu."

René Pujol
22 | 20 | 22 | $44

321 W. 51st St. (bet. 8th & 9th Aves.), 212-246-3023
■ A "trip to France without going to the airport", this Midtown veteran has "divine" French fare "at half the price of its East Side competitors"; what's more, "they take theater curtain times seriously"; it's "had a long run and for good reason."

Republic 🅂
16 | 15 | 14 | $19

2290 Broadway (bet. 82nd & 83rd Sts.), 212-579-5959
37 Union Sq. W. (bet. 16th & 17th Sts.), 212-627-7172
☑ "Cool", "quick" and "cheap" Pan-Asian noodle specialists; besides sitting "next to strangers" at "noisy" benches, the food is "hit or miss" as is service, but "at these prices you can't complain."

Restivo 🅂
∇ 17 | 16 | 16 | $26

209 Seventh Ave. (22nd St.), 212-366-4133
■ "Charming" little Chelsea Italian with a Joyce-handy location, "gay" clientele and low prices – you can't go wrong at $7.95 for lunch.

Rialto ◐🅂
– | – | – | M

265 Elizabeth St. (bet. Houston & Prince Sts.), 212-334-7900
An understated dining room with red leather banquettes and a "cozy garden" sets the scene for first-rate American food and a beautiful crowd at this SoHo newcomer; early visitors find it so cool, as in so hot.

Rice 'n' Beans 🅂
19 | 7 | 14 | $18

744 Ninth Ave. (bet. 50th & 51st Sts.), 212-265-4444
■ "A hole-in-the-wall, but not in your pocket", this tiny, far West Side Brazilian serves "good", "basic" "home cooking"; it's so "nice 'n' cheap", it "makes you want to samba."

Rincon de España 🅂
19 | 11 | 17 | $32

226 Thompson St. (bet. Bleecker & W. 3rd Sts.), 212-260-4950
■ This lively Villager is a tight fit, but "worth it" for "good", "filling", "authentic" Spanish food, "friendly" service and a roaming guitarist; it's so "dark" you can't see it "needs renovation."

Riodizio 🅂
417 Lafayette St. (bet. Astor Pl. & E. 4th St.), 212-529-1313

| 17 | 16 | 16 | $34 |

◼ "Don't eat for a week before you go" to this "bargain" AYCE East Village Brazilian rotisserie that's a "meat lovers' dream"; it's "best to do with a group" that's very hungry and ready to "party."

Rio Mar ◐🅂
7 Ninth Ave. (Little W. 12th St.), 212-242-1623

| 19 | 12 | 16 | $27 |

◼ A "secret", "sexy" West Village "gem" serving "cheap", "authentic", garlicky Spanish fare and free-flowing sangria; it's a "hip", "dark", deep "dive" with a jukebox that's a "treasure trove of Latin music."

River 🅂
345 Amsterdam Ave. (bet. 76th & 77th Sts.), 212-579-1888

| 19 | 17 | 17 | $26 |

◪ "Take a group and share orders" at this "tasty", "innovative", bamboo-decorated West Side Vietnamese; critics say it "doesn't stand out" from the "flood of like-named" competitors in the area.

RIVER CAFE (Brooklyn) ◐🅂
1 Water St. (Brooklyn Bridge), 718-522-5200

| 25 | 27 | 24 | $61 |

◼ This New American "celebration place" under the Brooklyn Bridge wins kudos all-around for its "picture-perfect" views of Manhattan, "wonderful", "creative" food, "crisp service" and "divinely romantic" ambiance that almost commands "hold hands."

Riverrun ◐🅂
176 Franklin St. (bet. Greenwich & Hudson Sts.), 212-966-3894

| 16 | 13 | 16 | $23 |

◪ "When you're feeling unpretentious", check out this casual TriBeCa "standby" for its brews and standard pub fare; its "loyal clientele" calls it a "neighborhood hangout" and a "good value."

Roberto's (Bronx) 🅂
632 Crescent Ave. (186th St. & Belmont Ave.), 718-733-9503

| ▽ 23 | 11 | 20 | $33 |

◼ A "favorite" Arthur Avenue–area Italian that's "worth the trip" for "fresh", "delicious" pasta at good prices; it's strictly "no-frills", but the staff "treats you like family" and as for the food – "now, that's Italian!"

Rocco 🅂
181 Thompson St. (bet. Bleecker & Houston Sts.), 212-677-0590

| ▽ 19 | 13 | 19 | $31 |

◪ Since 1922, this Village Italian "step into the past" has been dishing out "real home cooking" at "reasonable prices"; critics cite "lack of decor" and say it "was better years ago."

Rocking Horse Cafe Mexicano ◐🅂
182 Eighth Ave. (bet. 19th & 20th Sts.), 212-463-9511

| 19 | 15 | 16 | $25 |

◼ The "decor looks more Californian but the food is true Mexican" at this "cheap" "Chelsea find"; good food, mind-boggling margaritas and "fun waiters" combine to make this a rocking time.

Roettele A.G.
126 E. Seventh St. (bet. Ave. A & 1st Ave.), 212-674-4140

| 18 | 16 | 17 | $31 |

◪ You can "sit in the garden and pretend you're in the Alps" at this "charming", "cut-rate" East Village Swiss-German; its fans favor the "fabulous fondue" but others consider it "real cheesy."

Rolf's 🅂
281 Third Ave. (22nd St.), 212-477-4750

| 18 | 18 | 16 | $30 |

◼ "A must at Christmas" when it puts up "more lights than Rockefeller Center", this "old" German "favorite" serves "huge portions" of dishes such as roast goose, schnitzel and wurst; despite "slow service", it "just keeps rolling along."

ROSA MEXICANO ◐🅂   23 | 18 | 19 | $39
1063 First Ave. (58th St.), 212-753-7407
■ "Mouthwatering" guacamole and mega-margaritas make this "top-notch", "top-dollar" Midtown Mexican "popular" enough to produce "crowds and noise"; according to most, the "authentic", "refined" food and "personalized service" "never disappoint."

Rose Cafe 🅂   17 | 17 | 17 | $30
24 Fifth Ave. (9th St.), 212-260-4118
🆉 "Big, sunny windows" and a "prime location" on Fifth Avenue keep this American NYU neighbor "blooming"; while possibly "inconsistent", regulars call it "comfortable" and "affordable."

Rosemarie's   24 | 20 | 22 | $43
145 Duane St. (bet. Church St. & W. B'way), 212-285-2610
■ Come "escape for lunch" or "hide away" for dinner at this TriBeCa "treasure"; you'll be rewarded by "exceptional" Italian fare, "warm service" and "pleasingly understated decor."

Rose of India ◐🅂   18 | 15 | 16 | $17
308 E. Sixth St. (bet. 1st & 2nd Aves.), 212-533-5011
🆉 "Tacky plates, bright lights" and "365-day Christmas" decor make this "delicious, cheap and colorful" East Village Indian seem like "a bad Bombay acid trip"; for best results, "just tell them it's your birthday and then sit back and enjoy the show."

Rosewood 🅂   – | – | – | M
1319 Third Ave. (bet. 75th & 76th Sts.), 212-879-5000
Two good young chefs and an attractive, casual setting make this brand-new East Side American bistro a good bet; though expensive for daily use, it should make a good place for Sunday dinner.

Rossini's ◐🅂   19 | 17 | 20 | $40
108 E. 38th St. (bet. Lexington & Park Aves.), 212-683-0135
🆉 An "old-style" – some say "dull" and "dated" – Murray Hill Italian serving "consistently good", if "pricey", meals including "outstanding sauces" via "attentive staff"; there's opera on Saturdays.

Route 66 Cafe ◐🅂   ▽ 17 | 15 | 17 | $19
858 Ninth Ave. (bet. 55th & 56th Sts.), 212-977-7600
■ With "something on the menu for everyone", this "cheap", "bright" new Hell's Kitchen "diner with a theme and attitude" serves "healthy food", fruits, salads and terrific juices.

Royal Siam 🅂   21 | 12 | 17 | $23
240 Eighth Ave. (bet. 22nd & 23rd Sts.), 212-741-1732
■ "Tasty", "dependable" Thai food plus "helpful" service and fair prices make this Chelsean a "terrific value" – especially the "bargain lunch"; just ignore the "bleak" decor.

Rubyfruit Bar & Grill 🅂   ▽ 17 | 17 | 19 | $29
531 Hudson St. (bet. Charles & W. 10th Sts.), 212-929-3343
■ For "girls' night out", this "upscale" West Village lesbian fave has "good", if undistinguished, American fare at "reasonable prices" plus "cozy tables" downstairs and a "crowded bar" upstairs; we had trouble deciphering one surveyor's comment, i.e. "hit *or* miss" vs. "hit *on* miss."

Rungsit Thai 🅂   17 | 7 | 14 | $17
208 E. 34th St. (bet. 2nd & 3rd Aves.), 212-689-1479
161 E. 23rd St. (bet. 2nd & 3rd Aves.), 212-260-0704 ⇗
🆉 "For hot and spicy" food that's far from pricey, check out these tongue-teasing Thai twins; but "don't expect fancy here", we're talking "no-frills" decor and "sloppy service."

	F	**D**	**S**	**C**

Russian Samovar [S] — 19 | 17 | 18 | $38

256 W. 52nd St. (bet. B'way & 8th Ave.), 212-757-0168

■ "A taste of the old country", this Theater District Russian appeals to many Russian emigrés with its "satisfying food" and "helpful service"; after a few of its "killer vodkas" and a song or two, you should get into that old Moscow mood.

Russian Vodka Room ◐[S] — ▽ 20 | 23 | 21 | $36

265 W. 52nd St. (8th Ave.), 212-307-5835

■ Host-owner Dmitri is a "charmer" at this "unusual", "dark" new Midtown watering hole with more on-site-infused vodkas "than you can shake a babushka at"; the Russian food is also quite good.

Ruth's Chris Steak House ◐[S] — 22 | 19 | 20 | $50

148 W. 51st St. (bet. 6th & 7th Aves.), 212-245-9600

◪ To most "a carnivore's delight" with "succulent steaks" cooked in butter, this New Orleans–based Midtown chain steakhouse also has critics who find "lots of sizzle but no substance" and say "for tourists."

S'Agapo (Queens) ◐[S] — ▽ 21 | 16 | 18 | $30

34-21 34th Ave. (35th St.), 718-626-0303

◪ An "authentic" Astoria taverna offering "surprisingly sophisticated Greek food", "friendly service" and occasional Greek music.

Sahara (Brooklyn) ◐[S] — ▽ 20 | 10 | 15 | $21

2337 Coney Island Ave. (bet. Aves. U & T), 718-376-8594

■ You can't beat the "hearty Mideast fare" and "fabulous bread" at this Gravesend "el cheapo", but some locals say that "tacky wall paintings and poor service" make it "best for takeout."

Saigon Grill ◐[S] — 20 | 8 | 16 | $19

2381 Broadway (87th St.), 212-875-9072

■ Arguably "the best of the West Side Vietnamese" places, this "zero decor" joint serves "copious", "delicious food" at "easy-to-take prices"; tip: focus on the food, ignore the ambiance.

Saigon House and Bar [S] — ▽ 19 | 9 | 16 | $22

89-91 Bayard St. (Mulberry St.), 212-732-8988

■ Though sorely in need of a decorator's touch, this Downtown Vietnamese near City Hall has "huge, fresh and filling" noodle soups, grilled veggies and rock-bottom prices that make it fail-safe.

Sakagura ◐ — ▽ 20 | 21 | 18 | $38

211 E. 43rd St. (bet. 2nd & 3rd Aves.), 212-953-7253

■ "Casual" Midtown Japanese with an impressive sake array (200 kinds) and a charming "private club" ambiance; fans "adore" it.

Salaam Bombay [S] — 21 | 18 | 18 | $30

317-319 Greenwich St. (bet. Duane & Reade Sts.), 212-226-9400

■ "Knock-your-socks-off-Indian" food with "beautiful decor", live sitar music on weekends and a "pleasant" staff make this a TriBeCa favorite, especially for the $10.95 lunch buffet.

Salam Cafe & Restaurant [S] — ▽ 20 | 15 | 16 | $25

104 W. 13th St. (bet. 6th & 7th Aves.), 212-741-0277

◪ West Village locals like this "homestyle Middle Eastern" for its "flavorful", "hearty", reasonably priced cuisine and comfy setting; others say the staff is "in need of some schooling."

Sal Anthony's [S] — 18 | 17 | 18 | $33

55 Irving Pl. (bet. 17th & 18th Sts.), 212-982-9030

◪ This old Gramercy-area townhouse Italian is an "institution" beloved for its "robust" food, "noisy" but "comfortable" ambiance and "nice" sidewalk cafe; skeptics say it's "coasting", but even they admit that the $10.50 prix fixe lunch is "a steal."

Sal Anthony's S.P.Q.R. S
18 | 18 | 18 | $32
133 Mulberry St. (bet. Grand & Hester Sts.), 212-925-3120

☑ A "huge, [often] busy dining room" with high ceilings and exposed brick walls makes this "reliable", "old-style Italian" "brighter and cheerier" than most of its Little Italy competition; it's a "courthouse crowd" favorite but also a tourist destination.

Sala Thai S
20 | 13 | 17 | $26
1718 Second Ave. (bet. 89th & 90th Sts.), 212-410-5557

☑ "Dependably good neighborhood Thai" (some say "best on the Upper East Side") served by "gracious staff" at low prices; but even fans lament "sterile black lacquer decor" and "cramped" seating.

Saloon, The ●S
14 | 13 | 14 | $27
1920 Broadway (64th St.), 212-874-1500

☑ "Location is everything" at this "cavernous", "crowded" Lincoln Center "standby"; expect "noise, noise, noise", "brusque service" and a "vast menu" of "mediocre" American food in exchange for primo people-watching from the sidewalk cafe seats.

Salute! ●S
18 | 19 | 16 | $33
270 Madison Ave. (bet. 39th & 40th Sts.), 212-213-3440

☑ In an area "desperately needing a lunch spot", this new Murray Hill Tuscan's "tasty pizzas and munchies" are "a welcome addition" (for dinner too); it's already a "hopping" scene even if service needs work.

Samalita's Tortilla Factory S⇗ ▽
17 | 12 | 15 | $16
1429 Third Ave. (bet. 80th & 81st Sts.), 212-737-5070

☑ "Quaint little" Midtown Cal-Mex with "light, fresh" fare and "tasty takeout" that is a good "bang for the buck"; still, some claim "portions are small" and overall it's "nothing special."

Sambuca S
18 | 15 | 16 | $27
20 W. 72nd St. (bet. Columbus Ave. & CPW), 212-787-5656

☑ Whether they call it "a poor man's Carmine's" or a "better and quieter" alternative, no one can resist comparing this "family-style" Italian to that other popular Westsider; "inexpensive", "hearty" fare and a "festive" ambiance make it "perfect for large groups."

Sammy's Noodle Shop ●S
17 | 10 | 14 | $16
453 Sixth Ave. (11th St.), 212-924-6688

☑ "Bargain-basement prices" keep noodle lovers flocking to this "noisy" Chinese "cafeteria" in the Village; service may be "rude and rushed", but the create-your-own-plate option is "amazing."

Sammy's Roumanian S
18 | 10 | 15 | $42
157 Chrystie St. (Delancey St.), 212-673-0330

☑ "You have to go once in a lifetime" to this "kitschy", schmaltzy, loud Lower East Side "bar mitzvah" for its "Jewish soul food", "bad music" and laughable service; the gigantic grease-laden dishes are "a heart attack on a plate", so check with your cardiologist first.

Sam's Noodle Shop ●S
19 | 8 | 14 | $16
411 Third Ave. (29th St.), 212-213-2288

☑ Murray Hill Chinese featuring "huge portions" of "classic noodle shop fare" served "quick" and "cheap, cheap, cheap" in a setting that's "no-frills" at best.

San Domenico S
23 | 23 | 23 | $61
240 Central Park S. (bet. B'way & 7th Ave.), 212-265-5959

☑ "A class act"; loyal fans, including TV celeb regulars, love the "elegant", understated ambiance, "flawless" service and chef Odette Fada's "amazing" food at Tony May's "sophisticated Italian"; critics call it slightly "stuffy" and "expensive", unless you order the prix fixe.

San Giusto — 20 | 19 | 21 | $47
935 Second Ave. (bet. 49th & 50th Sts.), 212-319-0900
◪ "Beautiful interiors" and "excellent service" set the tone at this pricey Midtown Italian; it's a "real sleeper" with "wonderful specials."

San Pietro ◐ — 22 | 20 | 22 | $51
18 E. 54th St. (bet. 5th & Madison Aves.), 212-753-9015
■ Midtown Italian offering "excellent" (albeit "pricey") pastas and "made to order" dishes, "gracious service" and "elegant" decor to business and political "movers and shakers."

Santa Fe ◐[S] — 19 | 18 | 18 | $35
72 W. 69th St. (bet. Columbus Ave. & CPW), 212-724-0822
◪ "Reliable", "upscale" Lincoln Center Southwestern with "cozy", "soothing" peach pastel decor and a fireplace; the menu may be a bit "tired", but eating here is "the next best thing to being in Santa Fe."

Sant Ambroeus [S] — 19 | 16 | 17 | $41
1000 Madison Ave. (bet. 77th & 78th Sts.), 212-570-2211
◪ "Gelati to die for" and "wonderful" pastries draw raves for this East Side Milanese "hideaway"; on the downside, diners report "slow" service, "Italo-funereal" decor and "high prices."

Santorini [S] — ▽ 19 | 16 | 19 | $27
7 Washington Pl. (Mercer St.), 212-260-3066
◪ Washington Square–area Greek with a "cheerful" setting and "the nicest staff ever"; fans swear by the "fresh, expertly prepared" food, though a few say it's just "so-so."

Sapporo East ◐[S] — 20 | 11 | 14 | $22
245 E. 10th St. (1st Ave.), 212-260-1330
■ For "cheap and tasty", "superfresh" sushi, you can't beat this East Village Japanese with its "low-budget diner" setting and "confused staff"; it's "always crowded", so "plan to wait."

Sarabeth's [S] — 20 | 17 | 17 | $29
Hotel Wales, 1295 Madison Ave. (bet. 92nd & 93rd Sts.), 212-410-7335
Whitney Museum, 945 Madison Ave. (75th St.), 212-570-3670
423 Amsterdam Ave. (bet. 80th & 81st Sts.), 212-496-6280
■ Go early or brace for "eternal waiting" to sample "delicious baked goods" and other American fare at this trio of "precious" "perennial favorites"; the "flowery" "gingham" decor can trigger "Laura Ashley overload", but Sunday brunch is "a must."

Sardi's ◐ — 15 | 19 | 17 | $41
234 W. 44th St. (bet. B'way & 8th Ave.), 212-221-8440
◪ This Theater District mecca is as integral to NY "as the Empire State Building"; but its "overpriced" Italian "food needs rejuvenation" and it has "staff so old" they make Tony Randall look like a kid.

Sarge's Deli ◐[S] — 16 | 9 | 13 | $19
548 Third Ave. (bet. 36th & 37th Sts.), 212-679-0442
◪ "Typical", "no-frills" deli in Murray Hill where "surly waitresses are the daily special"; being open 24 hours a day makes it "a lifesaver."

Sarong Sarong Bar/Rest. ◐[S] — – | – | – | M
343 Bleecker St. (bet. Christopher & W. 10th Sts.), 212-989-0888
Men never looked better in dresses than at this West Village Malaysian-Chinese that clothes its festive staff in sarongs; both the food and decor are appealing, but don't skirt the popular happy hour.

Savann 🅂
414 Amsterdam Ave. (bet. 79th & 80th Sts.), 212-580-0202   21 | 14 | 17 | $37

Savann Est 🅂
181 E. 78th St. (bet. Lexington & 3rd Aves.), 212-396-9300
☑ West and East Side twins serving "beautifully presented", midpriced French-American "fusion" fare; foes find them "dark" and "deafening."

Savore ◐🅂
200 Spring St. (Sullivan St.), 212-431-1212   19 | 17 | 19 | $38
☑ "Creative" SoHo Tuscan with a "pretty" dining room and outdoor seating; most swear by the "top-of-the-line" fare and service, others swear at it – "noisy", "too full of themselves."

Savoy 🅂
70 Prince St. (Crosby St.), 212-219-8570   23 | 21 | 21 | $43
■ SoHo's "cozy" "little gem" may be "the most romantic spot in town", especially near the fireplace in winter; Peter Hoffman's seasonally changing American-Med menu is "almost perfect", particularly "upstairs for the fixed price dinner."

Sazerac House 🅂
533 Hudson St. (Charles St.), 212-989-0313   17 | 15 | 17 | $26
☑ For "a bit of N'Awlins in the West Village", try this "homey", "historic neighborhood favorite"; though "no Emeril's", the "copious portions" of "tasty Cajun" fare are "a great bargain."

Scaletta 🅂
50 W. 77th St. (bet. Columbus Ave. & CPW), 212-769-9191   21 | 19 | 22 | $41
■ A "quiet", "relaxing" and "roomy" West Side Italian where you can "have a serious conversation" "without raising your voice"; both food and service are "consistently first-rate", but "no bargain."

Scalinatella ◐🅂
201 E. 61st St. (bet. 2nd & 3rd Aves.), 212-207-8280   23 | 16 | 19 | $54
■ You feel "like you're in Italy" at this "beautiful" below-ground East Side "grotto" featuring "terrific", though "shockingly expensive", Italian cuisine and "friendly" service; it's a veritable "ace in a hole."

Scratch ◐🅂
150 Spring St. (bet. W. B'way & Wooster St.), 212-334-2338   14 | 16 | 13 | $33
☑ Suffering from delusions of adequacy, this "cool", Euro-Asian Eclectic yearling has more "happening bathrooms" than kitchen.

Screening Room, The ◐🅂
54 Varick St. (bet. Canal & Laight Sts.), 212-334-2100   21 | 21 | 19 | $36
☑ The red velvet "'30s Hollywood" aura and $30 prix fixe movie-dinner deal make this TriBeCa American yearling the ultimate "date place" – "a reel find" with "killer martinis" and "outstanding" food.

Scully on Spring ◐🅂
203 Spring St. (Sullivan St.), 212-965-0057   ▽ 20 | 18 | 19 | $38
☑ "Unpretentious" SoHo newcomer with a "cozy" ambiance, "fun bar" and "tasty" Mediterranean fare; some say it's "still working out kinks."

SeaGrill
Rockefeller Plaza, 19 W. 49th St. (bet. 5th & 6th Aves.), 212-332-7610   24 | 24 | 22 | $52
■ "Neptune could never do this well" say fans of chef Ed Brown's "fabulous" fish; they're "worth the price" especially given "gracious" service and a "romantic setting" next to Rockefeller Center's ice rink.

Seagrill of the Aegean ◐🅂
1562 Second Ave. (81st St.), 212-734-3125   18 | 13 | 16 | $32
☑ "You don't need an expense account" at this affordable Upper East Side "diner-style" Greek seafooder; most surveyors tout the fresh fish, but critics insist it's just "a step above Red Lobster."

Sea Gull ⓢ
▽ 21 | 23 | 21 | $49

140-148 Centre St. (Walker St.), 212-941-9292

☒ "Neighborhood treat" in TriBeCa that's "not a bad bet" for Malaysian food and occasional celebrity sightings ("JFK, Jr.", no less).

Seasons (Brooklyn) ⓢ
▽ 21 | 16 | 20 | $29

556 Driggs Ave. (N. 7th St.), 718-384-9695

■ Surveyors swoon over this Williamsburg French-Italian "little miracle in the middle of nowhere"; the "creative, subtle" bistro fare and "personal service" offer "value miles beyond the price."

Second Avenue Deli ◐ⓢ
21 | 9 | 14 | $20

156 Second Ave. (10th St.), 212-677-0606

■ Pastrami lovers still mourn the tragic murder of owner Abe Lebewohl, but "his spirit lives on" at this kosher deli "motherland" serving "the best corned beef, pastrami and chopped liver on earth."

Seeda Thai II ⓢ
18 | 13 | 16 | $22

309 W. 50th St. (bet. 8th & 9th Aves.), 212-586-4040

☒ Cheap Theater District Thai-Vietnamese serving "tasty", "extra-spicy" food in a setting that some call "quaint" and others call "seedy."

Sekku ⓢ
▽ 20 | 14 | 17 | $33

343 Lexington Ave. (bet. 39th & 40th Sts.), 212-697-9020

☒ "Unpretentious" but "very crowded" Murray Hill Japanese with "an excellent sushi bar" and live jazz on Sundays; it's a popular "lunch place", but some find it "overrated."

Sel et Poivre ⓢ
17 | 15 | 17 | $37

853 Lexington Ave. (bet. 64th & 65th Sts.), 212-517-5780

☒ East Side French bistro that many praise as "dependable" for "simple home cooking" and "gracious service"; however, disappointed diners can be harsh: "pedestrian", "snooty."

Senza Nome ⓢ
17 | 21 | 15 | $31

1675 Third Ave. (bet. 93rd & 94th Sts.), 212-410-4900

☒ The "sculpture garden" and "stylish" dining room win points for this Upper East Side Italian, but some feel the uninspired kitchen and "forgetful" service need work.

Sequoia ◐ⓢ
15 | 18 | 15 | $29

Pier 17, 89 Fulton St. (South St. Seaport), 212-732-9090

☒ "Who needs decor with the Brooklyn Bridge as a backdrop? – sit outside, if possible" to sip a drink and enjoy this Seaport standby's harbor views over "average American" fare.

Serendipity 3 ◐ⓢ
17 | 19 | 15 | $23

225 E. 60th St. (bet. 2nd & 3rd Aves.), 212-838-3531

■ Taste the "superdelicious" frozen hot chocolate and "everything is right with the world" at this "timeless", "whimsical" "dessert heaven"-cum-children's toy store near Bloomingdale's; it's worth braving lines, "spotty" service and "Tokyo prices.

Seryna
24 | 22 | 22 | $61

11 E. 53rd St. (bet. 5th & Madison Aves.), 212-980-9393

■ You'll find "Japanese elegance with the price to match" at this "exclusive" and "tranquil Midtown hideaway"; "exotic" dishes like Kobe beef cooked on a hot rock at your table are "magnificent", but "hard to cut without an expense account."

Sesumi ⓢ
▽ 19 | 15 | 18 | $29

1649 Second Ave. (bet 85th & 86th Sts.), 212-879-1024

☒ "Small neighborhood" Japanese on the Upper East Side with "competent" staff and "solid", "dependable if unexciting sushi" at "fair" prices; hard-to-please surveyors sniff "best of a poor crop."

Sette Mezzo ◗⧢⇄
21 | 16 | 18 | $43

969 Lexington Ave. (bet. 70th & 71st Sts.), 212-472-0400
■ "Always crowded" with the "chic" and "trendy", this "intimate"
East Side Italian wins praise for "lively salads, soups and pastas" – if
you can stomach the "attitude" that comes with it.

Sette MoMA ⧢
16 | 19 | 16 | $37

Museum of Modern Art, 11 W. 53rd St. (bet. 5th & 6th Aves.),
212-708-9710; after 5PM, enter at 12 W. 54th St.
☑ "Tranquil and lovely views" of the MoMA sculpture garden make
this mezzanine Italian a "civilized" "respite" for art buffs; however,
the "postmodern pastas" and "snobby staff" draw mixed reviews.

Sevilla ◗⧢
20 | 13 | 16 | $30

62 Charles St. (4th St.), 212-929-3189
☑ To "feel you're in the south of Spain" just stop into this "dark, cheap,
fun" "old West Village joint"; specializing in "robust", "garlicky" paella
and "superb sangria" for over 50 years, it's still going strong.

Shaan ⧢
22 | 22 | 21 | $37

Rockefeller Ctr., 57 W. 48th St. (bet. 5th & 6th Aves.), 212-977-8400
☑ "Quiet, elegant" "upscale Indian" where "you feel you're in a
palace" with a lunch buffet that's fit for a king; dissenters say curry
"should never be this expensive."

Shabu-Shabu 70 ⧢
18 | 13 | 16 | $30

314 E. 70th St. (bet. 1st & 2nd Aves.), 212-861-5635
☑ A "pleasant", "reasonable", "cook-your-own" East Side Japanese
BBQ that's "the cleanest of its kind", with "polite service" and "fresh"
food; still, a few call it "shabby-shabby."

Shabu-Tatsu ⧢
19 | 15 | 17 | $28

483 Columbus Ave. (bet. 83rd & 84th Sts.), 212-874-5633
1414 York Ave. (75th St.), 212-472-3322
216 E. 10th St. (bet. 1st & 2nd Aves.), 212-477-2972 ◗
■ "You play the chef" at these "affordable", "authentic" Japanese
BBQs featuring at-table cooking, "helpful" waiters and "minimalist
decor"; they're best "on a cold day" with the young and hungry.

Shaliga Thai Cuisine ⧢
▽ 19 | 14 | 16 | $30

834 Second Ave. (bet. 44th & 45th Sts.), 212-573-5526
☑ "Good" Thai food (but "nothing stunning") is presented by "friendly"
staff at this "undiscovered", moderately priced UN local.

Shanghai Manor ⧢
18 | 14 | 18 | $27

141 E. 55th St. (bet. Lexington & 3rd Aves.), 212-753-3900
■ "Dependable" East Midtown Chinese that is "vastly cheaper" than
its famous neighbor Shun Lee Palace; "imaginative cooking", "efficient
service" and the ability to get a table make it worth a try.

Shark Bar ◗⧢
19 | 15 | 16 | $30

307 Amsterdam Ave. (bet. 74th & 75th Sts.), 212-874-8500
■ "Come early to beat the crowd" at this "funky", "raucous" West
Side buppie "nightspot"; it's known as much for its atmosphere and
"celeb clientele" as for its "hearty" Soul Food.

Sharz Cafe & Wine Bar ⧢
20 | 14 | 18 | $29

177 E. 90th St. (bet. Lexington & 3rd Aves.), 212-876-7282
☑ "Small", "homey" East Side Mediterranean bistro with "delicious"
food, "low prices" and "knowledgeable" staff; popularity means the
place is often "cramped" and "noisy."

	F	D	S	C

Shinbashi
280 Park Ave. (48th St.), 212-661-3915   22 | 20 | 21 | $43

Shinbashi-an S
141 E. 48th St. (bet. Lexington & 3rd Aves.), 212-752-0505
☑ "Elegant" "minimalist decor" adds to the "serene teahouse feel" at this "pricey" Midtown Japanese "business" duo with "fresh-off-the-line" sushi and "charming staff"; while "not up to [the top Japanese] competition", it's only a thin slice below.

Shopsin's General Store ⇆
63 Bedford St. (Morton St.), 212-924-5160   ▽ 21 | 14 | 14 | $21
☑ A "huge menu" of "imaginative", "white trash" "home cookin'" and "endless soups made to order" make this "eccentric" West Village grocery "hangout" worth a visit – at least "once per Halley's Comet"; it's an "only in NY, surreal experience."

Short Ribs (Brooklyn) S
2707 86th St. (W. 11th St.), 718-449-4061   17 | 14 | 15 | $25
☑ "Always packed", this "noisy", "bargain" "Brooklyn hangout" specializes in "humongous portions" of "greasy, finger-lickin'" ribs and Cajun chicken; critics say it's "short on everything."

Shun Lee ◐S
43 W. 65th St. (bet. Columbus Ave. & CPW), 212-595-8895   23 | 21 | 21 | $41
■ "Outstanding", "sophisticated Chinese" near Lincoln Center with "sexy" black and white dragon decor; though "expensive" for its genre, it's "certainly the classiest Chinese" in the area.

Shun Lee Cafe ◐S
43 W. 65th St. (bet. Columbus Ave. & CPW), 212-769-3888   21 | 16 | 18 | $32
■ "Popular" for its dim sum, this black and white, "Formica deco" decor West Side Chinese is "great for a quickie before Lincoln Center."

SHUN LEE PALACE ◐S
155 E. 55th St. (bet. Lexington & 3rd Aves.), 212-371-8844   24 | 22 | 22 | $44
■ Michael Tong's East Midtown "perennial favorite" flagship is many surveyors' choice as "the best Chinese in NY"; though "expensive", its "inventive" food is "always excellent" and it "comes with all the flourishes", including attractive Adam Tihany–designed decor.

Siam Inn ◐S
854 Eighth Ave. (bet. 51st & 52nd Sts.), 212-757-4006   20 | 14 | 18 | $25
916 Eighth Ave. (bet. 54th & 55th Sts.), 212-489-5237
■ "Fast, fresh" "affordable" and "convenient for theatergoers", these twin Thais win praise for "attentive" service and "small", plain but pleasant dining rooms.

Sichuan Palace S
310 E. 44th St. (bet. 1st & 2nd Aves.), 212-972-7377   ▽ 21 | 17 | 18 | $33
☑ A favorite of "UN types" for what some call "the best Szechuan food outside of China"; critics clout it as "pricey" and "sterile."

Sido S
1608 Third Ave. (bet. 90th & 91st Sts.), 212-423-0654   17 | 10 | 15 | $18
403 Amsterdam Ave. (79th St.), 212-874-2075 ◐⇆
☑ For "cheap, quick and tasty" hummus and falafel, consider these "tiny" "Middle Eastern favorites" with coffee shop decor.

SIGN OF THE DOVE ◐S
1110 Third Ave. (65th St.), 212-861-8080   23 | 26 | 23 | $55
■ "The ultimate romantic restaurant" with chef Andrew D'Amico's "delectable", "nouveau" American-Continental fare and "fresh flowers everywhere"; given prices as "rich" as the menu, some save this East Side "landmark" "for special occasions"; for a "less expensive", more "casual" experience try the adjoining cafe.

Silk Road Palace 🇸🇿
18 | 8 | 15 | $18

447B Amsterdam Ave. (bet. 81st & 82nd Sts.), 212-580-6294

☑ There's "always a crowd" at this "bargain" Upper West Side Chinese and, with "delicious, freshly prepared food" and free white wine or soda, "who cares about atmosphere" or "the wait outside"?

Silver Palace 🇸
16 | 11 | 11 | $21

50 Bowery (Canal St.), 212-964-1204

☑ It's "like a mad mess hall" at this "cavernous" "Chinatown classic" offering "hot, tasty" dim sum at "fantastic values"; "go with a group" and "just point" at what you want to eat.

Silver Pond (Queens) ●🇸
20 | 10 | 13 | $22

56-50 Main St. (bet. Booth Memorial & 56th Aves.), 718-463-2888

☑ It "still looks like the diner" it once was, but "Flushing's answer to Chinatown" is "worth a visit" for its "divine" dim sum and seafood; however, "parking is a headache" as is "sullen" service.

Silver Spurs ●🇸
14 | 10 | 14 | $15

771 Broadway (E. 9th St.), 212-473-5517
490 La Guardia Pl. (W. Houston St.), 212-228-2333

☑ "Noisy" Villagers serving "juicy" burgers, pancakes and omelets; decor is one cut "above a coffee shop", but low prices "spur you on."

Silver Swan ●🇸
18 | 15 | 17 | $30

41 E. 20th St. (bet. B'way & Park Ave. S.), 212-254-3611

☑ For "hearty", "soul-warming German fare", try this "gemütlichkeit" Gramercy Teuton; besides "outstanding" schnitzel, wursts and strudel, it has "one of the best beer lists in town."

Sirabella's 🇸
21 | 14 | 19 | $33

72 East End Ave. (bet. 82nd & 83rd Sts.), 212-988-6557

■ This "quaint, romantic Italian" is "an East End Avenue secret" that's lauded by locals for its "wonderful staff", "gourmet pizzas" and "excellent pastas" despite a "teeny", "crowded" setting.

Sistina ●🇸
22 | 17 | 20 | $49

1555 Second Ave. (bet. 80th & 81st Sts.), 212-861-7660

☑ East Side Italian with a "creative" menu served in a "lovely", "unpretentious" setting; despite having been around for years, it's relatively little known, possibly because of its price.

Skylight Diner ●🇸
▽ 15 | 15 | 16 | $17

402 W. 34th St. (bet. 9th & 10th Aves.), 212-244-0395

☑ "Enormous portions" come at "minuscule prices" at this "'50s-style diner"; it's "a surprise" to find such "a decent place near Javits."

Sloppy Louie's 🇸
18 | 11 | 14 | $32

92 South St. (bet. Fulton & John Sts.), 212-509-9694

☑ Since 1930, this Seaport "landmark" has been serving "fresh seafood" in a "noisy", "no-frills" "Cape Cod" setting; skeptics cite "high prices", "cranky waiters" and too many tourists.

SMITH & WOLLENSKY ●🇸
23 | 17 | 19 | $51

797 Third Ave. (49th St.), 212-753-1530

■ Argentina never had it so good – for "boys' club business dining" on "T-rex–sized steaks" "with all the fixin's" and "wonderful wines", this "hectic", "bustling" two-floor steakhouse is still "*the* place to go" in Midtown; single women salivate over all the eligible meet.

S.O.B.'s 🇸
15 | 17 | 14 | $33

200 Varick St. (W. Houston St.), 212-243-4940

☑ "Food is the side order" at this "hip", "energetic" SoHo Brazilian; the real specialties are "terrific" live "Latino music", "excellent caipirinhas" and the chance to "dance the night away."

Sofia Fabulous Grill ◐[S] — – | – | – | M

29 E. 61st St. (bet. Madison & Park Aves.), 212-702-9898

Just opened and stylish Eastsiders are already swarming over this colorful, midpriced Tuscan grill and its attractive back terrace; so this is where all the models eat.

Sofia Fabulous Pizza ◐[S] — 18 | 17 | 13 | $31

1022 Madison Ave. (79th St.), 212-734-2676

◪ It's "noisy" and "crowded with good-looking" Eastsiders and Euros, but pizza lovers adore the "crispy", "thin-crust" pies and the terrace that's "an escape to Naples on a spring day."

SoHo Kitchen & Bar ◐[S] — 15 | 16 | 14 | $26

103 Greene St. (bet. Prince & Spring Sts.), 212-925-1866

◪ The "typical American bar fare" may be "underinspired", but "you have to love the flights of wine" at this "cavernous", "bare-brick" loft; go "for the scene" and ignore the "lackadaisical service."

Soho Steak [S]🚫 — 20 | 15 | 15 | $33

90 Thompson St. (bet. Prince & Spring Sts.), 212-226-0602

◪ "Popular bistro" serving "super" steak frites "at bargain prices"; it's "very French, right down to the smokers", and tables are so "squashed together" "you may butt elbows as you cut" your dinner.

Solera — 21 | 20 | 21 | $45

216 E. 53rd St. (bet. 2nd & 3rd Aves.), 212-644-1166

■ "Sophisticated" Midtown "haute" Spaniard that wins olés for its "unbelievable tapas", townhouse setting and smooth service.

Song ◐[S] — ▽ 18 | 19 | 17 | $23

107 MacDougal St. (bet. Bleecker & W. 3rd Sts.), 212-529-3808

◪ Regulars sing the praises of the "spectacular" fried green tea ice cream, "excellent" noodle soups and low tabs at this West Village Vietnamese; however, its quirky decor may be off-key.

Sonia Rose [S] — 24 | 21 | 22 | $48

132 Lexington Ave. (bet. 28th & 29th Sts.), 212-545-1777

■ "Candlelit charm" makes this Murray Hill townhouse arguably "the most romantic" "little hideaway" in NY; though the prix fixe Eclectic-French cuisine is "heavenly", "cramped" seating and "slow" service can cut into the otherwise "magical" experience.

Souen [S] — 17 | 13 | 14 | $21

28 E. 13th St. (bet. 5th Ave. & University Pl.), 212-627-7150

◪ "The bean sprout and Birkenstock crowd" tout the "inventive Vegetarian" cuisine at this "serene" macrobiotic standby; critics cite "rabbit food–bland" dishes with "dormitory-like decor and service."

Soul Cafe ◐[S] — ▽ 19 | 21 | 18 | $29

444 W. 42nd St. (bet. 9th & 10th Aves.), 212-244-7685

◪ A "cool, hip crowd" heads to West Midtown to try this newcomer's "outrageous" portions of "tasty", "upscale African-American Soul Food"; "chic decor" and live music are pluses.

Soul Fixins' 🚫 — ▽ 21 | 8 | 17 | $14

371 W. 34th St. (bet. 8th & 9th Aves.), 212-736-1345

■ "Sylvia's without the tour buses" describes this "bit of Georgia" near Penn Station; soulful foodies squeeze in to hear "old R&B music" while chowing down on "finger-licking-good ribs."

Souperman 🚫 — – | – | – | I

77 Pearl St. (Stone St.), 212-269-5777

Chef Johannes Sanzin has joined the city's soup craze, stirring up a storm at this easily affordable new Downtown lunch spot; though strictly counter service, it's hard to imagine getting more for less.

SOUP KITCHEN INTL. ⌀

| 27 | 4 | 8 | $13 |

259-A W. 55th St. (bet. 8th Ave. & B'way), 212-757-7730

■ "What can anyone say that Seinfeld hasn't covered?"; the soups are "legendary" and so is the "abuse" by chef Al Yeganeh (aka "the soup Nazi"); closed summers, it's takeout only, so "be quick" and "move to the left" – as "art imitates life, life imitates art."

Soup Nutsy

| 17 | 6 | 11 | $11 |

148 E. 46th St. (bet. Lexington & 3rd Aves.), 212-972-8800

☑ Purists dismiss it as a "copycat" "riding on the reputation" of the Soup Kitchen, but others say this "sleeper near the Waldorf" serves "tasty" soups "without the abuse."

Soup Pot ⌀

| ∇ 21 | 11 | 15 | $12 |

73 W. Broadway (bet. Murray & Warren Sts.), 212-962-7687

☑ If you "get over the claustrophobia", it's "like grandma's kitchen" at this pleasant Trade Center "lunch scene" serving "fresh soup and chile daily" along with "delicious wraps and desserts."

South Shore Country Club
(Staten Island)

| ∇ 22 | 24 | 21 | $38 |

200 Huguenot Ave. (W. Shore Expy., exit 4), 718-356-7017

☑ No one disputes the breathtaking "view overlooking the golf course" at this reception favorite; however, comments on the Italian-Continental food run the gamut from "excellent" to "mediocre."

SPARKS STEAK HOUSE

| 25 | 19 | 21 | $55 |

210 E. 46th St. (bet. 2nd & 3rd Aves.), 212-687-4855

☑ "Arteries be damned", this wood-paneled steakhouse standby is worth the cholesterol, crowds and "long waits" for a table; carnivores and oenophiles agree that you can't do much better for "succulent" lobster, aged steaks or fine wines; people literally die to come here.

Spartina ●

| 21 | 18 | 19 | $39 |

355 Greenwich St. (Harrison St.), 212-274-9310

■ "Hip", "laid-back and glamorous" TriBeCa cafe where a "beautiful staff" serves "beautiful customers" "excellent" thin-crust pizzas and other "creative", midpriced Mediterranean dishes; tastefully dressed up in a dress-down neighborhood, it gives all the appearances of being a long-term winner.

Spice Ⓢ

| – | – | – | I |

1411 Second Ave. (bet. 73rd & 74th Sts.), 212-988-5348

Spare, modern East Side Thai newcomer with a menu that includes a number of NY firsts, all at modest prices.

Spirit Cruises Ⓢ

| 11 | 19 | 15 | $50 |

Pier 62, W. 23rd St. (Hudson River), 212-727-2789

■ "Fantastic" views of the city "from every angle" make up for "overpriced", "mediocre" American food and the "cheesy" "middle America floor show" on these island harbor cruises.

Spring Street Natural ●Ⓢ

| 18 | 16 | 15 | $23 |

62 Spring St. (Lafayette St.), 212-966-0290

☑ "Marvelously tranquil" and "airy" "SoHo respite" with a "big", "reasonably priced" menu that "proves health food can be tasty"; unfortunately, "absentminded dancers" double as servers here.

Stage Deli ●Ⓢ

| 19 | 10 | 13 | $22 |

834 Seventh Ave. (bet. 53rd & 54th Sts.), 212-245-7850

☑ For "humongous" sandwiches with prices to match, stop by this "hectic", "crowded" Midtown deli; expect "rushed" waiters, "elbow-to-elbow" seating and "celebrity autographs on the walls."

F D S C

Standard Notions ●🅂   ▽ 18 | 16 | 16 | $16
161 Ludlow St. (bet. Houston & Stanton Sts.), 212-473-3535
☑ Locals say this "friendly" Lower East Side bargain newcomer is "trying hard and succeeding" with "well-prepared" Caribbean, Mexican, Cajun and American combos.

Starbucks 🅂   14 | 11 | 11 | $10
120 E. 87th St. (Lexington Ave.), 212-426-2580 ☾
1559 Second Ave. (81st St.), 212-472-7972
1117-1123 Lexington Ave. (78th St.), 212-517-8476
1445 First Ave. (75th St.), 212-472-7784
1290 Third Ave. (74th St.), 212-772-6903
1128 Third Ave. (66th St.), 212-472-6535
430 Park Ave. (bet. 55th & 56th Sts.), 212-317-1345
Sony Plaza, 550 Madison Ave. (bet. 55th & 56th Sts.), 212-833-6102
400 E. 54th St. (1st Ave.), 212-688-8951
1166 Sixth Ave. (45th St.), 212-354-3730
330 Madison Ave. (42nd St.), 212-682-1880
1100 Sixth Ave. (42nd St.), 212-398-4508
2379 Broadway (87th St.), 212-875-8470 ☾
2681 Broadway (102nd St.), 212-280-1811 ☾
2252 Broadway (81st St.), 212-721-4157 ☾
2045 Broadway (70th St.), 212-496-1551 ☾
152-154 Columbus Ave. (67th St.), 212-721-0470 ☾
322 W. 57th St. (bet. 8th & 9th Aves.), 212-399-0714
1656 Broadway (51st St.), 212-397-7124 ☾
750 Seventh Ave. (bet. 49th & 50th Sts.), 212-974-0032 ☾
1585 Broadway (47th St.), 212-541-7515 ☾
684 Eighth Ave. (bet. 43rd & 44th Sts.), 212-398-9702
585 Second Ave. (32nd St.), 212-684-1299
395 Third Ave. (28th St.), 212-686-2483 ☾
296-300 Third Ave. (23rd St.), 212-598-9651 ☾
304 Park Ave. S. (23rd St.), 212-475-9025
1372 Broadway (bet. 37th & 38th Sts.), 212-921-0827
370 Seventh Ave. (31st St.), 212-967-8463
124 Eighth Ave. (16th St.), 212-462-2020
684 Sixth Ave. (22nd St.), 212-691-1948
378 Sixth Ave. (bet. 8th St. & Waverly Pl.), 212-477-2690
93 Greenwich Ave. (Bank St.), 212-462-4697
21 Astor Pl. (Lafayette St.), 212-982-3563 ☾
141-143 Second Ave. (9th St.), 212-780-0024 ☾
78 Spring St. (Crosby St.), 212-219-2961
38 Park Row (Beekman St.), 212-587-8400
Battery Park, 24 State St. (Pearl St.), 212-482-1180
☑ Java junkies call these coffeehouses "a gift from the gods"; others fear "they're taking over the planet" with inefficiency and high prices.

Stardust Dine-O-Mat ●🅂   14 | 16 | 13 | $18
1491 Broadway (43rd St.), 212-768-3170
☑ It's like "dining with Richie and the Fonz" at this "kitschy", nostalgic Times Square diner featuring singing waiters and "comfort food" that kids love; critics say you "need out-of-state ID to enter."

Star Fish 🅂   19 | 17 | 16 | $40
1294 Third Ave. (bet. 74th & 75th Sts.), 212-744-5924
☑ On the piscatorially deprived East Side, many call this "neighborhood newcomer" "a great catch"; look for "amazingly fresh", though slightly "contrived", seafood and a "quality raw bar."

St. Dymphnas ●🅂   ▽ 19 | 18 | 17 | $17
118 St. Marks Pl. (bet. Ave. A & 1st Ave.), 212-254-6636
■ For "tasty Irish" fare try this East Villager; "a lovely garden", fish 'n' chips and the requisite pints of Guinness make it "authentic."

159

	F	D	S	C
Steak Frites ◐[S]	18	16	16	$35

9 E. 16th St. (bet. 5th Ave. & Union Sq. W.), 212-463-7101
◪ "A little taste of France", this "cheerful", "noisy" Union Square bistro has become a neighborhood "institution"; "stick to the basics" – "delicious" pommes frites and "inexpensive" steak.

Stella del Mare — 21 | 18 | 20 | $45
346 Lexington Ave. (bet. 39th & 40th Sts.), 212-687-4425
◪ This "old-time Italian" in Murray Hill is praised for its "lovely", "quiet" ambiance that's "perfect" for "advertising lunches" or "romantic" dinners; others say "disappointing for the price."

Stingy Lulu's ◐[S]≠ — 14 | 16 | 14 | $17
129 St. Marks Pl. (bet. Ave. A & 1st Ave.), 212-674-3545
◪ You "gotta love" the "kitsch", "old-time diner decor" and "cheap" American "comfort food" at this "dark and smoky" East Villager; hipsters warn "now that it has caught on, it's over."

St. Maggie's Cafe — 17 | 18 | 17 | $33
120 Wall St. (bet. Front & South Sts.), 212-943-9050
◪ "Elegant" 19th-century decor and a "reliable but not exciting" American menu make this "Wall Street eatery" "better than most" for "corporate lunches"; critics claim it "needs a good dusting."

St. Michel (Brooklyn) [S] — ▽ 22 | 19 | 22 | $39
7518 Third Ave. (bet. 75th & 76th Sts.), 718-748-4411
■ "France lives in Brooklyn" at this "romantic little bistro" with what surveyors call "consistently good" food "lovingly prepared" and served by "caring" staff; Bay Ridge residents are delighted.

Sugar Bar ◐[S] — – | – | – | M
254 W. 72nd St. (bet. B'way & West End Ave.), 212-579-0222
Ashford and Simpson's exotic West Side Mediterranean-African newcomer has an appealing menu, friendly staff, attractive African-style decor and a garden in back; despite being pricey by neighborhood standards, it's a buppie favorite.

Sukhothai West [S] — ▽ 18 | 18 | 17 | $26
411 W. 42nd St. (bet. 9th & 10th Aves.), 212-947-1933
◪ Theatergoers mildly tout this "convenient" Thai as "worth the visit" for "tasty", reasonably priced food in a cozy interior.

Sunny East [S] — ▽ 20 | 16 | 18 | $31
21 W. 39th St. (bet. 5th & 6th Aves.), 212-764-3232
■ "Good, reliable Chinese in the heart of the Garment District" with "professional" service and "bargain" lunch specials; "booked" solid at midday, it's "empty on weeknights."

Supper Club — 14 | 21 | 16 | $47
240 W. 47th St. (bet. B'way & 8th Ave.), 212-921-1940
◪ "Relive the glory days of the '40s" at this (weekend only) dinner club with "romantic" ballroom dancing, big bands and "glam decor"; the Continental food and service may be "amateurish", but it's still "fun" at this "dress-up" "B movie Rainbow Room."

Supreme Macaroni Co. — 18 | 14 | 16 | $26
511 Ninth Ave. (bet. 38th & 39th Sts.), 212-564-8074
◪ Celebrating its 50th anniversary, this "red sauce" trattoria in the back of a Hell's Kitchen grocery charms diners with "cheap", "tasty" pasta and "time warp" digs; foes say "deeply ordinary", "not supreme."

Sushi Bar ◐ — 21 | 15 | 17 | $33
256 E. 49th St. (2nd Ave.), 212-644-8750
■ Though it's not "for the purist", surveyors swoon over the "fresh" "sushi with a twist" and "helpful" chefs at this "cool" Midtowner

Sushiden
24 | 18 | 21 | $44

19 E. 49th St. (bet. 5th & Madison Aves.), 212-758-2700
123 W. 49th St. (bet. 6th & 7th Aves.), 212-398-2800

☑ "The best and freshest" sushi draws crowds to this Midtown duo; most give it "an 'A' for service", but some say "stuffy" and "noisy."

Sushi Hana 🅂
22 | 15 | 16 | $29

1501 Second Ave. (78th St.), 212-327-0582

■ "If you can stand the wait" and "abrupt service", you'll be rewarded with "huge portions" of "fresh, creative" sushi at "affordable prices"; fans call it "the best" Japanese on the East Side.

Sushihatsu ●🅂
24 | 13 | 18 | $45

1143 First Ave. (bet. 62nd & 63rd Sts.), 212-371-0238

☑ Die-hard fans swear this "classic" Japanese boasts "the freshest, best sushi in NYC", but you'll have to put up with "Park Avenue prices", "lackluster" service and "nondescript digs" for a taste.

SUSHISAY
26 | 18 | 21 | $49

38 E. 51st St. (bet. Madison & Park Aves.), 212-755-1780

■ "Bring the trust fund" to this Midtown favorite for "expensive" but "superb" "traditional sushi" that's "worth every cent"; the decor may be "sterile", but you can't argue with fish "so fresh" that it wins many votes as best sushi year after year.

Sushiya 🅂
– | – | – | M

28 W. 56th St. (bet. 5th & 6th Aves.), 212-247-5760

Bright, new Midtown Japanese with a midpriced sushi bar and a standard hot menu of tempura, teriyaki, udon soups, etc.; the presence of an obviously contented crowd suggests they're doing things right.

Sushi Zen
24 | 16 | 19 | $41

57 W. 46th St. (bet. 5th & 6th Aves.), 212-302-0707

■ "For people who like their lunch raw", the "fresh, fresh, fresh", "inventive" sushi at this "quick and efficient" Theater District "respite" is always "popular"; if it's "too dark" and "cramped" inside, check out the "charming little-known outdoor garden."

Svoboda ●🅂
– | – | – | M

248 E. Fifth St. (2nd Ave.), 212-387-0707

For Eclectic snacks, drinks of all kinds and a dark, sexy setting, head to this two-tiered East Villager where the restaurant is downstairs and cigar lounge upstairs.

Sweet Basil (Staten Island) 🅂
17 | 15 | 16 | $30

833 Annadale Rd. (bet. Amboy Rd. & Arden Ave.), 718-317-5885

■ "The reason why Staten Island deserves some culinary respect" say fans of the "exotic" game and seafood at this "crowded, comfortable" "storefront" Continental that's also popular for its "bargain" early-bird; N.B. ratings may have been affected by surveyor confusion with the Sweet Basil jazz club in the Village.

Sweet-n-Tart Cafe ●🅂⌷
▽ 19 | 8 | 13 | $14

76 Mott St. (Canal St.), 212-334-8088
136-11 38th Ave. (Main St.), Queens, 718-661-3380

☑ The adventuresome" tout the "refreshing" "mango shakes", "delicious health tonics", "congee and fried donuts" at this "cheap" and "cheery" Chinatown "basement dive"; the Flushing branch is new.

Swiss Inn
16 | 13 | 16 | $33

311 W. 48th St. (bet. 8th & 9th Aves.), 212-459-9280

☑ For a "quick", "good value" "heavy" fondue dinner, this "Theater District standby" is "a nice change of pace"; however, some complain that it's "a little musty" and "truly boring."

161

Sylvia's 🅂   18 | 13 | 17 | $26
328 Lenox Ave. (bet. 126th & 127th Sts.), 212-996-0660
■ The "queen" of Soul Food still packs busloads of "Nikon-toting tourists" and "yuppies" into her "colorful", "tacky" Harlem "landmark" for "dependable" "down-home" "finger-lickin' ribs", fried chicken, greens, sweet potato pie and old-time cakes; "all true NYers should try it", particularly for "the gospel brunch on Sunday."

Syrah 🅂   19 | 16 | 19 | $33
1400 Second Ave. (bet. 72nd & 73rd Sts.), 212-327-1780
☑ "This new kid on the [East Side] block tries hard" and, many say, "delivers" with "genial" service and "upbeat American cuisine"; locals love its wine tastings and "bargain" prix fixe brunches.

Szechuan Hunan Cottage ◑🅂   18 | 9 | 16 | $19
1588 York Ave. (bet. 83rd & 84th Sts.), 212-535-5223
■ Free wine and "very cheap prices" for "tasty" if "greasy" Chinese keep locals lining up outside this East Side "neighborhood standby."

Szechuan Kitchen 🅂≠   23 | 6 | 14 | $18
1460 First Ave. (76th St.), 212-249-4615
☑ "Packing them in for 20 years", this East Side Chinese offers "delicious", "plentiful", "extremely cheap" food in a tiny space that looks like a Kansas kitchen; to avoid the rush, try takeout.

Table d'Hôte 🅂   21 | 19 | 21 | $42
44 E. 92nd St. (bet. Madison & Park Aves.), 212-348-8125
☑ Charming little Carnegie Hill French-American that has good food, service and "tearoom" ambiance; "don't go if you're overweight – there isn't enough room."

Tai Hong Lau 🅂   ▽ 21 | 8 | 12 | $23
70 Mott St. (bet. Bayard & Canal Sts.), 212-219-1431
☑ Fans tout this "overly discovered" Chinatown dive's "fantastic", cheap dim sum, but knock "rude" service and "greasy walls."

Taiyo Japanese 🅂   ▽ 21 | 11 | 17 | $24
1374 York Ave. (bet. 73rd & 74th Sts.), 212-879-3805
■ This "tiny and unassuming" East Side "neighborhood Japanese" yearling boasts "real fresh" sushi and "very friendly" service; admirers call it a "dependable" "good value."

Taka 🅂   ▽ 24 | 15 | 20 | $30
61 Grove St. (bet. Bleecker St. & 7th Ave. S.), 212-242-3699
■ West Village chef-owner Takako Yoneyama "makes art out of sushi" and puts "unique" items on her menu"; but her restaurant is so "irritatingly small" that few surveyors have tried it.

Takahachi ◑🅂   21 | 13 | 16 | $28
85 Ave. A (bet. 5th & 6th Sts.), 212-505-6524
■ Offering "a peek at [East Village] chic" – and freak, this no-reserving Japanese "always has a line" for its "large portions" of "fresh, flavorful" sushi at "bargain" prices.

TakeSushi   21 | 14 | 17 | $37
71 Vanderbilt Ave. (bet. 45th & 46th Sts.), 212-867-5120
☑ Most diners find this midpriced, Grand Central Japanese standby still has the "best sushi and sashimi east of Osaka"; others lament it's "not the sparkler it once was."

Takino Japanese ◑🅂   ▽ 20 | 14 | 17 | $33
1026 Second Ave. (bet. 54th & 55th Sts.), 212-750-2108
☑ "Good homestyle Japanese" with the "best tempura since Tokyo" in a "small, unassuming" East Side "family restaurant"; service ranges from "friendly" to "phantom."

Taliesin ▽ 20 | 21 | 19 | $47

Millenium Hilton, 55 Church St. (bet. Dey & Fulton Sts.), 212-312-2000

◪ "One of the few decent restaurants in the Wall Street restaurant void", this "costly", upper-floor American hotel dining room offers "an excellent business lunch", good views and Frank Lloyd Wright–style space; "in Des Moines, you'd be thrilled", but this is NY.

Tam-Tam Bar ◐[S] – | – | – | M

Kimberly Hotel, 145 E. 50th St. (bet. Lexington & 3rd Aves.), 212-829-9000

Elegant French-Eclectic Midtown newcomer with grass cloth walls, delicate paper lamps, a '40s ambiance, classic jazz and the songs of Edith Piaf as the backdrop for interesting midpriced food.

Tang Pavilion [S] 22 | 18 | 19 | $31

65 W. 55th St. (bet. 5th & 6th Aves.), 212-956-6888

◪ You get "a taste of royal Shanghai" at this Midtown, "fast service", "white-tablecloth" Chinese; usually dining here is "impeccable" but a few notice "an occasional off night."

Tang Tang [S] 15 | 7 | 13 | $18

1328 Third Ave. (76th St.), 212-249-2102

243 Third Ave. (20th St.), 212-477-0460

◪ "Surprisingly good". "cheap", "fast" Chinese restaurants where fans say you "can't go wrong"; however, critics find them "run-of-the-mill" with too much grease.

Tanti Baci Caffé [S] 20 | 14 | 17 | $21

163 W. 10th St. (bet. 7th Ave. S. & Waverly Pl.), 212-647-9651

◪ This "crowded", cheap, "subterranean" Village Italian hideaway now has a wine license; most surveyors still savor the "simple but satisfying" pastas, yet some say they've been disappointed lately.

Taormina of Mulberry St. ◐[S] 20 | 16 | 18 | $36

147 Mulberry St. (bet. Grand & Hester Sts.), 212-219-1007

◪ "Ask what to have" at this Little Italy landmark; it's "one of the better restaurants in the area", and the handy parking lot is a plus, but it doesn't seem the same without John Gotti.

Tapas Lounge, The ◐[S] 16 | 19 | 14 | $31

1078 First Ave. (59th St.), 212-421-8282

◪ "Go with a small appetite and big wallet" because these "tiny tapas" can add up to an "expensive" meal at this Spanish lounge; if you're not tapas-ed out, you may enjoy the live flamenco dancers.

Tapastry [S] 18 | 18 | 19 | $30

575 Hudson St. (bet. Bank & W. 11th Sts.), 212-242-0003

◪ Best "with a big group", this "lively" American tapas specialist in a "gothic" West Village setting offers "real taste treats"; but some find it "not quite good enough" and "overpriced for tiny portions."

Tapika [S] 21 | 22 | 20 | $41

950 Eighth Ave. (56th St.), 212-397-3737

■ The handsome, high-ceilinged decor is "as innovative as the creative SW food" at this trendy restaurant near Carnegie Hall; with "flavors that kick butt", "fantastic margaritas" and "amazing beer choices" it's surprising that it isn't busier; try the brunch buffet.

Taprobane Sri Lankan [S] ▽ 17 | 14 | 18 | $24

234 W. 56th St. (bet. B'way & 8th Ave.), 212-333-4203

■ "The first Sri Lankan restaurant tastes fine but does not define its difference well"; admirers praise its "cheap", "exotic" cuisine (reminiscent of Indian) and "cordial" staff, but people "afraid to try the unknown" leave this Westsider underpatronized.

F	D	S	C

Tap Room Restaurant ◐[S] — | – | – | M
3 W. 18th St. (bet. 5th & 6th Aves.), 212-691-7666
Replacing Zip City, this new brewpub brings otherwise hard to find Austrian food and beers to the Flatiron area at accessible prices.

Taqueria de Mexico [S]≠ 19 | 12 | 15 | $18
93 Greenwich Ave. (bet. Bank & W. 12th Sts.), 212-255-5212
■ A West Village Mexican that serves "quick", "cheap", "greaseless", "muy authentico" "peasant" food and "awesome margaritas" in "a small, funky" space.

Tartine [S]≠ 22 | 15 | 15 | $22
253 W. 11th St. (W. 4th St.), 212-229-2611
■ "Really exceptional" French bistro fare and terrific brunch at low prices get diners to endure "long lines", "cramped" quarters and "surly" "Parisian service" at this West Village BYO "hidden jewel"; it's fun "making friends" with "supermodels" on line.

Tatany [S] 23 | 14 | 17 | $30
380 Third Ave. (bet. 27th & 28th Sts.), 212-686-1871
Tatany 52 ◐[S]
250 E. 52nd St. (bet. 2nd & 3rd Aves.), 212-593-0203
◪ "The best sushi for the buck" plus hot foods all get high marks at this Japanese duo; but service ("Japanese with French attitude") "could be better", "tables are too close" and waits can be "long."

Tatou 18 | 20 | 17 | $43
151 E. 50th St. (bet. Lexington & 3rd Aves.), 212-753-1144
◪ At this "elegant" Midtown East supper club, the French-accented New American food is "surprisingly good", but (except at lunch) the scene, floor show and dancing are the main draws.

Taverna Kyclades (Queens) ◐[S] ▽ 26 | 22 | 25 | $26
33-07 Ditmars Blvd. (bet. 33rd & 35th Sts.), 718-545-8666
■ According to the few surveyors who know it, the Greek food is "impressive" and decor "attractive" at this "crowded" Astoria seafood specialist; "they think a lot of themselves", fortunately "rightfully."

Taverna Vraka (Queens) ◐[S] ▽ 19 | 14 | 16 | $32
23-15 31st St. (bet. 23rd & 24th Aves.), 718-721-3007
■ "Generous portions" of "well-prepared" "basic Greek fare" are only part of the picture at this Astoria taverna; it can be "quiet as a churchyard" or "hopping" once the bouzouki band starts playing.

Tavern on Jane ◐[S] 16 | 15 | 17 | $26
31 Eighth Ave. (Jane St.), 212-675-2526
■ "Reasonably priced", "cozy" West Village "local hangout" that serves "good, hearty" American bar food, burgers and strong coffee along with a full bar.

TAVERN ON THE GREEN [S] 16 | 25 | 17 | $48
Central Park West (67th St.), 212-873-3200
◪ The "glitzy" "Hans Christian Andersen" "fairy-tale setting" at this Central Park American landmark "makes up for any shortcomings"; though critics consider it "touristy", most NYers delight in the "magical" ambiance of the Crystal Room and outdoor dining area as long as they keep their menu choices simple; in any event, "for celebrations" and private parties, it's hard to beat; with over 3,000 surveyors voting, this is obviously one of NY's most important dining destinations.

Tea & Sympathy 🅂

18 | 16 | 16 | $20

108 Greenwich Ave. (bet. 12th & 13th Sts.), 212-807-8329

☑ Anglophiles revel in this "quirky" British tea shop in the West Village, but some criticize "long waits" for "cramped" seating and "arrogant" service at this "$10 trip to England."

Tea Box, The

22 | 21 | 19 | $26

Takashimaya, 693 Fifth Ave. (bet. 54th & 55th Sts.), 212-350-0180

■ A "serene" Midtown "oasis" in the Takashimaya department store serving "terrific teas" and "precious", "gift-wrapped" Japanese bento box food that can be "divine", but is "gone in two bites."

Telephone Bar & Grill ◑🅂

15 | 15 | 14 | $23

149 Second Ave. (bet. 9th & 10th Sts.), 212-529-5000

☑ With a "cute London phone booth theme", this "noisy", "smoky" East Village low-budget "hangout" is "more bar than restaurant", but the "fun Brit food" and "college days" ambiance have their admirers.

Television City ◑🅂

▽ 13 | 15 | 13 | $27

74 W. 50th St. (6th Ave.), 212-333-3388

☑ "The novelty wears off fast" at this new, "loud" Midtown television theme restaurant; surveyors report that it already feels like a "rerun" and the inexpensive Eclectic menu is like a "TV dinner."

Telly's Taverna (Queens) ◑🅂⇗

23 | 11 | 17 | $27

28-13 23rd Ave. (bet. 28th & 29th Sts.), 718-728-9194

■ The "very simple", "cheap" Greek grills are "always wonderful" at this elemental Astoria joint; to fight the crowds, noise and smoke, try the outdoor garden.

TEMPLE BAR ◑🅂

15 | 25 | 17 | $28

332 Lafayette St. (bet. Bleecker & E. Houston Sts.), 212-925-4242

■ "Bogie would have swilled martinis" in this "sexy", "dark" NoHo watering hole that reeks of glamour and "seduction" ("models and investment bankers"); it has "perfect" giant cocktails and "good appetizers", but everyone asks "what food?"

Ten Kai 🅂

22 | 14 | 17 | $35

20 W. 56th St. (bet. 5th & 6th Aves.), 212-956-0127

■ "Sushi so fresh it's almost swimming" is the most noteworthy feature of this "cramped", "midlevel" Midtown Japanese business venue; N.B. the prix fixe lunch is a special bargain.

Tennessee Mountain 🅂

16 | 12 | 14 | $25

143 Spring St. (Wooster St.), 212-431-3993

☑ Hordes of carnivores dub this "down-home", "well-priced" SoHo BBQ "the Himalayas of ribs", chicken and other smoked meats; but didactic detractors dis the food ("take Zantac") and service for having gone down the mountain.

Teodora 🅂

▽ 22 | 18 | 20 | $37

141 E. 57th St. (bet. Lexington & 3rd Aves.), 212-826-7101

■ Off to a good start, this "small", "beautiful" new Midtown Northern Italian has "excellent" "country-style" food and "welcoming" ambiance.

Teresa's 🅂

18 | 9 | 14 | $17

80 Montague St. (Hicks St.), Brooklyn, 718-797-3996 ⇗
70-34 Austin St. (Continental Ave.), Queens, 718-520-2910

☑ "Loosen your belt" for "hearty", "cheap" Central European food; but the coffee shop decor "could use a going over" and "unsmiling" servers remind one of a "Polish automat."

TERRACE, THE
24 | 27 | 24 | $57

400 W. 119th St. (Amsterdam Ave. & Morningside Dr.), 212-666-9490
■ The "marvelous view plus excellent French food and service" keep this rooftop Morningside Heights institution a favorite both "for romance" and "special occasions"; valet parking is a lifesaver.

Tevere 84 S
21 | 18 | 19 | $46

155 E. 84th St. (bet. Lexington & 3rd Aves.), 212-744-0210
☑ "You'd never know" that this "amazing" Upper East Side Northern Italian is also kosher – that is, unless you ask for milk with your coffee; critics speculate "that's why it's overpriced."

T.G.I. Friday's
11 | 11 | 11 | $20

604 Fifth Ave. (48th St.), 212-630-0307 S
47 E. 42nd St. (bet. Madison & Vanderbilt Aves.), 212-922-5671 S
430 Lexington Ave. (bet. 42nd & 43rd Sts.), 212-922-5667
761 Seventh Ave. (50th St.), 212-767-8350 S
21 W. 51st St. (bet. 5th & 6th Aves.), 212-767-8352 S
1680 Broadway (53rd St.), 212-767-8326 ◑S
1450 Broadway (41st St.), 212-626-7399 S
484 Eighth Ave. (34th St.), 212-630-0308 S
47 Broadway (Trinity Pl.), 212-483-8322
☑ Champions of this "cheesy" chain consider it a "reliable" place for drinks, appetizers, burgers and other basic fare; its many detractors see it as "expensive competition for McDonald's."

Thady Con's S
▽ 16 | 23 | 20 | $24

915 Second Ave. (49th St.), 212-688-9700
☑ The "extremely charming" transporting Irish pub decor – complete with four working fireplaces – is the main draw of this new Midtowner; it's a "great place to go for beers", but the Irish food ("scones, mutton, salmon, etc.") is "authentic", "which means bland."

Thai Cafe (Brooklyn) S⊉
▽ 21 | 11 | 15 | $18

923-925 Manhattan Ave. (Kent St.), 718-383-3562
■ "Cheap" Thai food "bursting with flavor" puts this unassumng Greenpoint spot on the gastronomic map; the decor may be "garage sale", but "viewing the food preparation" is "mouthwatering."

Thai House Cafe ⊉
21 | 10 | 19 | $20

151 Hudson St. (Hubert St.), 212-334-1085
☑ "Let the owner-chef pick dishes for you" and this "cheerful" TriBeCa Thai produces "something great" that's "so cheap they practically give it away"; the "mediocre" decor barely matters.

Thailand Cafe S
▽ 19 | 15 | 17 | $23

95 Second Ave. (bet. 5th & 6th Sts.), 212-477-1872
■ There's "really creative cooking" at this "small", often "noisy" East Village Thai with early-bird specials and "friendly", "quick" service.

Thailand Restaurant ◑S
23 | 9 | 15 | $19

106 Bayard St. (Baxter St.), 212-349-3132
■ Despite bare "mess-hall seating", this Downtown cousin of Pongsri Thai is a "cheap" favorite for epicures on jury duty; many consider it "the best Thai in NY."

Thai Orchid S
16 | 11 | 16 | $24

936 First Ave. (bet. 51st & 52nd Sts.), 212-308-2111
☑ The "fresh and tasty" lunch buffet is "a good value" and the back garden "a nice surprise"; but critics decry "pretentious" dinners, "pushy" service and "bizarre" decor.

Thali Vegetarian S≠ ▽ 19 | 11 | 18 | $13

10 Greenwich Ave. (bet. Charles & W. 10th Sts.), 212-367-7411

◪ "Good for a frugal night out", this "tiny", "spartan" Greenwich Village Indian-Vegetarian newcomer has no regular menu, only "Krishna-esque" daily specials; though it's "noisy", singles like "tables so close you can't help starting a conversation."

Thé Adoré ≠ 19 | 16 | 14 | $16

17 E. 13th St., 2nd fl. (bet. 5th Ave. & University Pl.), 212-243-8742

■ "Cozy" two-story Village tea shop serving "wonderful" croissants, "exquisite" sandwiches and "perfect" French pastry; service is "quirky" and the ambiance is "civilized junk shop."

Theodore ◐S – | – | – | E

913 Broadway (bet. 20th & 21st Sts.), 212-673-6333

The Flatiron District's newest venture is a handsome, white-wainscoted, upscale New American with daily Viennese specials and serious prices.

Thomas' S 18 | 20 | 20 | $38

72 Bedford St. (Commerce St.), 212-627-4011

◪ Recently renovated, "cute little" West Village bistro that continues to serve "creative" New American food including "incredible brunch"; still, a few complain "quality has fallen off."

Tibetan Kitchen S 16 | 11 | 16 | $19

444 Third Ave. (bet. 30th & 31st Sts.), 212-679-6286

◪ Murray Hill "hole-in-the-wall" that gives novices a "cheap" and "soothing introduction to Tibetan food"; what some call "bland", others consider "a delightful alternative to Chinese or Thai."

Tibet Shambala S ▽ 19 | 11 | 18 | $18

488 Amsterdam Ave. (bet. 83rd & 84th Sts.), 212-721-1270

◪ This "drab", "mellow" Tibetan West Side "change of pace" has "cheap", "hearty", "interesting" food; though orders may "take forever", service is "caring" and there's soothing Tibetan music.

Tick Tock Diner ◐S ▽ 17 | 16 | 17 | $15

481 Eighth Ave. (34th St.), 212-268-8444

◪ "Very good diner food" and "courteous" service draw people "five nights a week" to this "much-needed", "clean", 24-hour Garment District newcomer; ticked-off diners find it "very suburban."

Tien Fu Guong S ▽ 16 | 15 | 16 | $21

180 Third Ave. (bet. 16th & 17th Sts.), 212-505-2000

◪ "Better than average Chinese", this "long-running" Gramercy "lacquer box" harks back to "fancy Chinese of yore"; a few critics say the food, though "good for the price", is "going downhill", but new owners may improve things.

Tierras Colombianas (Queens) S≠ ▽ 21 | 14 | 17 | $18

3301 Broadway (33rd St.), 718-956-3012

82-18 Roosevelt Ave. (82nd St.), 718-426-8868 ◐

■ Although this Queens pair serves up "mass quantities" of "hearty", "cheap" Colombian food, it's "so good" "there's never a need for a doggy bag"; "patient" staff will guide you through the menu.

Time Cafe ◐S 17 | 16 | 14 | $26

87 Seventh Ave. S. (Barrow St.), 212-220-9100

380 Lafayette St. (Great Jones St.), 212-533-7000

◪ "Trendy" NoHo "standby" that's a "cool" place to people-watch, but also has "healthful" California-style food that's "surprisingly pleasing" and "cheap"; the new West Side site has a roof terrace and both are "relaxing for brunch."

Tin Room Cafe (Brooklyn) 𝗦   ▽ 21 | 20 | 20 | $27
5 Front St. (Old Fulton St.), 718-246-0310
■ New, "already quaint" "Brooklyn find" mixing "delightful" Italian food with live opera in a "pleasant" garden; surveyors "can't understand how they do it at the price"; there's "nice brunch" too.

Tio Pepe ◐𝗦   18 | 17 | 18 | $26
168 W. Fourth St. (bet. 6th & 7th Aves.), 212-242-9338
◪ With "good standard" Spanish-Mexican cuisine, "tapas at the bar", "a pleasant garden room" and a strolling guitarist, this Village mainstay "hangs in" there, despite those who say it has "seen better days."

Titou 𝗦⇗   – | – | – | M
259 W. Fourth St. (bet. Charles & Perry Sts.), 212-691-9359
Decorated with architectural features, this ruddy, warm sibling of Tartine gives West Villagers good French bistro food at such a decent price you can come two or three times per week.

Toast ◐   ▽ 19 | 19 | 18 | $36
428 Lafayette St. (bet. Astor Pl. & 4th St.), 212-473-1698
◪ At this Village people-watching "scene" opposite the Public Theater, the Asian-accented Eclectic food "can be quite good" and there's a new theater/supper club; but it may be "trying too hard to be cool."

Tokyo 𝗦   ▽ 21 | 12 | 16 | $31
342 Lexington Ave. (bet. 39th & 40th Sts.), 212-697-8330
■ "Not just a sushi place", this "very Japanese restaurant" just south of Grand Central offers "very reliable", "interesting" food at "modest" prices; "go with someone who has lived in Japan."

Toledo   ▽ 22 | 21 | 20 | $39
6 E. 36th St. (bet. 5th & Madison Aves.), 212-696-5036
◪ But for its price, most say "olé!" to the "authentic", "classic" Spanish cuisine" at this Murray Hill re-creation of "Madrid in the '60s."

Tombola ◐   ▽ 17 | 13 | 19 | $26
1603 Second Ave. (bet. 83rd & 84th Sts.), 212-772-2161
◪ Despite its small size and "complete lack of decor", this Upper East Side family spot is a "happening place"; parents and kids are willing to stand in line for its "decent" Italian cooking.

Tommaso's (Brooklyn) 𝗦   21 | 16 | 20 | $37
1464 86th St. (bet. 14th & 15th Aves.), 718-236-9883
■ Surveyors say this Bensonhurst "old-world" Italian's food, "amazing wine list", "friendly" ambiance and live opera singing make them "want to live in Brooklyn."

TOMOE SUSHI   27 | 9 | 15 | $32
172 Thompson St. (bet. Bleecker & Houston Sts.), 212-777-9346
■ NYers in search of "simply the best sushi without having to fly to Tokyo" line up "from 6 PM" on at this little Village "zero decor" "hole-in-the-wall"; the "tantalizing" food is "cheap enough" and good enough to make the torturous wait and "rude" service "worthwhile" for all but a few – and they say "it's time to expand."

Tom's Restaurant (Brooklyn) ⇗ ▽ 20 | 15 | 20 | $13
782 Washington Ave. (Sterling Pl.), 718-636-9738
■ "You're treated like family" at this 1936 vintage luncheonette in Prospect Heights; it's "a step back in time" with some of the best diner food around, and an owner who's "one of the sweetest men in NY."

Tony's Di Napoli [S] — 17 | 13 | 16 | $25

1606 Second Ave. (bet. 83rd & 84th Sts.), 212-861-8686

◪ The "cheap" "pastas by the yard" and "family-style" ambiance inevitably remind surveyors of Carmine's; however, some think this spacious East Side trattoria is just a pale imitation.

Toons — 18 | 15 | 16 | $23

363 Greenwich St. (bet. Franklin & Harrison Sts.), 212-925-7440

Toons ◐[S]

417 Bleecker St. (Bank St.), 212-924-6420

◪ "Authentic", "inexpensive" Thai duo that's "reliable" and "yummy"; the West Village branch has "dark" but "homey" decor, while the TriBeCa site has a comfy "living room–like" setting.

Topaz Thai [S] — 22 | 15 | 18 | $24

127 W. 56th St. (bet. 6th & 7th Aves.), 212-957-8020

◪ "When the mood is Thai, the choice is Topaz", especially for a pre–Carnegie Hall dinner; other fans of this "gourmet Thai" "hidden treasure" find takeout preferable to "long waits" and "tight quarters."

TOP OF THE TOWER [S] — 16 | 26 | 19 | $39

Beekman Tower Hotel, 3 Mitchell Pl., 26th fl. (1st Ave. & 49th St.), 212-980-4796

◪ "Stunning", "nonpareil" 360-degree views from the "deco splendor" of this "ultraromantic" "Fred and Ginger"–type Beekman penthouse restaurant/piano bar overshadow the light American-Continental food that "should be better at these prices."

Toraya — ▽ 21 | 24 | 21 | $23

17 E. 71st St. (bet. 5th & Madison Aves.), 212-861-1700

■ "An oasis of calm" amid East Side shops and museums, this "simple but elegant", "Zen-like", Kyoto-style Japanese tearoom is "heaven" for "green tea and Japanese cakes" or "exquisite lunch."

Torre di Pisa NY ◐[S] — 19 | 23 | 17 | $43

19 W. 44th St. (bet. 5th & 6th Aves.), 212-398-4400

◪ This "asymmetrical" Midtown "power lunch"/pre-theater Italian sparks debate over David Rockwell's "Dali-esque" decor ("spectacular" vs. "psycho"), the food ("outstanding" vs. "uneven") and service ("friendly" vs. "slow"); all agree it "leans to the expensive side."

Tortilla Flats ◐[S] — 15 | 17 | 15 | $21

767 Washington St. (W. 12th St.), 212-243-1053

◪ Party-hardies tout "tons of fun", "loud music", margaritas and "cheap eats" – in that order – at this "wonderfully tacky" West Village Mexican; with bingo nights, hula hoop contests and late-night happy hours – well, you've got the point.

Tosca (Staten Island) [S] — ▽ 20 | 22 | 21 | $36

2071 Clove Rd. (bet. Fingerboard & Richmond Rds.), 718-442-6060

■ Surveyors applaud this "up-and-coming", opera-themed Italian as "Staten Island's shining star" because of its "witty" "Disney set" decor, "terrific" food and "personable service"; for a start, try brunch.

Toscana — 19 | 18 | 18 | $41

843 Lexington Ave. (bet. 64th & 65th Sts.), 212-517-2288

◪ "Well-prepared" Tuscan fare and "impeccable service" win fans for this "sedate" East Side Northern Italian; a few critics counter that it's "crowded", "slow" and "not worth the price."

TOTONNO PIZZERIA NAPOLITANO S

25 | 8 | 12 | $15

1544 Second Ave. (bet. 80th & 81st Sts.), 212-327-2800
1524 Neptune Ave. (bet. 15th & 16th Sts.), Brooklyn, 718-372-8606 ⊅
☑ Many consider the "legendary brick-oven pizza" at this Coney Island institution to be "the ultimate"; the recently opened East Side branch is both better appointed and more accommodating than the hard-edged original.

Tout Va Bien ●S

18 | 14 | 18 | $34

311 W. 51st St. (bet. 8th & 9th Aves.), 212-974-9051
■ Besides "consistent", "satisfying", "bargain" French bistro fare, this nearly 50-year-old "faded" Theater District spot serves nostalgia in the form of Edith Piaf records and "French farmhouse" ambiance.

Townhouse, The S

17 | 18 | 19 | $33

206 E. 58th St. (bet. 2nd & 3rd Aves.), 212-826-6241
■ "Everyone is welcome" at this "upscale but casual", gay East Side American townhouse; look for "surprisingly good" "well-priced" food and a $10 prix fixe lunch or $14.50 dinner that's "an incredible bargain"; "what goes on upstairs?" is nobody's business.

Tramps Cafe

– | – | – | M

45 W. 21st St. (bet. 5th & 6th Aves.), 212-633-9570
Live music, young crowds and moderately priced Southern comfort food keep this Flatiron loft hopping; check out who's playing.

Trattoria Alba S

19 | 17 | 18 | $32

233 E. 34th St. (bet. 2nd & 3rd Aves.), 212-689-3200
☑ "Low-key" Murray Hill "neighborhood" Northern Italian with "solid" food, a "comfortable" setting and "accommodating" service; its few critics consider it "just fair" with staff "out of a Scorsese movie."

TRATTORIA DELL'ARTE ●S

22 | 21 | 19 | $42

900 Seventh Ave. (57th St.), 212-245-9800
■ Best known for its body-parts art and celeb clientele, this moderately priced Midtown West Italian also has a "dazzling" antipasto bar and individual pizzas that keep Carnegie Hall–goers and power lunchers coming back; let's "meet under the left breast."

Trattoria del Portico ●S

19 | 16 | 18 | $32

1431 Second Ave. (bet. 74th & 75th Sts.), 212-794-1032
☑ The new "dressed-down", "country inn" setting at this East Side Italian is well suited to the "reasonably priced", "enticingly fresh" homemade pastas; however, some complain service "sometimes misses" and quality is "slipping."

Trattoria I Pagliacci ●S⊅

19 | 12 | 17 | $23

240 Park Ave. S. (bet. 19th & 20th Sts.), 212-505-3072
☑ At this "unpretentious", cash-only Flatiron Northern Italian, the food and prices make surveyors "sing"; but the murals of the namesake clown don't help decor ratings.

Trattoria Romana (Staten Island) S

– | – | – | M

1476 Hylan Blvd. (Benton Ave.), 718-980-3113
Packed nightly with a thirtysomething crowd downing pizzas or nibbling on low-cal dishes, this nondescript brick-oven Italian is worth trying if you're in the neighborhood.

Trattoria Rustica S

21 | 14 | 19 | $31

347 E. 85th St. (bet. 1st & 2nd Aves.), 212-744-1227
■ It's "hard to believe" such "fabulous pasta and fresh sauces" can come from such an "affordable", "homey" East Side "hole-in-the-wall"; despite "too few tables", these people "know how to run a restaurant."

Trattoria Spaghetto ●⧲⧸
18 | 12 | 15 | $25
232 Bleecker St. (Carmine St.), 212-255-6752
☑ This expanded West Village Italian is still packed with diners (inside and out) who appreciate "soup that's a meal" and "hearty pasta" that's more than a meal; the motto here should be "more for less" – with the caveat that bigger isn't always better.

Trattoria Venti Tre ⧲
▽ 19 | 16 | 17 | $26
23 Cleveland Pl. (bet. Spring & Kenmare Sts.), 212-941-0286
■ The interior of this SoHo Italian was renovated this year, but the garden remains the place to dine in summer; fans say you "can't beat the reasonably priced food that comes in megaportions."

Treehouse, The ⧲
– | – | – | M
436 Hudson St. (Morton St.), 212-989-1363
Fans of the Village Atelier will be happy with the smooth transition to this Village newcomer which is more kid-friendly and inherits its romantic space with the same chef, ownership and a similar but lower priced American-French menu; it's reminiscent of a New England inn.

Triangolo ●⧲⧸
20 | 15 | 19 | $30
345 E. 83rd St. (bet. 1st & 2nd Aves.), 212-472-4488
☑ Italian bargain lovers pack this "friendly", "bright" orangey, cash-only East Side "antidote to the pasta doldrums", but a critical minority prefers takeout to eating in this "cramped" space.

Tribeca Grill ⧲
22 | 20 | 19 | $44
375 Greenwich St. (Franklin St.), 212-941-3900
☑ "The limos now have to compete with the tourist buses" at Robert De Niro's "cool hot spot" in a former TriBeCa warehouse; while most surveyors think the New American food is at least as good as the "trendy" scene, skeptics call the place "overpriced" and "overrated."

Trionfo ●
19 | 17 | 20 | $40
224 W. 51st St. (bet. B'way & 8th Ave.), 212-262-6660
☑ This "expensive" Theater District "oasis" is "a fun place to enjoy above-average Italian food" and "friendly" service; however, recent changes, including a new chef and decor, put our ratings in doubt.

Triple Eight Palace ●⧲
18 | 12 | 12 | $22
E. Broadway Mall, 88 E. Broadway (bet. Division & Market Sts.), 212-941-8886
☑ "Dim sum like you've never had it – delicious, creative, limitless" – is why lunchers endure this "smoky, crowded, noisy" Chinatown "barn"; at dinner, it's funereal.

Triplets Old NY Steak House ⧲
17 | 14 | 18 | $40
11-17 Grand St. (6th Ave.), 212-925-9303
■ SoHo Jewish-Romanian that's "an instant bar mitzvah" party and "just what the doctor didn't order"; "embarrassingly corny" waiters sing and deliver "big portions" of "take a Pepcid" "fattening" food, but the triplets' story alone is worth the price of a meal.

Trois Canards ⧲
20 | 18 | 18 | $35
184 Eighth Ave. (bet. 19th & 20th Sts.), 212-929-4320
☑ With "lovely" "bargain" prix fixes, "beautiful" decor and smart service, this "busy" bistro "adds French savoir faire to Chelsea"; still, not all are impressed: "overpriced", "gushy waiters", "assembly line."

Trois Jean ⧲
20 | 19 | 18 | $46
154 E. 79th St. (bet. Lexington & 3rd Aves.), 212-988-4858
☑ Well-heeled locals crowd this recently renovated East Side duplex French bistro for "expensive", "va-ree Franch" food and service, plus "the best desserts in the galaxy."

Tropica Bar & Seafood House
22 | **19** | **19** | **$44**

MetLife Bldg., 200 Park Ave. (45th St. & Lexington Ave.), 212-867-6767

■ Grand Central commuters and business lunchers soak up "a ray of tropical sun" at this Key West–style seafooder with "creative, inventive" fish dishes by a new chef; closed weekends.

T Salon & T Emporium S
18 | **21** | **15** | **$25**

11 E. 20th St. (bet. 5th Ave. & Broadway), 212-358-0506

☑ Look for "heady teas" and accompanying "good", simple food at this "cozy" new Chelsea tea shop with garden; but for "overwired" service, it would have "terrific karma."

Tsampa ◑S
19 | **19** | **20** | **$22**

212 E. Ninth St. (bet. 2nd & 3rd Aves.), 212-614-3226

■ "Mood-altering", "Zen-like" East Village "sleeper" that "brings Tibetan serenity" and "healthful", "delicate" food to a "frenetic neighborhood"; it's the kind of place where you can "bring your meditation" beads and "eat a momo."

Tse Yang S
23 | **24** | **22** | **$51**

34 E. 51st St. (bet. Madison & Park Aves.), 212-688-5447

■ The "benchmark for elegant Chinese cuisine", this "swanky" Midtowner is "a dynasty of its own"; besides "fantastic Peking duck", they'll "make anything you ask for", but inevitably it's "expensive."

T.S. Ma S
18 | **14** | **18** | **$23**

Five Penn Plaza (8th Ave. & 33rd St.), 212-971-0050

☑ "Satisfying", "quick" Chinese at "fair prices" in the Madison Square Garden "culinary desert" accounts for the crowds before games; fans call it "the only game in town."

Tsunami S
17 | **18** | **15** | **$28**

70 W. Third St. (bet. La Guardia Pl. & Thompson St.), 212-475-7770

☑ The "gimmick" of sushi on toy boats floating around a central bar charms patrons of this Village Japanese, but others say it's "smile over substance" and question food that's circled without takers.

Tucci ◑S
17 | **16** | **17** | **$31**

206 E. 63rd St. (bet. 2nd & 3rd Aves.), 212-355-9100

☑ "Erratic" Italian food and language-barrier service cause some to give this East Side trattoria a "thumbs-down"; however, others praise it as an "inexpensive", "unheralded" "side-street find."

Turkish Cuisine ◑S
18 | **13** | **17** | **$26**

631 Ninth Ave. (bet. 44th & 45th Sts.), 212-397-9650

■ Theatergoers "gorge on appetizers" at this low-cost, "tacky", BYO Hell's Kitchen Turk; though "no big deal", it's "fast", "inexpensive" and "good" for kebabs, meze and stuffed grape leaves.

Turkish Kitchen S
21 | **18** | **19** | **$32**

386 Third Ave. (bet. 27th & 28th Sts.), 212-679-1810

Turkish Grill ◑S
193 Bleecker St. (MacDougal St.), 212-674-8833

☑ This Murray Hill mecca offers "delightfully exotic" Turkish food "fit for a sultan" and "solicitous" staffers who ease the way for novices; however, the live music on Tuesdays isn't for everyone; P.S. the less fancy newer Village Grill is "a bargain."

Turtle Bay Grill & Lounge S
∇ **15** | **13** | **15** | **$21**

987 Second Ave. (bet. 52nd & 53rd Sts.), 212-223-4224

☑ The "decent" burgers and other low-cost pub fare are secondary to the "party" feel at this new cigar-friendly, "speakeasy"-style East Side "pickup scene."

Tuscan Square ⓢ

− | − | − | E

16 W. 51st St. (bet. 5th & 6th Aves.), 212-977-7777
Pino Luongo's new Rockefeller Center Tuscan restaurant/market is handy for both workers and tourists who can dine upstairs, pick up breads, sweets, coffee and takeout on the lower level, and browse through myriad shoppables (candles, pottery, clothes, etc.); though too new to rate, it's already crowded.

TUSCANY GRILL (Brooklyn) ⓢ

25 | 18 | 20 | $35

8620 Third Ave. (bet. 86th & 87th Sts.), 718-921-5633
■ "Why go to Italy" when "authentic", "delicious" Tuscan food and "caring service" can be found at this "charming" Bay Ridge grill?; despite the crowds and noise, this "winner" is "worth a trip."

Tutta Pasta ⓢ

16 | 12 | 15 | $21

26 Carmine St. (bet. Bedford & Bleecker Sts.), 212-463-9653 ●
504 La Guardia Pl. (bet. Bleecker & Houston Sts.), 212-420-0652 ●
8901 Third Ave. (bet. 89th & 90th Sts.), Brooklyn, 718-238-6066
160 Seventh Ave. (bet. 1st St. & Garfield Pl.), Brooklyn, 718-788-9500 ●
108-22 Queens Blvd. (71st St.), Queens, 718-261-8713
☑ Reviews for this far-flung pasta minichain are all over the map, ranging from "tops in NYC for cheap pasta" to "bland" and "not tutta gooda anymora"; however, "for a quick bowl of pasta", it's "not bad."

Tutto Sapori ⓢ

▽ 19 | 17 | 18 | $31

245 E. 84th St. (bet. 2nd & 3rd Aves.), 212-517-8365
☑ "Enjoyable" East Side Italian "standby" serving "wonderful" "brick-oven specialties in a warm" and "pretty" setting; the surveyor who said his fish was "better than sex" obviously needs help.

12th St. Bar & Grill (Brooklyn) ⓢ

▽ 21 | 19 | 19 | $28

1123 Eighth Ave. (12th St.), 718-965-9526
■ Now in its second year, this "upscale" but modestly priced American bistro with a "limited but tasty menu" is "worth a trip" to Park Slope; there are good reasons why it gets "crowded."

20 Mott Street ⓢ

20 | 9 | 13 | $22

20 Mott St. (bet. Chatham Sq. & Pell St.), 212-964-0380
☑ "Expect to wait" for "some of the best dim sum in town" at this "cheap", "crowded and noisy" multilevel "Chinese dive"; it improves "if you bring someone who speaks" Chinese and sit upstairs.

"21" CLUB

21 | 22 | 22 | $55

21 W. 52nd St. (bet. 5th & 6th Aves.), 212-582-7200
■ Although this "NY landmark" is still criticized as "clubby" and "pricey", under new management it's doing a lot "to make newcomers feel welcome" with chef Erik Blauberg's "better than ever" American food, "famous people-watching" and prix fixe meals that are "a wonderful deal"; as always, private parties here are impressive; in short, "it's back and better than ever."

Two Boots ⓢ

19 | 12 | 14 | $15

37 Ave. A (bet. 2nd & 3rd Sts.), 212-505-2276
514 Second St. (bet. 7th & 8th Aves.), Brooklyn, 718-499-3253 ●

Two Boots Pizzeria ●ⓢ
42 Ave. A (bet. 3rd & 4th Sts.), 212-254-1919

Two Boots To Go-Go ●ⓢ
74 Bleecker St. (B'way), 212-777-1033

Two Boots to Go West ●ⓢ
201 W. 11th St. (Greenwich Ave. & 7th Ave. S.), 212-633-9096
■ Sophisticated as these cheap, "funky, cool pizzerias with a Cajun twist" may seem, they're also "child magnets"; as a result, many prefer to get their cornmeal-crusted pizza or crawfish calzones to go.

F | D | S | C

Two Rooms ◐[S] ▽ 18 | 22 | 17 | $41

313 E. 58th St. (bet. 1st & 2nd Aves.), 212-223-1886

◪ This trendy East Side newcomer stirs up controversy; fans love the African-International cuisine and "romantic" "colonial" setting, especially after 11 PM when "young lovelies" make the scene; foes feel "totally ripped off" by "arrogant" service and "mediocre" food.

Two Toms (Brooklyn) ⊄ 22 | 9 | 16 | $25

255 Third Ave. (bet. President & Union Sts.), 718-875-8689

◪ "Like a family party", this "noisy", out-of-the way, "spartan" Boerum Hill Italian is not for the faint of heart; with no menus, "the waiter tells you what's available" and "mammoth portions" of inexpensive food follow; for best results, bring 10 or more friends.

Two Two Two [S] 24 | 22 | 22 | $54

222 W. 79th St. (bet. Amsterdam Ave. & B'way), 212-799-0400

◪ Ardent admirers of this French-accented Continental in a handsome West Side townhouse would rate it "one, one, one" for food, decor and service; however, some surveyors feel it's "too too too", as in crowded, noisy and expensive.

Typhoon Brewery 18 | 17 | 14 | $32

22 E. 54th St. (bet. 5th & Madison Aves.), 212-754-9006

■ Despite dropping ratings, the "pricey", "devilishly spicy" Thai food and house-brewed beers get good reviews at this "sleek", "trendy" Midtown "yuppie" hangout; it's often as "noisy" as a typhoon.

Ubol's Kitchen (Queens) [S] ▽ 23 | 11 | 21 | $22

24-42 Steinway St. (25th Ave.), 718-545-2874

◪ Thai it, "you'll like it" – "even the medium spicy is hot" at this "friendly", low-budget Astoria "find"; however, it has "off nights – maybe the chef was on vacation."

Ukrainian East Village [S]⊄ 18 | 9 | 13 | $20

140 Second Ave. (bet. 9th St. & St. Marks Pl.), 212-529-5024

■ At this "grubby" East Village "dive", you'll find "plain but substantial", "great value" Eastern European "homestyle cooking", e.g. pierogi, barley vegetable soup, potato pancakes – enough said.

Uncle George's (Queens) ◐[S]⊄ 19 | 8 | 13 | $19

33-19 Broadway (34th St.), 718-626-0593

■ "Plates of great classics" (grilled fish is "sensational") come to you at this lines-out-the-door, 24-hour Astoria Greek – a "cheap", "boisterous", "upscale diner" that's a "late-night lifesaver."

Uncle Jack's Steakhouse (Queens) – | – | – | E

39-40 Bell Blvd. (40th Ave.), 718-229-3400

There's a Manhattan feel to this new, upscale Queens steakhouse with a hopping bar, "21" Club–veteran waiters, Kobe beef, single-malt scotches and a cigar room that's a modern take on Victorian decor; early visitors say it brings class to Bayside.

Uncle Nick's [S] 21 | 12 | 16 | $25

747 Ninth Ave. (bet. 50th & 51st Sts.), 212-245-7992

569 Hudson St. (W. 11th St.), 212-206-3951

◪ "The only thing missing is a sea view" at this "authentic" Greek taverna (with a new Village offshoot); while most tout the "great value" grilled fish, kebabs and salads, others say it's "not up to its hype."

Union Pacific

_– | – | – | E_

111 E. 22nd St. (bet. Lexington & Park Aves.), 212-995-8500
The Flatiron District's most ambitious newcomer, from the owners of Rain and Main Street Uptown, brings back chef Rocco DiSpirito, whose Dava fans still savor his American fare with a global twist; the former C.T. space has been reconstructed and is more inviting than ever; the only question is whether foodies, bankers or models will dominate here.

UNION SQUARE CAFE S

27 | 24 | 26 | $53

21 E. 16th St. (bet. 5th Ave. & Union Sq. W.), 212-243-4020
☑ Once again rated NY's Most Popular restaurant, because "it all clicks" at Danny Meyer's "urbane", "feel good", "quintessential" NYC landmark off Union Square; over 4,400 surveyors report that it "deserves all possible superlatives" for chef Michael Romano's American-Eclectic cooking, unusually "reasonable prices" that are $10 to $20 below the competition and Meyer's "relaxed", "gracious" direction which is reflected in high service ratings.

Universal Grill ◑S

16 | 16 | 17 | $27

44 Bedford St. (bet. Carmine & Leroy Sts.), 212-989-5621
☑ "Campy, gay" "West Village spin on a diner" that's "a hoot for the hip": "every night is New Year's Eve" with "creative" American food served by young tambourine-banging waiters.

Urban Hero ⊄

▽ 18 | 4 | 12 | $11

245 W. 38th St. (bet. 7th & 8th Aves.), 212-719-0665
■ Only open for lunch, this unusual Midtown hero shop has the "ugliest decor" but serves cheap, "fresh, flavorful" heros made from the likes of poultry sausages, plus soups and salads.

Üsküdar S

21 | 12 | 19 | $29

1405 Second Ave. (bet. 73rd & 74th Sts.), 212-988-2641
■ This "terrific" East Side Turkish "closet" has a "talented chef", "reasonable prices" and "helpful staff"; however, a few find it "a little too tight for comfort."

Va Bene S

20 | 17 | 18 | $40

1589 Second Ave. (bet. 82nd & 83rd Sts.), 212-517-4448
■ "You'd never notice" it's kosher, assert customers of this somewhat formal East Side dairy Italian; though it's a bit "pricey", those who keep kosher and have limited dining options say it's "worth it."

V&T Pizzeria ◑S

19 | 8 | 13 | $15

1024 Amsterdam Ave. (bet. 110th & 111th Sts.), 212-663-1708
☑ "A Columbia tradition", this "Energizer Bunny of college hangouts" serves "cheap", cheesy, chewy pizza to cholesterol addicts who hardly notice its "surly" service and "needs-a-boost" decor.

Van West ◑S

17 | 14 | 18 | $20

247-249 W. 72nd St. (bet. B'way & West End Ave.), 212-579-6828
☑ Free wine with dinner, a greenhouse back room, "sensible prices" and civil service draw Westsiders to this otherwise "typical" Chinese-Vietnamese yearling; in sum, it's "good but not great."

Vatan S

20 | 22 | 21 | $29

409 Third Ave. (29th St.), 212-689-5666
■ Murray Hill Indian with a "storybook" "Indian village setting" serving an AYCE prix fixe Vegetarian "feast"; still, some gripe about the no-choice set menu and price that's "over the top" – for Indian food.

Vegetarian's Paradise 🅂
18 | 11 | 14 | $18
33 Mott St. (Pell St.), 212-406-6988
144 W. Fourth St. (bet. MacDougal St. & 6th Ave.), 212-260-7130
☑ At this stark Chinese duo, they serve vegetarian dishes with "faux" meat; fans find the tofu switch a "delicious" "novelty" at "bargain prices", but foes say "it gets boring" and you "pay more for less fat."

Velvet Restaurant & Lounge ◗🅂
— | — | — | M
223 Mulberry St. (bet. Prince & Spring Sts.), 212-965-0439
Sleek and sexy sums up this SoHo newcomer featuring a creative Continental menu; though the tab for dinner and drinks can add up, the locale and upstairs lounge fully compensate.

Velvet Room ◗🅂
14 | 23 | 13 | $28
209 E. 76th St. (bet. 2nd & 3rd Aves.), 212-628-6633
☑ A "smoky", "sexy" East Side Spanish-Med where wine, desserts and tapas are secondary to "vampy" "*Addams Family*" decor; go for "romantic" "mood dining" – "picture the inside of Jeannie's bottle."

VENIERO'S ◗🅂
23 | 13 | 13 | $13
342 E. 11th St. (bet. 1st & 2nd Aves.), 212-674-7070
☑ "When calories don't count" "you can have your cake and eat it too" at this inexpensive 1894 East Village Italian bakery/cafe; lines and "touristy" ambiance don't deter those dreaming of "sweets."

Vera Cruz (Brooklyn) ◗🅂
— | — | — | M
195 Bedford Ave. (bet. 6th & 7th Sts.), 718-599-7914
Little known outside its Williamsburg neighborhood, this hip but also family-friendly Mexican-cum-garden serves authentic south-of-the-border food with modest prices to match.

Verbena 🅂
23 | 22 | 21 | $50
54 Irving Pl. (bet. 17th & 18th Sts.), 212-260-5454
■ Diane Forley creates "savory", "sophisticated" seasonal dishes at her Gramercy New American where "spare, elegant" decor and a "secret garden" "oasis" lull diners into forgiving high prices and well-meaning "actors . . . I mean waiters."

Vergina
∇ 19 | 17 | 20 | $32
231 E. 53rd St. (bet. 2nd & 3rd Aves.), 212-317-1566
■ An "authentic", "friendly" East Midtown Greek newcomer that's a good bet for a "festive" meal of "serious garlic" in a "lovely townhouse"; so far few have found it, making ratings less reliable.

Vermouth ◗🅂
∇ 17 | 18 | 15 | $26
355 Amsterdam Ave. (77th St.), 212-724-3600
■ "Trendy" new West Side scene that scores with "killer martinis", "diverting decor" and New American cuisine; not surprisingly some "never make it to the food" and "crawl out – wasted."

Veselka ◗🅂
17 | 12 | 13 | $15
144 Second Ave. (9th St.), 212-228-9682
☑ Though the recent rehab of this East Village Ukrainian classic receives mixed reviews, it remains a "hearty" blintz and borscht "paradise" with "gentle prices" that's both "divey and delicious."

Vespa Cibobuono ◗🅂
∇ 21 | 19 | 19 | $31
1625 Second Ave. (bet. 84th & 85th Sts.), 212-472-2050
■ A "simple" East Side Italian "neighborhood staple" with a "wonderful garden" and NY's "most unique host"; it's touted as "great for a first date" over "homestyle" pastas.

Via Brasil ◐[S] ▽ 18 | 14 | 18 | $32
34 W. 46th St. (bet. 5th & 6th Aves.), 212-997-1158
■ Surveyors say "we had fun" at this "lively" Midtown Brazilian serving "large", "meaty" portions of "authentic", "inventive" dishes; live music nights keep everyone in a south-of-the-border mood.

Viand [S] 16 | 7 | 14 | $16
300 E. 86th St. (2nd Ave.), 212-879-9425 ◐
1011 Madison Ave. (78th St.), 212-249-8250
673 Madison Ave. (bet. 61st & 62nd Sts.), 212-751-6622 🚫
■ "Tops in coffee shops" with "the best turkey sandwich in NY", these independently owned, "cheap" but "deluxe" spots satisfy locals looking for a "fast and good" no-fuss, no-frills meal.

Via Oreto [S] 23 | 15 | 21 | $36
1121 First Ave. (bet. 61st & 62nd Sts.), 212-308-0828
■ "Sometimes simplicity works" – it certainly does at this "cozy" East Side "neighborhood Italian" with mama-style "home cooking" and "gracious" mother and son hosts; "like eating with relatives who care", it "never misses a beat."

Viceroy, The ◐[S] 14 | 17 | 14 | $27
160 Eighth Ave. (18th St.), 212-633-8484
◪ "Oh, you're supposed to eat?" ask those who cruise this Chelsea American gay scene with "glam" art deco ambiance and "easy-on-the-eyes" waiters; so what if the food is only "fair?"

Vico ◐[S]🚫 21 | 14 | 18 | $41
1302 Madison Ave. (bet. 92nd & 93rd Sts.), 212-876-2222
◪ "Clubby" but "kid-friendly" Carnegie Hill Italian standby that pleases neighborhood "members" with "consistently tasty" pastas; it draws mixed reviews from nonregulars as "pricey" and "stuffy."

Victor's Cafe 52 ◐[S] 19 | 18 | 18 | $38
236 W. 52nd St. (bet. B'way & 8th Ave.), 212-586-7714
■ For "good" but "not great, not cheap" Cuban food and "relaxing" "Havana in the '50s ambiance", try this Theater District "mainstay"; skirt steak, roast pig, ropa vieja and sangria all score well.

Viet-Nam [S] 22 | 8 | 16 | $18
11-13 Doyers St. (bet. Bowery & Pell St.), 212-693-0725
◪ "Fresh", "exotic" and "cheap" sing surveyors about this "spicy, satisfying" Chinatown Vietnamese; despite "minimalist", "grungy" decor, most diners consider the food the "best" of its kind in NY.

VIEW, THE [S] 19 | 26 | 20 | $46
Marriott Marquis Hotel, 1535 Broadway (bet. 45th & 46th Sts.), 212-704-8900
◪ "Appropriately named", this Times Square Continental's rotating rooftop "view is the headliner"; however, its "surprisingly good" food and "fantastic" AYCE buffet draw NYers as well as sightseers.

Villa Berulia 22 | 19 | 23 | $40
107 E. 34th St. (bet. Lexington & Park Aves.), 212-689-1970
■ A "miracle on 34th Street" say regulars of this "intimate" Murray Hill Northern Italian "standby" with "you ask for it, you get it" service and "always steady", "good" food.

Village Bistro [S] ▽ 21 | 17 | 20 | $27
92 Seventh Ave. S. (bet. Barrow & Grove Sts.), 212-255-6665
◪ You "can't go wrong" since the beer may be the "best in town" at this West Village New American with "surprisingly" good food; those in the know feel it's fine for a burger and brew.

Village Grill ◐ [S] ▽ 16 | 16 | 15 | $25

518 La Guardia Pl. (Bleecker St.), 212-228-1001

◪ "Average" is the consensus on this West Village French-American "hangout" with a "convenient" NYU location and "passable" food; service is "unbelievably slow even when the place is empty."

Villa Mosconi 19 | 15 | 19 | $34

69 MacDougal St. (bet. Bleecker & W. Houston Sts.), 212-673-0390

■ An "old West Village favorite", this "hearty", "consistent" Italian "family place" serves "earthy" standards that are "still good after all these years"; surveyors also laud the new back garden.

Vince and Eddie's ◐ [S] 19 | 17 | 18 | $40

70 W. 68th St. (bet. Columbus Ave. & CPW), 212-721-0068

◪ "Go early or late" to avoid the Lincoln Center "crush" and "rush" at this "homey" American where chef Scott Campbell creates reliably "good"meals, including a "standout" brunch; reactions to the setting range from "cozy" "country home" to "sardine can."

Vinegar Factory Restaurant [S] 20 | 13 | 14 | $23

431 E. 91st St., 2nd fl. (bet. 1st & York Aves.), 212-987-0885

■ Eli Zabar's weekend-only Upper East Side brunch and bread spot above his food emporium is a "family-friendly" "yuppieville" serving "the best French toast on the planet"; though the mezzanine setting is "bare-bones", his food is "fresh" and "healthy."

Vinnie's Pizza ◐ [S] ≠ 21 | 6 | 13 | $11

285 Amsterdam Ave. (bet. 73rd & 74th Sts.), 212-874-4382

◪ "A perfect slice of NY" is found at this West Side pizzeria possessing the "best pies" and "worst ambiance"; super "cheesy" toppings and thick crusts have locals insisting "there is no better."

Vintage ◐ [S] ▽ 16 | 20 | 20 | $23

753 Ninth Ave. (bet. 50th & 51st Sts.), 212-581-4655

◪ A Hell's Kitchen newcomer serving American tapas in a "hip", "dark", "sophisticated" space to a "mellow crowd"; it's "up and coming", but currently more "comfy" lounge than restaurant.

Virage ◐ [S] ▽ 19 | 14 | 17 | $25

118 Second Ave. (bet. 7th & 8th Sts.), 212-253-0425

◪ This "funky", modestly priced East Village Eclectic newcomer earns mixed reviews, from "sublimely fresh" to "mediocre"; "they're still trying to get it right", with "lots of room for improvement."

Virgil's Real BBQ [S] 19 | 14 | 16 | $26

152 W. 44th St. (bet. B'way & 6th Ave.), 212-921-9494

■ "Enormous portions" of "greasy but great" BBQ attract "urban cowboys" (and girls) to this Times Square "hog heaven", "heart attack headquarters"; "bring a big appetite and some wet naps."

Vittorio Cucina [S] ▽ 24 | 19 | 20 | $33

308-310 Bleecker St. (bet. Grove St. & 7th Ave. S.), 212-463-0730

■ A "sleeper" with what some call "incredible" food and a "lovely" garden, this West Village Italian is a "comfortable", "old-fashioned" experience; one inevitably wonders why it's "usually empty."

Vivolo ◐ 20 | 19 | 20 | $39

140 E. 74th St. (bet. Lexington & Park Aves.), 212-737-3533

■ "Beautiful" East Side Italian townhouse that's a "reliable" "old friend" to seniors soothed by its "dark", firelit downstairs dining room and bargain pre- and post-theater prix fixe menus.

Volare
▽ 22 | 18 | 23 | $35

147 W. Fourth St. (bet. 6th Ave. & Washington Sq. Park), 212-777-2849

■ "Unexpectedly romantic", "very hospitable" West Village Italian where the staff is like "family" and the food is "hearty" and "old-fashioned"; it's a bit pricey, but "always a pleasure."

VONG 🅂
25 | 25 | 22 | $52

200 E. 54th St. (3rd Ave.), 212-486-9592

☑ A "one-of-a-kind" "adventure" awaits at this Midtown "destination"; here Thai meets French in an "elegant", "exotic" (some say "zany") "fantasy" setting and the resulting "innovative" flavors are enjoyed by a "hip", "sexy" crowd; but for "attitude, attitude, attitude" and "high prices", it would be perfect.

Vynl Diner 🅂
16 | 15 | 16 | $18

824 Ninth Ave. (54th St.), 212-974-2003

☑ Plan on Asian-accented coffee shop fare at this "groovy" Hell's Kitchen diner and brunch specialist; the "funky hipster" ambiance and "original" eats aren't for the fainthearted or easily heartburned.

Walker's ◐🅂
15 | 14 | 15 | $22

16 N. Moore St. (Varick St.), 212-941-0142

☑ An "old, reliable" 1890 vintage TriBeCa pub where local artists, Wall Streeters and stars "mingle over beers" and burgers in a "genuine old NY" room.

Wall St. Kitchen & Bar
14 | 15 | 13 | $27

70 Broad St. (Beaver St.), 212-797-7070

☑ "More yuppie than yummy", this "new", weekday-only American "fills a real need" in the culinarily "desolate" Financial District; it "finally brings a little trendiness below Chambers Street."

Wally's and Joseph's ◐
20 | 15 | 20 | $45

249 W. 49th St. (bet. B'way & 8th Ave.), 212-582-0460

☑ "If you're a man's man who loves steaks and lobsters" simply "step back in time and enjoy" this "clubby" Theater District surf and turf standby; critics call it plastic and tired, but they're outvoted.

Washington Place 🅂
– | – | – | M

75 Washington Pl. (bet. 6th Ave. & Washington Sq. Park), 212-539-1776

This Village newcomer in a "romantic brownstone setting" clearly has potential; American-Mediterranean specialties are the draw.

WATER CLUB, THE ◐🅂
22 | 25 | 21 | $52

500 E. 30th St. (East River), 212-683-3333

■ Located on an East River barge, Buzzy O'Keeffe's "romantic", pricey American offers "amazing seafood" in a handsome, "clubby" setting with a "breathtaking view" that makes it a popular "place for special occasions" and parties; try the "dynamite brunch."

Waterfront Ale House 🅂
16 | 12 | 15 | $20

540 Second Ave. (30th St.), 212-696-4104
155 Atlantic Ave. (bet. Henry & Clinton Sts.), Brooklyn, 718-522-3794

☑ "Go for the happy hour" at either of these pubs; boasting "large selections of microbrews" and gametime TVs, both serve as "second homes" for the beer and burger crew.

Waterloo Brasserie ◐🅂
– | – | – | M

145 Charles St. (Washington St.), 212-352-1119

A spin-off from the popular Le Zoo nearby, this Belgian West Villager has been hopping with a smart young crowd since day one, offering an affordable menu led by mussels and frites; there's a happening bar too.

F D S C

WATER'S EDGE (Queens) 23 26 23 $52
44th Dr. & East River (Vernon Blvd.), 718-482-0033
■ Starting with the free ferry ride, this "elegant", highly rated Long Island City American offers "spectacular views of the Manhattan skyline" and an "enormously romantic" space; "aka Weddings-R-Us."

Well's ◐[S] ▽ 18 13 16 $23
2247-49 Seventh Ave. (bet. 132nd & 133rd Sts.), 212-234-0700
■ Devotees delight in the "dee-lish" food at this "congenial and spirited" Harlem Soul Fooder serving "slammin'" fried chicken and waffles; it also has live jazz and dancing (Mondays and Fridays).

West Bank Cafe ◐[S] 16 15 16 $28
Manhattan Plaza, 407 W. 42nd St. (bet. 9th & 10th Aves.), 212-695-6909
■ "The famous and soon to be" can be spotted consuming the New American fare at this "comfortable, casual" Theater District cafe; at night you can enjoy the live music here without blowing a lot of cash.

West End Cottage ◐[S] 15 10 15 $17
212 W. 72nd St. (bet. B'way & West End Ave.), 212-874-6556
◪ "Quick", "above-average", "cheap" Chinese fare and "free-flowing wine" draw many Westsiders to this "neighborhood place"; however, the "tacky decor" encourages takeout.

West 63rd St. Steakhouse ◐[S] 21 22 21 $51
Radisson Empire Hotel, 44 W. 63rd St. (bet. B'way & Columbus Ave.), 212-246-6363
◪ Besides its handy Lincoln Center location, what makes this steakhouse a "cut above the rest" is its "quiet", "elegant setting" that appeals to older clients; still, some beef about portions that "elevate your cholesterol count" and lower your bank account.

White Horse Tavern ◐[S]≠ 12 14 13 $20
567 Hudson St. (11th St.), 212-989-3956
■ Come "with friends" to drink and enjoy a burger at this "old NY" Dylan Thomas haunt West Village pub; the outside tables provide a "great place to hang out" and people-watch.

Wilkinson's Seafood [S] 23 18 21 $46
1573 York Ave. (bet. 83rd & 84th Sts.), 212-535-5454
■ "Yorkville's best-kept secret" lures in a "classy clientele" with "delectable seafood" and "very good wines" in a "serene Mondrian-esque setting"; since the food is "pricey", you may want to try the $21.95 early-bird special.

Willow [S] 20 20 20 $43
1022 Lexington Ave. (73rd St.), 212-717-0703
◪ In a "nicely lit" duplex townhouse, this "charming", "unhurried" Eastsider serves a pleasing New American–French menu that gives you that "home-away-from-home feeling"; "intimate and comfortable", it's the "ideal place" for a "lovely, quiet dinner."

Wilson's ◐[S] 15 15 16 $28
201 W. 79th St. (Amsterdam Ave.), 212-769-0100
■ Though some find the "straight-ahead" American food only "so-so" in this "lofty" West Side grill, the "young, hungry, partying crowd" enjoys the "bar scene", "huge martinis" and live music.

Windows on India ◐[S] 19 16 16 $21
344 E. Sixth St. (1st Ave.), 212-477-5956
■ Being the "prettiest" restaurant on Curry Row doesn't say much, but having some of the best Indian food does; "stay away from the vindaloo unless you have a cast-iron stomach."

WINDOWS ON THE WORLD 🅂   20 | 26 | 21 | $55

One World Trade Ctr., 107th fl. (West St.), 212-524-7000

■ "It's the view, stupid" that brings diners from all over the world to this reopened 107th-floor New American; if the high-priced "food doesn't match the view", that's no criticism, and the recent arrival of chef Michael Lomonaco may address the problem; besides the main restaurant, there's a host of other facilities including The Greatest Bar on Earth, Cellar in the Sky and numerous private party rooms.

Wollensky's Grill ●🅂   21 | 16 | 18 | $40

201 E. 49th St. (3rd Ave.), 212-753-0444

■ "For a casual encounter with meat", "clubby carnivores" herd next door to Smith & Wollensky's "cheaper" but equally good sibling; it's also popular for its outdoor tables and late hours.

Wong Kee 🅂⊘   22 | 6 | 12 | $15

113 Mott St. (bet. Canal & Hester Sts.), 212-966-1160

■ Chinatown's "consistent", "fresh", "delicious Cantonese" at real "low prices" compels fans to say "to hell with the ambiance" and "I wish I lived closer."

Won Jo ●🅂   21 | 11 | 13 | $25

23 W. 32nd St. (bet. B'way & 5th Ave.), 212-695-5815

■ "Huge portions" from a "huge menu" "satisfy Korean cravings" at this 24-hour BBQ joint on the 32nd Street Korean strip; "bring a translator, wear an old dirty shirt" and plan to grill your own meal.

Woo Chon ●🅂   22 | 13 | 14 | $28

8-10 W. 36th St. (bet. 5th & 6th Aves.), 212-695-0676
41-19 Kissena Blvd. (Main St.), Queens, 718-463-0803

■ "Spice up your life with some Korean food" at this 24-hour duo that serves some of the "finest and smokiest" BBQ in town; a "full color photo menu is helpful in ordering" for novices.

World Yacht 🅂   13 | 22 | 16 | $57

Pier 81, W. 41st St. (Hudson River), 212-630-8100

☑ Although the sights are "spectacular" on this wining, dining and dancing yacht, the "mediocre", cafeteria-like Continental cuisine is a turnoff; dinner cruises are $67 and up, Sunday brunch, a mere $39.

Wraparama 🅂⊘   ▽ 16 | 11 | 13 | $13

163 First Ave. (bet. 10th & 11th Sts.), 212-358-9727

☑ East Village newcomer offering multiethnic burritos that include "delicious ingredients" and healthy choices; "easy on the wallet", it's a "neat" alternative to fast food.

Wu Liang Ye 🅂   21 | 13 | 15 | $27

215 E. 86th St. (bet. 2nd & 3rd Aves.), 212-534-8899
36 W. 48th St., 2nd fl. (bet. 5th & 6th Aves.), 212-398-2308
338 Lexington Ave. (bet. 39th & 40th Sts.), 212-370-9647

■ "Chinese heaven is hot, hot, hot" according to fans who find nirvana at these "spicy" Szechuan shops; they give you a taste of Chinatown "without having to travel there."

Wylie's Ribs ●🅂   16 | 10 | 14 | $26

891 First Ave. (50th St.), 212-751-0700

☑ Though surveyors "blow hot and cold" over this East Midtown BBQ joint, kids especially love the "huge" beef ribs that "look like they come from dinosaurs."

Xando Coffee & Bar ●🅂   – | – | – | I

2160 Broadway (76th St.), 212-328-2501

While some may find this caffeinated newcomer merely a Starbucks without the franchise incarnations, other bean buffs are sure to be swayed by its colorful decor and generous tea and coffee menu.

F | D | S | C

Xunta [S] 20 | 14 | 14 | $22
174 First Ave. (bet. 10th & 11th Sts.), 212-614-0620
◪ "Your taste buds will dance" along with the "festive staff" as you enjoy the "fantastic" tapas and sangria at this "noisy and crowded", "bargain" East Village Spaniard; to get a seat, "go early."

Yaffa Cafe ◐[S] 15 | 17 | 13 | $17
97 St. Marks Pl. (bet. Ave. A & 1st Ave.), 212-674-9302
◪ The "pierced" crowd finds the garden of this "cheap", "laid-back" 24-hour East Village semi-Vegetarian the perfect place to "compose angst-ridden poems" while munching on salads and veggie burgers.

Yaffa's ◐[S] 17 | 17 | 14 | $21
353 Greenwich St. (Harrison St.), 212-274-9403
Yaffa's Tea Room ◐[S]
19 Harrison St. (Greenwich St.), 212-966-0577
■ Hip "artists and yuppies" love to linger at the well-spaced tables of this affordable TriBeCa Eclectic duo with "funky" "opium parlor" ambiance; for best results, keep it simple and take it slow.

YAMA 26 | 11 | 14 | $31
122 E. 17th St. (Irving Pl.), 212-475-0969
92 W. Houston St. (bet. La Guardia Pl. & Thompson St.), 212-674-0935 ◐[S]
◪ Gramercy Japanese (with a new Village spin-off) revered for "bargain", "whale-sized" sushi so tender you "don't need teeth" and so fresh it's "still moving"; on the downside: "horrific" waits, "rushed service" and "claustrophobia."

Yamaguchi 19 | 14 | 17 | $30
212 E. 52nd St. (bet. 2nd & 3rd Aves.), 212-754-4840
35 W. 45th St. (bet. 5th & 6th Aves.), 212-840-8185
■ "Basic" Midtown Japanese that are popular as "reasonably priced" "business lunch destinations"; while the "samurai" decor doesn't dazzle, you can cut a good deal here.

Yankee Clipper, The [S] 16 | 16 | 16 | $36
170 John St. (South St.), 212-344-5959
◪ A "quiet", "comfortable" Seaport seafooder drawing tourists and the "bar food" crowd; the chow's "inconsistent" but "if you need to have seafood in the area", the prix fixe menu is a good option.

Yan Van Van ▽ 17 | 19 | 19 | $33
335 Madison Ave. (on Vanderbilt Ave., bet. 43rd & 44th Sts.), 212-973-0461
◪ Besides "typical" Japanese-Korean-Chinese fare, "you can grill your own" food tableside at this "undiscovered" restaurant opposite Grand Central; the young American staff explains what you're eating.

Yellowfingers ◐[S] 15 | 13 | 14 | $27
200 E. 60th St. (3rd Ave.), 212-751-8615
◪ A post-movie/Bloomingdale's Eclectic that's "reliable" for a "quick" light meal; there's "people-watching" by the windows, but "strained service", deafening "din" and "tiny" tables cost points.

Yet Jip [S] ▽ 19 | 13 | 14 | $26
5 W. 36th St. (bet. 5th & 6th Aves.), 212-629-4466
◪ Though the staff speaks "minimal English" and service could "improve", that shouldn't stop you from enjoying "authentic" Korean BBQ and other "traditional" dishes at this Midtowner.

Ye Waverly Inn [S] 16 | 21 | 17 | $30
16 Bank St. (Greenwich Ave.), 212-929-4377
◪ On a "cold winter night" "bring a date" and "sit by one of the fireplaces" (or try the garden in summer) at this "cozy", "romantic", historic West Village American comfort food standby; some surveyors prefer to drink here and eat elsewhere.

York Grill S
19 | 19 | 19 | $36

1690 York Ave. (bet. 88th & 89th Sts.), 212-772-0261
■ Upper East Side "neighborhood" New American that's "embraced" by locals for its "solid", "dependable" food, "simple", "cozy" ambiance and service "without attitude"; it stands out since "there's not much competition" in the area.

Yoshi ●S
– | – | – | M

201 E. Houston St. (bet. Ludlow & Orchard Sts.), 212-539-0225
Adjoining Katz's Deli to the west, this brand new Lower East Side Japanese couldn't be more different from its neighbor; it's a clean, quiet, understated, modern place – only its modest prices compare to Katz's.

Yuka S
16 | 9 | 14 | $25

1557 Second Ave. (bet. 80th & 81st Sts.), 212-772-9675
☑ Despite a "shabby", "claustrophobic" setting, all-Yukan-eat sushi ($18) is still the big draw at this "busy" East Side Japanese; critics say the sushi's quality is "not what it once was."

Yura & Co.
19 | 12 | 14 | $24

1645 Third Ave. (92nd St.), 212-860-8060
☑ Carnegie Hill residents say Yura missing out if you haven't tried this "informal", "child-friendly" BYO Eclectic's famed early-bird special ($8.98); but "dreary" decor causes some to opt for "gourmet takeout."

Zarela S
21 | 17 | 16 | $36

953 Second Ave. (bet. 50th & 51st Sts.), 212-644-6740
■ "It's a party every night" at this "bright" Midtown Mexican with a "deafening" downstairs bar area; upstairs and lunch are quieter, but both floors offer the same "delicious", "nonclichéd" food that has made Zarela a perennial NYC Mexican favorite.

Zenith Vegetarian Cuisine S
19 | 17 | 18 | $24

888 Eighth Ave. (52nd St.), 212-262-8080
■ "Best of its kind" is the verdict on this affordable, "soothing" Midtown Asian-Vegetarian; still, at least one surveyor would prefer to "go to the Sheep Meadow and graze."

Zen Palate S
19 | 19 | 17 | $25

2170 Broadway (bet. 76th & 77th Sts.), 212-501-7768
663 Ninth Ave. (46th St.), 212-582-1669
34 Union Sq. E. (16th St.), 212-614-9291
■ "Poetry with veggies", the "artful use of tofu", "beautiful", modern minimalist decor and "relaxing", "Zen-like" ambiance account for this original minichain's enormous popularity.

Zephyr Grill S
18 | 17 | 19 | $33

Beekman Tower, 3 Mitchell Pl. (1st Ave. & 49th St.), 212-223-4200
■ If looking for a UN "neighborhood place" for "quiet conversation" and a "harmless" but "dependable" lunch, this "relaxed", "cheery" Eclectic-American should satisfy.

Zinno S
18 | 18 | 19 | $36

126 W. 13th St. (bet. 6th & 7th Aves.), 212-924-5182
■ A "laidback" but "grown-up" "neighborhood" Greenwich Village Italian with a harmonious blend of "excellent" nightly jazz and "simple" but surprisingly "decent" midpriced food.

Zito's East S
– | – | – | I

211-213 First Ave. (bet. 12th & 13th Sts.), 212-473-3400
"A real success story for the East Village", this West Village bakery's new offspring offers thin-crust pizzas, pastas and nightly specials in a plain bare-brick setting; BYO makes this bargain a steal.

Zócalo 🅂
174 E. 82nd St. (bet. Lexington & 3rd Aves.), 212-717-7772

20 | 18 | 18 | $37

■ "Vibrant colors draw you in" to this "upscale", "stylish" East Side Mexican while "unusual", "inspired" dishes and wild margaritas keep you there; most neighbors are grateful it's not another Italian.

Zoë 🅂
90 Prince St. (bet. B'way & Mercer St.), 212-966-6722

22 | 20 | 20 | $42

■ The "beautiful people" assert there's "always an awesome meal" at this "airy", "hip", "open kitchen" SoHo New American; besides a constantly changing, "exciting" menu, there's a "well-informed", "caring" staff and "fantastic wine list."

Zucca 🅂
227 Tenth Ave. (bet. 23rd & 24th Sts.), 212-741-1970

20 | 17 | 17 | $39

☑ Seasonal fruits and vegetables figure prominently in chef Eric Stapleman's Mediterranean menu at this "sparse yet slick" West Chelsea venue favored by the "waiting to be discovered" crowd.

Zucchero ◐🅂
1464 Second Ave. (bet. 76th & 77th Sts.), 212-517-2541

18 | 14 | 17 | $26

■ A "basic", "solid", "friendly" East Side Italian standby appreciated by locals as a "value"; despite "zip" decor, it's still a "notch above the other pastarias on Second Avenue."

Zuni ◐🅂
598 Ninth Ave. (43rd St.), 212-765-7626

19 | 14 | 17 | $28

■ "Colorful" decor, "reasonable prices" and a "wide variety" of "creative", "cleanly presented" Southwestern dishes make this a good Theater District choice; it's "short on space but long on taste."

Zutto 🅂
77 Hudson St. (bet. Harrison & Jay Sts.), 212-233-3287

19 | 16 | 17 | $30

■ Looking to "satisfy your raw cravings"?; then head to this "peaceful" TriBeCa neighborhood Japanese; it's "reliable" and "never crowded" with service that's improving.

Indexes to Restaurants

Special Features and Appeals

TYPES OF CUISINE

Afghan
Afghan Kebab House
Bamiyan
Caravan
Kabul Cafe
Khyber Pass
Pamir

African
La Baraka
Sugar Bar

American (New)
ABC Parlour Cafe
Across the Street
Aja
Alley's End
Alva
Ambassador Grill
American Festival
An American Place
Ansonia
Aquagrill
Arcadia
Aureole
Bar Nine
B Bar
Bel-Air
Boathouse Cafe
Botany
Bridge Cafe
Broome St. Bar
Bryant Park Cafe
Bryant Park Grill
Bubble Lounge
Butterfield 81
Cafe Aubette
Café Botanica
Cafe Colonial
Cafe Luxembourg
Cafe S.F.A.
Candela
Cascabel
Cellar in the Sky
Charlotte
Cheetah
Circa
City Bakery
City Crab
City Wine & Cigar
Clementine
Coconut Grill
Columbus Bakery
Coming or Going
Contrapunto
Cornelia St. Cafe
Cosí Sandwich
C3
Cub Room/Café
Decade
Dojo
Duane Park Cafe

East of Eighth
Ed Sullivan's
85 Down
Elephant & Castle
Evelyn
Factory Cafe
Fez at Time Cafe
57, 57
First
Flowers
44
Fraunces Tavern
Fred's at Barneys
Friend of a Farmer
Garage
Garden Cafe
Globe
Gotham B&G
Gramercy Tavern
Granville
Grove
Grove St. Brasserie
Halcyon
Harbour Lights
Harley Davidson
Heights Cafe
Henry's End
Hudson Corner
Hudson Grill
Indigo
Iridium Jazz
Island
Janine's
Josephina
JUdson Grill
Kalio
Katch
Lake Cafe
Le Bar Bat
Le Max
Lenox Room
Levana
Liam
Library
Lincoln Tavern
Lipstick Cafe
Lobster Club
London Lennie's
Luma
Luxia
M & R Bar
Man Ray
March
Marguery Grill
Mark's
Mary's
Match
Match Uptown
Max & Moritz
Merchants, N.Y.
Merlot B&G

Mid City Grill
Mike & Tony's
Monkey Bar
New City Cafe
New Prospect Cafe
New World Grill
NoHo Star
Nola
Nova Grill
Oaks
Oceana
147
Onieals Grand St.
Oyster Bar
Pageant
Park
Park Avalon
Park Ave. Cafe
Planet Hollywood
Quilty's
Rachel's
Rainbow Room
Redeye Grill
Regency
Rialto
River Cafe
Rose Cafe
Rosewood
Rubyfruit B&G
Saloon
Sarabeth's
Savann
Savoy
Screening Room
SeaGrill
Seasons
Sign of the Dove
Spring St. Natural
Stingy Lulu's
Syrah
Table d'Hôte
Taliesin
Tapastry
Tatou
Tavern on Green
Temple Bar
Theodore
Thomas'
Time Cafe
Top of the Tower
Townhouse
Tribeca Grill
Tropica Bar
"21" Club
Union Pacific
Union Square Cafe
Universal Grill
Verbena
Vermouth
Viceroy
Village Bistro
Village Grill
Vinegar Factory

Vintage
Wall St. Kitchen
Washington Pl.
Water's Edge
West Bank Cafe
West 63rd Steak
Willow
Windows on World
Yellowfingers
York Grill
Zephyr Grill
Zoë
Zuni

American (Regional)
Acme B&G
Aggie's
America
An American Place
Arizona 206/Cafe
Baby Jake's
Brother Jimmy's
Brothers BBQ
Cafe Beulah
Canal House
City Crab
Cooking With Jazz
Copeland's
Cowgirl Hall of Fame
Dallas BBQ
Drovers Tap Room
Emily's
Fishin Eddie
Grange Hall
Great Jones Cafe
Grill Room
Hog Pit
Home
Hotel Galvez
Hudson River Club
Hurricane Island
Independent
Jezebel
Josie's
Justin's
Little Jezebel
Lola
Lupe's East L.A.
Man Ray
Mary Ann's
Mekka
Mesa City
Mesa Grill
Michael's
Miracle Grill
Motown Cafe
Old Devil Moon
Pearl Oyster Bar
Pearson's Texas BBQ
Pink Tea Cup
Saloon
Santa Fe
Short Ribs
Soul Cafe

Soul Fixins'
Standard Notions
St. Maggie's
Sugar Bar
Tapastry
Tennessee Mountain
Tramps Cafe
Treehouse
Tropica Bar
Turtle Bay Grill
Vince and Eddie's
Virgil's Real BBQ
Well's

American (Traditional)

ABC Parlour Cafe
Abigael's
Aggie's
Algonquin Hotel
All State Cafe
America
Amy's Bread
Anglers & Writers
Annie's
Ben Benson's
Billy's
Brooklyn Diner
Bubby's
Busby's
Chadwick's
Chat 'n Chew
Chelsea Feast
Chelsea Grill
Chumley's
Clarke's, P.J.
Cody's B&G
Coffee Shop
Comfort Diner
Community B&G
Corner Bistro
Cupcake Cafe
Dan Maxwell's
Delano Drive
Ear Inn
E.A.T.
Edison Cafe
Eighteenth & Eighth
EJ's Luncheonette
Empire Diner
Fashion Cafe
Frankie & Johnnie's
Fraunces Tavern
Fred's
Friend of a Farmer
Gallagher's
Gills
Good Enough to Eat
Great Jones Cafe
Hard Rock Cafe
Harley Davidson
Heartland Brewery
Hooters
Hot Tomato
Hourglass Tavern

Houston's
Hunters
Hurley's
Island Burgers
Jackson Hole
Jekyll & Hyde
Jerry's
J.G. Melon
Joe Allen
Joe Jr.'s
King Cole
Kitchenette
Knickerbocker B&G
La Boulangere
Lake Cafe
Landmark Tavern
London Lennie's
Louie's Westside
Lucky Strike
Luke's B&G
Main Street
Maloney & Porcelli
Mama's Food Shop
Manhattan Grille
Matthew's
Mayfair
Mayrose
McSorley's
Mercantile Grill
Metropolitan Cafe
Mickey Mantle's
Mike's American
Minetta Tavern
Moran's Chelsea
Morgan Court
Mortimer's
Motown Cafe
Muggs
Museum Cafe
Neary's
Night Gallery
Oak Room
Odeon
Official All Star
Old Homestead
Old Town Bar
Oyster Bar
Palm
Paris Commune
Patroon
Pete's Tavern
Pietro's
Planet Hollywood
Plaza Oyster Bar
Pop Heaven & Hell
Popover Cafe
Post House
Riverrun
Ruth's Chris
Saloon
Sarabeth's
Sazerac House
Screening Room

Sequoia
Serendipity 3
Short Ribs
Silver Spurs
Smith & Wollensky
SoHo Kitchen
Spirit Cruises
Tap Room
Tavern on Jane
T.G.I. Friday's
Tom's Restaurant
Treehouse
T Salon
12th St. B&G
"21" Club
Vince and Eddie's
Walker's
Water Club
Waterfront Ale Hse.
West 63rd Steak
White Horse
Wilson's
Wollensky's Grill
Wylie's Ribs
Yankee Clipper
Ye Waverly Inn

Argentinean
Novecento
Old San Juan

Asian
Adrienne
Aja
Asia de Cuba
Asiana
Bright Food Shop
Cafe Asean
Colony
E & O
Eat & Drink
Estihana
Helianthus
Katch
Kelley & Ping
Kokachin
Lespinasse
Lucky Cheng's
Mangez Avec Moi
Match
Match Uptown
Mirezi
NoHo Star
O.G.
Orienta
Oriental Garden
Rain
Republic
Yan Van Van
Zenith

Austrian
Max & Moritz
Tap Room
Theodore

Bakeries
City Bakery
Columbus Bakery
Cupcake Cafe
La Boulangere
Payard Pâtisserie
Veniero's
Zito's East

Bar-B-Q
Brother Jimmy's
Brothers BBQ
Churr. Plataforma
Dallas BBQ
Emily's
Green Field
Hog Pit
Live Bait
Master Grill Intl.
Mid City Grill
Pearson's Texas BBQ
Riodizio
Short Ribs
Tennessee Mountain
Virgil's Real BBQ
Waterfront Ale Hse.
Wylie's Ribs

Belgian
Café de Bruxelles
Le Pain Quotidien
Petite Abeille
Pommes Frites
Waterloo Brasserie

Brazilian
Brasilia
Cabana Carioca
Cafe Colonial
Casa Brasil
Churr. Plataforma
Circus
Coffee Shop
Fiamma
Green Field
Ipanema
Master Grill Intl.
Rice 'n' Beans
Riodizio
S.O.B.'s
Via Brasil

Burmese
Mingala Burmese
Mingala West

Cajun/Creole
Acadia Parish
Acme B&G
Baby Jake's
Cajun
City Crab
Cooking With Jazz
Gage & Tollner
Granville
Great Jones Cafe

Jean Lafitte
La Belle Epoque
Louisiana Comm. B&G
Mardi Gras
107 West
Orleans
Sazerac House
Standard Notions
Two Boots
Well's

Californian

California Burrito
Calif. Pizza Kitchen
China Grill
Ernie's
Martini's
Michael's
Original Calif. Taq.
Samalita's

Cambodian

Cambodian Cuisine

Caribbean

Bambou
Brawta Caribbean
B. Smith's
Cabana
Caribe
Delia's
Emily's
Island Spice
Justin's
Les Deux Lapins
Mekka
Negril
Old San Juan
Standard Notions
Tropica Bar

Chilean

Pomaire

Chinese

Asia de Cuba
August Moon
Au Mandarin
Bayamo
Big Wong
Bill Hong's
Bruce Ho's
Canton
Charlie Mom
Chef Ho's
Chiam
China Fun
Chin Chin
Dish of Salt
Eastern Villa
East Lake
Empire Szechuan
Evergreen Cafe
Excellent Dumpling Hse.
First Wok
Flor de Mayo

Flower Drum
Fortune Garden
Fuleen Seafood
Fu's House
Ginger House
Golden Monkey
Golden Unicorn
Goody's
Great Shanghai
HSF
Hunan Balcony
Hunan Park
Jade Plaza
Jimmy Sung's
Jing Fong
Joe's Shanghai
J. Sung Dynasty
Kam Chueh
K.B. Garden
Keewah Yen
Kum Gang San
Kum Kau Kitchen
La Caridad 78
Little Szechuan
Mama Buddha
Mandarin Court
Maple Garden
Mee Noodle Shop
Mr. Chow
Mr. Tang
New Chao Chow
Nice Restaurant
Noodles on 28
NY Noodle Town
Ocean Palace
Ollie's
Orienta
Oriental Garden
Our Place
Pacifica
Peking Duck House
Peking Park
Phoenix Garden
Pig Heaven
Sammy's Noodle
Sam's Noodle
Sarong Sarong
Shanghai Manor
Shun Lee
Shun Lee Cafe
Shun Lee Palace
Sichuan Palace
Silk Rd. Palace
Silver Palace
Silver Pond
Sunny East
Szechuan Hunan
Szechuan Kitchen
Tai Hong Lau
Tang Pavilion
Tang Tang
Tien Fu Guong
Triple Eight

Tse Yang
T.S. Ma
20 Mott Street
Van West
Vegetarian Paradise
West End Cottage
Wong Kee
Wu Liang Ye

Coffeehouses
Cafe Lalo
Cafe Mona Lisa
Caffe Bianco
Caffe Biondo
Caffe Rafaella
Caffe Reggio
Caffe Vivaldi
Cupcake Cafe
Drip
DT•UT
Ferrara
Le Figaro Cafe
Le Gamin
Le Pain Quotidien
New World Coffee
Pasqua Coffee
Starbucks
Veniero's
Xando Coffee

Coffee Shops/Diners
Barking Dog Lunch.
Brooklyn Diner
Burger Heaven
Christine's
Comfort Diner
Edison Cafe
Eisenberg Sandwich
EJ's Luncheonette
Empire Diner
Grey Dog's
Joe Jr.'s
Kings Plaza Diner
Lenox Hill Grill
Mayrose
Odessa
Pop Heaven & Hell
Silver Spurs
Skylight Diner
Stardust Dine-O-Mat
Tick Tock Diner
Tom's Restaurant
Viand
Vynl Diner

Colombian
Tierras Colombianas

Continental
Bull Run
Cafe du Pont
Cafe Europa
Cafe Inferno
Cafe Nicholson
Cafe Remy
Carlyle

Champagne's
Cloister Cafe
Cupping Room
Decade
Demi
Fantino
Ferrara
Four Seasons
F•stop
Garden Cafe
Harry's/Hanover Sq.
King Crab
Kings' Carriage Hse.
La Cigale
Leopard
Marina Cafe
Marion's
Marylou's
Mont Blanc
Novecento
Old Bermuda Inn
O'Neals'
One if by Land
Palm Court
Parsonage
Pete's Downtown
Petrossian
Pier 25A
Rasputin
Raymond's Cafe
Riverrun
Sarabeth's
Sardi's
Sign of the Dove
South Shore
Supper Club
Sweet Basil
Top of the Tower
Two Two Two
Velvet Restaurant
View
Wally's and Joseph's
World Yacht

Cuban
Asia de Cuba
Bayamo
Cabana
Cafe Con Leche
Calidad Latina
Havana Chelsea
Havana Tea/Cigar
La Caridad 78
La Rosita
Victor's Cafe 52

Delis
Barney Greengrass
Ben's Kosher
Carnegie Deli
E.A.T.
Eisenberg Sandwich
Ess-a-Bagel
Fine & Schapiro

Grabstein's Deli
Junior's
Kaplan's
Katz's Deli
Manganaro's
Pastrami King
Sarge's Deli
Second Ave. Deli
Stage Deli

Dim Sum
Chiam
China Fun
Chin Chin
E & O
East Lake
Empire Szechuan
Evergreen Cafe
Fortune Garden
Fu's House
Golden Unicorn
HSF
Jade Plaza
Jing Fong
K.B. Garden
Mandarin Court
Nice Restaurant
Ocean Palace
Ollie's
Oriental Garden
Our Place
Pacifica
Peking Duck House
Sam's Noodle
Shun Lee Cafe
Silver Palace
Silver Pond
Sunny East
Sweet-n-Tart
Tai Hong Lau
Triple Eight
20 Mott Street
Vegetarian Paradise

Eclectic/International
ABC Parlour Cafe
Across the Street
Alexi on 56
Anton's
Bamcafe
Bar & Books
Bar 89
Blue Ribbon
Bodega
Boom
Cafe Gitane
Cafe Margaux
Cafe Remy
Cafe S.F.A.
Café Word of Mouth
Caffe Bianco
Cal's
Camille's Clover Hill
Carol's Cafe

Caviarteria
Chelsea Grill
Chez Le Chef
China Grill
Cibar
City Wine & Cigar
Club Macanudo
Columbus Bakery
Community B&G
Cupping Room
Daydream Cafe
Delegates' Dining Room
Divine Bar
Druids
East of Eighth
Emerald Planet
Empire Diner
Etats-Unis
Fanelli
Fashion Cafe
Flute
Fred's Beauty
Galaxy
Garden Cafe
Global 33
Globe
Indigo
It's a Wrap
Jekyll & Hyde
Josephina
Josie's
Kalio
Lansky Lounge
Le Bar Bat
Le Figaro Cafe
L'Ermitage
Life Cafe
Lips
Lola
Lucky Cheng's
Match
Match Uptown
Maxwell's
Meli Melo
Nadine's
New Prospect Cafe
Night Gallery
NoHo Star
Pascalou
Planet Hollywood
Popover Cafe
Route 66 Cafe
Rubyfruit B&G
Scratch
Sharz Cafe
Shopsin's
Sonia Rose
Spring St. Natural
Star Fish
St. Dymphnas
Svoboda
Tam-Tam Bar
Television City

Thé Adoré
Toast
Two Rooms
Union Pacific
Union Square Cafe
Urban Hero
Velvet Restaurant
Velvet Room
Virage
Vynl Diner
Wraparama
Yaffa's
Yellowfingers
Yura & Co.
Zenith
Zephyr Grill

Egyptian
Casa La Femme

English
Havana Tea/Cigar
Lady Mendl's
Landmark Tavern
Tea & Sympathy
Telephone B&G

Ethiopian
Meskerem

Filipino
Cendrillon

Fondue
Golden Pot
Melting Pot
Swiss Inn

French
Adrienne
Annam
Bel-Air
Bouley Bakery
Bouterin
Box Tree
Café des Artistes
Cafe Margaux
Café Pierre
Caffé Lure
CamaJe
Can
Capsouto Frères
Carlyle
Champagne's
Chanterelle
Chez Es Saada
Chez Napoléon
Daniel
Delia's
Destinée
Franklin Station
Gertrude's
Ici
Indochine
Iridium Jazz
Jean Claude
Jean Georges

Jean Lafitte
Jo Jo
Kitchen Club
Kokachin
La Baraka
La Boheme
La Bonne Soupe
La Boulangere
L'Absinthe
La Caravelle
La Colombe d'Or
La Côte Basque
La Folie
La Grenouille
La Maison Japonaise
La Metairie
La Nouvelle Justine
La Petite Auberge
L'Ardoise
La Reserve
Le Bernardin
Le Biarritz
Le Bistrot de Maxim's
Le Boeuf à la Mode
Le Chantilly
Le Cirque 2000
L'Ecole
Le Grenadin
Leopard
Le Perigord
Le Pescadou
Le Refuge
Le Refuge Inn
Le Régence
Le Relais
Le Rivage
L'Ermitage
Les Célébrités
Lespinasse
Les Pyrénées
Les Routiers
Le Taxi
Le Zoo
Luma
Lutèce
Mark's
Merlot B&G
Métisse
Montrachet
Park Bistro
Pascalou
Peacock Alley
Poisson
Rasputin
René Pujol
Savann
Sonia Rose
St. Michel
Table d'Hôte
Tam-Tam Bar
Tatou
Terrace
Thé Adoré

Treehouse
Trois Jean
Village Grill
Vong
Willow

French Bistro
Aesop's Tables
Alison on Dominick
Au Troquet
Balthazar
Bar Six
Between the Bread
Bienvenue
Bistro Carré
Bistro du Nord
Bistro Le Steak
Bistro 39
Bistrot Margot
Cafe Centro
Café Crocodile
Café de Bruxelles
Café de Paris
Cafe du Pont
Café Loup
Cafe Luxembourg
Cafe Noir
Café St. John
Cafe Un Deux Trois
Capsouto Frères
Chelsea Bistro
Chez Brigitte
Chez Jacqueline
Chez Josephine
Chez Le Chef
Chez Ma Tante
Chez Michallet
Chez Suzette
Cornelia St. Cafe
Country Café
Danal
Demarchelier
Elephant
Félix
Ferrier
Flea Market Cafe
Florent
French Roast
Frontière
Gascogne
Grove
Jacques' Bistro
Jo Jo
Jubilee
Jules
Kiosk
La Belle Epoque
La Boite en Bois
La Bouillabaisse
L'Absinthe
L'Acajou
La Crêpe
La Goulue
La Jumelle

La Lunchonette
La Mangeoire
La Mediterranée
La Mirabelle
La Petite Auberge
L'Ardoise
La Ripaille
Le Beaujolais
Le Bilboquet
Le Boeuf à la Mode
Le Bouchon
Le Gamin
Le Gigot
Le Jardin Bistro
Le Madeleine
Le Marais
Le Max
L'Entrecote
Le Pescadou
Le Petit Hulot
Le Quercy
Le Rivage
Les Deux Gamins
Les Halles
Le Singe Vert
Les Sans Culottes
Le Taxi
Le Veau D'Or
L'Express
Lucky Strike
Madison Bistro
Manhattan Bistro
Max & Moritz
Mme. Romaine
Montrachet
Opaline
Park Bistro
Payard Pâtisserie
Perry Bistro
Petite Crevette
Pierre au Tunnel
Pitchoune
Provence
Quatorze Bis
Raoul's
Raphaël
Red Light Bistro
Seasons
Sel et Poivre
Soho Steak
Steak Frites
Tartine
Titou
Tout Va Bien
Trois Canards
Trois Jean

German
Hallo Berlin
Heidelberg
Killmeyer's
Mayfair
Roettele A.G.
Rolf's
Silver Swan

Greek

Agrotikon
Akroyiali
Artos
Athens Cafe
Cafe Greco
Christos Hasapo
Dionysos
Elias Corner
Eros
Fish Market
Greek Captain
Gus' Place
Ithaka
Joe Jr.'s
Karyatis
Kings Plaza Diner
Meltemi
Milos
Molyvos
Niko's
Periyali
Rafina
S'Agapo
Santorini
Seagrill /Aegean
Taverna Kyclades
Taverna Vraka
Telly's Taverna
Uncle George's
Uncle Nick's
Vergina

Hamburgers

All State Cafe
Burger Heaven
Cal's
Chelsea Grill
Clarke's, P.J.
Corner Bistro
Ear Inn
Fanelli
Hard Rock Cafe
Island Burgers
Jackson Hole
Jekyll & Hyde
J.G. Melon
Joe Allen
Junior's
Mickey Mantle's
Official All Star
Old Town Bar
Planet Hollywood
Silver Spurs
Telephone B&G
Television City
T.G.I. Friday's
"21" Club
Viand
Waterfront Ale Hse.
White Horse

Health Food

(Most restaurants will cook to
health specifications; see also
Vegetarian)
Angelica Kitchen
Caravan of Dreams
Daydream Cafe
Dojo
Herban Kitchen
Josephina
Josie's
Quantum Leap
Souen
Spring St. Natural
Sweet-n-Tart
Tsampa
Yaffa Cafe
Zen Palate

Hot Dogs

Gray's Papaya
Papaya King

Hungarian

Mocca Hungarian
Red Tulip

Indian

AJ's Niota
Akbar
Baluchi's
Bay Leaf
Bombay Palace
Darbar
Dawat
Diwan Grill
Haveli
India Grill
Jackson Diner
Jewel of India
Karahi
Malika
Mavalli Palace
Mitali East/West
Mughlai
Nirvana
Passage to India
Rose of India
Salaam Bombay
Shaan
Thali Vegetarian
Vatan
Windows on India

Indonesian

Bali Nusa Indah

Irish

Fitzers
Hunters
Landmark Tavern
McSorley's
Neary's
St. Dymphnas
Thady Con's

Israeli
Rectangles
Sido

Italian
(N=Northern; S=Southern; N&S=Includes both)
Abbracciamento (N)
Acappella (N)
Al Bacio (N&S)
Al Dente (N)
Allegria (N)
Allora (N)
Alonzo's (N&S)
Amarone (N&S)
Anche Vivolo (N&S)
Angelina's (N&S)
Angelo's (N&S)
Angels (N&S)
Aperitivo (N)
Areo (N&S)
Aria (N)
Arlecchino (N&S)
Armani Cafe (N&S)
Arqua (N)
Arté (N&S)
Artepasta (N&S)
Arturo's Pizzeria (S)
Artusi (N&S)
Baci (S)
Ballato's (S)
Baraonda (N)
Barbetta (N)
Bardolino (N&S)
Barocco (N)
Barolo (N)
Bar Pitti (N)
Basilica (N)
Basta Pasta (N&S)
Beatrice Inn (N)
Becco (N)
Bella Blu (N&S)
Bella Donna (N)
Bella Luna (N)
Bellissima (N&S)
Bello (N)
Belluno (N)
Benito I (S)
Benito II (S)
Bice (N)
Biricchino (N)
Bona Fides (N&S)
Bondini (N)
Bora (N)
Borgo Antico (N)
Bosco (N&S)
Bravo Gianni (N&S)
Bricco (S)
Brio (N&S)
Bruno (N&S)
Bussola B&G (S)
Cafe Cento Sette (N&S)
Cafe Fiorello's (N&S)
Cafe Nosidam (N&S)

Cafe Trevi (N)
Caffé Bondí (N&S)
Caffe Buon Gusto (N&S)
Caffe Cielo (N)
Caffe Grazie (N&S)
Caffe Popolo (N&S)
Caffe Rosso (N&S)
Caffé Taci (N)
Caffé Torino (N&S)
Calla Larga (N)
Campagna (N)
Campagnola (N&S)
Candido Pizza (N&S)
Cara Mia (N&S)
Carino (N)
Carmen Pagina (N&S)
Carmine's (S)
Casa del Pescatore (N&S)
Casa Di Pre (N&S)
Casa Mia (N&S)
Castellano (N)
Cellini (N&S)
Cent'Anni (N)
Cheetah (N&S)
Chelsea Ristorante (N)
Chianti (N&S)
Christina's (N&S)
Ciao Bella Cafe (N&S)
Ciao Europa (N&S)
Cibo (N&S)
Ciccio & Tony's (N&S)
Cinquanta (N&S)
Cinque Terre (N)
Ci Piace (N&S)
Circo, Osteria del (N)
Ciro Trattoria (N)
Ci Vediamo (N)
Coco Marina (N&S)
Coco Opera (N)
Coco Pazzo (N&S)
Coco Pazzo Teatro (N&S)
Col Legno (N)
Contrapunto (N)
Cortina (N)
Cucina (N&S)
Cucina Della Fontana (N)
Cucina della Nonna (N)
Cucina di Pesce (N)
Cucina Stagionale (N)
Cucina Vivolo (N&S)
Da Ciro (N&S)
Da Mario (N&S)
D'Angelo, Osteria (N)
Da Nico (N&S)
Daniella (N)
Da Silvano (N&S)
Da Tommaso (N)
Da Umberto (N)
Da Vittorio (N)
DeGrezia (N)
Delano Drive (N&S)
DeRosa (S)
Diva (N)

Divina Commedia (N)
Divino (N)
Dolce (N)
Dominick's (S)
Don Giovanni (N&S)
Downtown (N)
Due (N)
East River Cafe (N)
Ecco (N)
Ecco-La (N)
Elaine's (N&S)
Elio's (N)
Emilios (N&S)
Ennio & Michael (N&S)
Erminia (N&S)
Ernie's (N)
Est! Est!! Est!!! (N)
Fantino (N)
Farfalle Trattoria (S)
Felidia (N)
Ferdinando's (S)
Ferrara (N&S)
Fiamma (N&S)
F.illi Ponte (N&S)
Fino (N)
Fiorentino's (S)
Firenze (N)
Focacceria (N&S)
Follonico (N&S)
Fontana di Trevi (N)
Freddie & Pepper's (S)
Fred's at Barneys (N&S)
Fresco by Scotto (N)
Frico (N)
Frontière (N)
Frutti di Mare (N)
Gabriel's (N)
Gargiulo's (S)
Gemelli (N&S)
Gene's (N)
Gennaro (N&S)
Giambelli (N&S)
Giando (N&S)
Gigino (N&S)
Gino (S)
Giovanni (N)
Giovanni 25 (N)
Girasole (N&S)
Goodfella's (N&S)
Grace's Trattoria (S)
Grand Ticino (N&S)
Grano Trattoria (N&S)
Graziella (N&S)
Grifone (N)
Harry Cipriani (N&S)
Hosteria Fiorella (N)
Il Bagatto (N&S)
Il Boschetto (S)
Il Cantinori (N)
Il Corallo (N&S)
Il Cortile (N&S)
Il Faro (S)
Il Fornaio (N&S)

Il Gabbiano (N&S)
Il Giglio (N&S)
Il Menestrello (N)
Il Monello (N&S)
Il Mulino (N)
Il Nido (N&S)
Il Palazzo (N&S)
Il Pellicano (S)
Il Postino (N&S)
Il Tinello (N)
Il Toscanaccio (N)
Il Vagabondo (N)
Il Valentino (N)
In Padella (N)
Isle of Capri (N&S)
Isola (N&S)
I Tre Merli (N)
I Trulli (S)
Japas 47 (N)
Joanna's (N&S)
Joe's Pizza (N&S)
John's of 12th St. (N&S)
Joseph's (N&S)
Julian's (N&S)
La Boheme (N)
La Collina (N)
La Fenice (N&S)
La Focaccia (N)
La Fontana (N)
La Giara (N&S)
La Gioconda (N&S)
La Granita (N)
La Lanterna (N&S)
Lamarca (S)
La Mela (N&S)
Lanza Restaurant (N&S)
La Pizza Fresca (N&S)
La Primavera (N)
La Rivista (N&S)
La Traviata (N)
Lattanzi (N&S)
La Vela (N&S)
Le Madri (N&S)
Lento's (N&S)
Letizia (N&S)
Limoncello (N&S)
Loui Loui (N&S)
L'Ulivo (N)
Lumi (N&S)
Lusardi's (N)
Luxia (N&S)
Manducatis (N&S)
Manganaro's (N&S)
Mangia (N)
Mangia e Bevi (S)
Mappamondo (N)
Marchi's (N)
Marco Polo (N&S)
Maria Elena (N)
Marinella (N&S)
Mario's (N&S)
Martini's (N&S)
Massimo (N&S)

Mazzei (N&S)
Mediterraneo (N)
Medusa (N)
Meridiana (S)
Messina Cafe (N)
Mezzaluna (N&S)
Mezzanotte (S)
Mezzogiorno (N&S)
Minetta Tavern (N&S)
Montebello (N)
Monte's (S)
Monzù (N&S)
Moreno (N&S)
Nanni Il Valletto (N)
Nanni's (N)
Naples 45 (S)
Nello (N)
Nicola Paone (N)
Nicola's (N&S)
Nino's (N)
Noodle Pudding (N&S)
Northside Cafe (N&S)
Notaro (N)
Novitá (N&S)
101 (N&S)
Orologio (N)
Orso (N)
Osso Buco (N&S)
Osteria al Doge (N)
Osteria Fiorentina (N)
Palio (N&S)
Panarella's (N)
Paola's (N)
Paper Moon Express (N)
Paper Moon Milano (N&S)
Pappardella (N)
Parioli Romanissimo (N)
Park Side (N&S)
Parma (N)
Pasta Lovers (N&S)
Patrissy's (N&S)
Patsy's (S)
Patsy's Pizza (N)
Paul & Jimmy's (N&S)
Pellegrino's (N&S)
Pescatore (N)
Pesce & Pasta (N&S)
Petaluma (N&S)
Pete's Downtown (N&S)
Pete's Tavern (N&S)
Picasso Cafe (N&S)
Piccola Venezia (N)
Piccolino (N&S)
Piccolo Angolo (N)
Pierino (S)
Pietrasanta (N)
Pietro's (N)
Pizzeria Uno (N&S)
Pó (N&S)
Pomodori (N&S)
Pomodoro Rosso (N&S)
Portobello (N&S)
Primavera (N&S)

Primola (N&S)
Provi, Provi (N)
Puccini (N&S)
Puttanesca (N&S)
Quattro Gatti (S)
Queen (N&S)
Rafaella Rist. (N)
Raffaele (S)
Rao's (S)
Remi (N)
Restivo (N&S)
Roberto's (N&S)
Rocco (S)
Rosemarie's (N)
Rossini's (N)
Sal Anthony's (N&S)
Sal Anthony's SPQR (N&S)
Salute! (N)
Sambuca (N&S)
San Domenico (N&S)
San Giusto (S)
San Pietro (S)
Sant Ambroeus (N)
Savore (N)
Scaletta (N)
Scalinatella (N&S)
Seasons (N)
Senza Nome (N)
Sette Mezzo (N&S)
Sette MoMA (N&S)
Sirabella's (N)
Sistina (N)
Sofia Fabulous Grill (N&S)
Sofia Fabulous Pizza (N)
South Shore (N)
Stella del Mare (N)
Supreme Macaroni (N&S)
Tanti Baci Caffé (N&S)
Taormina (N&S)
Teodora (N)
Tevere 84 (N&S)
Tin Room (N)
Tombola (N&S)
Tommaso's (N&S)
Tony's Di Napoli (S)
Torre di Pisa (N)
Tosca (N)
Toscana (N)
Totonno Pizzeria (S)
Trattoria Alba (N&S)
Trattoria Dell'Arte (N&S)
Trattoria del Portico (N&S)
Trattoria I Pagliacci (N)
Trattoria Romana (N&S)
Trattoria Rustica (N&S)
Trattoria Spaghetto (N&S)
Trattoria Venti Tre (N&S)
Triangolo (N)
Trionfo (N&S)
Tucci (N)
Tuscan Square (N)
Tuscany Grill (N&S)
Tutta Pasta (N&S)

Tutto Sapori (N&S)
Two Boots (N&S)
Two Toms (S)
Va Bene (S)
V&T Pizzeria (N)
Veniero's (N&S)
Vespa Cibobuono (N)
Via Oreto (S)
Vico (N&S)
Villa Berulia (N)
Villa Mosconi (N&S)
Vittorio Cucina (N&S)
Vivolo (N&S)
Volare (N&S)
Yellowfingers (N)
Zinno (N)
Zito's East (N&S)
Zucchero (N&S)

Japanese
Avenue A
Azusa of Japan
Benihana
Blue Ribbon Sushi
Chikubu
Choga
Choshi
Dojo
East
Empire Szechuan
Estihana
Fujii
Fujiyama Mama
Garden Cafe
Haikara Grill
Hakata
Hamachi
Han Sung
Haru
Hasaki
Hatsuhana
Hatsune
Honmura An
Hyotan Nippon
Ikeno Hana
Inagiku
Iso
Japonica
Jo-An Japanese
Kan Pai
Katsuhama
Kiiroi-Hana
Kitaro
Kitchen Club
Korea Palace
Kum Gang San
Kuruma Zushi
La Maison Japonaise
Lan
Lenge
Menchanko-tei
Meriken
Mishima
Momoyama

Monster Sushi
Mottsu
Nadaman Hakubai
Nakagawa
Nippon
Nobu
Oikawa
Omen
Onigashima
Otabe
Sakagura
Sapporo East
Sekku
Seryna
Sesumi
Shabu-Shabu
Shabu-Tatsu
Shinbashi
Souen
Sushi Bar
Sushiden
Sushi Hana
Sushihatsu
Sushisay
Sushiya
Sushi Zen
Taiyo Japanese
Taka
Takahachi
TakeSushi
Takino
Tatany
Tea Box
Ten Kai
Tokyo
Tomoe Sushi
Toraya
Tsunami
Yama
Yamaguchi
Yoshi
Yuka
Zutto

Jewish
(See also Kosher)
Barney Greengrass
Ben's Kosher
Carnegie Deli
E.A.T.
Eisenberg Sandwich
Ess-a-Bagel
Fine & Schapiro
Kaplan's
Karahi
Katz's Deli
Lattanzi
Pastrami King
Ratners
Sammy's Roumanian
Sarge's Deli
Second Ave. Deli
Stage Deli
Triplets Old NY

Korean

Choga
Dok Suni
Empire Korea
Guh Ho
Hangawi
Han Sung
Kang Suh
Korea Palace
Kum Gang San
Mill Korean
Mirezi
Won Jo
Woo Chon
Yet Jip

Kosher

Abigael's
Alexi on 56
Ben's Kosher
Bissaleh
Estihana
Fine & Schapiro
Grabstein's Deli
Haikara Grill
La Fontana
Le Marais
Levana
Pastrami King
Provi, Provi
Ratners
Rectangles
Second Ave. Deli
Tevere 84
Va Bene

Laotian

Mangez Avec Moi

Lebanese

Al Bustan

Malaysian

Franklin Station
Malayboo
Nyonya
Penang
Sarong Sarong
Sea Gull

Mediterranean

Aesop's Tables
Alexandre
Arioso
Artos
Azure
Bouterin
Cafe Centro
Café Crocodile
Cafe Greco
Cafe Inferno
Cafe Noir
Cal's
Caravan of Dreams
Casa Di Pre
Casa La Femme

Circa
Corsica
Cucina & Co.
Danal
Delphini
Dionysos
Divine Bar
Edgar's Cafe
Epices du Traiteur
Fish Market
Giorgio's
Gus' Place
Helena's
Il Buco
Isabella's
Isola
Japas 47
Lafayette Grill & Bar
La Mangeoire
La Mediterranée
Layla
Mangia
Matthew's
Medusa
Messina Cafe
Metronome
Mezze
Nica's
Nick & Toni's
Niko's
Oznot's Dish
Park Avalon
Park Bistro
Picasso Cafe
Picholine
Pitchoune
Pó
Provence
Red Light Bistro
Savoy
Scully on Spring
Sharz Cafe
Spartina
Sugar Bar
Terrace
Velvet Room
Verbena
Washington Pl.
Zucca

Mexican/Tex-Mex

Benny's Burritos
Blockhead's Burritos
Bodega
Burritoville
California Burrito
Canyon Road
Cowgirl Hall of Fame
El Parador Cafe
El Rio Grande
El Teddy's
Fresco Tortilla
Gabriela's
Hotel Galvez

Johnny Tejano's
La Cocina
Lupe's East L.A.
Mamá Mexico
Mary Ann's
Maya
Maz Mezcal
Mi Cocina
Mi Nidito
107 West
Original Calif. Taq.
Rocking Horse
Rosa Mexicano
Samalita's
Santa Fe
Taq. de Mexico
Tio Pepe
Tortilla Flats
Vera Cruz
Zarela
Zócalo

Middle Eastern
Al Bustan
Bissaleh
Casa La Femme
Kabul Cafe
Khyber Pass
Layla
Lemon Tree Cafe
Magic Carpet
Moustache
Oznot's Dish
Rectangles
Salam Cafe
Sido

Moroccan
Bar Six
Café Fès
Chez Es Saada
Country Café
Little Village
Lotfi's Moroccan
Mezze

Noodle Shops
Big Wong
Bo-Ky
East
Honmura An
Kelley & Ping
Mee Noodle Shop
Menchanko-tei
New Chao Chow
Noodles on 28
NY Noodle Town
Ollie's
Republic
Sammy's Noodle
Sam's Noodle
Sweet-n-Tart

Nuevo Latino
Bistro Latino
Erizo
Patría

Persian
Persepolis

Peruvian
El Pollo
Flor de Mayo

Pizza
Arturo's Pizzeria
Calif. Pizza Kitchen
Candido Pizza
Chelsea Ristorante
Da Ciro
Da Nico
Denino's Tavern
Don Giovanni
Freddie & Pepper's
Goodfella's
Joe's Pizza
John's Pizzeria
La Granita
La Pizza Fresca
Le Madri
Lento's
Little Italy Pizza
Lombardi's
Loui Loui
Mediterraneo
Moustache
Nick's Pizza
Oven
Patsy Grimaldi's
Patsy's
Patsy's Pizza
Pintaile's Pizza
Pizzeria Uno
Sofia Fabulous Pizza
Totonno Pizzeria
Tutto Sapori
Two Boots
V&T Pizzeria
Vinnie's Pizza
Zito's East

Polish
Christine's
Teresa's

Portuguese
Fado
Ipanema
Luzia's
Pao!

Puerto Rican
La Taza de Oro
Old San Juan

Romanian
Sammy's Roumanian
Triplets Old NY

Russian
Andrusha
Caviar Russe
FireBird
L'Ermitage

201

Petrossian
Pravda
Rasputin
Russian Samovar
Russian Vodka Rm.
Ukrainian

Scandinavian
Aquavit
Christer's

Seafood
Acadia Parish
Akroyiali
Anglers & Writers
Aquagrill
Bangkok Cuisine
Ben Benson's
Billy's
Blue Ribbon
Blue Water Grill
Bosco
Bridge Cafe
Captain's Table
Casa del Pescatore
City Crab
Cucina di Pesce
Docks
Elias Corner
El Quijote
Erizo
Fish
Fishin Eddie
Fish Market
Foley's Fish House
Francisco's C.V.
Frutti di Mare
Fuleen Seafood
Gage & Tollner
Giando
Gills
Greek Captain
Harbour Lights
Hosteria Fiorella
Hurricane Island
Jade Plaza
Kam Chueh
Katch
King Crab
La Bouillabaisse
Le Bernardin
Lobster Box
Lobster Club
London Lennie's
Lundy Bros.
Mad Fish
Maloney & Porcelli
Manhattan Grille
Manhattan Ocean
Marina Cafe
Marinella
Marylou's
Meltemi
Milos

Moran's Chelsea
Oceana
Ocean Grill
Ocean Palace
Oriental Garden
Oyster Bar
Oznot's Dish
Pacifico
Pearl Oyster Bar
Pearl Room
Pescatore
Petite Crevette
Pier 25A
Pietro's
Pisces
Plaza Oyster Bar
Poisson
Rafina
Redeye Grill
SeaGrill
Seagrill/Aegean
Sequoia
Silver Pond
Sloppy Louie's
Sofia Fabulous Grill
Star Fish
Stella del Mare
Sweet Basil
Taverna Kyclades
Telly's Taverna
Tropica Bar
Wally's and Joseph's
Water Club
Wilkinson's
Yankee Clipper

Soups
Daily Soup
Hale & Hearty
La Bonne Soupe
Mr. Soup
Souperman
Soup Kitchen Intl.
Soup Nutsy
Soup Pot

South American
Bistro Latino
Boca Chica
Cabana Carioca
El Pollo
Erizo
Green Field
Master Grill Intl.
Riodizio
S.O.B.'s

Southern/Soul
Brother Jimmy's
Brothers BBQ
B. Smith's
Bubby's
Cafe Beulah
Copeland's
Cowgirl Hall of Fame

Emily's
Jezebel
Justin's
Little Jezebel
Live Bait
Lola
Mekka
Motown Cafe
Old Devil Moon
Pink Tea Cup
Shark Bar
Soul Cafe
Soul Fixins'
Sylvia's
Tramps Cafe
Well's

Southwestern
Arizona 206/Cafe
Bright Food Shop
Canyon Road
Citrus B&G
Cowgirl Hall of Fame
El Rio Grande
Hotel Galvez
Hudson Grill
Island Burgers
Mesa City
Mesa Grill
Mickey Mantle's
Miracle Grill
Santa Fe
Tapika
Zuni

Spanish
Barcelona
Bolo
Cafe Español
Cafe Riazor
Calidad Latina
Domingo
El Charro
El Cid
El Faro
El Pote Español
El Quijote
Flor de Sol
Francisco's C.V.
Helena's
La Paella
Malaga
Marichu
Ñ 33 Crosby
Olé
Rincon de España
Rio Mar
Sevilla
Solera
Tapas Lounge
Tio Pepe
Toledo
Velvet Room

Sri Lankan
Lakruwana
Taprobane

Steakhouses
Akroyiali
Angelo & Maxie's
Ben Benson's
Benihana
Billy's
Bobby Van's
Bull & Bear
Christos Hasapo
Cité
Cité Grill
Dan Maxwell's
Embers
Florent
Frankie & Johnnie's
Frank's
Gage & Tollner
Gallagher's
Jake's Steakhouse
Keens Steakhouse
Knickerbocker B&G
Le Marais
Maloney & Porcelli
Manhattan Grille
Mid City Grill
Mike & Tony's
Moran's Chelsea
Morton's
Old Homestead
Palm
Pen & Pencil
Peter Luger
Pietro's
Post House
Ruth's Chris
Smith & Wollensky
Soho Steak
Sparks Steak House
Triplets Old NY
Uncle Jack's
Wally's and Joseph's
West 63rd Steak
Wollensky's Grill

Swiss
Golden Pot
Mont Blanc
Roettele A.G.
Swiss Inn

Tapas
Cafe Español
Cafe Noir
Divine Bar
El Cid
Frico
Global 33
Helena's
Il Buco
Japas 47
La Paella

Ñ 33 Crosby
Tapas Lounge
Tapastry
Velvet Room
Xunta

Thai
Bangkok Cafe
Bangkok Cuisine
Chanpen Thai
Chili Pepper
Elephant
Empire Szechuan
Holy Basil
Jai-Ya Thai
Kin Khao
Lemongrass Grill
Mangez Avec Moi
Mueng Thai
Orienta
Owen Thai
Plan Eat Thailand
Pongsri Thai
Puket
Q, a Thai Bistro
Rain
Regional Thai
River
Royal Siam
Rungsit Thai
Sala Thai
Seeda Thai II
Shaliga Thai
Siam Inn
Spice
Sukhothai West
Thai Cafe
Thai House Cafe
Thailand Cafe
Thailand Rest.
Thai Orchid
Toons
Topaz Thai
Typhoon Brewery
Ubol's Kitchen
Vong
Vynl Diner

Tibetan
Tibetan Kitchen
Tibet Shambala
Tsampa

Tunisian
La Baraka

Turkish
Deniz a la Turk
Istanbul
Marti
Pasha
Sahara
Turkish Cuisine

Turkish Kitchen
Üsküdar

Ukrainian
Kiev
Odessa
Ukrainian
Veselka

Vegetarian
Angelica Kitchen
Candle Cafe
Caravan of Dreams
Dojo
Hangawi
Helianthus
Herban Kitchen
Mama Buddha
Mavalli Palace
Mi Nidito
Oznot's Dish
Poti Vegetarian
Quantum Leap
Souen
Spring St. Natural
Thali Vegetarian
Vatan
Vegetarian Paradise
Yaffa Cafe
Zenith
Zen Palate

Vietnamese
Annam
Bo-Ky
Can
Cuisine de Saigon
Cyclo
Hué
Indochine
Le Colonial
Little Saigon
Mangez Avec Moi
MeKong
Miss Saigon
Monsoon
Nam Phuong
New Pasteur
Nha Trang
Orienta
Pho Bang
Pho Tu Do
Pho Viet Huong
Rain
River
Saigon Grill
Saigon House
Seeda Thai II
Song
Van West
Viet-Nam

LOCATIONS

Restaurant name followed by its street location.
(A = Avenue; s = Street, e.g. 1A/116s = First Ave. at 116th St.,
3A/82-3s = Third Ave. between 82nd & 83rd Sts.)

East 90s & Up
(East of Fifth Avenue)
Across the Street *91s/1A-York*
Al Bacio *3A/94-5s*
Andrusha *Lex/90-1s*
Barcelona *Mad/91-2s*
Barking Dog *3A/94s*
Bistro du Nord *Mad/93s*
Brother Jimmy's *3A/92-3s*
Burritoville *3A/90-1s*
Busby's *92s/Mad*
Demi *Mad/93s*
Ecco-La *3A/93s*
El Pollo *1A/90-1s*
Emily's *5A/111s*
Island *Mad/92-3s*
Jackson Hole *Mad/91s*
Joanna's *92s/5A-Mad*
Johnny Tejano's *3A/93s*
La Collina *Lex/92s*
Pascalou *Mad/92-3s*
Patsy's Pizza *1A/117-8s*
Piccolo Pomodoro *2A/90-1s*
Pintaile's Pizza *91s/Mad-5A*
Rao's *114s/Pleasant*
Sarabeth's *Mad/92-3s*
Senza Nome *3A/93-4s*
Sharz Cafe *90s/3A-Lex*
Sido *3A/90-1s*
Table d'Hôte *92s/Mad-Park*
Vico *Mad/92-3s*
Vinegar Factory *91s/York-1A*
Yura & Co. *3A/92s*

East 80s
(East of Fifth Avenue)
Baluchi's *2A/81-2s*
Bella Donna II *1A/86-7s*
Bistro Carré *1A/82-3s*
Butterfield 81 *81s/Lex-3A*
Cafe Trevi *1A/81-2s*
Caffe Grazie *84s/Mad-5A*
Calif. Burrito *3A/80s*
Candido *1A/83-4s*
Carino *2A/88-9s*
Chef Ho's *2A/89-90s*
Ci Piace *3A/81s*
Ci Vediamo *3A/81s*
Dan Maxwell's *2A/88-9s*
Demarchelier *86s/Mad-Park*
Divino *2A/80-1s*

DT•UT *2A/84-5s*
East *3A/80-1s*
E.A.T. *Mad/80-1s*
Elaine's *2A/88-9s*
Elio's *2A/84-5s*
Erminia *83s/2-3A*
Etats-Unis *81s/2-3A*
Firenze *2A/82-3s*
First Wok *3A/88s*
Gills *1A/81-2s*
Giovanni 25 *83s/Mad-5A*
Girasole *82s/Lex-3A*
Heidelberg *2A/85-6s*
India Grill *81s/2-3A*
Jackson Hole *2A/83-4s*
Jacques' Bistro *85s/3A*
Jasmine *2A/84s*
Kings' Carriage *82s/2-3A*
La Folie *3A/80-1s*
La Fontana *83s/1-2A*
Le Boeuf à la Mode *81s/York-E. End*
Lenge *3A/82-3s*
Le Pain Quotidien *Mad/84-5s*
Le Refuge *82s/Lex-3A*
Lobster Club *80s/Mad-5A*
Maxwell's *Lex/85-6s*
Maz Mezcal *86s/1-2A*
Mazzei *2A/81-2s*
Miss Saigon *3A/80-1s*
Mocca Hungarian *2A/82-3s*
Momoyama *2A/81-2s*
New World *3A/89-90s; Lex/84s*
Nica's *5A/81s*
Nicola's *84s/Lex-3A*
Orleans *3A/81-2s*
Our Place *3A/82s*
Paola's *85s/1-2A*
Papaya King *86s/3A*
Parioli Romanissimo *81s/5A-Mad*
Penang *2A/83s*
Pesce & Pasta *3A/87-8s*
Pig Heaven *2A/80-1s*
Pintaile's Pizza *York/83-4s*
Pizzeria Uno *86s/2-3A*
Primavera *1A/82s*
Quattro Gatti *81s/2-3A*
Sala Thai *2A/89-90s*
Samalita's *3A/80-1s*
Seagrill of Aegean *2A/81s*

Sesumi *2A/85-6s*
Sirabella's *E. End/82-3s*
Sirocco *Mad/85-6s*
Sistina *2A/80-1s*
Starbucks *2A/81s; 87s/Lex*
Szechuan Hunan *York/83-4s*
Tevere 84 *84s/Lex-3A*
Tombola *2A/83-4s*
Tony's Di Napoli *2A/83-4s*
Totonno *2A/80-1s*
Trattoria Rustica *85s/1-2A*
Triangolo *83s/1-2A*
Tutto Sapori *84s/2-3A*
Va Bene *2A/82-3s*
Vespa *2A/84-5s*
Viand *86s/2A*
Wilkinson's *York/83-4s*
Wu Liang Ye *86s/2-3A*
York Grill *York/88-9s*
Yuka *2A/80-1s*
Zócalo *82s/Lex-3A*

East 70s
(East of Fifth Avenue)
Afghan Kebab Hse. *2A/70-1s*
Allora *1A/71s*
Annie's *3A/78-9s*
Bar & Books *Lex/73s*
Baraonda *2A/75s*
Bardolino *2A/77-8s*
Bella Blu *Lex/70-1s*
Bella Donna *77s/1-2A*
Bellissima *2A/73-4s*
Bissaleh *2A/74-5s*
Bistro Le Steak *3A/75s*
Boathouse Cafe *E. Park Dr./72s*
Bosco *Lex/74-5s*
Brother Jimmy's *1A/76s*
Burritoville *1A/77-8s*
Café Crocodile *74s/1-2A*
Cafe Greco *2A/71-2s*
Café Word of Mouth *Lex/72-3s*
Caffe Bianco *2A/77-8s*
Caffe Buon Gusto *77s/2-3A*
Campagnola *1A/73-4s*
Candle Cafe *3A/74-5s*
Canyon Road *1A/76-7s*
Carlyle *76s/Mad*
Charlie Mom *1A/77-8s*
Coconut Grill *2A/77s*
Coco Pazzo *74s/Mad*
Cortina *2A/75-6s*
Cucina Vivolo *74s/Lex-Park*
Dallas BBQ *3A/72-3s*

Daniel *76s/5A-Mad*
Due *3A/79-80s*
EJ's Luncheonette *3A/73s*
Fiamma *1A/77-8s*
First Wok *3A/78s*
Fish Market *2A/74-5s*
Golden Monkey *1A/73-4s*
Grace's *71s/3A*
Hatsune *73s/1A*
Havana Tea/Cigar *78s/2-3A*
Hunan Balcony *2A/74s*
Hunters *3A/78-9s*
Hurricane Island *3A/74-5s*
Ikeno Hana *Lex/72-3s*
Il Monello *2A/76-7s*
J.G. Melon *3A/74s*
Kan Pai *2A/77-8s*
Katch *75s/1-2A*
Kiosk *Lex/72-3s*
La Granita *2A/77s*
Lenox Hill *Lex/77-8s*
Lenox Room *3A/73-4s*
Le Petit Hulot *Lex/70-1s*
Letizia *1A/72-3s*
Loui Loui *3A/75s*
Luke's B&G *3A/79-80s*
Lumi *Lex/70s*
Lusardi's *2A/77-8s*
Malaga *73s/1A-York*
Mark's *77s/Mad*
Mary Ann's *2A/78-9s*
Mezzaluna *3A/74-5s*
Mortimer's *Lex/75s*
Nino's *1A/72-3s*
Orienta *75s/2-3A*
Owen Thai *1A/77-8s*
Pacifico *2A/77-8s*
Pamir *2A/74-5s*
Parma *3A/79-80s*
Payard *Lex/73-4s*
Persepolis *2A/74-5s*
Petaluma *1A/73s*
Pintaile's Pizza *York/76-7s*
Pomodori *2A/74-5s*
Quatorze Bis *79s/1-2A*
Rafina *York/78-9s*
Red Tulip *75s/1A-York*
Rosewood *3A/75-6s*
Sant Ambroeus *Mad/77-8s*
Sarabeth's *Mad/75s*
Savann Est *78s/Lex-3A*
Sette Mezzo *Lex/70-1s*
Shabu-Shabu 70 *70s/1-2A*
Shabu-Tatsu *York/75s*

Sofia Fab. Pizza *Mad/79s*
Spice *2A/73-4s*
Starbucks *Lex/78s; 1A/75s; 3A/74s*
Star Fish *3A/74-5s*
Sushi Hana *2A/78s*
Syrah *2A/72-3s*
Szechuan Kitchen *1A/76s*
Taiyo *York/73-4s*
Tang Tang *3A/76s*
Toraya *71s/5A-Mad*
Tratt. del Portico *2A/74-5s*
Trois Jean *79s/Lex-3A*
Uskudar *2A/73-4s*
Velvet Room *76s/2-3A*
Viand *Mad/78-9s*
Vivolo *74s/Park-Lex*
Willow *Lex/73s*
Zucchero *2A/76-7s*

East 60s
(East of Fifth Avenue)
Angels *1A/62-3s*
Arcadia *62s/5A-Mad*
Arizona 206 & Cafe *60s/2-3A*
Aureole *61s/Mad-Park*
Bellissima *2A/62-3s*
Bravo Gianni *63s/2-3A*
Brio *Lex/61-2s*
Cabana *3A/60-1s*
Cafe Nosidam *Mad/66s*
Café Pierre *61s/5A-Mad*
Cal. Pizza Kitchen *60s/3A*
China Fun *2A/65s*
Circus *Lex/62-3s*
Club Macanudo *63s/Park-Mad*
Colony *1A/65s*
Contrapunto *60s/3A*
Decade *1A/61s*
Destinée *61s/Lex-Park*
East *66s/1-2A*
East River Cafe *1A/61s*
Evergreen, Cafe *1A/69-70s*
Ferrier *65s/Mad-Park*
Fred's at Barneys *61s/5A-Mad*
Gertrude's *61s/Mad-Park*
Gino *Lex/60-1s*
Hale & Hearty *Lex/64-5s*
Hosteria Fiorella *3A/63-4s*
Ici *69s/Mad-Park*
Il Pellicano *62s/1A-York*
Il Vagabondo *62s/1-2A*
Isle of Capri *3A/61s*
Jackson Hole *64s/2-3A*
Jake's Stkhse. *3A/67-8s*
John's Pizzeria *64s/1A-York*

Jo Jo *64s/Lex-3A*
Kitaro *1A/63-4s*
L'Absinthe *67s/2-3A*
La Goulue *Mad/64-5s*
L'Ardoise *1A/65-6s*
Le Bilboquet *63s/Mad-Park*
Le Bistrot Maxim's *Mad/61-2s*
Le Régence *64s/Mad-Park*
Le Relais *Mad/63s*
Le Taxi *60s/Park-Mad*
Le Veau D'Or *60s/Park-Lex*
Library *Park/61s*
Manhattan Grille *1A/63-4s*
Marguery Grill *65s/Park-Lex*
Marti *1A/68-9s*
Match Uptown *60s/Mad-Park*
Matthew's *3A/61s*
Maya *1A/64-5s*
Mediterraneo *2A/66s*
Merchants, N.Y. *1A/62s*
Mesa City *3A/62-3s*
Mme. Romaine *61s/Park-Lex*
Muggs *64s/1A-York*
Nanni II *61s/Park-Lex*
Nello *Mad/62-3s*
New World *3A/67-8s; 3A/61-2s*
Park Ave. Cafe *63s/Park-Lex*
Patsy's Pizza *2A/69s*
Post House *63s/Mad-Park*
Primola *2A/64-5s*
Regency *Park/61s*
Scalinatella *61s/2-3A*
Sel et Poivre *Lex/64-5s*
Serendipity 3 *60s/2-3A*
Sign of the Dove *3A/65s*
Sofia Fab. Grill *61s/Mad-Park*
Starbucks *3A/66s*
Sushihatsu *1A/62-3s*
Toscana *Lex/64-5s*
Tucci *63s/2-3A*
Viand *Mad/61-2s*
Via Oreto *1A/61-2s*
Yellowfingers *60s/3A*

East 50s
(East of Fifth Avenue)
Akbar *Park/57-8s*
Al Bustan *3A/50-1s*
Alexandre *54s/Lex-Park*
Anche Vivolo *58s/2-3A*
Aria *52s/2A*
Armani Cafe *Mad/57-8s*
Artos *53s/1-2A*
Bar & Books *1A/50s*
Benihana *56s/Park-Lex*

Between the Bread 56s/Lex-3A
Bice 54s/5A-Mad
Bill Hong's 56s/2-3A
Billy's 1A/52-3s
Blockhead's 2A/50-1s
Bouterin 59s/1A-Sutton Pl.
Bruce Ho's 57s/Park-Lex
Bruno Ristorante 58s/2-3A
Burger Heaven Mad/54-5s;
   53s/5A-Mad
Cafe du Pont 1A/56-7s
Cafe Nicholson 58s/1-2A
Caffe Buon Gusto 2A/53-4s
Casa Brasil 53s/1-2A
Casa del Pescatore 2A/50-1s
Caviar Russe Mad/54-5s
Caviarteria Park/59s
Cellini 54s/Mad-Park
Chianti 2A/55s
Cinquanta 50s/Park-Mad
Clarke's, P.J. 3A/55s
Columbus Bakery 1A/52-3s
Coming or Going 58s/Mad-Park
Cosí Sandwich 52s/3A-Lex;
   56s/Mad-Park
Dawat 58s/2-3A
DeGrezia 50s/2-3A
Deniz a la Turk 57s/1A-Sutton Pl.
Divine Bar 51s/2-3A
Eros 1A/58-9s
Ess-a-Bagel 3A/50-1s
Felidia 58s/2-3A
57, 57 57s/Park-Mad
Fitzers Lex/56-7s
Four Seasons 52s/Park-Lex
Fresco by Scotto 52s/Park-Mad
Fresco Tortillas 2A/51-2s
Fu's House 2A/51-2s
Giambelli 50s/Mad-Park
Haikara Grill 2A/53-4s
Harry Cipriani 5A/59-60s
Houston's 53s/Lex-3A
Hyotan Nippon 59s/Lex-Park
Il Gabbiano 58s/2-3A
Il Menestrello 52s/5A-Mad
Il Nido 53s/2-3A
Il Toscanaccio 59s/5A-Mad
Il Valentino 56s/1-2A
Jubilee 54s/1-2A
Kaplan's 59s/Mad-Park
King Cole 55s/5A-Mad
Kokachin 52s/5A-Mad
Korea Palace 54s/Park-Lex
La Gioconda 53s/2-3A

La Grenouille 52s/5A-Mad
La Mangeoire 2A/53-4s
La Mediterranée 2A/50-1s
Le Chantilly 57s/Park-Lex
Le Cirque 2000 Mad/50-1s
Le Colonial 57s/Lex-3A
L'Entrecote 1A/57-8s
Leopard 50s/2-3A
Le Perigord 52s/1A-FDR Dr.
Lespinasse 55s/Mad-5A
Les Sans Culottes 2A/57-8s
Lipstick Cafe 3A/54s
Lutèce 50s/2-3A
Maloney & Porcelli 50s/Park-Mad
Maple Garden 53s/2-3A
March 58s/1A-Sutton Pl.
Mayfair 1A/53s
Meltemi 1A/51s
Metropolitan Cafe 1A/52-3s
Monkey Bar 54s/Park-Mad
Montebello 56s/Park-Lex
Mr. Chow 57s/1-2A
Neary's 57s/1-2A
New World 57s/Lex; 5A/51s; 3A/51s
Nippon 52s/Lex-3A
Oceana 54s/Mad-Park
Oikawa 3A/50s
Otabe 56s/Park-Mad
Pamir 1A/58s
Paper Moon Express 58s/Mad-Park
Paper Moon Milano 58s/Mad-Park
Park, The 56s/Lex-Park
Pasqua Coffee 53s/Park-Mad;
   3A/54-5s
Pescatore 2A/50-1s
Pesce & Pasta 1A/59s
Puket 2A/50-1s
Raffaele 1A/57-8s
Rosa Mexicano 1A/58s
San Pietro 54s/5A-Mad
Seryna 53s/5A-Mad
Shanghai Manor 55s/Lex-3A
Shun Lee Palace 55s/Lex-3A
Solera 53s/2-3A
Starbucks 54s/1A; Park/55-6s;
   Mad/55-6s
Sushisay 51s/Mad-Park
Takino 2A/54-5s
Tam-Tam Bar 50s/Lex-3A
Tapas Lounge 1A/59s
Tatany 52s/2-3A
Tatou 50s/Lex-3A
Tea Box 5A/54-5s
Teodora 57s/Lex

208

Thai Orchid *1A/51-2s*
Townhouse *58s/2-3A*
Tse Yang *51s/Mad-Park*
Turtle Bay Grill *2A/52s*
Two Rooms *58s/1-2A*
Typhoon Brewery *54s/Mad-5A*
Vergina *53s/2-3A*
Vong *54s/3A*
Wylie's Ribs *1A/50s*
Yamaguchi *52s/2-3A*
Zarela *2A/50-1s*

East 40s
(East of Fifth Avenue)
Alonzo's *45s/1-2A*
Ambassador Grill *UN Plaza/1-2A*
Azusa of Japan *44s/5A-Mad*
Bobby Van's *Park/46s*
Box Tree *49s/2-3A*
Bull & Bear *Park/49s*
Burger Heaven *Mad/40-1s;*
 49s/5A-Mad
Cafe Centro *45s/Lex-Vanderbilt*
Cafe de Paris *2A/49s*
Cafe SFA *5A/49-50s*
Calif. Burrito *Park/46s*
Captain's Table *2A/46s*
Carmen Pagina Uno *49s/1-2A*
Chiam *48s/Lex-3A*
Chikubu *44s/5A-Mad*
Chin Chin *49s/2-3A*
Cibo *2A/41-2s*
Comfort Diner *45s/2-3A*
Cosí Sandwich *45s/Mad-Vanderbilt*
Cucina & Co. *45s/Lex-Vanderbilt*
Daily Soup *41s/5A-Mad; 43s/Lex-3A*
Da Mario *1A/49-50s*
Delegates' Din. Rm.-UN *1A/46s*
Diwan Grill *48s/Lex-3A*
Docks Oyster Bar *3A/40s*
Dolce *49s/Mad-Park*
Domingo *49s/2-3A*
East *44s/2-3A*
Flower Drum *2A/45-6*
Fortune Garden *2A/45-6s*
Grifone *46s/2-3A*
Hatsuhana *Park/46s; 48s/5A-Mad*
Hurley's *6A/49s*
Il Postino *49s/1-2A*
Inagiku *49s/Lex-Park*
Japas 47 *47s/3A-Lex*
Jimmy Sung's *44s/2-3A*
J. Sung Dynasty *Lex/48s*
Katsuhama *47s/5A-Mad*
Kuruma Zushi *47s/5A-Mad*

Little Italy *Vanderbilt/45-6s*
Malika *43s/2-3A*
Mangia *48s/Mad-5A*
Marichu *46s/1-2A*
Mee Noodle Shop *2A/49s*
Menchanko-tei *45s/Lex-3A*
Mezze *44s/Mad-5A*
Mid City Grill *47s/5A*
Morton's *5A/45s*
Nanni's *46s/Lex-3A*
Naples 45 *45s/Lex-Vanderbilt*
New World *Mad/48s; 3A/45s;*
 Mad/43-4s
Oyster Bar *42s/Vanderbilt*
Palm *2A/44-5s*
Palm Too *2A/44-5s*
Pasqua Coffee *Mad/43s; Lex/44-5s*
Patroon *46s/Lex-3A*
Peacock Alley *Park/49-50s*
Peking Park *Park/40s*
Pen & Pencil *45s/2-3A*
Phoenix Garden *40s/2-3A*
Pietro's *43s/2-3A*
Sakagura *43s/2-3A*
San Giusto *2A/49-50s*
Shaliga Thai *2A/44-5s*
Shinbashi *Park/48s*
Shinbashi-an *48s/3A-Lex*
Sichuan Palace *44s/1-2A*
Smith & Wollensky *49s/3A*
Soup Nutsy *46s/3A-Lex*
Sparks *46s/2-3A*
Starbucks *Mad/42s*
Sushi Bar *49s/2A*
Sushiden *49s/5A-Mad*
TakeSushi *Vanderbilt/45-6s*
T.G.I. Friday's *Lex/42-3s;42s/Mad*
Thady Con's *2A/49s*
Top of Tower *Mitchell Pl.: 1A/49s*
Tropica *45s/Lex-Vanderbilt*
Wollensky's Grill *49s/3A*
Yan Van Van *Vanderbilt/43-4s*
Zephyr Grill *Mitchell Pl.: 1A/49s*

West 90s & Up
(West of Fifth Avenue)
Cafe Con Leche *Amst./95-6s*
Cafe St. John *110s/Amst.*
Caffé Taci *Bway/110s*
Carmine's *Bway/90-1s*
Copeland's *145s/Bway-Amst.*
Empire Szechuan *Bway/170-1s;*
 Bway/100s; Bway/97s
Farfalle *Col./93s*
Fish *Bway/108s*

Flor De Mayo *Bway/100-1s*
Gabriela's *Amst./93s*
Gennaro *Amst./92-3s*
Hunan Balcony *Bway/98s*
Hunan Park *Col./95s*
Jo-An Japanese *Bway/103-4s*
Krispy Kreme *125s/8A*
La Cocina *Bway/98-9s*
La Rosita *Bway/108-9s*
Lemongrass Grill *Bway/94-5s*
Mamá Mexico *Bway/101-2s*
Mary Ann's *Bway/91s*
Meridiana *Bway/105-6s*
Métisse *105s/Bway-Amst.*
Mill Korean *Bway/112-3s*
Monsoon *Bway/110-1s*
New World *Bway/114s*
Ollie's *Bway/116s*
107 West *Bway/107-8s*
Starbucks *Bway/102s*
Sylvia's *Lenox/126-7s*
Terrace *119s/Amst.-Morningside*
V&T Pizzeria *Amst./110-1s*
Well's *7A/132-3s*

West 80s
(West of Central Park)
Al Dente *Amst./80s*
Azure *Amst./83-4s*
Barney Greengrass *Amst./86-7s*
Bella Luna *Col/88-9s*
Cafe Con Leche *Amst./80-1s*
Cafe Lalo *83s/Amst.-Bway*
Columbus Bakery *Col./82-3s*
Delphini *Col./85s*
Docks Oyster Bar *Bway/89-90s*
Drip *Amst./83-4s*
Edgar's Cafe *84s/Bway-W.End*
EJ's Luncheonette *Amst./81-2s*
Evelyn, The *Col./78s*
Fred's *Amst./83s*
French Roast *Bway/85s*
Fujiyama Mama *Col./82-3s*
Good Enough to Eat *Amst./83-4s*
Haru *Amst./80-1s*
Isola *Col./83-4s*
Jackson Hole *Col./85s*
La Cocina *85s/Bway-Amst.*
La Mirabelle *86s/W. End-Riverside*
Lemongrass Grill *Amst./84s*
Les Routiers *Amst./87-8s*
Little Jezebel *Col./86s*
Louie's Westside *Amst./81s*
Luzia's *Amst./80-1s*
Main Street *Col./81-2s*

Merchants, N.Y. *Col./85-6s*
Miss Saigon *Col./82-3s*
Monsoon *Amst./81s*
New World *Col./80s*
Nola *Amst./80-1s*
Nova Grill *Bway/85s*
Ollie's *Bway/84s*
Panarella's *Col./84-5s*
Pho Bang *86s/Col.*
Pizzeria Uno *Col./81s*
Popover Cafe *Amst./86-7s*
Puccini *Col./83s*
Rain *82s/Col.-Amst.*
Republic *Bway/82-3s*
Saigon Grill *Bway/87s*
Sarabeth's *Amst./80-1s*
Shabu-Tatsu *Col./83-4s*
Silk Road Palace *Amst./81-2s*
Starbucks *Bway/81s; Bway/87s*
Tibet Shambala *Amst./83-4s*

West 70s
(West of Central Park)
All State Cafe *72s/Bway-W End*
Ansonia *Col./75-6s*
Artepasta *73s/Col.-Amst.*
Baci *Amst./79-80s*
Baluchi's *Col./73-4s*
Bissaleh *72s/Amst.-Col.*
Burritoville *72s/Amst.-Col.*
Cafe Luxembourg *70s/Amst.-W. End*
Caffe Buon Gusto *71s/Col.-CPW*
Caffe Popolo *Col./76-7s*
Calif. Burrito *Bway/71-2s*
China Fun *Col./71-2s*
Citrus B&G *Amst./75s*
Dallas BBQ *72s/CPW-Col.*
Emack & Bolio's *Amst./78-9s*
Empire Szechuan *72s/Bway-W. End*
Epices *70s/Col.-Bway*
Ernie's *Bway/75-6s*
Estihana *79s/Bway-Amst.*
Fine & Schapiro *72s/Bway-Col.*
Fishin Eddie *71s/Col.-CPW*
Freddie & Pepper's *Amst./74-5s*
Gray's Papaya *Bway/72s*
Hunan Park *Col./70-1s*
Isabella's *Col./77s*
Istanbul *Amst./79-80s*
Janine's *Col./74-5s*
Josie's *Amst./74s*
La Caridad 78 *Bway/78s*
La Vela *Amst./77-8s*
Mad Fish *Bway/77-8s*
Matsuri *72s/Amst.-Col.*

Mingala West *Amst./75-6s*
Mughlai *Col./75s*
Museum Cafe *Col./77s*
New World *Bway/75-6s*
Niko's *Bway/76s*
Ocean Grill *Col./78-9s*
Pappardella *Col./74-5s*
Pasha *71s/Col.-CPW*
Patsy's Pizza *74s/Col.-CPW*
Penang *Col./71s*
Pomodoro Rosso *Col./70-1s*
Provi, Provi *72s/Bway-W. End*
River *Amst./76-7s*
Sambuca *72s/CPW-Col.*
Savann *Amst./79-80s*
Scaletta *77s/CPW-Col.*
Shark Bar *Amst./74-5s*
Sido *Amst./79s*
Starbucks *Bway/70s*
Sugar Bar *72s/Bway-W. End*
Two Two Two *79s/Bway-Amst.*
Van West *72s/Bway-W. End*
Vermouth *Amst./72s*
Vinnie's Pizza *Amst./73s*
West End Cottage *72s/Bway-W. End*
Wilson's *79s/Amst.*
Xando Coffee *Bway/76s*
Zen Palate *Bway/76-7s*

West 60s
(West of Fifth Avenue)
Café des Artistes *67s/CPW-Col.*
Cafe Fiorello's *Bway/63-4s*
Coco Opera *65s/CPW-Col.*
Empire Szechuan *Col./68-9s*
Gabriel's *60s/Bway-Col.*
Iridium *63s/Col.-Bway*
It's a Wrap *Bway/68-9s*
Jean Georges *CPW/60-1s*
John's Pizzeria *65s/CPW-Col.*
Josephina *Bway/63-4s*
La Boite en Bois *68s/CPW-Col.*
La Fenice *Bway/68-9s*
Lenge *Col./69s*
Levana *69s/Bway/Col.*
Lincoln Tavern *64s/Bway-CPW*
Merlot *63s/Col.-Bway*
New World *Col./67s*
Nick & Toni's *67s/Bway-Col.*
Ollie's *Bway/67s*
O'Neals' *64s/Bway-CPW*
Picholine *64s/Bway-CPW*
Saloon *Bway/64s*
Santa Fe *69s/CPW-Col.*
Shun Lee *65s/CPW-Col.*

Shun Lee Cafe *65s/CPW-Col.*
Starbucks *Col./67s*
Tavern on Green *CPW/67s*
Vince & Eddie's *68s/Col.-CPW*
West 63rd Steak *63s/Bway-Col.*

West 50s
(West of Fifth Avenue)
Adrienne *5A/55s*
Afghan Kebab Hse. *9A/51-2s*
Alexi on 56 *56s/5-6A*
Allegria *55s/6A*
American Festival *50s/5-6A*
Aperitivo *56s/5-6A*
Aquavit *54s/5-6A*
Artusi *52s/5-6A*
August Moon *58s/6-7A*
Baluchi's *56s/Bway-8A*
Bangkok Cuisine *8A/52-3s*
Bar & Books *56s/6-7A*
Bar 9 *9A/53-4s*
Bay Leaf *56s/5-6A*
Bello *9A/56s*
Ben Benson's *52s/6-7A*
Benihana *56s/5-6A*
Bistro Latino *Bway/54s*
Blockhead's *50s/8-9A*
Bombay Palace *52s/5-6A*
Bricco *56s/8-9A*
Brooklyn Diner *57s/Bway-7A*
Café Botanica *CPS/6-7A*
Cafe Europa *57s/7A*
Caffe Cielo *8A/52-3s*
Carnegie Deli *7A/55s*
Castellano *55s/6-7A*
Champagne's *55s/5-6A*
Chanpen Thai *9A/51s*
Chez Napoleon *50s/8-9A*
China Grill *53s/6A*
Christer's *55s/6-7A*
Ciao Europa *54s/5-6A*
Circo, Osteria del *55s/6-7A*
Cité *51s/6-7A*
Cité Grill *51s/6-7A*
D'Angelo, Osteria *56s/Bway-8A*
Darbar *56s/5-6A*
Da Tommaso *8A/53-4s*
Daydream Cafe *51s/9-10A*
Divina Commedia *9A/50s*
Druids *10A/50-1s*
East *55s/Bway-8A*
Ed Sullivan's *Bway/53-4s*
Fantino *CPS/6-7A*
Fashion Cafe *51s/5-6A*

Ferrara *Bway/53s*
Flute *54s/Bway-7A*
Fontana di Trevi *57s/6-7A*
Fresco Tortillas *9A/51-2s; 10A/56-7s*
Gallagher's *52s/Bway-8A*
Giovanni *55s/5-6A*
Halcyon *54s/6-7A*
Hale & Hearty *56s/5-6A*
Hallo Berlin *51s/9-10A*
Hard Rock Cafe *57s/Bway-7A*
Harley Davidson *6A/56s*
Hooters *56s/7A-B'way*
Il Tinello *56s/5-6A*
Island Burgers *9A/51-2s*
Jean Lafitte *58s/6A*
Jekyll & Hyde Club *6A/57-8s*
JUdson Grill *52s/6-7A*
Julian's *9A/53-4s*
Kabul Cafe *54s/Bway-8A*
Keewah Yen *56s/5-6A*
Kiiroi-Hana *56s/5-6A*
King Crab *8A/52s*
La Bonne Soupe *55s/5-6A*
La Caravelle *55s/5-6A*
La Côte Basque *55s/5-6A*
La Crêpe de Bretagne *56s/5-6A*
Le Bar Bat *57s/8-9A*
Le Bernardin *51s/6-7A*
Le Biarritz *57s/8-9A*
Le Bouchon *51s/8-9A*
Lemon Tree *9A/51-2s*
Le Quercy *55s/5-6A*
L'Ermitage *56s/5-6A*
Les Célébrités *58s/6-7A*
Les Pyrénées *51s/Bway-8A*
Les Sans Culottes *51s/8-9A*
Mangia *57s/5-6A*
Mangia e Bevi *9A/53s*
Manhattan Ocean *58s/5-6A*
Martini's *7A/53s*
Mee Noodle Shop *9A/53s*
Menchanko-tei *55s/5-6A*
Michael's *55s/5-6A*
Mickey Mantle's *CPS/5-6A*
Milos *55s/6-7A*
Mi Nidito *8A/51s*
Molyvos *7A/55-6s*
Motown Cafe *57s/6-7A*
Nirvana *CPS/5-6A*
Oak Room/Bar *5A/59s*
Old San Juan *9A/51-2s*
Onigashima *55s/5-6A*
Palio *51s/6-7A*
Palm Court *5A/59s*

Pasqua Coffee *6A/54-5s; 6A/51-2s*
Pasta Lovers *58s/6-7A*
Patsy's *56s/Bway-8A*
Petrossian *58s/7A*
Planet Hollywood *57s/6-7A*
Plaza Oyster Bar *58s/5-6A*
Puttanesca *9A/56s*
Raphaël *54s/5-6A*
Redeye Grill *7A/56s*
Remi *53s/6-7A*
René Pujol *51s/8-9A*
Rice 'n' Beans *9A/50-1s*
Route 66 Cafe *9A/55-6s*
Russian Samovar *52s/Bway-8A*
Russian Vodka Room *52s/Bway-8A*
Ruth's Chris *51s/6-7A*
San Domenico *CPS/Bway-7A*
Seeda Thai *50s/8-9A*
Sette MoMA *53s/5-6A*
Siam Inn *8A/54-5s; 8A/51-2s*
Soup Kitchen Intl. *55s/Bway-8A*
Stage Deli *7A/53-4s*
Starbucks *Bway/51s; 57s/8-9A*
Sushiya *56s/5-6A*
Tang Pavilion *55s/5-6A*
Tapika *56s/8A*
Taprobane *56s/Bway-8A*
Television City *6A/50s*
Ten Kai *56s/5-6A*
T.G.I. Friday's *7A/50s; 51s/5-6A; Bway/53s*
Topaz Thai *56s/6-7A*
Tout Va Bien *51s/8-9A*
Trattoria dell'Arte *7A/56-7s*
Trionfo *51s/Bway-8A*
Tuscan Sq. *51s/5-6A*
"21" Club *52s/5-6A*
Uncle Nick's *9A/50-1s*
Victor's Cafe *52s/Bway-8A*
Vintage *9A/50-1s*
Vynl Diner *9A/54s*
Zenith *8A/52s*

West 40s
(West of Fifth Avenue, including Theater District)
Afghan Kebab Hse. *46s/6-7A*
Algonquin Hotel *44s/5-6A*
Amarone *9A/47-8s*
Amy's Bread *9A/46-7s*
Bali Nusa Indah *9A/45-6s*
Barbetta *46s/8-9A*
Basilica *9A/46-7s*
Becco *46s/8-9A*
Brasilia *45s/5-6A*

Bryant Park Cafe *42s/5-6A*
Bryant Park Grill *40s/5-6A*
B. Smith's *8A/47s*
Cabana Carioca *45s/6-7A*
Cafe Europa *6A/46s*
Cafe Un Deux Trois *44s/6A-Bway*
Calif. Burrito *7A/49s; 8A/40-1s*
Cara Mia *9A/45-6s*
Caravan *8A/46-7s*
Carmine's *44s/Bway-8A*
Charlotte *44s/6A-Bway*
Chez Josephine *42s/9A-Dyer*
Chez Suzette *46s/8-9A*
Churr. Plataforma *49s/8-9A*
Ciro *8A/49s*
Coco Pazzo Teatro *46s/Bway-8A*
Così Sandwich *42s/5-6A*
Dish of Salt *47s/6-7A*
Don Giovanni *44s/8-9A*
Edison Cafe *47s/Bway-8A*
Ferrara *42s/7A*
FireBird *46s/8-9A*
Foley's Fish House *7A/47-8s*
44 *44s/5-6A*
Frankie & Johnnie's *45s/Bway-8A*
Fresco Tortilla *42s/6A-Bway*
Frico Bar *43s/9A*
Guh Ho *46s/5-6A*
Hakata *47s/Bway-8A; 48s/Bway-8A*
Hourglass Tavern *46s/8-9A*
Ipanema *46s/5-6A*
Island Spice *44s/9-10A*
Jewel of India *44s/5-6A*
Jezebel *9A/45s*
Joe Allen *46s/8-9A*
John's Pizzeria *44s/Bway-8A*
La Cocina *8A/46-7s*
Lakruwana *44s/8-9A*
Landmark Tavern *11A/46s*
La Primavera *48s/Bway-8A*
La Reserve *49s/5-6A*
La Rivista *46s/8-9A*
Lattanzi *46s/8-9A*
Le Beaujolais *46s/8-9A*
Le Madeleine *43s/9-10A*
Le Marais *46s/6-7A*
Le Max *43s/6A-Bway*
Le Rivage *46s/8-9A*
Les Sans Culottes *46s/8-9A*
Limoncello *7A/50-1s*
Little Italy *45s/6A*
Little Saigon *46s/8-9A*
Lotfi's Moroccan *46s/8-9A*
Luxia *48s/8-9A*

Meskerem *47s/9-10A; 11A/49s*
Mike's American B&G *10A/45-6s*
Mont Blanc *48s/8-9A*
Mr. Soup *44s/Bway-6A*
Nakagawa *44s/5-6A*
New World Grill *49s/8-9A*
Official All Star Cafe *Bway/45s*
Ollie's *44s/Bway-8A*
Orso *46s/8-9A*
Osteria al Doge *44s/6-7A*
Pasta Lovers *49s/6-7A*
Pierre au Tunnel *47s/Bway-8A*
Pietrasanta *9A/47s*
Poisson *44s/6-7A*
Pomaire *46s/8-9A*
Pongsri Thai *48s/Bway-8A*
Rachel's *9A/43-4s*
Rainbow Room *Rock Pl./49-50s*
Sardi's *44s/Bway-8A*
SeaGrill *49s/5-6A*
Shaan *48s/5-6A*
Soul Cafe *42s/9-10A*
Starbucks *7A/49-50s; Bway/47s;*
  6A/45s; 8A/43-4s; 6A/42s
Stardust Dine-O-Mat *Bway/43s*
Sukhothai West *42s/9-10A*
Supper Club *47s/Bway-8A*
Sushiden *49s/6-7A*
Sushi Zen *46s/5-6A*
Swiss Inn *48s/8-9A*
T.G.I. Friday's *Bway/41s*
Torre di Pisa *44s/5-6A*
Turkish Cuisine *9A/44-5s*
Via Brasil *46s/5-6A*
View *Bway/45-6s*
Virgil's Real BBQ *44s/6-7A*
Wally's & Joseph's *49s/Bway-8A*
West Bank Cafe *42s/9-10A*
World Yacht *41s/Hudson River*
Wu Liang Ye *48s/5-6A*
Yamaguchi *45s/5-6A*
Zen Palate *9A/46s*
Zuni *9A/43s*

Murray Hill
(40th to 30th Sts., East of Fifth Ave.)
An American Place *32s/Park-Mad*
Asia de Cuba *Mad/37-8s*
Belluno *Lex/39-40s*
Bienvenue *36s/5A-Mad*
Bistro 39 *2A/39s*
Blockhead's *3A/33-4s*
Bora *Mad/33-4s*
Christina's *2A/33-4s*

Ciccio & Tony's East *3A/37-8s*
Cinque Terre *38s/Mad-Park*
Da Ciro *Lex/33-4s*
East *38s/5A-Mad*
El Parador Cafe *34s/1-2A*
El Pote Español *2A/38-9s*
El Rio Grande *38s/3A*
Emilios *33s/3A-Lex*
Empire Korea *32s/5A-Mad*
Fino *36s/5A-Mad*
Fresco Tortillas *3A/36-7s; 2A/38-9s*
Garden Cafe-Kitano *38s/Park*
Hangawi *32s/5A-Mad*
Jackson Hole *3A/35s*
La Giara *3A/33-4s*
La Maison Japon. *39s/Park-Lex*
Le Grenadin *37s/5A-Mad*
Madison Bistro *Mad/37-8s*
Marchi's *31s/2-3A*
Mee Noodle Shop *2A/31s*
Messina Cafe *3A/37-8s*
Mishima *Lex/30-1s*
Morgan Court *Mad/36-7s*
Nadaman Hakubai *Park/38s*
Nicola Paone *34s/2-3A*
Notaro *2A/34-5s*
Patsy's Pizza *3A/34-5s*
Piccolino *36s/5A-Mad*
Rossini's *38s/Lex-Park*
Rungsit II *34s/2-3A*
Salute *Mad/39s*
Sarge's Deli *3A/36-7s*
Sekku *Lex/39-40s*
Starbucks *2A/32s*
Stella del Mare *Lex/39-40s*
Tibetan Kitchen *3A/30-1s*
Tokyo *Lex/39-40s*
Toledo *36s/5A-Mad*
Trattoria Alba *34s/2-3A*
Tre Pomodori *34s/2-3A*
Villa Berulia *34s/Park-Lex*
Water Club *30s/East River*
Wu Liang Ye *Lex/39-40s*

Gramercy Park
(30th to 24th Sts., East of Fifth
Ave., and 24th to 14th Sts., East
of Park Ave. S.)
Abigael's *37s/5A-Mad*
Bamiyan *3A/26s*
Cafe Aubette *27s/Lex-Park S.*
Candela *16s/Irving Pl.-Park S.*
Chez Le Chef *Lex/28-9s*
Choshi *Irving Pl./19s*
Christine's *2A/26s*

Cibar *Irving Pl./17-8s*
Daily Soup *Park S./24-5s*
Delano Drive *Waterside Plaza/East R.
   & 25s*
DeRosa *2A/29-30s*
East *3A/26-7s*
Empire Szechuan *3A/27-8s*
Ess-a-Bagel *1A/21s*
Fresco Tortilla *Lex/23-4s*
Friend of Farmer *Irving Pl./18-9s*
Galaxy *Irving Pl./15s*
Globe *Park S./26-7s*
Hué *23s/2-3A*
I Trulli *27s/Park S.-Lex*
Jai-Ya Thai *3A/28-9s*
La Colombe d'Or *26s/Lex-3A*
Lady Mendl's *Irving Pl./17-8s*
Lamarca *22s/3A*
La Petite Auberge *Lex/27-8s*
Les Halles *Park S./28-9s*
Malayboo *3A/27-8s*
Marti *24s/2-3A*
Mavalli Palace *29s/Park S.-Mad*
Meli Melo *Mad/29-30s*
Moreno *Irving Pl./18s*
Mr. Soup *23s/Lex-Park S.*
Noodles on 28 *3A/28s*
Olé *2A/24-5s*
Park Bistro *Park S./28-9s*
Paul & Jimmy's *18s/Park S.-Irv.*
Pete's Tavern *18s/Irving Pl.*
Pitchoune *3A/19s*
Pongsri Thai *2A/18s*
Rolf's *3A/22s*
Rungsit Thai *23s/3A-Lex*
Sal Anthony's *Irving Pl./17-8s*
Sam's Noodle *3A/29s*
Sonia Rose *Lex/28-9s*
Starbucks *3A/28s; 3A/23s*
Tang Tang *3A/20s*
Tatany *27s/2-3A*
Tien Fu Guong *3A/16-7s*
Turkish Kitchen *3A/27-8s*
Union Pacific *22s/Park S.-Lex*
Vatan *3A/28-9s*
Verbena *Irving Pl./17-8s*
Waterfront Ale *2A/30s*
Yama *17s/Irving Pl.*

Garment District & Chelsea
(40th to 24th Sts., West of Fifth
Ave., and 24th to 14th St., West
of Sixth Ave.)
Alley's End *17s/8-9A*
Amy's Bread *9A/15-6s*

Appetito *39s/5-6A*
Arioso *23s/6-7A*
Ben's Kosher Deli *38s/7-8A*
Biricchino *29s/8A*
Bright Food Shop *8A/21s*
Burritoville *23s/7-8A*
Cafe Inferno *8A/18-9s*
Cafe Riazor *16s/7-8A*
Cajun *8A/16s*
Calidad Latina *9A/18s*
Calif. Burrito *7A/20-1s*
Chelsea Bistro *23s/8-9A*
Chelsea Feast *23s/10-1A*
Chelsea Grill *8A/16-7s*
Chelsea Ristorante *8A/15-6s*
Community B&G *7A/22-3s*
Cupcake Cafe *9A/39s*
Daniella *8A/26s*
Da Umberto *17s/6-7A*
Don Giovanni *10A/22-3s*
East of Eighth *23s/7-8A*
Eighteenth & 8th *8A/18s*
El Cid *15s/8-9A*
El Quijote *23s/7-8A*
Empire Diner *10A/22s*
Francisco's C.V. *23s/6-7A*
Frank's *10A/15s*
Fresco Tortilla *14s/7-8A; 8A/22-3s;*
   6A/25-6s; 9A/39-40s
Gascogne *8A/17-8s*
Ginger House *7A/28-9s*
Hale & Hearty *9A/15-6s*
Han Sung *35s/5-6A*
Havana Chelsea *8A/19-20s*
Il Faro *39s/5-6A*
Kang Suh *Bway/32s*
Keens Stkhse. *36s/5-6A*
Krispy Kreme *23s/7-8A*
La Lunchonette *10A/18s*
La Nouvelle Justine *23s/7-8A*
La Taza de Oro *8A/14-5s*
La Traviata *23s/9-10A*
Le Gamin *9A/21s*
Le Madri *18s/7A*
Le Singe Vert *7A/19-20s*
Luma *9A/22-3s*
Manganaro's *9A/37-8s*
Mangia *34s/Herald Sq.*
Man Ray *8A/18-9s*
Mary Ann's *8A/16s*
Merchants, N.Y. *7A/16-7s*
Meriken *7A/21s*
Monster Sushi *23s/6-7A*

Moran's *10A/19s*
Negril *23s/8-9A*
New World *7A/34-5s*
Old Homestead *9A/14-5s*
147 *15s/6-7A*
Petite Abeille *18s/6-7A*
Pop Heaven & Hell *8A/25-6s*
Raymond's Cafe *7A/15-6s*
Red Light Bistro *9A/14-5s*
Regional Thai *7A/22s*
Restivo *7A/22s*
Rocking Horse *8A/19-20s*
Royal Siam *8A/22-3s*
Skylight Diner *34s/9-10A*
Soul Fixins' *34s/9A*
Spirit Cruises *23s/Hudson River*
Starbucks *Bway/37-8s; 7A/31s; 8A/16s*
Sunny East *39s/5-6A*
Supreme Macaroni *9A/38-9s*
T.G.I. Friday's *8A/34s*
Tick Tock Diner *8A/34s*
Trois Canards *8A/19-20s*
T.S. Ma *Penn Pl.:33s/8A*
Urban Hero *38s/7-8A*
Viceroy *8A/18s*
Won Jo *32s/5A-Bway*
Woo Chon *36s/5-6A*
Yet Jip *36s/5-6A*
Zucca *10A/23-4s*

Flatiron District/ Union Square

(Between Chelsea & Gramercy
Park, bounded by 24th and
14th Sts., between 6th Ave. and
Park Ave. S.)
ABC Parlour Cafe *19s/Bway-Park S.*
Aja *Bway/22s*
Alva *22s/Park S.-Bway*
America *18s/5A-Bway*
Angelo & Maxie's *Park S./19s*
Bangkok Cafe *20s/Park S.-Bway*
Basta Pasta *17s/5-6A*
Bella Donna *23s/Bway-Mad*
Blue Water Grill *Union Sq. W./16s*
Bolo *22s/Park S.-Bway*
Cafe Beulah *19s/Park S.-Bway*
Caffé Bondi *20s/5-6A*
Calif. Burrito *Park S./23s*
Cal's *21s/5-6A*
Campagna *21s/Park S.-Bway*
Chat 'n Chew *16s/Union Sq. W.-5A*
Cheetah *21s/5-6A*
Chili Pepper *Park S./19-20s*
City Bakery *17s/Bway-5A*

City Crab *Park S./19s*
Coffee Shop *Union Sq. W./16s*
Daily Soup *17s/Bway-5A*
Da Vittorio *20s/Park S.-Bway*
Dionysos *5A/15-6s*
Eisenberg *5A/22-3s*
Flowers *17s/5-6A*
Follonico *24s/5-6A*
Fred's Beauty *22s/5-6A*
F•stop *20s/5-6A*
Giorgio's *21s/Park S.-Bway*
Gramercy Tavern *20s/Park S.-Bway*
Granville *20s/Park S.-Bway*
Hamachi *20s/Park S.-Bway*
Heartland Brew. *Union Sq. W./16-7s*
Hot Tomato *6A/21s*
Justin's *21s/5-6A*
La Boulangere *21s/Park S.-Bway*
L'Acajou *19s/5-6A*
La Pizza Fresca *20s/Bway-Park S.*
L'Express *Park S./20s*
Live Bait *23s/Bway-Mad*
Lola *22s/5-6A*
Mayrose *Bway/21s*
Medusa *Park S./19-20s*
Mesa Grill *5A/15-6s*
Metronome *Bway/21s*
Novitá *22s/Park S.-Lex*
Old Town Bar *18s/Park S.-Bway*
Park Avalon *Park S./18-9s*
Patría *Park S./20s*
Periyali *20s/5-6A*
Republic *Union Sq. W./16-7s*
Silver Swan *20s/Park S.-Bway*
Starbucks *6A/21-2s; Park S./23s*
Steak Frites *16s/Union Sq. W.-5A*
Tap Room *18s/5-6A*
Theodore *Bway/20-1s*
Tramps Cafe *21s/5-6A*
Tratt. I Pagliacci *Park S./19-20s*
T Salon *20s/Bway-5A*
Union Sq. Cafe *16s/Union Sq. W.-5A*
Zen Palate *Union Sq. E./16s*

Greenwich Village
(14th to Houston Sts., West of Fifth)
Aggie's *Houston/MacDougal*
Anglers & Writers *Hud./St. Luke's Pl.*
Annam *Carmine/Bleecker-Bedford*
Anton's *4s/Perry*
Arlecchino *Bleecker/6A-MacDougal*
Artepasta *Greenwich A/Bank*
Arturo's Pizzeria *Houston/Thompson*
Au Troquet *12s/Greenwich s*
Baluchi's *6A/Washington Pl.*

Bar & Books *Hudson/Horatio-Jane*
Bar Pitti *6A/Bleecker-Houston*
Bar Six *6A/12-3s*
Beatrice Inn *12s/4s*
Benny's Burritos *Greenwich A/Jane*
Bondini *9s/5-6A*
Botany *Greenwich A/Perry*
Brothers BBQ *Varick/Clarkson*
Cafe Asean *10s/6A*
Cafe de Bruxelles *Greenwich A/13s*
Cafe Español *Carmine/7A; Bl/Mac*
Café Fès *4s/Charles*
Cafe Loup *13s/6-7A*
Cafe Mona Lisa *Bleecker/7A S.*
Caffe Lure *Sullivan/Bleecker-Houston*
Caffe Rafaella *7A S./10s-Charles*
Caffe Reggio *MacDougal/3s-Bleecker*
Caffe Rosso *12s/4s*
Caffe Torino *10s/Greenwich A-7A*
Caffe Vivaldi *Jones/Bleecker-W. 4s*
CamaJe
    MacDougal/Bleecker-Houston
Caribe *Perry/Greenwich s*
Cent'Anni *Carmine/Bleecker-Bedford*
Charlie Mom *6A/8-9s; 6A/11-2s;
    7A S./Bleecker-Morton*
Chez Brigitte *Greenwich A/Bank-7A*
Chez Jacqueline *Mac/Bl-Houston*
Chez Ma Tante *10s/4s-Bleecker*
Chez Michallet *Bedford/Grove*
Choga *Bleecker/La Guardia-Thompson*
Chumley's *Bedford/Barrow*
Cornelia St. Cafe *Cornelia/4s*
Corner Bistro *4s/Jane*
Corsica *4s/Bank-12s*
Cowgirl Hall *Hudson/10s*
C3 *Waverly Pl./MacDougal*
Cucina Della Fontana *Bleecker/Char*
Cucina Stagionale *Bleecker/6-7A*
Cuisine de Saigon *13s/6-7A*
Da Silvano *6A/Bleecker-Houston*
Drovers *Jones/Bleecker-4s*
E & O *Houston/La Guardia-Thompson*
East *Barrow/7A S./4s*
EJ's Luncheonette *6A/9-10s*
El Charro *Charles/Greenwich A-7A*
Elephant & Castle *Greenwich A/11s*
El Faro *Greenwich s/Horatio*
Empire Szechuan *7A S./11s; GrA/6A*
Est! Est!! Est!!! *Carmine/Bedford-7A S.*
Factory Cafe *Christopher/Bleecker*
Ferrara *Greenwich A/Christopher*
Florent *Gansevoort/Greenwich s*
Focacceria *MacDougal/Bl-Houston*

French Roast *11s/6A*
Fujii *Greenwich A/7A-11s*
Garage *7A S./Grove-Barrow*
Gene's *11s/5-6A*
Golden Pot *Greenwich A/Bank-12s*
Grand Ticino *Thompson/3s-Bleecker*
Grange Hall *Commerce/Barrow*
Grano Trattoria *Greenwich A/10s*
Gray's Papaya *6A/8s*
Graziella *Greenwich A/Charles-Perry*
Grey Dog's Coffee *Carmine/Bleecker*
Grove *Bleecker/Grove*
Grove St. Brasserie *Grove/7A S.*
Gus' Place *Waverly Pl./6A*
Hog Pit *9A/13s*
Home *Cornelia/Bleecker-4s*
Hudson Corner *Hudson/Perry-11s*
Il Mulino *3s/Thompson-Sullivan*
Indigo *10s/7A S.-Waverly Pl.*
Ithaka *Barrow/Bedford-Bleecker*
Jekyll & Hyde *7A S./Barrow-Grove*
Joe Jr.'s *6A/11-2s*
Joe's Pizza *Bl/Carmine; Carmine/6A*
John's Pizzeria *Bleecker/6A-7A S.*
La Boheme *Minetta Ln./3s-Bleecker*
La Focaccia *Bank/4s*
La Lanterna *MacDougal/3-4s*
La Metairie *10s/4s*
La Paella *Hudson/11s-Perry*
La Ripaille *Hudson/12s-Bethune*
Le Figaro *Bleecker/MacDougal*
Le Gigot *Cornelia/Bleecker-4s*
Lemongrass Grill *Barrow/7A S.*
Les Deux Gamins *Waverly Pl./Grove*
Le Zoo *11s/Greenwich s*
Liam *Thompson/Bleecker-Houston*
Lips *Bank/Greenwich A*
Magic Carpet *Carmine/6A-7A S.*
Mama Buddha *Hudson/Bank*
Mappamondo *Hudson/Bank; 8A/12s;
    MacDougal/3s-Bleecker*
Maria Elena *13s/6-7A*
Marinella *Carmine/Bedford*
Marylou's *9s/5-6A*
Mary's *Bedford/Carmine-Leroy*
Massimo *Thompson/Bleecker-3s*
Mi Cocina *Jane/Hudson*
Minetta Tavern *MacDougal/3s*
Miracle B&G *Bleecker/11s-Bank*
Mirezi *5A/12-3s*
Mitali West *Bleecker/7A S.*
Moustache *Bedford/Grove-Barrow*
Nadine's *Bank/Greenwich s*

New World *6A/11-2s; 6A/12s*
Night Gallery *7A S./4s-10s*
Oaks *Grove/7A S.-Bleecker*
One if by Land *Barrow/7A S.-4s*
Orig. Cal. Taqueria *Hud/10s*
Osteria Fiorentina *Bleecker/Jones*
Paris Commune *Bleecker/11s-Bank*
Pearl Oyster *Cornelia/Bleecker-4s*
Perry Bistro *Hudson/Perry*
Pesce & Pasta *Bleecker/6A-7A S.*
Petite Abeille *Hud/Barrow; 14s/9A*
Picasso Cafe *Bleecker/Charles*
Piccolo Angolo *Hudson/Jane*
Pink Tea Cup *Grove/Bedford*
Pizzeria Uno *6A/8s-Waverly Pl.*
Pó *Cornelia/Bleecker-4s*
Portobello *Thompson/Bleecker-3s*
Quantum Leap *3s/Sullivan-Thompson*
Rafaella *Bleecker/Perry-Charles*
Rinçon de España *Thompson/3s*
Rio Mar *9A/Little W. 12s*
Rocco *Thompson/Houston-Bleecker*
Rubyfruit *Hudson/Charles-10s*
Salam Cafe *13s/6-7A*
Sammy's Noodle *6A/11s*
Sarong Sarong *Bleecker/10s*
Sazerac House *Hudson/Charles*
Sevilla *Charles/4s*
Shopsin's *Bedford/Morton*
Song *MacDougal/3s-Bleecker*
Starbucks *6A/Waverly Pl.-8s;
    Greenwich A/Bank*
Taka *Grove/7A S.-Bleecker*
Tanti Baci *10s/7A S.-Waverly Pl.*
Tapastry *Hudson/Bank-11s*
Taq. de Mexico *Greenwich A/12s*
Tartine *11s/4s*
Tavern on Jane *8A/Jane*
Tea & Sympathy *Greenwich A/12-3s*
Thali *Greenwich A/10s-Charles*
Thomas' *Bedford/Commerce*
Time Cafe *7A S./Barrow*
Tio Pepe *4s/6A-7A S.*
Titou *4s/Charles-Perry*
Tomoe *Thompson/Bl-Houston*
Toons *Bleecker/Bank*
Tortilla Flats *Washington/12s*
Tratt. Spaghetto *Bleecker/Carmine*
Treehouse *Hudson/Morton*
Tsunami *3s/La Guardia Pl.-Thompson*
Turkish Grill *Bleecker/Mac-6A*
Tutta Pasta *Carmine/Bedford*
Two Boots West *11s/GrA*

Uncle Nick's *Hudson/11s*
Universal Grill *Bedford/Leroy*
Vegetarian's Paradise *4s/6A*
Village Bistro *7A S./Bl-Grove*
Villa Mosconi *MacDougal/Houston*
Vittorio *Bleecker/7A S.-Grove*
Volare *4s/6A-MacDougal*
Washington Place *Wash Pl./6A*
Waterloo Brasserie *Charles/Wash*
White Horse Tavern *Hudson/11s*
Yama *Houston/La Guardia-Thompson*
Ye Waverly Inn *Bank/Waverly Pl.*
Zinno *13s/6-7A*

Central Village/NoHo
(14th to Houston Sts., Fifth to
Third Aves.)
Acme B&G *Gr. Jones/Bway*
Arté *9s/Univ Pl.-5A*
Bayamo *Bway/4s-Wash. Pl.*
B Bar *4s/Bowery-Lafayette*
Borgo Antico *13s/5A-Univ Pl.*
Bussola *4A/9-10s*
Clementine *5A/8s*
Dallas BBQ *Univ Pl./8s*
Danal *10s/3-4A*
Dojo *W. 4s/Bway-Mercer*
Emerald Planet *Gr. Jones/Bway*
Ennio & Michael *La Guardia/3s*
Fez *Lafayette/Great Jones-4s*
Gotham B&G *12s/5A-Univ. Pl.*
Great Jones Cafe *Gr. Jones/Bowery*
Helena's *Lafayette/Astor Pl.-4s*
Il Buco *Bond/Lafayette-Bowery*
Il Cantinori *10s/Bway-Univ. Pl.*
Indochine *Lagayette/Astor Pl.-4s*
Japonica *Univ. Pl./12s*
Knickerbocker *Univ. Pl./9s*
La Belle Epoque *Bway/12-3s*
Lemongrass Grill *Univ. Pl/11s*
Louisiana Commun. *Bway/Bl*
Marion's *Bowery/Gr. Jones-4s*
NoHo Star *Lafayette/Bleecker*
Osso Bucco *Univ. Pl./11-2s*
Pageant B&G *9s/3-4A*
Patsy's Pizza *Univ. Pl./10-1s*
Riodizio *Lafayette/Astor Pl.-4s*
Rose Cafe *5A/9s*
Santorini *Wash. Pl./Mercer*
Silver Spurs *Bway/9s;*
  La Guardia/Houston
Souen *13s/5A-Univ Pl.*
Starbucks *Astor Pl./Lafayette*
Temple Bar *Lafayette/Houston*
Thé Adoré *13s/5A-Univ. Pl.*

Time Cafe *Lafayette/Gr. Jones-4s*
Toast *Lafayette/4s-Astor Pl.*
Tutta Pasta *La Guardia/Houston*
Two Boots *Bleecker/Bway*
Village Grill *La Guardia/Bleecker*

East Village
(14th to Houston Sts., East of
Third Ave.)
Agrotikon *14s/1-2A*
Angelica Kitchen *12s/1-2A*
Asiana *Ave. A/4s*
Avenue A *Ave. A/6-7s*
Baby Jake's *1A/1-2s*
Bambou *14s/2-3A*
Bel-Air *St. Marks Pl./Ave. A-1A*
Bendix Diner *1A/10-1s*
Benny's Burritos *Ave. A/6s*
Boca Chica *1A/1s*
Bona Fides *2A/3-4s*
Burritoville *2A/8-9s*
Cafe Cento Sette *3A/13s*
Cafe Margaux *Ave. B/11s*
Caravan of Dreams *6s/1A-Ave. A*
Chez Es Saada *1s/1-2A*
Christine's *1A/12-3s*
Circa *2A/6s*
Cloister Cafe *9s/2-3A*
Col Legno *9s/2-3A*
Cucina di Pesce *4s/2-3A*
Cyclo *1A/12-3s*
Dallas BBQ *2A/St. Marks Pl.*
Delia's *3s/Aves. A-B*
Dojo *St. Marks Pl./2-3A*
Dok Suni *1A/7s-St. Marks Pl.*
85 Down *Ave. A/5-6s*
Elephant *1s/1-2A*
First *1A/5-6s*
Flea Market Cafe *Ave. A/9s*
Frutti di Mare *4s/2A*
Global 33 *2A/5-6s*
Hasaki *9s/2-3A*
Haveli *2A/5-6s*
Holy Basil *2A/9-10s*
Hotel Galvez *Ave. B/6-7s*
Il Bagatto *2s/Ave. A-B*
In Padella *2A/9s*
Iso *2A/11s*
John's of 12th *12s/2A*
Jules *St. Marks Pl./1-2A*
Khyber Pass *St. Marks Pl./2-3A*
Kiev *2A/7s*
Lan *3A/10-1s*
Lanza *1A/10-1s*

La Paella *9s/2-3A*
Les Deux Lapins *5s/Aves. A-B*
Life Cafe *10s/Ave. B*
Lucky Cheng's *1A/1-2s*
Mama's Food Shop *3s/Aves. A-B*
Mary Ann's *2A/5s*
McSorley's *7s/2-3A*
Mee Noodle Shop *1A/13s*
Mekka *Ave. A./Houston-2s*
Mingala Burmese *7s/2-3A*
Miracle Grill *1A/6-7s*
Mitali East *6s/1-2A*
Moustache *10s/1A-Ave. A*
Odessa *Ave. A/7s-St. Marks Pl.*
O.G. *6s/Aves. A-B*
Old Devil Moon *12s/Aves. A-B*
Opaline *Ave. A/5-6s*
Orologio *Ave. A/10-1s*
Oven *2A/3-4s*
Pasqua Coffee *Astor Pl./3A*
Passage to India *6s/2A*
Penang B&G *3A/11s*
Pisces *Ave. A/6s*
Pizzeria Uno *3A/10-1s*
Pommes Frites *2A/7s-St. Marks Pl.*
Rectangles *2A/10s*
Roettele A.G. *7s/1A-Ave. A*
Rose of India *6s/1-2A*
Sapporo East *10s/1A*
Second Ave. Deli *2A/10s*
Shabu-Tatsu *10s/1-2A*
Starbucks *2A/9s*
St. Dymphnas *St. Marks Pl./Ave. A-1A*
Stingy Lulu's *St. Marks Pl./Ave. A-1A*
Svoboda *2A/5s*
Takahachi *Ave. A/5-6s*
Telephone B&G *2A/9-10s*
Thailand Cafe *2A/5-6s*
Tsampa *9s/2-3A*
Two Boots *Ave. A/2-3s*
Ukrainian *2A/St. Marks Pl.-9s*
Veniero's *11s/1-2A*
Veselka *2A/9s*
Virage *2A/7s*
Windows on India *6s/1A*
Wraparama *1A/10s*
Xunta *1A/10-1s*
Yaffa Cafe *St. Marks Pl./1A-Ave. A*
Zito's East *1A/12-3s*

Lower East Side
(Houston to Canal Sts., East of Bowery)
Katz's Deli *Houston/Ludlow*
Lansky Lounge *Norfolk/Delancey*
Ratners *Delancey/Norfolk-Suffolk*
Sammy's Roumanian *Chrystie/Delan*
Standard Notions
   Ludlow/Houston-Stanton
Yoshi *Houston/Ludlow-Orchard*

SoHo – Little Italy
(Houston to Canal Sts., West of Bowery)
AJ's Niota *W. Bway/Grand*
Alison *Dominick/Hudson-Varick*
Angelo's *Mulberry/Hester-Grand*
Aquagrill *Spring/6A*
Ballato's *Houston/Mott-Mulberry*
Balthazar *Spring/Crosby*
Baluchi's *Spring/Sullivan-Thompson*
Bar 89 *Mercer/Spring-Broome*
Barolo *W. Bway/Spring-Broome*
Benito I *Mulberry/Broome*
Benito II *Mulberry/Grand-Broome*
Bistrot Margot *Prince/Mott*
Blue Ribbon *Sullivan/Prince-Spring*
Blue Ribbon Sushi *Sullivan/Prince*
Boom *Spring/Wooster-W. Bway*
Broome St. Bar *W. Bway/Broome*
Cafe Gitane *Mott/Prince*
Cafe Noir *Grand/Thompson*
Caffe Biondo *Mulberry/Grand-Hester*
Can *W. Bway/Houston*
Canal House *W. Bway/Grand*
Casa La Femme *Wooster/Prince*
Cascabel *Lafayette/Spring-Broome*
Cendrillon *Mercer/Broome-Grand*
Cody's B&G *Hudson/Dominick*
Country Cafe *Thompson/Spring*
Cub Room *Sullivan/Prince*
Cub Room Cafe *Prince/Sullivan*
Cucina della Nonna *Grand/Mercer*
Cupping Room *W. Bway/Grand*
Da Nico *Mulberry/Broome-Grand*
Diva *W. Bway/Broome-Grand*
Downtown *W. Bway/Broome*
Ear Inn *Spring/Washington*
Eat & Drink *Mercer/Houston-Prince*
El Pollo *Broome/Wooster*
Erizo *W. Bway/Prince-Spring*
Fanelli *Prince/Mercer*
Félix *W. Bway/Grand*
Ferrara *Grand/Mott-Mulberry*
Frontière *Prince/Sullivan-MacDougal*
Helianthus *MacDougal/Prince*
Herban Kitchen *Hudson/Spring*
Honmura An *Mercer/Houston-Prince*
Hudson Grill *Hudson/King*
Il Corallo *Prince/Thompson-Sullivan*

Il Cortile *Mulberry/Canal-Hester*
Il Fornaio *Mulberry/Hester-Grand*
Il Palazzo *Mulberry/Hester-Grand*
I Tre Merli *W. Bway/Houston-Prince*
Jean Claude *Sullivan/Houston*
Jerry's *Prince/Greene-Mercer*
Karahi *Broome/W. Bway*
Kelley & Ping *Greene/Prince*
Kin Khao *Spring/W. Bway-Thompson*
Kitchen Club *Prince/Mott*
La Boulangere *Bway/Spring*
La Cigale *Mott/Prince-Spring*
La Jumelle *Grand/Wooster-W. Bway*
La Mela *Mulberry/Grand-Broome*
L'Ecole *Bway/Grand*
Le Gamin *MacDougal/Houston-Prince*
Le Jardin *Cleve. Pl./Spring*
Le Pescadou *King/6A*
Little Italy *Varick/Charlton-King*
Lombardi's *Spring/Mulberry-Mott*
Lucky Strike *Grand/Wooster-W. Bway*
L'Ulivo *Spring/Thompson*
Lupe's East L.A. *6A/Watts*
M & R *Elizabeth/Houston-Prince*
Manhattan Bistro *Spring/Wooster*
Match *Mercer/Houston-Prince*
MeKong *Prince/Mott-Mulberry*
Mezzogiorno *Spring/Sullivan*
Monzù *Mercer/Prince*
Mottsu *Mott/Houston-Prince*
New World *W. Bway/Prince-Spring*
Novecento *W. Bway/Grand-Broome*
Ñ 33 Crosby *Crosby/Grand-Broome*
Nyonya *Grand/Mott*
Omen *Thompson/Prince-Spring*
Onieals *Grand/Centre-Mulberry*
Pao! *Spring/Greenwich s*
Patrissy's *Kenmare/Mulberry-Centre*
Pellegrino's *Mulberry/Hester-Grand*
Penang *Spring/Greene-Mercer*
Pravda *Lafayette/Prince-Houston*
Provence *MacDougal/Prince-Houston*
Quilty's *Prince/Sullivan-Thompson*
Raoul's *Prince/Sullivan-Thompson*
Rialto *Elizabeth/Houston-Prince*
Sal's SPQR *Mulberry/Hester-Grand*
Savore *Spring/Sullivan*
Savoy *Prince/Crosby*
Scratch *Spring/Wooster-W. Bway*
Scully on Spring *Spring/Sullivan*
S.O.B.'s *Varick/Houston*
SoHo Kitchen *Greene/Prince-Spring*
Soho Steak *Thompson/Prince-Spring*
Spring St. Natural *Spring/Lafayette*

Starbucks *Spring/Crosby*
Taormina *Mulberry/Grand-Hester*
Tennessee Mtn. *Spring/Wooster*
Tratt. Venti Tre *Cleve. Pl./Spring*
Triplets *Grand/6A*
Velvet *Mulberry/Prince-Houston*
Zoë *Prince/Bway-Mercer*

Chinatown

(South of Hester St., East of
Lafayette St.; west of Allen &
Pike Sts.)

Big Wong *Mott/Canal-Bayard*
Bo-Ky *Bayard/Mott-Mulberry*
Cafe Colonial *Houston/Elizabeth*
Canton *Division/Bowery-Market*
Eastern Villa *Mott/Bayard-Canal*
Excellent Dumpling *Lafayette/Canal*
Fuleen Seafood *Division/E. Bway*
Golden Unicorn *E. Bway/Catherine*
Great Shanghai *Division/Bowery*
HSF *Bowery/Canal*
Jing Fong *Elizabeth/Canal-Bayard*
Joe's Shanghai *Pell/Mott-Bowery*
Kam Chueh *Bowery/Bayard*
Little Szechuan *E. Bway/Chatham Sq.*
Mandarin Court *Mott/Canal-Bayard*
Mr. Tang *Mott/Bayard*
Mueng Thai *Pell/Mott-Bowery*
New Chao Chow *Mott/Canal-Hester*
New Pasteur *Baxter/Canal-Bayard*
Nha Trang *Baxter/Canal-Bayard*
Nice Rest. *E. Bway/Market*
NY Noodle Town *Bowery/Bayard*
Oriental Garden *Elizabeth/Canal*
Pacifica *Lafayette/Canal*
Peking Duck Hse. *Mott/Chatham Sq.*
Pho Bang *Chatham Sq./Mott;*
Mott/Canal; Pike/Canal-Division
Pho Tu Do *Bowery/Grand*
Pho Viet Huong *Mulberry/Canal*
Saigon House *Bayard/Mulberry*
Sea Gull *Centre/Walker-White*
Silver Palace *Bowery/Canal*
Sweet-n-Tart *Mott/Canal*
Tai Hong Lau *Mott/Canal-Bayard*
Thailand Rest. *Bayard/Baxter*
Triple Eight *E. Bway/Division-Mkt*
20 Mott St. *Mott/Chatham Sq.-Pell*
Vegetarian's Paradise *Mott/Pell*
Viet-Nam *Doyers/Pell-Bowery*
Wong Kee *Mott/Canal-Hester*

TriBeCa – Downtown

(South of Canal Street, including Wall St. area)

Acappella *Hudson/Chambers*
Arqua *Church/White*
Au Mandarin *WFC: Vesey/West*
Barocco *Church/Walker*
Bodega *W. Bway/Thomas-Duane*
Bouley Bakery *W. Bway/Duane-Reade*
Bridge Cafe *Water/Dover*
Bubble Lounge *W. Bway/N. Moore*
Bubby's *Hudson/N. Moore*
Bull Run *William/Pine*
Burritoville *Water/Broad;*
    Chambers/W. Bway-Greenwich s
Cafe Remy *Greenwich s/Carlisle*
Calif. Burrito *WFC: Vesey*
Capsouto Frères *Washington/Watts*
Cellar in Sky *WTC/West*
Chanterelle *Harrison/Greenwich s*
City Wine *Laight/Greenwich s*
Coco Marina *WFC: West/Liberty-Vesey*
Daily Soup *John/Dutch-Nassau*
Duane Park Cafe *Duane/Hudson*
Ecco *Chambers/W. Bway-Church*
El Teddy's *W. Bway/Franklin-White*
Fado *Canal/Greenwich s-Washington*
F.illi Ponte *Desbrosses/W. Side Hwy.*
Flor de Sol *Greenwich s/Harrison*
Franklin Station *W. Bway-Franklin*
Fraunces Tavern *Pearl/Broad*
Fresco Tortilla *Chambers/Bway*
Gemelli *WTC #4: Church/Dey*
Gigino *Greenwich s/Duane-Reade*
Grill Room *WFC: Liberty/West*
Harbour Lights *Seaport*
Harry's *Hanover Sq./Pearl*
Hudson River Club *WFC: Vesey*
Il Giglio *Warren/Greenwich s*
Independent *W. Bway/Worth*
Joseph's *Hanover Sq./Pearl-Water*

Kitchenette *W. Bway/Warren*
Lafayette G&B *Franklin/Lafayette*
Layla *W. Bway/Franklin*
Little Italy *Park Pl./Bway-Church*
Mangez Avec Moi *W. Bway/Murray*
Menchanko-tei *WTC/WTC Concourse*
Mercantile Grill *Pearl/Hanover Sq.*
Montrachet *W. Bway/Walker-White*
Morton's *West St./Liberty-Albany*
Nam Phuong *6A/Walker-White*
New World *Wall/Water; NY Plaza/*
    S. Ferry; Bway/Battery Pl.
Nobu *Hudson/Franklin*
Odeon *W. Bway/Thomas*
Pasqua Coffee *WFC: Vesey;*
    Church/Barclay; Bway/Liberty
Pierino *Reade/W. Bway-Church*
Pizzeria Uno *Seaport: South St.*
Riverrun *Franklin/Greenwich s*
Rosemarie's *Duane/W. Bway-Church*
Salaam Bombay *Greenwich s/Duane*
Screening Room *Varick/Canal*
Sequoia *Fulton/South St.*
Sloppy Louie's *South St./Fulton-John*
Souperman *Pearl/Stone*
Soup Pot *W. Bway/Murray-Warren*
Spartina *Greenwich s/Harrison*
Starbucks *Park Row/Beekman;*
    State/Pearl
St. Maggie's Cafe *Wall/South St.*
Taliesin *Church/Fulton-Dey*
T.G.I. Friday's *Bway/Trinity Pl.*
Thai House Cafe *Hudson/Hubert*
Toons *Greenwich s/Franklin*
Tribeca Grill *Greenwich s/Franklin*
Walker's *N. Moore/Varick*
Wall St. Kitchen *Broad/Beaver*
Windows on World *WTC/West*
Yaffa's *Greenwich s/Harrison*
Yankee Clipper *John/South St.*
Zutto *Hudson/Jay-Harrison*

BRONX

Dominick's *Arthur/186-7s*
Il Boschetto *Gun Hill/Tiemann*
Le Refuge Inn *City Is./Sutherland*

Lobster Box *City Is./Belden-Rochelle*
Mario's *Arthur/184-6s*
Roberto's *Crescent/186s-Belmont*

BROOKLYN

Bay Ridge

Areo *3A/84s*
Chadwick's *3A/88-9s*
Chianti *3A/86s*
Embers *3A/95-6s*
Goodfella's *3A/96s*
Lento's *3A/Ovington*

Mr. Tang *3A/76s*
101 *4A/101s*
Pearl Room *3A/82-3s*
Pizzeria Uno *4A/92s*
St. Michel *3A/75-6s*
Tuscany Grill *3A/86-7s*
Tutta Pasta *3A/89-90s*

Bensonhurst
Mr. Tang *86s/19A*
Tommaso's *86s/14-5A*

Boerum Hill
Brawta Cafe *Atlantic/Hoyt*
Moustache *Atlantic/Bond-Nevins*
Two Toms *3A/Union*

Brighton Beach
Paradise *Emmons/Nostrand*

Brooklyn Heights
Acadia Parish *Atlantic/Clinton-Henry*
Caffe Buon Gusto *Montague/Henry*
Gage & Tollner *Fulton/Jay*
Heights Cafe *Montague/Hicks*
Henry's End *Henry/Cranberry*
La Bouillabaisse *Atlantic/Henry*
Noodle Pudding *Henry/Middagh*
Orig. Cal. Taqueria *Bergen/Court*
Patsy Grimaldi's *Old Fulton/Water*
Pete's Downtown *Old Fulton/Water*
Petite Crevette *Atlantic/Henry*
Queen *Court/Livingston*
River Cafe *Water/Bklyn Bridge*
Teresa's *Montague/Hicks*
Tin Room Cafe *Front/Old Fulton*
Waterfront Ale *Atlantic/Henry*

Canarsie
Abbracciamento *Rockaway P'way*
Grabstein's Deli *Rockaway P'way*

Carroll Gardens
Ferdinando's *Union/Hicks-Col.*
Marco Polo *Court/Union*

Clinton Hill
Kum Kau *Myrtle/Washington*

Cobble Hill
Camille's *Court/Kane-DeGraw*
Kalio *Court/Kane-Butler*

Coney Island
Gargiulo's *15s/Surf-Mermaid*
Mr. Tang *Coney Is. A/Ave. X*
Rasputin *Coney Is. A/Ave. X*
Totonno Pizzeria *Neptune/15-6s*

Downtown
Bamcafe *Lafayette/Ashland Pl.*
Junior's *Flatbush Ext./DeKalb*

Astoria
Akroyiali *Bway/33s*
Athens Cafe *30A/32s*
Christos Hasapo *23A/41-2s*
Elias Corner *31s/24A*

Fort Greene
Cambodian Cuisine *S. Elliot Pl./Lafayette-Fulton*
New City Cafe *DeKalb/Vanderbilt*

Gravesend
Fiorentino's *Ave. U/McDonald-West*
Sahara *Coney Island/T-U*

Greenpoint
Thai Cafe *Manhattan A/Kent*

Kings Plaza
Kings Pl. Diner *Ave. U/Coleman*

Ocean Parkway
Ocean Palace *Ave. U/14-5s*
Short Ribs *86s/11s*

Park Slope
Cucina *5A/Garfield Pl.-Carroll*
Lemongrass *7A/Lincoln Pl.*
Lento's *Union/6-7A*
Max & Moritz *7A/14-5s*
Mike & Tony's *5A/Carroll*
Monte's *Carroll/Nevins-3A*
New Prospect Cafe *Flatbush A/Plaza*
New World *7A/Carroll*
Orig. Cal. Taqueria *7A/9-10s*
Petite Crevette *7A/1s*
Twelfth St. B&G *8A/12s*
Two Boots *2s/7-8A*

Prospect Heights
Garden Cafe *Vanderbilt/Prospect Pl.*
Tom's *Washington/Sterling Pl.*
Tutta Pasta *7A/Garfield Pl.-1s*

Sheepshead Bay
Lundy Bros. *Emmons/Ocean A*

Sunset Park
Jade Plaza *8A/60-1s*
Ocean Palace *8A/55s*

Williamsburg
Giando on Water *Kent/Bway*
Northside Cafe *Kent/7s*
Oznot's Dish *Berry/9s*
Peter Luger *Bway/Driggs*
Plan Eat Thailand *Bedford/7s*
Seasons *Driggs/7s*
Vera Cruz *Bedford/6-7s*

QUEENS

Greek Captain *36A/32s*
Jackson Hole *Astoria/70s*
Karyatis *Bway/35-6s*
Little Village *Steinway/25-28A*
Mezzanotte *Bway/32-3s*

Piccola Venezia *28A/Steinway*
S'Agapo *34A/35s*
Taverna Kyclades *Ditmars/33-5s*
Taverna Vraka *31s/23A*
Telly's Taverna *23A/28-9s*
Tierras Colomb. *Bway/33s*
Ubol's Kitchen *Steinway/25A*
Uncle George's *Bway/34s*

Bayside
Ben's Kosher Deli *26A/211-2s*
Frankie & Johnnie's *Northern/194s*
Pier 25A *Northern/215-6s*
Pizzeria Uno *Bell/39A*
Uncle Jack's *Bell/40A*

Corona
Greek Captain *Van Doren/108s*
Green Field *Northern/108s*
Park Side *Corona/108s-51A*

Elmhurst
Goody's *Bway/83s*
Greek Captain *82s/Roosevelt*
Jai-Ya Thai *Bway/81s*
Pho Bang *Bway/Elmhurst*

Flushing
East Lake *Main/Franklin*
Golden Monkey *Roosevelt/Prince*
Joe's Shanghai *37A/Main-138s*
K.B. Garden *39A/Main-Union*
Kum Gang San *Northern/Main*
Master Grill *College Pt./34-5A*
Pasqua Coffee *La Guardia A'port-*
USAir Shuttle Term.
Penang *Prince/Roosevelt*
Pho Bang *Kissena/Main*
Poti *Main/41 Rd.-Sanford*

Quantum Leap *Fr. Meadow Ln./67A*
Silver Pond *Main/56A*
Sweet-n-Tart *38A/Main*
Woo Chon *Kissena/Main*

Forest Hills
Cabana *70 Rd./108s-Yellowstone*
Mardi Gras *Austin/70 A*
New World *Continental/Austin-Queens*
Nick's Pizza *Ascan/Austin-Burns*
Pizzeria Uno *70 Rd./108s-Yellowstone*
Q, a Thai Bistro *Ascan/Austin-Burns*
Teresa's *Austin/Continental*
Tutta Pasta *Queens/71 Rd.*

Forest Hills Gardens
Melting Pot *Station Sq./Burns*

Jackson Heights
Jackson Diner *74s/37A-Roosevelt*
Tierras Colomb. *Roosevelt/82s*

Kew Gardens
Pastrami King *Queens/82A*

Little Neck
La Baraka *Northern/Little Neck*

Long Island City
Jackson Ave. Stkhse.
  Jackson/Q'boro
Manducatis *Jackson/21s-47A*
Pearson's BBQ *51A/Vernon*
Water's Edge *44 Dr./East River*

Rego Park
Goody's *63 Dr./Booth-Saunders*
London Lennie's *Woodhaven/63 Dr.*

Whitestone
Cooking With Jazz *154s/12A*

STATEN ISLAND

Aesop's Tables *Bay/Maryland*
Angelina's *Jefferson/Drumgode*
Carmen's *Barclay/Hylan*
Carol's *Richmond/Seaview*
Denino's *Pt. Richmond/Hooker Pl.*
Goodfella's *Hylan/Seaview*
Killmeyer's *Arthur Kill/Sharrotts*
Lake Cafe *Clove/Victory*

Marina Cafe *Mansion/Hillside*
Old Bermuda Inn *Arthur Kill/Rossville*
Parsonage *Arthur Kill/Clarke*
South Shore *Huguenot/W. Shore Exp'wy*
Sweet Basil *Annadale/Arden-Amboy*
Tosca *Clove/Fingerboard-Richmond*
Trattoria Romana *Hylan/Benton*

SPECIAL FEATURES AND APPEALS

Breakfast
(All hotels and the following standouts)
ABC Parlour Cafe
Aggie's
American Festival
Anglers & Writers
Barney Greengrass
Brooklyn Diner
Café Botanica
Cafe Con Leche
Café Pierre
Carlyle
City Bakery
E.A.T.
EJ's Luncheonette
57, 57
Fraunces Tavern
French Roast
Globe
Good Enough to Eat
Junior's
La Boulangere
Mark's
Michael's
Naples 45
NoHo Star
Regency
Sarabeth's
Starbucks
Tick Tock Diner
Tuscan Square
Veselka
Viand

Brunch
(Best of many)
Ambassador Grill
America
Anglers & Writers
Aquagrill
Aquavit
Arizona 206/Cafe
Blue Water Grill
Bryant Park Grill
B. Smith's
Bubby's
Butterfield 81
Café Botanica
Café de Bruxelles
Café des Artistes
Cafe Luxembourg
Capsouto Frères
Carlyle
Coco Pazzo
Danal
Ear Inn
Empire Diner
Friend of a Farmer
Grange Hall
Grove

Hudson River Club
Independent
Isabella's
Island
La Belle Epoque
La Cigale
Landmark Tavern
Lenox Room
Le Régence
Lola
Maloney & Porcelli
Mark's
Marylou's
Matthew's
Mesa Grill
NoHo Star
Ocean Grill
O'Neals'
Palm Court
Park Avalon
Park Ave. Cafe
Petrossian
Rainbow Room
Redeye Grill
River Cafe
Sarabeth's
Screening Room
Sylvia's
Tapika
Tartine
Treehouse
Trois Jean
Vince and Eddie's
Water Club
Zephyr Grill
Zoë

Cheese Trays
Alva
Ansonia
Aureole
Cellar in the Sky
Chanterelle
Fred's at Barneys
Gramercy Tavern
Herban Kitchen
Jean Georges
Lenox Room
Les Célébrités
Lespinasse
Picholine

Cigar Friendly
Alva
Angelo & Maxie's
Asia de Cuba
Bar & Books
Bar Six
Ben Benson's
Billy's
Blue Water Grill
Bobby Van's

Bruno
Bubble Lounge
Bull & Bear
Café des Artistes
Campagna
Cibar
City Wine & Cigar
Clarke's, P.J.
Club Macanudo
Decade
F.illi Ponte
Flute
Four Seasons
Frank's
Fred's Beauty
Granville
Grove St. Brasserie
Harry's/Hanover Sq.
Havana Tea/Cigar
JUdson Grill
Keens Steakhouse
King Cole
Le Bar Bat
Maloney & Porcelli
Michael's
Monkey Bar
Morton's
Old Town Bar
Patroon
Post House
Redeye Grill
Remi
Russian Vodka Rm.
Smith & Wollensky
Tatou
Torre di Pisa
"21" Club
Wall St. Kitchen
Water Club
West 63rd Steak
Wollensky's Grill
World Yacht

Coffeehouses/Desserts
(See *Hotels* & *Teas*, plus the
following best bets)
ABC Parlour Cafe
Amy's Bread
Anglers & Writers
Café des Artistes
Cafe Europa
Cafe Lalo
Cafe Mona Lisa
Café Word of Mouth
Caffe Bianco
Caffe Biondo
Caffe Rafaella
Caffe Reggio
Caffe Vivaldi
Carlyle
Cupcake Cafe
Cupping Room
Drip
DT•UT

Edgar's Cafe
Emack & Bolio's
Ferrara
French Roast
Krispy Kreme
La Lanterna
Le Figaro Cafe
Le Gamin
Lipstick Cafe
New World Coffee
Palm Court
Pasqua Coffee
Payard Pâtisserie
Pink Tea Cup
Sant Ambroeus
Starbucks
Tea & Sympathy
T Salon
Veniero's
Xando Coffee

Dancing/Entertainment
(Check days, times and
performers for entertainment;
D=dancing; best of many)
Ambassador Grill (piano)
Bayamo (D/mambo)
Bissaleh (comedy)
Blue Water Grill (jazz/r&b)
Bruno (piano)
B. Smith's (jazz)
Café Pierre (piano)
Cajun (Dixieland jazz)
Campagnola (piano)
Carlyle (cabaret/piano)
Cheetah (cabaret)
Chez Josephine (jazz)
Citrus B&G (band)
Cooking With Jazz (jazz)
Copeland's (jazz)
Gertrude's (jazz)
Jezebel (piano)
Jules (jazz)
Knickerbocker B&G (jazz)
La Belle Epoque (jazz)
La Nouvelle Justine (mock s&m)
La Traviata (piano)
Layla (belly dancer)
Le Bar Bat (D)
Lips (drag queens)
Lola (blues/gospel)
Match (jazz)
Match Uptown (jazz)
Merchants, N.Y. (jazz)
Metronome (jazz)
Oaks (piano)
147 (jazz)
One if by Land (piano)
Opaline (jazz)
Park (jazz)
Rainbow Room (bands,D)
Red Tulip (varies)
River Cafe (piano)
Sign of the Dove (jazz)

S.O.B.'s (D/world beat)
Stella del Mare (piano/singer)
Supper Club (D/big bands)
Tatou (D/jazz)
Tavern on Green (D/jazz)
Top of the Tower (piano/singer)
Tramps Cafe (blues)
Tsunami (jazz)
Walker's (jazz)
Water Club (piano)
World Yacht (D/bands)
Zinno (jazz)
Zócalo (guitar/singer)

Delivers*/Takeout

(Nearly all Asians, coffee
shops, delis, diners and
pasta/pizzerias deliver or do
takeout; here are some
interesting possibilities;
D=delivery, T=takeout; call to
check range and charges,
if any)
ABC Parlour Cafe (D,T)
Acadia Parish (T)
Afghan Kebab House (D,T)
Angelica Kitchen (D,T)
Arizona 206/Cafe (D)
Armani Cafe (D,T)
Baluchi's (D,T)
Bayamo (D,T)
Bay Leaf (D,T)
Ben's Kosher (D,T)
Between the Bread (D,T)
Bice (D)
Billy's (T)
Blockhead's Burritos (T)
Brio (D,T)
Brooklyn Diner (D,T)
Brother Jimmy's (D,T)
Cafe Greco (D,T)
California Burrito (D,T)
Campagnola (D)
Carnegie Deli (D,T)
Chin Chin (D,T)
Circa (D,T)
Coco Marina (D,T)
Coming or Going (D,T)
Cosí Sandwich (D,T)
Cucina Della Fontana (D,T)
Cucina di Pesce (D,T)
Cucina Stagionale (D,T)
Dawat (D,T)
E.A.T. (D,T)
Fine & Schapiro (D,T)
Florent (D,T)
Frank's (D,T)
Globe (D,T)
Grill Room (D,T)
Hatsuhana (D,T)
Jackson Hole (D,T)
Japonica (D)
Jewel of India (D,T)
Jimmy Sung's (D,T)

Junior's (D,T)
Kiiroi-Hana (D,T)
Le Madri (D,T)
Le Marais (D,T)
Lola (D,T)
Mangia (D,T)
Mi Cocina (D,T)
Miss Saigon (D,T)
Mitali East/West (D,T)
Odessa (D,T)
Orienta (D,T)
Our Place (D)
Pamir (D,T)
Park Bistro (D,T)
Pascalou (D,T)
Pearson's Texas BBQ (D,T)
Petaluma (D,T)
Piccolo Angolo (D)
Pig Heaven (D,T)
Popover Cafe (D,T)
Provi, Provi (D,T)
Queen (D,T)
Ratners (D,T)
Remi (D)
Republic (D,T)
River (D,T)
Route 66 Cafe (T)
Salaam Bombay (D,T)
Sal Anthony's (D,T)
Second Ave. Deli (D,T)
Sharz Cafe (D,T)
Shun Lee (D,T)
Shun Lee Palace (D,T)
Spring St. Natural (D,T)
Stage Deli (D,T)
Sunny East (D,T)
Sushiden (D,T)
Sushi Hana (D,T)
Sylvia's (D,T)
Tam-Tam Bar (D,T)
Tapika (D,T)
Tartine (D,T)
Tennessee Mountain (D,T)
Thai Orchid (D,T)
Toscana (D,T)
Tuscan Square (D,T)
20 Mott Street (D,T)
Uncle Nick's (D,T)
Urban Hero (D,T)
Üsküdar (D,T)
Viet-Nam (D,T)
Virgil's Real BBQ (D,T)
Yankee Clipper (D,T)
Zarela (D,T)

Dining Alone

(Other than hotels, coffee
shops, sushi bars and counter
service places)
ABC Parlour Cafe
Al Dente
Amy's Bread
Anglers & Writers
Aquagrill

Aquavit
Aria
Armani Cafe
Bouterin
Busby's
Café Botanica
Cafe S.F.A.
Carlyle
Coming or Going
Cosí Sandwich
Darbar
Drovers Tap Room
EJ's Luncheonette
Elephant & Castle
FireBird
Fred's at Barneys
Good Enough to Eat
Gotham B&G (at the bar)
Gramercy Tavern (at the bar)
Gray's Papaya
Gus' Place
Hudson River Club
JUdson Grill
La Caravelle
La Fenice
Lespinasse
Mangia
Mme. Romaine
Naples 45
Nick & Toni's
Oceana
Ollie's
Oyster Bar
Pearl Oyster Bar
Pommes Frites
Sarabeth's
Sette MoMA
Soup Kitchen Intl.
Sushisay
Sushiya
Tea & Sympathy
T Salon
Tuscan Square
Union Square Cafe
Vinnie's Pizza
Wall St. Kitchen
Zen Palate

Family Style
Allegria
Becco
Canton
Carmine's
Chiam
China Grill
Chin Chin
Churr. Plataforma
Copeland's
Dawat
Drovers Tap Room
Green Field
Jackson Diner
John's Pizzeria
Kum Gang San

Le Colonial
Lemongrass Grill
Main Street
Master Grill Intl.
Mitali East/West
Monsoon
Nobu
NY Noodle Town
Ollie's
Orienta
Oriental Garden
Owen Thai
Penang
Riodizio
Sambuca
Siam Inn
Tony's Di Napoli

Fireplaces
(Best of many)
Asia de Cuba
Barbetta
Box Tree
Cafe Centro
Camille's Clover Hill
Chelsea Bistro
Christer's
Circus
Cornelia St. Cafe
Demi
Evelyn
Gertrude's
I Trulli
Keens Steakhouse
Landmark Tavern
March
Marchi's
Merchants, N.Y.
Moran's Chelsea
New City Cafe
Old Bermuda Inn
O'Neals'
One if by Land
Paris Commune
René Pujol
Savoy
Thady Con's
Vittorio Cucina
Vivolo
Water Club
Ye Waverly Inn

Game In Season
(The following are
recommended)
An American Place
Aquavit
Arcadia
Aureole
Borgo Antico
Bouterin
Cafe Centro
Café Crocodile
Café des Artistes

Daniel
Da Umberto
Felidia
FireBird
Gotham B&G
Gramercy Tavern
Henry's End
Hudson River Club
Jean Georges
Jo Jo
Keens Steakhouse
La Caravelle
La Grenouille
La Reserve
Le Cirque 2000
Le Madri
Le Perigord
Lutèce
Massimo
Picholine
Primavera
San Domenico
Trois Jean
"21" Club
Two Two Two
Union Square Cafe

Health/Spa Menus
(Most top places cook to
order to meet any dietary
request; call in advance to
check; besides Asians, the
following are good bets)
Adrienne
Aria
Aureole
Bouley Bakery
Café Pierre
Candle Cafe
Caravan of Dreams
Chiam
Chin Chin
Cub Room/Café
Daily Soup
Daniel
57, 57
Flower Drum
Four Seasons
Gramercy Tavern
Halcyon
Herban Kitchen
It's a Wrap
Jean Georges
Josephina
Josie's
Le Cirque 2000
Le Madri
Little Szechuan
Lobster Club
Lutèce
Mangia
Mark's
Marylou's
Matthew's

Milos
Nirvana
Nobu
Ocean Grill
Persepolis
Picholine
Popover Cafe
Quantum Leap
Quilty's
Shanghai Manor
Shun Lee
Shun Lee Palace
Souen
Soup Kitchen Intl.
Tang Pavilion
Theodore
Trionfo
Tuscan Square
Vong
Wraparama
Zen Palate

Holiday Meals
(Special prix fixe meals
offered at major holidays)
Adrienne
Algonquin Hotel
American Festival
An American Place
Aquavit
Box Tree
Café Botanica
Café des Artistes
Café Pierre
Carlyle
Charlotte
Clementine
Destinée
Duane Park Cafe
Ed Sullivan's
Fantino
57, 57
FireBird
44
Four Seasons
Fresco by Scotto
Gotham B&G
Halcyon
Hudson River Club
JUdson Grill
Le Chantilly
Le Régence
Les Célébrités
Lespinasse
Mark's
Neary's
Oak Room
Ocean Grill
One if by Land
Park
Park Ave. Cafe
Peacock Alley
Regency
River Cafe

San Domenico
SeaGrill
Sign of the Dove
Sonia Rose
Taliesin
Tavern on Green
Terrace
Trois Jean
View
Water Club

Hotel Dining
Algonquin Hotel
  Algonquin Hotel
Beekman Tower
  Top of the Tower
  Zephyr Grill
Box Tree
  Box Tree
Cambridge
  La Mirabelle
Carlyle
  Carlyle
Club Quarters
  Bull Run
Delmonico Hotel
  Caviarteria
Edison Hotel
  Edison Cafe
Elysée Hotel
  Monkey Bar
Essex House
  Café Botanica
  Les Célébrités
Fitzpatrick Manhattan
  Fitzers
Four Seasons
  57, 57
Holiday Inn Downtown
  Pacifica
Inn at Irving Place
  Cibar
  Lady Mendl's
Jolly Madison
  Cinque Terre
Kitano
  Garden Cafe
  Nadaman Hakubai
Le Refuge Inn
  Le Refuge Inn
Lexington Hotel
  J. Sung Dynasty
Lombardy
  Park
Lowell Hotel
  Post House
Mark Hotel
  Mark's
Marriott Marquis
  View
Michelangelo
  Limoncello
Millenium Hilton
  Taliesin
Millennium Broadway
  Charlotte

Morgans Hotel
  Asia de Cuba
New York Palace
  Le Cirque 2000
Omni Berkshire Place
  Kokachin
Paramount Hotel
  Coco Pazzo Teatro
Peninsula Hotel
  Adrienne
Pierre Hotel
  Café Pierre
Plaza Athénée
  Le Régence
Plaza Hotel
  Oak Room
  Palm Court
  Plaza Oyster Bar
Radisson Empire Hotel
  Iridium Jazz
  Merlot B&G
  West 63rd Steak
Regal UN Plaza
  Ambassador Grill
Regency Hotel
  Library
  Regency
Renaissance NY Hotel
  Foley's Fish House
Rihga Royal Hotel
  Halcyon
Ritz-Carlton
  Fantino
Royalton Hotel
  44
Sherry Netherland
  Harry Cipriani
Shoreham Hotel
  La Caravelle
SoHo Grand Hotel
  Canal House
Stanhope Hotel
  Nica's
St. Regis Hotel
  King Cole
  Lespinasse
Surrey Suite Hotel
  Daniel
Sutton Residence Hotel
  Il Valentino
Trump Intl. Hotel/Tower
  Jean Georges
Waldorf-Astoria
  Bull & Bear
  Inagiku
  Peacock Alley
Wales Hotel
  Sarabeth's
Warwick Hotel
  Ciao Europa
Washington Sq. Hotel
  C3

"In" Places

Across the Street
Angelo & Maxie's
Aquagrill
Asia de Cuba
Balthazar
Blue Ribbon
Blue Water Grill
Bouley Bakery
Bubble Lounge
Café des Artistes
Cheetah
Chez Es Saada
Cibar
City Wine & Cigar
Clementine
Da Umberto
Decade
Evelyn
FireBird
Flute
44
Gabriel's
Gertrude's
Globe
Gramercy Tavern
Independent
Indochine
Jean Georges
Justin's
La Cigale
La Grenouille
Lansky Lounge
Le Cirque 2000
Le Colonial
Lenox Room
Le Singe Vert
Maloney & Porcelli
Medusa
Milos
Molyvos
Nobu
Ocean Grill
147
Park
Patroon
Payard Pâtisserie
Rain
Rao's
Redeye Grill
Rialto
Scully on Spring
Sofia Fabulous Grill
Union Pacific
Waterloo Brasserie

Late Late – After 12:30
(All hours are AM)
Arturo's Pizzeria (1)
Athens Cafe (1)
Avenue A (2)
Balthazar (2)
Bar & Books (2)
Baraonda (12:30)

230

Bar 89 (1)
Bar Nine (2)
Barocco (2)
Bar Six (2)
B Bar (1)
Between the Bread (24 hrs.)
Bissaleh (1)
Blue Ribbon (4)
Blue Ribbon Sushi (2)
Blue Water Grill (12:30)
Broome St. Bar (1:30)
Bubble Lounge (1)
Cafe Europa (2)
Cafe Lalo (2)
Cafe Mona Lisa (2)
Cafe Noir (4)
Cafe Riazor (1)
Caffé Lure (1)
Caffe Rafaella (1)
Caffe Reggio (2)
Caffe Vivaldi (1)
CamaJe (1)
Carnegie Deli (24 hrs.)
Casa La Femme (3)
Chez Josephine (1)
Clarke's, P.J. (3:45)
Clementine (3:15)
Cloister Cafe (2)
Coconut Grill (12:30)
Coffee Shop (6)
Corner Bistro (4)
Cupping Room (1)
Decade (1)
Diva (4)
Divine Bar (1)
Dojo (1)
Drip (1)
E & O (2)
Ear Inn (1)
East Lake (2)
East of Eighth (2)
Edgar's Cafe (12:45)
85 Down (2)
Elaine's (2)
Empire Diner (24 hrs.)
Empire Korea (2)
Fanelli (1)
Ferrier (2)
First (2)
Florent (24 hrs.)
French Roast (24 hrs.)
Fuleen Seafood (4)
Galaxy (2:30)
Garage (2)
Global 33 (1)
Gray's Papaya (24 hrs.)
Harbour Lights (1:30)
Havana Tea/Cigar (1)
Hot Tomato (1)
Hunan Balcony (1)
Independent (2)
I Tre Merli (1)
Jackson Hole (1)

Jake's Steakhouse (2)
Jekyll & Hyde (1)
J.G. Melon (2:30)
Joe Jr.'s (1)
Joe's Pizza (4)
Jules (1)
Junior's (1)
Kam Chueh (4:30)
Kang Suh (24 hrs.)
Kan Pai (2)
Kiev (24 hrs.)
Knickerbocker B&G (1)
Kum Gang San (24 hrs.)
La Caridad 78 (1)
La Jumelle (1)
La Lanterna (3)
Lansky Lounge (3)
Le Figaro Cafe (1:30)
Le Madri (12:30)
Le Singe Vert (1)
L'Express (24 hrs.)
Library (1)
Life Cafe (1)
Live Bait (1)
Lucky Cheng's (1)
Lucky Strike (4)
Luke's B&G (1)
M & R Bar (2)
Marion's (2)
Match (4)
Match Uptown (2)
McSorley's (1)
Medusa (4)
Menchanko-tei (12:30)
Merchants, N.Y. (2)
Mezzaluna (1)
Mezzogiorno (1)
Monzù (2)
Neary's (1:30)
Night Gallery (3)
Nirvana (1)
Novecento (1)
Ñ 33 Crosby (1:30)
NY Noodle Town (4)
Odeon (2)
Odessa (24 hrs.)
Official All Star (1)
Oikawa (1:30)
Ollie's (2)
Onigashima (12:30)
Opaline (2)
Oriental Garden (1:30)
Park (1)
Park Avalon (12:30)
Pizzeria Uno (1)
Planet Hollywood (1)
Pravda (2:30)
Rainbow Room (1)
Raoul's (2)
Red Light Bistro (1)
Rio Mar (1:30)
Rose of India (12:30)
Russian Vodka Rm. (3)

Sahara (1)
Sakagura (2)
Sapporo East (12:45)
Sarge's Deli (24 hrs.)
Stage Deli (1)
Standard Notions (1)
Stingy Lulu's (5)
Sushi Bar (2:30)
Sushihatsu (3:30)
Takahachi (12:45)
Takino (1:30)
Tapas Lounge (3)
Tatany (3:30)
Tavern on Jane (1)
Telephone B&G (12:30)
Tick Tock Diner (24 hrs.)
Turkish Kitchen (2)
Two Boots (1)
Uncle George's (24 hrs.)
Velvet Room (1)
Veselka (24 hrs.)
Viand (24 hrs.)
Village Grill (1)
Vinnie's Pizza (1)
Vintage (3)
Virage (2)
Walker's (1)
Well's (1)
West Bank Cafe (1)
White Horse (1)
Wollensky's Grill (2)
Won Jo (24 hrs.)
Woo Chon (24 hrs.)
Yaffa Cafe (24 hrs.)
Yaffa's (2)
Yamaguchi (2:30)
Yellowfingers (1)

Meet for a Drink
(Most top hotels and the
following standouts)
Alexandre
Algonquin Hotel
Alva
America
Balthazar
Bar & Books
Bar Six
B Bar
Bella Blu
Bice
Box Tree
B. Smith's
Bubble Lounge
Café des Artistes
Café Pierre
Caffe Rafaella
Carlyle
Champagne's
Chez Es Saada
Circo, Osteria del
Clarke's, P.J.
Clementine
Cub Room/Café

Dock's (Downtown)
Fanelli
Fantino
57, 57
FireBird
Flute
Four Seasons
44
Freds at Barneys
Gotham B&G
Gramercy Tavern
Grill Room
Harbour Lights
Harry's/Hanover Sq.
Heartland Brewery
Iridium Jazz
I Tre Merli
Jean Georges
JUdson Grill
Keens Steakhouse
King Cole
Landmark Tavern
Le Cirque 2000
Le Colonial
Library
Mark's
McSorley's
Merchants, N.Y.
Metronome
Monkey Bar
Nola
Oak Room
Old Town Bar
O'Neals'
Palm Court
Park
Patroon
Peacock Alley
Pete's Tavern
Pravda
Regency
Sign of the Dove
Tap Room
Temple Bar
Top of the Tower
"21" Club
Union Square Cafe
Vermouth
Vintage
Vong
West 63rd Steak
White Horse
Windows on World
Wollensky's Grill

Noteworthy Newcomers (276)

(Name, *cuisine*; * Not open yet, but looks promising)
Across the Street, *American*
Al Bacio, *Italian*
Alex*, *French/American*
Alexandre, *Med./French*
Alexi on 56, *Glatt kosher*

Amarone, *Italian*
American Park/Battery*, *American*
Angelo & Maxie's, *steakhouse*
Annam, *Vietnamese*
Arioso, *Mediterranean*
Asia de Cuba, *Chinese-Latino*
Asiana, *Asian*
August Bar/Rest.*, *American*
August Moon, *Chinese*
Azure, *Mediterranean*
Baby Jupiter*, *Cajun*
Balthazar, *French*
Bamcafe, *International*
Barcelona, *Mediterranean*
Bardolino, *Italian*
Bar Nine, *American*
Bateaux New York*, *American*
Bel-Air, *French/American*
Belluno, *Italian*
Ben's Kosher Deli, *Kosher*
Bentley's,* *Japanese*
Bissaleh, *Middle Eastern Kosher*
Bistro Carré, *French*
Bistro 39, *French*
Blue Ribbon Bakery*, *American*
Bop*, *Korean*
Botany, The, *American*
Bouley Bakery, *French*
Bricco, *Italian*
Cafe Gregory*, *Eclectic*
Cafe Inferno, *Med./Continental*
Café Montaigne*, *French*
Cafe Pappagallo, *Italian*
Cafe Remy, *Continental*
Cafeteria*, *American*
CamaJe, *French*
Cara Mia, *Italian*
Carmen Pagina Uno, *Italian*
Casa Brasil, *Brazilian*
Caviar Russe, *Russian*
Cellar in the Sky, *American*
Champagne's, *French/Continental*
Chanpen, *Thai*
Cheetah, *American*
CHE 2020*, *American*
Chez Es Saada, *Moroccan*
Chez Le Chef, *French*
Chili Pepper, *Thai*
Choga, *Korean/Japanese*
Churrascaria Plataforma, *Brazilian*
Cibar, *American*
Ciccio & Tony's East, *Italian*
Cigarnaya*, *Russian*
Ciro, *Italian*
Citrus Bar & Grill, *Southwestern*
City Wine/Cigar, *International*
Clementine, *American*
Coco Marina, *Italian*
Coco Opera, *Italian*
Copperfield's Magic*, *American*
Corsica, *French*

C^2*, *Eclectic*
Cyclo, *Vietnamese*
Da Mario, *Italian*
D'Angelo, Osteria, *Italian*
Danube*, *Viennese*
Decade, *Continental*
Del Frisco's*, *Steakhouse*
DeRosa, *Italian*
Destinée, *French*
Diamond Horseshoe*, *Steakhouse*
Dionysos, *Greek*
Divina Commedia, *Italian*
Domingo, *Spanish*
Drovers Tap Room, *American*
East of Eighth, *American*
85 Down, *American*
Elephant, The, *French/Thai*
Eleven Madison Park*, *American*
Epices du Traiteur, *Med.*
Estihana, *Kosher Asian*
Evelyn, The, *American*
Exchange Club*, *American*
Factory Cafe, *American*
Fado, *Portuguese*
Fiamma, *Brazilian/Italian*
FireBird, *Russian*
FireBird Cafe*, *Russian*
Fish Market, *Greek Seafood*
Flea Market Cafe, *French*
Flor de Sol, *Spanish*
Flute, *International*
Focacceria, *Italian*
14 Wall Street*, *French*
Franz Joseph*, *Austrian*
Fred's, *American*
Fred's Beauty, *Eclectic*
Fuleen Seafood, *Chinese*
Gemelli, *Italian*
Gennaro, *Italian*
Gertrude's, *French*
Gills, *Seafood*
Globe, The, *American*
Golden Pot, The, *Swiss Fondue*
Grace's Trattoria, *Italian*
Grand Central Café*, *American*
Grand Central*, *Steakhouse*
Grano Trattoria, *Italian*
Grey Dog's Coffee, *Coffeehouse*
Grill Room, The, *Steakhouse*
Grove St. Brasserie, *American*
Guh Ho, *Korean*
Haru, *Japanese*
Helena's, *Spanish*
Holy Basil, *Thai*
Hooters, *American*
Hotel Galvez, *Southwestern*
Houston's, *American*
Il Faro, *Mediterranean*
Il Postino, *Italian*
Independent, The, *American*
Istanbul, *Turkish*
It's a Wrap, *International*
Jacques' Bistro, *French*

Japas 47, *Mediterranean*
Jazz Standard, The*, *American*
Jean Georges, *French*
Joanie's*, *French*
Joanna's, *Continental*
Johnny Tejano's, *Tex-Mex*
Justin's, *Caribbean/Southern*
Karahi, *Indian/Jewish*
Katch, *American*
Killmeyer's, *German*
Kitaro, *Japanese*
La Crêpe de Bretagne, *French*
Lafayette, *American*
La Giara, *Italian*
Lan, *Japanese*
La Nouvelle Justine, *French*
Lansky Lounge, *Kosher Eclectic*
La Pizza Fresca, *Italian*
Le Cirque 2000, *French*
Le Gigot, *French*
Le Pain Quotidien, *Belgian*
Les Deux Lapins, *Caribbean*
Le Singe Vert, *French*
Liam, *American*
Little Jezebel, *Southern*
Little Village, *Moroccan*
Lot 61*, *International*
Luna Blu*, *Italian*
Mamá Mexico, *Mexican*
MarcoPierre*, *European*
Master Grill, *Brazilian*
Max & Moritz, *French-American*
Maximillian*, *Continental*
Maxwell's, *Continental*
Maya, *Mexican*
Medusa, *Italian/Med.*
Messina Cafe, *Mediterranean*
Metronome, *Mediterranean*
Mica Bar*, *Eclectic*
Mid City Grill, *American*
Milos, *Greek Seafood*
Minton's Playhouse*, *American*
Molyvos, *Greek*
Momoyama, *Japanese*
Monster Sushi, *Japanese*
Moomba*, *American*
Mottsu, *Japanese*
Mr. K's*, *Chinese*
Muggs, *American*
Nation*, *International*
Nica's, *Mediterranean*
Nick & Toni's Cafe, *Med.*
99 Second*, *American*
Nola, *American*
Oaks, The, *American*
Obeca-Li*, *International*
Ocean Grill, *Seafood*
Old San Juan, *Puerto Rican*
147, *American*
Onigashima, *Japanese*
Orienta Downtown*, *Asian*
Owen Thai, *Thai*
Pacific East*, *Asian*

Pacifico, *Seafood*
Paggio*, *Italian*
Paper Moon Express, *Italian*
Park, The, *American*
Pasha, *Turkish*
Pasta Break*, *Italian*
Patroon, *American*
Payard, *French*
Pearl Oyster Bar, *Seafood*
Pearl Room, *Seafood*
Perry Bistro, *French*
Petite Abeille, *Belgian*
Petite Crevette, *French Seafood*
Pisello*, *Italian*
Poisson, *French Seafood*
Polistino's*, *Italian*
Pommes Frites, *Belgian*
Pondicherry*, *French Colonial*
Pop Heaven & Hell, *Coffeehouse*
Poti, *Vegetarian*
Quilty's, *Mediterranean*
Rainforest Cafe*, *American*
Red Light Bistro, *Med.*
Rialto, *American*
Robiola*, *Italian*
Rosewood, *American*
Route 66 Cafe, *Southwestern*
Russian Vodka Room, *Russian*
Salt*, *American/Eclectic*
Salute!, *Italian*
Sarong Sarong, *Malaysian*
Scully on Spring, *Mediterranean*
Seagrill of the Aegean, *Greek*
Sea Gull, *Vietnamese-Malaysian*
7th Avenue South, *American*
Sofia Fabulous Grill, *Italian*
Soul Cafe, *Southern*
Souperman, *Soups*
Soup Pot, *Soups*
Spice, *Thai*
Standard Notions, *American*
Star Fish, *Seafood*
Steak Brokers*, *Steakhouse*
Step Mama*, *American*
Sugar Bar, *Mediterr./African*
Sushi Generation*, *Japanese*
Sushiya, *Japanese*
Svoboda, *International*
Tabla*, *American*
Tam-Tam Bar, *Eclectic*
Tapastry, *American*
Tap Room Restaurant, *Viennese*
Tazza*, *Mediterranean*
Television City, *American*
Tennessee Mtn.*, *Barbecue*
Teodora, *Italian*
Thady Con's, *Irish*
Thali Vegetarian, *Indian*
Theodore, *American*
Tick Tock Diner, *Diner*
Tin Room Cafe, *Italian*
Titou, *French*
Tonic, The*, *American*

Torch*, *French/S. American*
Treehouse, The, *American/French*
T Salon & T Emporium, *Tea*
Turtle Bay Grill, *American*
Tuscan Square, *Italian*
Two Rooms, *International*
Uncle Jack's, *Steakhouse*
Union Pacific, *American*
Velvet Rest./Lounge, *Continental*
Vermouth, *American*
Village Bistro, *American*
Vintage, *American*
Virage, *Amer./Med.*
Wall St. Kitchen & Bar, *American*
Washington Place, *American*
Waterloo Brasserie, *Belgian*
Watermark*, *Seafood*
Wraparama, *International*
Xando Coffee & Bar, *Coffeehouse*
Yoshi, *Japanese*
Zito's East, *Italian*

Noteworthy Closings (92)
Alejandra's
AmerAsia
Angry Monk
Aquamarine
Arlo's
@Cafe
Au Bon Coin
Avanti
Bangkok Thai
Bar Anise
Bella Blair
Biscotti
Black Sheep
Blue Plate
Brighton Grill
Cafe Equense
Cafe Masada
Casanis
Central Park South
Century Cafe
Chantal Cafe
Charlton's
Cha Yen
Chock Full o' Nuts
Christo's Steak House
Ci Vediamo-E. Village
Claire
Dacche
Dolcetto
Eden Rock
Edwardian Room
Food Bar
Genji
Gianni's
Girafe
Infinito
Itcho
Jaraf
Jim McMullen
J's Grill
Katana

Kumkapi
La Bonne Place
La Fondue
La Gallerie
La Poste
La Serre
La Spaghetteria
L'Auberge du Midi
Laurita's Cafe Soul
Leda
Let's Do Lunch
Lucky Dog Diner
Marnie's Noodle Shop
Maxim's
Mimosa
Mistral
9 Jones
Nine Muses Cafe
Old Roma
10021 Bar & Grill
Opus II
Paradis
Pasta Eater, The
Pedro Paramo
Pelago
Perry's End
Phoebe's
Quisisana
Rush'n Express
Rusty Staub's on Fifth
Sahara Classic
Saranac
Sfuzzi
Sonia et Josephine
Sorrentino's
Stanhope Restaurant
Stingray
SushiWorks
Tallulah
Tammany Hall
13 Barrow St.
37th St. Hideaway
Tiziano
Tompkins 131
Tre Amici
Twigs
Ugly Joe's
Voulez-Vous
What's Cookin'
Ying
Zip City Brewing Co.

Offbeat
Acadia Parish
Afghan Kebab House
Annam
Baby Jake's
Ben's Kosher
Bissaleh
Boca Chica
Cabana Carioca
Casa La Femme
Chez Le Chef
Copeland's

Deniz a la Turk
Dominick's
Drip
Eastern Villa
Elephant
Elias Corner
El Pollo
Fiamma
Franklin Station
Grabstein's Deli
Green Field
Hallo Berlin
Havana Tea/Cigar
La Caridad 78
La Nouvelle Justine
La Taza de Oro
Le Bar Bat
Lips
Lucky Cheng's
Marion's
Master Grill Intl.
Melting Pot
Michael's
NY Noodle Town
Pommes Frites
Pop Heaven & Hell
Rasputin
Red Tulip
Rolf's
Shopsin's
Stingy Lulu's
Sylvia's
Tramps Cafe
Uncle George's
Vinegar Factory
Well's

Old New York
(50+ yrs.; year opened;
* building)
1716 Old Bermuda Inn*
1726 One if by Land*
1763 Fraunces Tavern
1801 Bridge Cafe*
1812 Lobster Box*
1817 Ear Inn
1853 Moran's Chelsea*
1854 McSorley's*
1855 Parsonage*
1864 Pete's Tavern
1868 Landmark Tavern
1868 Old Homestead
1870 Billy's
1872 Fanelli
1875 Harry's/Hanover Sq.
1879 Gage & Tollner
1880 White Horse
1885 Keens Steakhouse
1887 Peter Luger
1888 Katz's Deli
1890 Clarke's, P.J.
1890 Walker's
1892 Ferrara
1892 Hurley's

1892	Old Town Bar
1894	Veniero's
1896	Rao's
1902	Algonquin Hotel
1902	Angelo's
1904	Ferdinando's
1904	Lanza Restaurant
1905	Ratners
1906	Barbetta
1906	Monte's (Brooklyn)
1907	Gargiulo's
1907	Oak Room
1907	Palm Court
1908	Barney Greengrass
1908	John's of 12th St.
1913	Oyster Bar
1917	Café des Artistes
1919	Gene's
1919	Grand Ticino
1919	Mario's
1920	Ye Waverly Inn
1921	Sardi's
1922	Rocco
1924	Totonno Pizzeria
1925	Beatrice Inn
1926	Frankie & Johnnie's
1926	Palm
1927	Caffe Reggio
1927	El Faro
1927	Fine & Schapiro
1927	Gallagher's
1928	Chumley's
1929	Eisenberg Sandwich
1930	"21" Club
1930	El Quijote
1930	El Charro
1930	Marchi's
1930	Sloppy Louie's
1931	Café Pierre
1931	Peacock Alley
1932	Patsy's Pizza
1932	Pen & Pencil
1932	Pietro's
1933	Lento's
1934	John's Pizzeria
1934	Papaya King
1934	Rainbow Room
1934	Tavern on Green
1936	Tom's Restaurant
1937	Carnegie Deli
1937	Denino's Tavern
1937	Le Veau D'Or
1937	Minetta Tavern
1937	Patrissy's
1937	Stage Deli
1938	Heidelberg
1938	Well's
1941	Sevilla
1944	Patsy's
1945	Gino
1945	Tout Va Bien
1945	V&T Pizzeria

Outdoor Dining

(G=garden; P=patio;
S=sidewalk; T=terrace;
W=waterside; our
recommendations)

Abbracciamento (P)
Aesop's Tables (G)
American Festival (G)
Anton's (S)
Aquagrill (T)
Aureole (G)
Barbetta (G)
Barolo (G,T)
Bar Pitti (S)
B Bar (G,P,T)
Ben Benson's (S)
Benny's Burritos (S)
Bistro Margot (G)
Blue Water Grill (P,S)
Boathouse Cafe (G)
Bona Fides (G)
Bouterin (T)
Bryant Park Cafe (G,T)
Bryant Park Grill (G,P,T)
Cafe Centro (S)
Cafe Fiorello (S)
Cafe Margaux (G)
Caffe Bianco (G,S)
Caffé Bondí (G)
Caffe Rafaella (S)
Caffe Reggio (S)
Cascabel (S)
Chelsea Feast (G)
Chez Jacqueline (S)
Chez Ma Tante (S)
Circo, Osteria del (P)
Cloister Cafe (G)
Coco Marina (G,W)
Coffee Shop (S)
Cucina di Pesce (G,S)
Da Silvano (S)
Delphini (S)
Downtown (T)
El Rio Grande (P)
Empire Diner (S)
Evelyn (S)
Ferrier (S)
Flowers (T)
Gascogne (G)
Grove (G)
Harbour Lights (T)
Helena's (G)
Home (G)
Il Cantinori (P)
Il Palazzo (G,S)
Isabella's (S)
I Trulli (G)
Jean Georges (T)
Josephina (G,S)
Julian's (G,S)
Killmeyer's (G)
La Cigale (G,P,T)

Lake Cafe (P,W)
Lattanzi (G)
La Vela (S)
Le Cirque 2000 (P)
Le Jardin Bistro (G)
Le Madeleine (G)
Le Madri (P)
Le Petit Hulot (G)
Le Refuge (G)
Le Refuge Inn (G)
Le Relais (T)
M & R Bar (G)
March (G)
Maria Elena (G)
Marichu (G,P)
Martini's (S)
Medusa (P)
Mekka (G)
Meridiana (G,S)
Metropolitan Cafe (G)
Mezzogiorno (P,S)
Miracle Grill (G)
Moreno (S)
Moustache (G)
Naples 45 (P)
New City Cafe (G)
New World Grill (P)
Ocean Grill (S)
Old Bermuda Inn (G,P,T)
Osteria Fiorentina (S)
Pete's Tavern (S)
Picasso Cafe (G)
Pisces (S)
Poisson (T)
Provence (G)
Redeye Grill (T)
Remi (P)
Rialto (G)
River Cafe (T)
Roettele A.G. (G)
Rosewood (S)
Saloon (S)
SeaGrill (G)
Seasons (G)
Sofia Fabulous Grill (T)
Sofia Fabulous Pizza (T)
Tartine (S)
Tavern on Green (G,P,T)
Thai Orchid (G)
Trattoria Spaghetto (S)
Trattoria Venti Tre (G)
Trionfo (S)
Tutta Pasta (S)
Vera Cruz (G)
Verbena (G)
Village Grill (S)
Vittorio Cucina (G)
Water Club (T,W)
Water's Edge (W)
White Horse (S)
Wollensky's Grill (S)
Ye Waverly Inn (G,S)

Parties & Private Rooms
(Any nightclub or restaurant charges less at off-times; * indicates private rooms available; best of many)
Ansonia*
Aquavit*
Artos*
Artusi*
Asia de Cuba
Barbetta*
Barolo*
Bayamo
Becco*
Belluno*
Benihana
Billy's*
Boathouse Cafe*
Bombay Palace*
Box Tree*
Bricco*
Brother Jimmy's*
Bryant Park Grill*
B. Smith's*
Bubble Lounge*
Cafe Centro*
Cafe Nicholson
Carmine's*
Champagne's*
Cheetah*
Chez Es Saada
Chez Josephine*
Chez Le Chef*
Chiam*
Chin Chin*
Clementine
Coffee Shop*
Cowgirl Hall of Fame
Decade*
Domingo*
Elaine's
El Teddy's*
Evelyn*
FireBird*
Flowers*
Foley's Fish House*
Four Seasons*
Fresco by Scotto*
Gabriel's*
Gallagher's*
Gertrude's*
Girasole*
Golden Unicorn*
Gramercy Tavern*
Harbour Lights*
Harry's/Hanover Sq.*
Heartland Brewery
Hudson River Club*
Il Cortile*
I Tre Merli*
I Trulli*
Jekyll & Hyde
Keens Steakhouse*

237

Kings' Carriage Hse.*
La Belle Epoque
La Côte Basque*
La Grenouille*
Landmark Tavern*
La Reserve*
Le Bar Bat
Le Bernardin*
Le Cirque 2000*
L'Ecole
Leopard*
Le Perigord*
Les Célébrités*
Levana*
Live Bait
Lola*
Lutèce*
Maloney & Porcelli*
Manhattan Ocean*
Marguery Grill*
Marylou's*
Metropolitan Cafe
Michael's*
Mickey Mantle's*
Milos*
Montrachet*
Moran's Chelsea*
Moreno*
Mortimer's*
Nirvana*
Nobu*
Oceana*
Official All Star*
O'Neals'*
147*
One if by Land*
Palio*
Park*
Park Ave. Cafe*
Patroon*
Pen & Pencil*
Periyali
Picholine*
Planet Hollywood*
Post House
Primavera*
Provence*
Rain*
Rainbow Room*
Raoul's*
Remi*
Riodizio
River Cafe*
Russian Vodka Rm.*
Sal Anthony's SPQR*
San Domenico*
Sardi's*
Screening Room*
Serendipity 3*
Sette MoMA*
Shun Lee Palace*
Sign of the Dove*
Smith & Wollensky*

S.O.B.'s
Sofia Fabulous Grill
Spirit Cruises*
Supper Club*
Sushisay*
Sylvia's*
Tapika*
Tatou*
Tavern on Green*
Tennessee Mountain*
Terrace*
Top of the Tower*
Torre di Pisa*
Trattoria Dell'Arte*
Treehouse
Tribeca Grill*
Triplets Old NY*
"21" Club*
Two Rooms*
Typhoon Brewery*
Union Pacific*
Virgil's Real BBQ
Vivolo*
Water Club*
Water's Edge*
Willow*
Windows on World*
World Yacht*
Zarela*

People-Watching
Balthazar
B Bar
Bice
Blue Ribbon
Blue Ribbon Sushi
Blue Water Grill
B. Smith's
Bubble Lounge
Chez Es Saada
China Grill
Circo, Osteria del
Clementine
Club Macanudo
Daniel
Domingo
Elio's
Evelyn
Ferrier
FireBird
44
Fresco by Scotto
Gabriel's
Independent
Indochine
Justin's
La Grenouille
Lansky Lounge
Le Bar Bat
Le Bernardin
Le Cirque 2000
Le Colonial
Le Relais
Le Singe Vert

Match
Mesa Grill
Metronome
Monkey Bar
Nobu
Odeon
147
Orienta
Park Avalon
Patría
Patroon
Pravda
Rain
Sofia Fabulous Grill
Waterloo Brasserie

Power Scenes
Ben Benson's
Carlyle
Cellar in the Sky
Daniel
Elio's
FireBird
Four Seasons
Gabriel's
Grill Room
Harry Cipriani
Il Mulino
Il Nido
Jean Georges
La Caravelle
La Côte Basque
La Grenouille
La Reserve
Le Bernardin
Le Cirque 2000
Les Célébrités
Lespinasse
Maloney & Porcelli
Oceana
Ocean Grill
Park Ave. Cafe
Patroon
Peter Luger
Post House
Rao's
Regency (breakfast)
Smith & Wollensky
Sparks Steak House
Trattoria Dell'Arte
"21" Club

Pre-Theater/Prix Fixe Menus
(Best of many; call to check prices, days and times;
B = brunch, L = lunch,
D = dinner, * indicates dinner prix fixe is pre-theater only;
also see pp. 21 and 22)
Akbar (L)
Anche Vivolo (L)*
Ansonia*
Aquagrill (L)

Aquavit (L,D)
Arcadia (D)
Aria*
Arizona 206/Cafe (L)
Arqua (L,D)
Artos (L)*
Aureole (L,D)
Barbetta*
Bar Six (B)*
Bay Leaf (L)*
Becco (L,D)
Bouterin (L)
Brother Jimmy's (D)
Bryant Park Grill (B)*
Café Botanica (B,L,D)
Cafe Centro (D)
Café Crocodile (D)
Café des Artistes (L,D)
Cafe Luxembourg (B,L,D)
Cafe Nicholson (D)
Café Pierre (B,L,D)
Chanterelle (L,D)
Chez Ma Tante (B)
Chez Michallet*
Chez Napoléon*
Chin Chin (L)
Christer's (L)*
Churr. Plataforma (L,D)
Circus (L)
Cité (D)
Cooking With Jazz (D)
Cucina di Pesce (D)
Daniel (L,D)
Darbar (L)*
Destinée (L,D)
Felidia (L)
57, 57 (L,D)
44*
Four Seasons*
Gotham B&G (L)
Hatsune (L,D)
Honmura An (L,D)
Hourglass Tavern (D)
Hudson River Club (B)*
Jewel of India (L,D)
Josephina (D)
Kings' Carriage Hse. (L,D)
Kiosk*
La Boite en Bois (B,D)
La Caravelle (L,D)
La Colombe d'Or (D)
La Côte Basque (L,D)
La Goulue (B)
La Grenouille (L,D)
La Maison Japonaise (L,D)
La Mangeoire (L,D)
La Mediterranée (L,D)
La Petite Auberge (D)
L'Ardoise (L,D)
La Reserve (L,D)
Le Beaujolais (L,D)
Le Bernardin (L,D)
Le Boeuf à la Mode (D)

Le Cirque 2000 (L)
L'Ecole (L,D)
Le Colonial*
Le Perigord (L,D)
Le Refuge (B,L)
Les Sans Culottes (L,D)
Levana (L,D)
Lutèce (L,D)
Man Ray (L)
March (D)
Marguery Grill (L,D)
Mark's (B,L,D)
Michael's*
Mitali East/West (B,L)
Mughlai (B,L)
Nirvana (L,D)
Nobu (L)
Onigashima (D)
Osteria Fiorentina (L)*
Our Place (L)*
Palio*
Park Ave. Cafe (D)
Park Bistro (L)*
Pascalou (B,D)
Patsy's (L)*
Paul & Jimmy's (L,D)
Peacock Alley (B,L,D)
Petrossian (B,L,D)
Pierre au Tunnel (D)
Pietro's (L)
Pisces*
Quatorze Bis (B,L)
Rainbow Room (B)*
Regency*
René Pujol (D)
Riodizio (D)
River Cafe (D)
Roettele A.G. (D)
Rungsit Thai (L)
Sal Anthony's (L,D)
Sal Anthony's SPQR (L,D)
San Domenico (L)*
SeaGrill*
Shaan (L)*
Sign of the Dove (L)*
Solera (L,D)
Sonia Rose (L,D)
Supper Club*
Table d'Hôte*
Tapika (B)*
Tatou (L)*
Tavern on Green (L)*
Torre di Pisa*
Tout Va Bien*
Trattoria Alba (L)*
Tribeca Grill (B,L)
Trois Jean (B,L,D)
Turkish Kitchen (L,D)
Tutta Pasta (L)
"21" Club (L)*
View (D)
Vivolo*
Vong (L)*

Water Club (B,L)*
Wilkinson's (D)
Willow*
Ye Waverly Inn (B,L)

Pubs/Bars/Microbreweries
Bar & Books
Bar Nine
Bar Six
B Bar
Broome St. Bar
Chumley's
Cité Grill
City Wine & Cigar
Clarke's, P.J.
Corner Bistro
Ed Sullivan's
Fanelli
Ferrier
Flute
Gramercy Tavern
Heartland Brewery
Hog Pit
Hunters
Hurley's
J.G. Melon
Joe Allen
Killmeyer's
King Cole
Knickerbocker B&G
Landmark Tavern
Luke's B&G
Match
McSorley's
Mesa City
Metronome
Monkey Bar
Oak Room (bar)
Old Town Bar
O'Neals'
Oyster Bar (saloon)
Palio (downstairs)
Park
Pete's Tavern
Pravda
Russian Vodka Rm.
Shark Bar
Tap Room
Telephone B&G
Thady Con's
"21" Club
Typhoon Brewery
Vermouth
Walker's
White Horse
Windows on World
Wollensky's Grill

Quiet Conversation
ABC Parlour Cafe
Adrienne
Akbar
Alley's End
Andrusha

Aquavit
Aria
August Moon
Bar & Books
Barbetta
Boathouse Cafe
Box Tree
Café Botanica
Cafe Nicholson
Café Pierre
Cafe Trevi
Carlyle
Caviar Russe
Chanterelle
Chelsea Bistro
Chez Le Chef
Chez Michallet
Destinée
Domingo
57, 57
FireBird
Flute
Four Seasons
Gertrude's
Globe
Gus' Place
Hudson River Club
Il Giglio
Il Monello
Il Tinello
Isle of Capri
Keens Steakhouse
Kings' Carriage Hse.
La Reserve
Le Bernardin
Le Boeuf à la Mode
Le Chantilly
Le Régence
L'Ermitage
Les Célébrités
Lespinasse
March
Montrachet
Morton's
Oak Room
One if by Land
Palio
Palm Court
Park
Pen & Pencil
Petrossian
Picholine
Primavera
Regency
San Domenico
SeaGrill
Seryna
Sign of the Dove
Temple Bar
Terrace
Top of the Tower
T Salon
Tse Yang

Water's Edge
West 63rd Steak
Zen Palate
Zucca

Raw Bars
(Best of many)
Angelo & Maxie's
Aquagrill
B Bar
Blue Ribbon
Blue Water Grill
Brother Jimmy's
Brothers BBQ
Bubble Lounge
Circa
City Crab
Cooking With Jazz
Docks
Ed Sullivan's
Fish
Fishin Eddie
Fish Market
Fujiyama Mama
Fuleen Seafood
Gage & Tollner
Gills
Globe
Grove St. Brasserie
Harbour Lights
Hatsuhana
Hosteria Fiorella
Independent
Jo-An Japanese
Kuruma Zushi
La Cocina
Lenox Room
Live Bait
London Lennie's
Lundy Bros.
Mad Fish
Manhattan Ocean
Merchants, N.Y.
Milos
Nola
Oceana
Ocean Grill
Onigashima
Oyster Bar
Pacifico
Pearl Oyster Bar
Pearl Room
Pisces
Plaza Oyster Bar
Star Fish
T.S. Ma
Water Club

Romantic Spots
ABC Parlour Cafe
Alexandre
Arcadia
Bar & Books
Barbetta

Box Tree
Bryant Park Grill
Bubble Lounge
Café des Artistes
Cafe Nicholson
Caviar Russe
Cellar in the Sky
Champagne's
Chez Josephine
Chez Michallet
Domingo
Erminia
FireBird
Flowers
Flute
Harbour Lights
I Trulli
Jezebel
King Cole Bar
La Belle Epoque
La Colombe d'Or
La Côte Basque
La Goulue
La Grenouille
Le Colonial
Le Jardin Bistro
Le Refuge
Les Célébrités
March
Marichu
Mark's
Marylou's
Match
Merchants, N.Y.
Metronome
One if by Land
Paola's
Provence
Rainbow Room
River Cafe
Sign of the Dove
Sonia Rose
Tavern on Green
Temple Bar
Terrace
Water's Edge
Windows on World
World Yacht

Saturday – Best Bets
(B=brunch; L=lunch;
best of many)
ABC Parlour Cafe (B)
Ambassador Grill (L)
America (B)
Anglers & Writers (B,L)
Aquagrill (B)
Aquavit (L)
Arcadia (L)
Arizona 206/Cafe (B,L)
Balthazar (B,L)
Barney Greengrass (B,L)
Barocco (L)
Barolo (L)

Bayamo (B,L)
Bay Leaf (L)
Bice (L)
Billy's (B,L)
Blue Water Grill (L)
Bouley Bakery (L)
Box Tree (B,L)
Bryant Park Grill (B)
Café Botanica (L)
Café des Artistes (B,L)
Café Pierre (L)
Cafe Un Deux Trois (B,L)
Caffe Rafaella (B,L)
Caffe Rosso (B,L)
Canal House (B)
Capsouto Frères (B)
Carlyle (L)
Carnegie Deli (L)
Caviarteria (B,L)
Cendrillon (B)
Chiam (B,L)
Circa (B)
Circo, Osteria del (L)
Cité Grill (B,L)
Coco Pazzo Teatro (L)
Coming or Going (B,L)
Cosí Sandwich (L)
Daniel (L)
Dawat (L)
Docks (B,L)
E & O (B,L)
E.A.T. (L)
85 Down (B)
EJ's Luncheonette (B,L)
Elephant & Castle (B)
El Rio Grande (B,L)
Ennio & Michael (L)
Erizo (B,L)
57, 57 (B)
Flowers (B)
Friend of a Farmer (B,L)
Gertrude's (L)
Globe (B)
Good Enough to Eat (B,L)
Grange Hall (B)
Grove (B)
Hard Rock Cafe (L)
Harry Cipriani (L)
Honmura An (L)
Hosteria Fiorella (B,L)
Il Monello (L)
Il Nido (L)
Independent (B)
Isabella's (L)
Island (B,L)
Jewel of India (L)
Josephina (B)
J. Sung Dynasty (L)
L'Absinthe (B)
La Côte Basque (L)
La Goulue (L)
La Grenouille (L)
La Metairie (L)

Le Bilboquet (L)
Le Cirque 2000 (L)
Le Madri (L)
Lenox Room (B)
Le Relais (B,L)
Les Halles (B,L)
Le Singe Vert (B,L)
Lespinasse (L)
Les Pyrénées (L)
Lobster Club (L)
Maloney & Porcelli (B,L)
Mark's (L)
Matthew's (B)
Medusa (B,L)
Mesa Grill (B)
Milos (L)
Miracle Grill (B)
Mitali East/West (B,L)
Mme. Romaine (L)
Molyvos (L)
Monzù (B)
NoHo Star (B)
O'Neals' (B,L)
Oriental Garden (B,L)
Palm Court (L)
Payard Pâtisserie (L)
Petaluma (B,L)
Pete's Tavern (B,L)
Petrossian (B)
Planet Hollywood (L)
Provence (B,L)
Quatorze Bis (B,L)
Redeye Grill (L)
River Cafe (B)
Saloon (B,L)
Sarabeth's (B,L)
Second Ave. Deli (L)
Serendipity 3 (L)
Sette MoMA (L)
Shark Bar (B)
Shun Lee Cafe (L)
Sign of the Dove (B)
Sofia Fabulous Grill (L)
Sylvia's (B,L)
Table d'Hôte (B)
Tartine (B,L)
Tavern on Green (B)
Trattoria Dell'Arte (B,L)
Trois Jean (L)
Tse Yang (L)
Verbena (B)
Veselka (B,L)
Vince and Eddie's (B)
Vinegar Factory (B)
Virgil's Real BBQ (L)
Walker's (B)
White Horse (L)
Willow (B)
Wollensky's Grill (L)
Zen Palate (L)

Sunday Dining – Best Bets
(B=brunch; L=lunch;
D=dinner; plus all hotels and
most Asians)
Across the Street (D)
Afghan Kebab House (D)
Aja (D)
Alva (D)
America (D)
Angelo & Maxie's (D)
Anglers & Writers (L,D)
Aquagrill (D)
Aquavit (B,L,D)
Arizona 206/Cafe (L,D)
Arqua (D)
Balthazar (L,D)
Baluchi's (L,D)
Barocco (L,D)
Barolo (L,D)
Bayamo (L,D)
Bay Leaf (L,D)
Becco (L,D)
Ben Benson's (D)
Bice (L,D)
Billy's (L,D)
Bistro du Nord (D)
Bistrot Margot (L,D)
Blue Water Grill (B,D)
Bouley Bakery (L,D)
Bouterin (D)
Bravo Gianni (D)
B. Smith's (B,L,D)
Butterfield 81 (B,D)
Cafe Beulah (D)
Café Botanica (B,D)
Café de Bruxelles (L,D)
Café des Artistes (L,D)
Cafe Noir (L,D)
Caffe Rafaella (L,D)
Caffe Vivaldi (L,D)
Campagnola (D)
Carlyle (B,L,D)
Carmine's (D)
Carnegie Deli (L,D)
Chez Ma Tante (B,D)
Chez Michallet (B,D)
Chiam (L,D)
Chin Chin (D)
Circo, Osteria del (D)
Circus (D)
Cité (D)
City Wine & Cigar (D)
Clarke's, P.J. (L,D)
Clementine (B,D)
Coconut Grill (B,D)
Dallas BBQ (L,D)
Dawat (D)
Demarchelier (B,L,D)
Dominick's (L,D)
EJ's Luncheonette (L,D)
Elias Corner (D)
El Rio Grande (L,D)
Empire Szechuan (L,D)

Erizo (L,D)
Ess-a-Bagel (L,D)
Etats-Unis (D)
Firenze (D)
First (B,D)
Flowers (L,D)
44 (B,L,D)
Gabriela's (L,D)
Gallagher's (L,D)
Gertrude's (L,D)
Good Enough to Eat (L,D)
Gotham B&G (D)
Gramercy Tavern (D)
Grand Ticino (B,L,D)
Grange Hall (D)
Gus' Place (B,L,D)
Hakata (D,L)
Henry's End (D)
Honmura An (D)
Hosteria Fiorella (L,D)
Ici (B,L,D)
Il Bagatto (D)
Il Cantinori (D)
Il Monello (L,D)
Independent (D)
Indochine (D)
Japonica (L,D)
Jewel of India (L,D)
J.G. Melon (L,D)
Jimmy Sung's (L,D)
John's Pizzeria (L,D)
Jubilee (B,D)
Junior's (L,D)
Katz's Deli (L,D)
Knickerbocker B&G (B,L,D)
La Bouillabaisse (L,D)
La Caridad 78 (L,D)
La Côte Basque (D)
La Goulue (B,L,D)
La Metairie (L,D)
L'Ardoise (B,L,D)
Le Boeuf à la Mode (D)
Le Cirque 2000 (L,D)
Le Madri (D)
Lemongrass Grill (D,L)
Lenox Room (D)
Le Perigord (D)
Le Relais (L,D)
Le Zoo (B,D)
Lola (B,D)
Lombardi's (L,D)
Lusardi's (D)
Maloney & Porcelli (L,D)
Manhattan Grille (B,D)
March (D)
Marguery Grill (D)
Mark's (B,L,D)
Maya (D)
Mazzei (D)
Mesa Grill (D)
Mi Cocina (B,D)
Milos (L,D)
Miracle Grill (D)

Mitali East/West (L,D)
Molyvos (L,D)
Monkey Bar (D)
Montrachet (D)
Moreno (L,D)
Neary's (B,D)
Nicola's (D)
Nippon (L,D)
Nirvana (L,D)
Nobu (D)
NY Noodle Town (L,D)
Ocean Grill (B,D)
Odessa (L,D)
Ollie's (L,D)
Our Place (L,D)
Palm (L,D)
Park Avalon (B,D)
Park Ave. Cafe (B,D)
Park Side (L,D)
Patsy Grimaldi's (L,D)
Peter Luger (L,D)
Piccola Venezia (L,D)
Pó (L,D)
Primavera (D)
Primola (D)
Provence (L,D)
Rainbow Room (B,D)
Raoul's (D)
Rasputin (L,D)
Ratners (L,D)
Redeye Grill (B,L,D)
Sarabeth's (D,L)
Savore (L,D)
Savoy (D)
Second Ave. Deli (L,D)
Sette Mezzo (L,D)
Shun Lee Cafe (L,D)
Shun Lee Palace (L,D)
Sofia Fabulous Grill (L,D)
Sofia Fabulous Pizza (L,D)
Sylvia's (D)
Szechuan Hunan (L,D)
Szechuan Kitchen (D)
Table d'Hôte (D)
Taormina (L,D)
Tavern on Green (D)
Tennessee Mountain (L,D)
Thai Orchid (L,D)
Torre di Pisa (L,D)
Trattoria Dell'Arte (L,D)
Trois Jean (B,L,D)
Tse Yang (L,D)
Union Square Cafe (D)
Veselka (L,D)
Virgil's Real BBQ (L,D)
Vong (D)
Water Club (B,L,D)
Wilkinson's (D)
Wilson's (B,D)
Windows on World (L,D)
Zarela (D)
Zoë (D)

244

Senior Appeal
Adrienne
Ambassador Grill
Andrusha
Aureole
Barbetta
Billy's
Box Tree
Bruce Ho's
Café Botanica
Café des Artistes
Cafe Trevi
Carlyle
Castellano
Caviar Russe
Christer's
Coco Opera
Daniel
Darbar
Dawat
Deniz a la Turk
Destinée
Duane Park Cafe
Embers
Felidia
57, 57
FireBird
Follonico
Four Seasons
Gallagher's
Gertrude's
Giovanni
Girasole
Hosteria Fiorella
Hudson River Club
Il Cortile
Il Menestrello
Il Monello
Il Nido
Il Tinello
Jean Georges
J. Sung Dynasty
La Caravelle
La Colombe d'Or
La Côte Basque
La Grenouille
La Mangeoire
La Mediterranée
La Petite Auberge
La Reserve
La Rivista
Lattanzi
Le Bernardin
Le Chantilly
L'Ecole
Le Perigord
Le Régence
Les Célébrités
Lespinasse
Levana
Lusardi's
Lutèce
Manhattan Grille

March
Mark's
Milos
Mme. Romaine
Neary's
Nippon
Oak Room
Oceana
Otabe
Oyster Bar
Palm
Palm Court
Park
Peter Luger
Picholine
Primavera
Red Tulip
Remi
Rosa Mexicano
Russian Samovar
Shun Lee
Shun Lee Palace
Sign of the Dove
Solera
St. Maggie's
Sushisay
Tavern on Green
Tse Yang
"21" Club
Two Two Two
Union Pacific
Union Square Cafe
Vivolo
West 63rd Steak
Wilkinson's
World Yacht

Singles Scenes
Acme B&G
Aja
Ansonia
Aquagrill
Balthazar
Bar & Books
Bar 89
Bar Six
B Bar
Benny's Burritos
Blue Water Grill
Boca Chica
Boom
Bubble Lounge
Canal House
Chez Es Saada
Cibar
Cité Grill
Clarke's, P.J.
Clementine
Cub Room/Café
Docks
Drip
DT•UT
El Teddy's
Ernie's

Ferrier
First
Heartland Brewery
Independent
Isabella's
I Trulli
JUdson Grill
Jules
La Goulue
Le Bar Bat
Live Bait
Luke's B&G
Marion's
Match Uptown
Merchants, N.Y.
Mesa City
Miracle Grill
Monkey Bar
Old Town Bar
147
Onieals Grand St.
Park Avalon
Pete's Tavern
Pravda
Shark Bar
S.O.B.'s
Tatou
Thady Con's
Tortilla Flats
Tribeca Grill
Universal Grill
Velvet Room
Vermouth
Viceroy
Walker's
Waterloo Brasserie
White Horse
Zarela

Sleepers
(Good to excellent food,
but little known)
Belluno
Botany
CamaJe
Carol's Cafe
D'Angelo, Osteria
Daydream Cafe
DeRosa
Eastern Villa
Fujii
Han Sung
Havana Chelsea
Ikeno Hana
Jade Plaza
Kam Chueh
Kitaro
Kum Gang San
La Crêpe
Lady Mendl's
Lafayette Grill & Bar
La Fontana
La Giara
Little Szechuan

Mardi Gras
Massimo
Messina Cafe
Mezzanotte
Mishima
Mueng Thai
Nadaman Hakubai
Osteria Fiorentina
Oven
Pacifica
Parsonage
Pierino
Russian Vodka Rm.
S'Agapo
Sahara
Sakagura
Sea Gull
Soup Pot
South Shore
Taiyo Japanese
Takino
Taverna Kyclades
Teodora
Thai Cafe
Tierras Colombianas
Tokyo
Tom's Restaurant
Toons
Tosca
Ubol's Kitchen
Village Bistro
Vittorio Cucina

Teflons
(Gets lots of business, despite
so-so food, i.e. they have
other attractions that prevent
criticism from sticking)
Acme B&G
Algonquin Hotel
All State Cafe
America
Artepasta
Bar & Books
Bar 89
Bayamo
B Bar
Boathouse Cafe
Boom
Brooklyn Diner
Broome St. Bar
Brothers BBQ
Bubble Lounge
Bull & Bear
Burger Heaven
Busby's
Cafe Europa
Caffe Reggio
California Burrito
Calif. Pizza Kitchen
China Fun
Chumley's
Clarke's, P.J.
Coffee Shop

Cowgirl Hall of Fame
Dallas BBQ
Dojo
Drip
Ear Inn
E.A.T.
Elaine's
Empire Diner
Fanelli
Fashion Cafe
Fine & Schapiro
Fraunces Tavern
French Roast
Hard Rock Cafe
Harley Davidson
Heartland Brewery
Hunters
Iridium Jazz
Jekyll & Hyde
La Bonne Soupe
Le Bar Bat
Lincoln Tavern
Live Bait
Lucky Cheng's
Luke's B&G
Martini's
Mayrose
McSorley's
Merchants, N.Y.
Mickey Mantle's
Mortimer's
Motown Cafe
Museum Cafe
New World Coffee
Official All Star
Old Town Bar
Pasqua Coffee
Pasta Lovers
Pete's Tavern
Pizzeria Uno
Planet Hollywood
Saloon
Sardi's
SoHo Kitchen
Starbucks
Telephone B&G
T.G.I. Friday's
Tortilla Flats
Viceroy
White Horse
World Yacht

Tasting Menus
Alexi on 56 ($50)
Ansonia ($40)
Aquavit ($75)
Aureole ($85)
Barbetta ($65 & up)
Bouley Bakery ($75)
Caviar Russe ($55)
Chanterelle ($89)
Chiam ($30 & up)
Circo, Osteria del ($60 & up)
Cub Room/Café ($65)

Daniel ($69 & up)
First ($34)
Follonico ($48 & up)
Gramercy Tavern ($72)
Honmura An ($43)
Hudson River Club ($75)
Inagiku ($58)
Jean Georges ($95)
Jo Jo ($55)
JUdson Grill ($58)
Kokachin ($45)
La Caravelle ($85)
La Côte Basque ($80)
La Grenouille ($95)
La Mangeoire ($44)
La Reserve ($85)
Layla ($42)
Le Chantilly ($75)
Le Cirque 2000 ($90)
L'Ecole ($25)
Le Perigord ($75)
Les Célébrités ($95)
Lespinasse ($130)
Luma ($60)
Lutèce ($85)
Montrachet ($75)
Monzù ($65)
Nadaman Hakubai ($80 & up)
Nino's ($60)
Nirvana ($65)
Nobu ($60 & up)
Oceana ($80)
One if by Land ($75)
Park Ave. Cafe ($67)
Picholine ($63)
Pó ($35)
Raphaël ($75)
Rialto ($38 & up)
River Cafe ($85)
Savoy ($48)
St. Michel ($35)
Tapika ($50)
Trionfo ($43)
"21" Club ($85)
Two Two Two ($100 & up)
Verbena ($55)
Vong ($65)

Teas
(See also *Hotels* and
Coffeehouses/Desserts; the
following are highly touted)
ABC Parlour Cafe
Adrienne
Anglers & Writers
Cafe Mona Lisa
Café Pierre
Café Word of Mouth
Carlyle
Caviar Russe
C3
Danal
Havana Tea/Cigar
Kings' Carriage Hse.

Lady Mendl's
La Goulue
Library
Mark's
Morgan Court
Nirvana
Palm Court
Tea & Sympathy
Tea Box
Trois Jean
T Salon
Yaffa's

Teenagers & Other Youthful Spirits
Aggie's
America
Angelo & Maxie's
Benny's Burritos
Ben's Kosher
Bridge Cafe
Brother Jimmy's
Bryant Park Cafe
Cafe Lalo
Carmine's
Carnegie Deli
Cowgirl Hall of Fame
Cucina Stagionale
Dallas BBQ
EJ's Luncheonette
Emack & Bolio's
Empire Diner
Empire Szechuan
Ernie's
First Wok
Globe
Good Enough to Eat
Goodfella's
Hallo Berlin
Hard Rock Cafe
Harley Davidson
Houston's
Island Burgers
Jackson Hole
Jerry's
John's Pizzeria
Katz's Deli
Krispy Kreme
Landmark Tavern
Little Saigon
Lupe's East L.A.
Main Street
Manganaro's
Mangia e Bevi
Master Grill Intl.
Maya
Mickey Mantle's
Motown Cafe
Nirvana
NoHo Star
Official All Star
Ollie's
Papaya King
Pig Heaven

Pizzeria Uno
Planet Hollywood
Salute!
Sammy's Roumanian
Screening Room
Second Ave. Deli
Serendipity 3
Shun Lee Cafe
Stage Deli
Sylvia's
Szechuan Hunan
Szechuan Kitchen
Tap Room
Tavern on Green
Television City
Tennessee Mountain
Totonno Pizzeria
Tramps Cafe
Tuscan Square
Tutta Pasta
Uncle Nick's
Urban Hero
Vinnie's Pizza
Virgil's Real BBQ
Windows on World
World Yacht
Zarela

Theme Restaurants
Brooklyn Diner
Fashion Cafe
Hard Rock Cafe
Harley Davidson
Jekyll & Hyde
La Nouvelle Justine
Le Bar Bat
Mickey Mantle's
Motown Cafe
Night Gallery
Official All Star
Planet Hollywood
Stardust Dine-O-Mat
Television City

Transporting Experiences
ABC Parlour Cafe
Afghan Kebab House
Akbar
Anglers & Writers
Aquavit
Balthazar
Barolo (garden)
Boathouse Cafe
Bouterin
Box Tree
Café des Artistes
Cafe Nicholson
Caribe
Cellar in the Sky
Chez Es Saada
Chez Josephine
Chez Michallet
FireBird
Gramercy Tavern

Heidelberg
Honmura An
Jezebel
Jimmy Sung's
Keens Steakhouse
Kelley & Ping
Kings' Carriage Hse.
La Belle Epoque
L'Absinthe
La Colombe d'Or
La Côte Basque
La Goulue
La Grenouille
Landmark Tavern
Le Colonial
L'Entrecote
Les Halles
Le Singe Vert
Manhattan Grille
Mark's
McSorley's
Nirvana
Palm Court
Pravda
Provence
Rainbow Room
Rao's
Raoul's
Red Tulip
Rosa Mexicano
Serendipity 3
Sylvia's
Tavern on Green
Temple Bar
Thady Con's
Top of the Tower
Vong
Windows on World
World Yacht
Zen Palate

Visitors on Expense Accounts
Aquavit
Arcadia
Aureole
Balthazar
Bice
Bouley Bakery
Cafe Centro
Café des Artistes
Carnegie Deli
Cellar in the Sky
Chanterelle
Chin Chin
Daniel
Da Umberto
Felidia
FireBird
Four Seasons
Gotham B&G
Gramercy Tavern
Harry Cipriani
Hudson River Club

Il Mulino
Il Nido
Jean Georges
Jo Jo
Kuruma Zushi
La Caravelle
La Côte Basque
La Grenouille
La Reserve
Le Bernardin
Le Chantilly
Le Cirque 2000
Les Célébrités
Lutèce
Manhattan Ocean
March
Mesa Grill
Milos
Montrachet
Nobu
Oceana
147
One if by Land
Palm
Park
Park Ave. Cafe
Patría
Patroon
Periyali
Peter Luger
Rainbow Room
Remi
River Cafe
San Domenico
Shun Lee Palace
Sign of the Dove
Smith & Wollensky
Sparks Steak House
Sushisay
Tavern on Green
Terrace
Trattoria Dell'Arte
Tribeca Grill
"21" Club
Union Square Cafe
Vong
Water Club
Windows on World
World Yacht

Wheelchair Access
(Recommended on the basis
of overall quality and ease of
access. The data re access
comes from the restaurants
and has not been verfied by
personal inspections. Thus,
it makes sense to call
in advance.)
Alva
An American Place
Asia de Cuba
Balthazar
Barolo

Billy's
Boathouse Cafe
Bolo
Bouley Bakery
Bouterin
Bryant Park Grill
B. Smith's
Café Botanica
Cafe Centro
Cafe S.F.A.
Cellar in the Sky
Chanterelle
Chiam
Cité
Cité Grill
City Wine & Cigar
Clementine
Coco Pazzo
Ernie's
57, 57
Frank's
Fred's at Barneys
Gabriel's
Gramercy Tavern
Jean Georges
Kokachin
Le Bernardin
Milos
Palio
Patroon
Republic
River Cafe
Sette MoMA
Starbucks
Union Pacific
Virgil's Real BBQ
Windows on World

Winning Wine Lists

Alison on Dominick
An American Place
Aquavit
Arcadia
Aureole
Barbetta
Barolo
Ben Benson's
Blue Ribbon
Bull & Bear
Cafe Centro
Carlyle
Cellar in the Sky
Chanterelle
Chiam
Circa
Circo, Osteria del
Cité
Coco Pazzo
Daniel
Felidia
57, 57
Four Seasons
Fresco by Scotto
Gabriel's

Gotham B&G
Gramercy Tavern
Halcyon
Harry's/Hanover Sq.
Henry's End
Hudson River Club
Il Cantinori
I Tre Merli
I Trulli
Jean Georges
JUdson Grill
La Caravelle
La Colombe d'Or
La Côte Basque
La Reserve
Le Bernardin
Le Cirque 2000
L'Ecole
Le Madri
Lenox Room
Le Perigord
Les Célébrités
Lespinasse
Levana
Luma
Lutèce
Maloney & Porcelli
Manhattan Ocean
March
Mark's
Merlot B&G
Michael's
Monkey Bar
Montrachet
Morton's
Nicola Paone (Italian)
Ñ 33 Crosby
Oak Room
Oceana
One if by Land
Oyster Bar (white)
Palio
Park Ave. Cafe
Patría
Peacock Alley
Piccola Venezia
Post House
Provence
Rainbow Room
Raoul's
Remi
René Pujol
River Cafe
Ruth's Chris
San Domenico
Savoy
SeaGrill
Sign of the Dove
Smith & Wollensky
SoHo Kitchen
Sparks Steak House
Tavern on Green
Terrace

Tommaso's
Tribeca Grill
Trois Jean
Tropica Bar
Tse Yang
"21" Club
Union Square Cafe
Verbena
Water Club
Windows on World
Wollensky's Grill
Zoë

Young Children
(Besides the normal fast-food places; * indicates children's menu available)
ABC Parlour Cafe
Acadia Parish*
America
American Festival*
Amy's Bread
Anglers & Writers*
Arqua
Barking Dog Lunch.
Bella Luna*
Benihana
Ben's Kosher*
Blockhead's Burritos*
Boathouse Cafe*
Bodega*
Brooklyn Diner
Brother Jimmy's*
Bryant Park Cafe
B. Smith's*
Bubby's
Caffe Popolo*
Chat 'n Chew*
Chelsea Feast*
Churr. Plataforma*
Coco Marina*
Comfort Diner*
Cowgirl Hall of Fame*
Dallas BBQ
EJ's Luncheonette*
Ernie's
Florent*
Foley's Fish House*
Friend of a Farmer*
Gabriela's*
Gene's
Globe*
Good Enough to Eat
Green Field
Harbour Lights*
Hard Rock Cafe*
Harley Davidson*

Il Vagabondo
Jackson Hole*
Jekyll & Hyde
John's Pizzeria
Katz's Deli
Kelley & Ping
La Bonne Soupe
La Cocina*
La Fenice*
Lake Cafe*
Lobster Box*
London Lennie's*
Main Street*
Mezzaluna*
Mezzanotte*
Mickey Mantle's*
Mi Cocina
Motown Cafe
Mueng Thai*
Museum Cafe*
Nadine's*
Nola*
Odeon*
Odessa*
Official All Star
O'Neals'
Patsy's Pizza
Pizzeria Uno
Planet Hollywood*
Popover Cafe*
Republic*
Rose Cafe*
Sambuca*
Sarabeth's
Second Ave. Deli
Serendipity 3
Shopsin's*
Short Ribs*
Skylight Diner
Stage Deli*
Stardust Dine-O-Mat
Sylvia's*
Tavern on Green*
Television City*
Tennessee Mountain*
T.G.I. Friday's*
Tortilla Flats*
Treehouse*
Tribeca Grill*
Triplets Old NY*
Two Boots*
Uncle Jack's*
V&T Pizzeria*
Virgil's Real BBQ
Walker's*
Wylie's Ribs

Wine Vintage Chart 1985-1996

This chart is designed to help you select wine to go with your meal. It is based on the same 0 to 30 scale used throughout this *Survey*. The ratings (prepared by our friend Howard Stravitz, a law professor at the University of South Carolina) reflect both the quality of the vintage and the wine's readiness for present consumption. Thus, if a wine is not fully mature or is over the hill, its rating has been reduced. We do not include 1987 because, with the exception of '87 cabernets, those vintages are not recommended.

	'85	'86	'88	'89	'90	'91	'92	'93	'94	'95	'96
WHITES											
French:											
Burgundy	27	28	20	29	24	18	26	19	25	25	26
Loire Valley	–	–	–	25	24	15	19	22	23	24	24
Champagne	28	25	24	26	28	–	–	24	–	25	26
Sauternes	22	28	29	25	26	–	–	–	18	22	24
California:											
Chardonnay	–	–	–	–	23	21	26	25	22	23	22
REDS											
French:											
Bordeaux	27	26	25	28	28	–	19	23	24	25	24
Burgundy	24	–	26	27	29	21	23	25	22	23	24
Rhône	26	20	26	28	27	26*	16	23*	23	24	22
Beaujolais	–	–	–	–	–	22	13	21	22	24	21
California:											
Cab./Merlot	27	26	16	22	28	26	25	24	24	23	22
Zinfandel	–	–	–	–	–	20	20	20	22	20	21
Italian:											
Tuscany	27	16	25	–	26	19	–	20	19	24	19
Piedmont	26	–	24	27	27	–	–	19	–	25	25

*Rating and recommendation is only for Northern Rhône wine in 1991 and Southern Rhône wine in 1993.

Bargain sippers take note: Some wines are reliable year in, year out, and are reasonably priced as well. These wines are best bought in the most recent vintages. They include: Alsatian Pinot Blancs, Côtes du Rhône, Muscadet, Bardolino, Valpolicella and inexpensive Spanish Rioja and California Zinfandel.